The Basic Grammar Preparation for English Tests

시험대비 영문법

정연재

중앙대학교 영어영문학과와 같은 학교 대학원 영어영문학과를 졸업하였다.
고등학교 영어교사, 토플·토익 강사로 여러 해 영어를 가르쳤고,
도서출판 고려원 부설「고려원어학연구원」원장으로 재직하면서
많은 영어 교재들을 연구하고 개발하였다.
저서로는《좋은 지문 다 모은 테마영문독해》(전7권)
《좋은 지문 다 모은 주니어 테마영문독해》(전6권)
《TOEFL에 자주 나오는 1000단어》《TOEFL 초보를 위한 기본독해》
《처음문법 40단계》《처음독해 40테마》《영미문화사전》등이 있다.

시험대비 영문법

편저자 정연재
2007년 7월 1일 초판 1쇄 발행
발행처 영어포럼
발행인 정연재

(우) 121-883 서울시 마포구 합정동 91-11호 2층
(전화) 02-323-7901 (팩스) 02-323-7902
(홈페이지) www.englishforum.co.kr
등록 1999년 2월 2일 제 11-169호
The Basic Grammar Preparation for English Tests ⓒ Jung Yun Jae 2007 Printed in Korea
ISBN 978-89-88891-45-2 54740

값 15,000원
저자와 출판사의 사권 승인없이 책의 내용이나 표지 등을 복제, 인용할수 없습니다.
파본은 교환해 드립니다.

THE BASIC GRAMMAR PREPARATION *for* ENGLISH TESTS

시험대비 영문법

정연재 편저

영어포럼

책을 시작하면서

★·★ 《시험대비 영문법》은 각종 영어시험을 준비하는 학습자의 문법학습을 위하여 만들어졌다.

이 책은 TOEFL, TOEIC, TEPS공무원, 편입 시험 등의 각종 영어시험을 준비하는 학습자들이 문법 부분을 효과적으로 공략하는데 도움을 주기위한 문법서로 기획되었다. 이 책은 문장을 구성하는 각 요소별로 문법을 설명하고, 적절한 연습문제와 기출문제를 풀어보도록 하여, 공부한 내용을 철저히 점검할 수 있도록 만들어졌다.

★·★ 효과적인 영어학습을 위해서는 문장구조를 습득하는 것이 필요하다.

모르는 단어가 있더라도 문장이나 단락으로 된 글의 내용을 이해하는 것은 어려울 것 없다. 영어의 문장구조를 정확하게 습득하고 있으면 된다. 단어는 단순히 문자기호일 뿐 단어 하나하나가 정확한 뜻을 가진 경우는 드물기 때문이다. 단어는 다른 단어들과 조합을 이루는 가운데 나름대로 확정된 뜻을 가지는데 문장이나 문단으로 구성될 때, 더욱 구체적인 내용이 된다.

이때 단어들이 절(clause) 또는 문장(sentence)을 이루기 위해 결합되는 순서가 있는데, 이를 '어순'(word order) 또는 '문장구조'(sentence structure)라고 한다.

★★★ 문법이란 문장구조를 체계화 시키는 것이다.

단어를 어떤 순서에 따라 조합하도록 하는 문장규칙이 바로 문법이다. 문법을 알면 정확하고 빠른 독해를 할 수 있으며, 자신의 생각을 분명하고 효과적으로 표현하는 데 큰 도움이 된다. 문법을 제대로 공부하지 않으면 영어를 제대로 이해할 수 없다. 또한 문장구조를 정확하게 파악하지 못하게 되므로, 글을 정확하고 효과적으로 읽기 어려운 것은 물론, 제대로 된 글을 쓸 수도 없다. 듣기와 말하기도 마찬가지다. **그래서 TOEFL, TOEIC, TEPS, 편입, 공무원 시험 등 문법 파트는 바로 이 문장구조를 학습자들이 어느 정도 습득하고 있는지를 측정하려는 것이다.** 꼭 문법사항을 묻는 문제만 아니라, 각종 영어시험에서 높은 점수를 얻기 위해서는 문법학습이 필수적이다.

★★★ 문법학습은 영어식 사고구조를 갖추는 것이다.

영어시험을 준비하는 학습자들은 영어식 사고구조에 익숙해져야 한다. 듣기, 말하기, 쓰기, 읽기 등 영어학습의 모든 영역을 영어식 사고구조에 익숙해지지 않으면 잘 할 수 없다. 문법이 필요 없다고 말하는 사람도 있으나, 문법 학습은 영어학습 모든 영역의 기초가 된다.

★★★ 따라서 문법 학습이란

1. 영어의 문장구조인 어순을 습득하는 과정이다.
2. 영어 문장의 어순은 주어가 첫째 자리, 동사가 두 번째 자리를 차지하는 것이 대원칙이다. 의문문이나 명령문, 도치문 등은 어순이 바뀌는 변형문들이다.
3. 기능어(관사, 대명사, 전치사, 접속사, 관계사, 조동사, be동사 등)와 의미어(명사, 동사, 형용사, 부사, 의문사 등)의 조합 과정을 익힌다.

★★★ 그래서 《시험대비 영문법》은 다음과 같이 구성하였다.

1. 영어에 대한 큰 틀(구조)을 먼저 세운 후 문법요소 상호간의 관계를 이해해나가는 것이 올바른 문법학습이다. 따라서 이 책은 구문편과 품사편을 별도로 구성하여 문장구조에 대한 학습이 먼저 이루어지도록 구성하였다. 구문편을 별도로 구성하여 비중 있게 다룬 것은 이 책이 다른 문법서와 가장 크게 차별되는 점이다.

2. 문법을 설명하는 중간 중간에 적절한 Exercise를 두어 효과적인 학습이 되도록 하였다. 문법을 공부한 즉시, 관련 문제를 다루어 보는 것은 문법사항에 대한 깊이 있는 이해를 가능하게 하며, 각종 시험에도 쉽게 적응할 수 있게 할 것이다.

3. 각 Unit의 끝에 Actual Test를 두어 각종 시험(TOEFL, TOEIC, 편입, 공무원 시험)에 대비하도록 하였다. Actual Test에 수록된 문제들은 여러 시험에 출제된 기출 문제여서, 앞에서 학습한 문법사항에 대한 확인은 물론이고, 시험에 적응할 수 있는 좋은 기회를 줄 것이다.

★★★ 다시 한번 강조하지만, 영어시험을 준비하는 학습자 여러분은

영어시험에 대비한 효과적인 영어 학습을 위해서는 문법을 먼저 이해해야 한다. 각종 영어 시험을 준비하는 학습자들은 단편적인 문법지식 습득에 매달릴 것이 아니라 영어에 대한 큰 틀을 먼저 갖추어야 한다. 가능하다면 빠르게 읽어 나가며 꾸준하게 공부한다면 여러분의 영문법 실력은 극대화 될 것이다. 그리고 그 극대화 된 실력은 바로 좋은 점수로 여러분 앞에 되돌아올 것이다.

Contents

The Basic Grammar
Preparation for
English Tests

Part I 구문편

Unit	1	문장 구조	13
Unit	2	문장의 종류	25
Unit	3	단문	47
Unit	4	중문	65
Unit	5	복문	77
Unit	6	특수문형	111
Unit	7	일치	149

Part II 품사편

Unit 8	명사	169
Unit 9	관사	185
Unit 10	대명사	197
Unit 11	한정사와 수량표시	207
Unit 12	형용사	227
Unit 13	부사	247
Unit 14	전치사	267
Unit 15	동사	287
Unit 16	조동사	307
Unit 17	부정사와 동명사	327

정답과 해설   350

The Basic Grammar
Preparation for English Tests

Part I

구문편
Sentence Structure

- Unit 1 문장구조
- Unit 2 문장의 종류
- Unit 3 단문
- Unit 4 중문
- Unit 5 복문
- Unit 6 특수문형
- Unit 7 일치

Unit 1

문장 구조

◀ **문장의 구조**(sentence structure or word order)

분류	구성	예
letter (철자)	· 알파벳 자모	a, b, c, d, e, f, g … t, u, v, w, x, y, z
Word (단어)	· letter+letter · 자음과 모음의 조합	· (의미어) apple, love, tree · (기능어) the, for, which
Phrase (구)	· word+word · 단어와 단어의 조합 · 일정한 어순에 따라 조합된다.	· a pretty young girl · for my love · will be going
Clause (절)	· 단어들이 일정한 어순에 따라 조합된다. · 반드시 하나 이상의 동사를 갖춘다. · 문장의 일부로서 역할을 한다.	· she was sad · who lives here · until the summer ends
Sentence (문장)	· 단어들이 일정한 어순에 따라 조합된다. · 하나 이상의 주어와 동사를 갖춘다. · 하나의 완전한 의미를 전달한다. · 대문자로 시작하고 마침표로 끝난다.	· You love me. · I love John who lives next door. · Tom went to the movies, but I went to the circus.

Basic Grammar for English Tests

◀ 구(phrases)

"구"는 주어와 서술어(predicate, 또는 동사 verb)의 구성이 없는 단순한 단어의 조합이다.

구의 어순 (phrase structure)

1. 관사, 소유격, 한정사 등은 반드시 명사 앞에 온다.

   - a boy (o)
   - boy a (x)

   - the world (o)
   - world the (x)

   - my favorite food (o)
   - food my favorite (x)

   - these three books (o)
   - these books three (x)

2. 전치사구 : 전치사는 언제나 명사 앞에 온다.

   - for me (o)
   - me for (x)

   - on time (o)
   - time on (x)

   - by the desk (o)
   - the desk by (x)

3. 동사구

   (1) 조동사+원형동사

   - must go (o)
   - go must (x)
   - must went (x)

   - will write (o)
   - will written (x)

   - will be going (o)
   - be will going (x)

   (2) have/has/had+p.p.(동사의 과거분사형)

   - have done (o)
   - have do (x)
   - have did (x)

   - had gone (o)
   - had went (x)
   - had go (x)

   - shall have finished (o)
   - shall have finish (x)

구의 종류

1. 명사구(noun phrases) : 주어, 보어, 목적어 역할

   The President's decision to resign was welcomed by the people.
   I don't have **the least interest in his plans**.

   대통령의 사임결정은 국민들에게 환영받았습니다. / 저는 그의 계획에 최소한의 관심도 가지고 있지 않습니다.

2. 동사구(verb phrases) : 동사 역할

   She **will write** a letter to her father.
   I **shall have finished** this work by five o'clock.

   그녀는 자기 아버지께 편지를 쓸 것입니다. / 저는 이 작업을 5시까지는 마치게 될 것입니다.

3. 형용사구(adjective phrases) : 형용사 역할(보어 역할 및 명사 수식)

   The teachers' strike is **of interest**.
   Relatives **from Chicago** visited us for a week.
   Dozens of magazines **in the waiting room** are ten years old.

   교사들의 파업은 재미있습니다. / 시카고의 친척들이, 1주일간 우리를 방문하였습니다. / 대기실에 있는 10여 권의 잡지들은 10년이 넘은 것들입니다.

4. 부사구(adverb phrases) : 부사 역할

   My puppy slept **by the chair**.
   The spectators cheered **for me**.
   Jane sings **with enthusiasm**.

   제 강아지가 의자 옆에서 잠을 잤습니다. / 구경꾼들이 나를 위해 응원을 하였습니다. / 제인은 열정적으로 노래를 부릅니다.

외형적인 구분

1. 동명사구(gerund phrases) : 동사+ing

   We lost the game by **failing to score enough points**.
   Lying to your friend is a serious mistake.
   My ultimate goal is **winning the history prize**.

   우리는 충분한 점수를 따내는 데 실패함으로써 게임에 졌습니다. / 친구에게 거짓말을 하는 것은 중대한 잘못입니다. / 저의 최종 목표는 역사학상을 수상하는 것입니다.

2. 전치사구(prepositional phrases)

   He stood **by the desk**.
   The woman drove **around the town**.
   I have just read it **in the morning newspaper**.

   그는 책상 옆에 서 있었습니다. / 그 여자는 시 외곽을 드라이브하였습니다. / 저는 아침 신문에서 그것을 읽었습니다.

3. 분사구(participial phrases) : 문장 전체를 수식하는 부사 역할

   Straightening his tie, John welcomed his guests.
   Leaving before sunrise, we reached Denver that night.
   The village, **ravaged by the tornado**, was like a ghost town.

   넥타이를 고쳐 매면서 존은 손님들을 맞이하였습니다. / 해뜨기 전에 출발을 하였기 때문에, 우리는 그날 밤에 덴버에 도착하였습니다. / 그 마을은 토네이도가 휩쓸고 가서 유령의 도시 같았습니다.

4. 부정사구(infinitive phrases) : to+동사원형

   The soldiers plan **to attack soon**. (목적어)
   To attend Harvard University is John's great desire. (주어)

Basic Grammar for English Tests

Michael's decision is **to visit his employment office**. (보어)
The plumber insists there is a method **to solve the leak**. (a method를 수식)
Laura claims that she is too busy **to attend the dance**. (busy를 수식)

_{병사들은 곧 공격할 계획을 짜고 있습니다. / 하버드대학에 다니는 것이 존의 큰 바램입니다. / 마이클의 결정은 그의 고용사무실을 방문하는 것입니다. / 배관공은 누수를 해결하는 방법이 있다고 주장합니다. / 로라는 자기가 너무 바빠서 무도회에 참석할 수 없다고 주장합니다.}

Exercise 1 다음 글을 읽으며 전치사를 찾아 ○표시 하시오.

ⓐt certain times men were fascinated by more particular problems within the general philosophic framework of these larger questions. For example, towards the end of the Middle Ages, that is in the fourteenth and fifteenth centuries, some critics of the then accepted Aristotelian system became specially interested in the problems of movement—why did a projectile continue to move after it had left the bow or sling and why did it gradually fall to the ground? Aristotle's explanations were no longer accepted as satisfactory, and the way was opened for a whole new philosophy to creep into men's minds through the small hole made in the accepted theory of motion.

Exercise 2 다음 보기를 참고하여 전치사구와 부정사를 구별하시오.

1. to laugh (부정사)
2. to town (전치사구)
3. to trip
4. to notify
5. to the park
6. to be angry
7. to park
8. to shout
9. to the shore
10. to the supermarket
11. to save
12. to drive
13. to run
14. to the drive
15. to peace
16. to the walk
17. to her laugh
18. to pieces
19. to his shout
20. to tear

Exercise 3 다음 문장에 쓰인 구의 종류를 알아보시오. (명사구, 동명사구, 동사구, 전치사구, 분사구, 부정사구)

1. <u>Many students</u> <u>have to work</u> <u>during school vacations</u>.
         명사구   동사구   전치사구

2. All of us hoped to remain calm during the test.
3. Having finished the work, the agent sent for a heavy meal.
4. At last a heavy rain fell on the parched ground.
5. An attitude of anxiety does not appeal to anyone.
6. Teaching a small puppy is a good way to develop patience.
7. To get an A is the goal of many students.
8. Putting all her strength into the effort, Ann did her best.
9. He has a large family to support.
10. The student remained in the library for two hours.

◀ 절(clauses)

절(clauses)은 주어와 서술어(동사)로 구성되어 문장의 일부로 표현되는 형식이다. 동사가 없으면 절이 성립되지 않으므로 동사 없는 절은 없다.

절의 어순 (clause structure)

1. 주절(독립절) : 주어(명사)+동사

   ⎡ car costs a lot of money (o)
   ⎢ costs car a lot of money (x)
   ⎣ costs a lot of money car (x)

2. 종속절

   (1) 종속접속어+동사

   ⎡ who lives in Oregon
   ⎣ which is used to make chewing gum

   (2) 종속접속어+주어+동사

   ⎡ after the game was over
   ⎣ because he was born in Texas

절의 종류

1. 주절 (main clause)

   한 문장에서 어떤 상황이나 행위에 대한 서술의 중심이 되는 절이다.
   독립절(independent clause)이라고도 한다.

Basic Grammar for English Tests

When the cheering stopped, **John was sad**.
The children play in the streets where there is no traffic.

응원이 끝나자 존은 슬펐습니다. / 어린이들은 자동차가 다니지 않는 거리에서 놉니다.

2. 등위절 (coordinate clause)

중문(compound sentences)에서는 주절, 종속절의 개념 없이 등위절이라고 한다.
등위접속사 · 상관접속사 : 등위절을 연결하는 접속어 and, but, both … and, not only …but also 등

Tom went to the movies, *but* John went to the circus.
Not only does she make a contribution herself, *but* she will *also* ask her friends.

* not only A, but also B : A 뿐만 아니라 B도 역시. Not only 가 문두에 올 때는 주어 동사가 도치된다.

톰은 영화보러 갔지만, 존은 서커스에 갔습니다. / 그녀는 혼자 봉사를 할 뿐만 아니라, 자기 친구들에게도 요구합니다.

3. 종속절 (subordinate clause or dependent clause)

주절을 수식한다.
종속절을 만드는 여러 가지 접속어로 인도된다.
종속접속어(subordinate conjunctions) : 모든 접속어는 절과 절을 연결하는 역할을 한다.

종속접속어(subordinate introductory signals)의 종류

명사절 인도		when where who whom whose what why how whether if that which
형용사절 인도		who whom where when that which
부사절 인도	시간	after before when while as by the time (that) since until as soon as once as/so long as whenever every time (that) the first time (that) the last time (that) the next time (that)
	원인 · 결과	because since now that as as/so long as insomuch as so (that) in order that
	양보	even though although though whereas while
	조건	if unless only if whether …or not even if in case(that) providing (that) provided (that) in the event(that)

Exercise **4** 다음 각 글을 읽고 구와 절을 구별하시오.

1. cars cost a lot of money (절)
2. in terms of population (구)
3. walking home takes time
4. spelling irregular verbs

5. to dream of better days
6. the man ate quickly
7. cars needing many repairs
8. winter nights chill the bones
9. to enter costs ten dollars
10. after the last dance
11. radial tires are expensive
12. from ten to twenty years

Exercise 5 다음 각 글을 읽고 종속절과 구를 구별하시오.

1. before finishing dinner (구)
2. if the doctors operate soon (종속절)
3. whom the committee chose
4. after the last class
5. as the sun set behind the hill
6. because he was born in Texas
7. standing in a long line
8. which the driver hit
9. an inexpensive Japanese model
10. before the rain had stopped
11. driving fifty-five miles an hour
12. which he passed easily

Exercise 6 다음 각 글을 읽고 주절, 종속절, 구를 구별하시오.

1. the water is used for irrigation (주절)
2. which is used to make chewing gum (종속절)
3. a famous talk show host (구)
4. her hopes for the future
5. the population increased greatly
6. a brain infection causing jerking
7. the fourth largest city of the state
8. although the law was repealed
9. who lived in Oregon
10. several different writing systems
11. when the radio was invented
12. the first ships were only logs

◀ 문장(sentence)

문장의 개념

1. 개념
   - (1) 주어와 서술어(동사)로 구성되어 완전한 의미를 전달하는 단어들의 조합이다.
   - (2) 문장은 적어도 주어와 동사 하나씩은 반드시 가지고 있다.
   - (3) 동사가 없으면 문장이 성립되지 않으니, 동사 없는 문장은 없다.

2. 명사어구절
   - (1) 주어 역할을 하는 것으로 명사(구), 대명사, 동명사(구), 부정사(구), 명사절 등이다.
   - (2) 이들을 넓은 의미의 명사라고 할 수 있다.

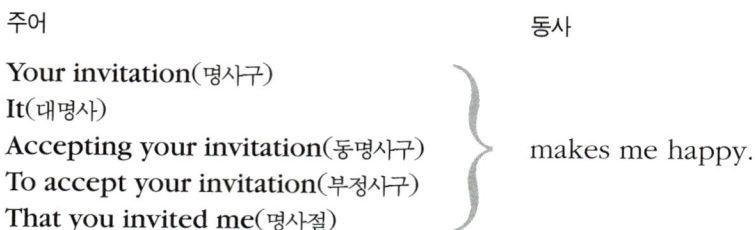

주어 / 동사

Your invitation(명사구)
It(대명사)
Accepting your invitation(동명사구) } makes me happy.
To accept your invitation(부정사구)
That you invited me(명사절)

명사어의 위치와 식별

1. 관사(articles: a/an, the)가 붙은 말
   an engineer, a desk, a beautiful chinese girl, the theater, the west
2. 소유격(possessive case)으로 시작된 말
   my cousin, her horse, your daughter, their house, its name, one's own idea
3. 전치사(prepositions) 뒤에 오는 말
   in the morning, of dust, to Kansas City, except you, against my opinion
4. 문장의 머리글자가 아니어도 대문자로 시작된 말
   English, April, Spring, Asher Benjamin, Christmas
5. 대명사는 물론 명사 역할을 한다
   I, you, she, they, their, it, him, her, me
6. 지시사를 포함하여 한정사(determiners)로 수식되는 말
   - 지시형용사(any-, each-, every-, some- 등) 뒤에 오는 말
     anyone, each student, everything, something, some coffee
   - 지시형용사(this, that, these, those 등)가 수식하는 말
     this guy, that building, those people

3. 어순 : 문장에서 동사(구)의 위치는 주어 다음 자리가 원칙이다.

You love me. (o)
Love you me. (x)

She tears the cloth.
Tears ran down her cheeks.

Buses come on time.
She buses the dishes.

그녀는 천을 찢고 있습니다. / 눈물이 그녀의 뺨을 타고 흘러내렸습니다. / 버스는 정각에 옵니다. / 그녀는 접시를 나릅니다.

John **drives** too fast.
John **is going to** Miami tomorrow.
Jane **has been reading** that book.
She **will go** to Boston next week.
She **must have gone** to the bank.

존은 너무 빨리 운전을 합니다. / 존은 내일 마이애미로 갑니다. / 제인은 그 책을 읽고 있었습니다. / 그녀는 다음 주에 보스턴에 갑니다. / 그녀는 분명히 은행에 갔었습니다.

Exercise 7 다음 문장들에서 주어를 찾아 밑줄을 치시오.
(전치사구와 명사구 등 각종 구를 먼저 찾은 뒤에 동사(구)를 찾으면 쉽다.)

1. _Courtesy_ demands a prompt apology
2. He is the new director of the institute.
3. To drive more than fifty five miles per hour is illegal.
4. Walking to the university takes twenty minutes.
5. Whoever wins the race will receive a trophy.
6. Cemeteries are frightening places at night.
7. Rollerskating has recently become very popular.
8. That all the passengers survived the crash is miraculous.
9. To get angry is not the solution.
10. These appear to be photographs of a North African village.

Exercise 8 다음 문장들에서 동사(구)를 찾아 밑줄을 치시오.

1. The municipal auditorium _is located_ on the shores of Town Lake.
2. That new book will interest football fans.
3. There are several new apartment complexes west of the university.
4. Near the auditorium stand the city coliseum and the fair grounds.
5. Buses depart from the station every half hour.

Basic Grammar for English Tests

6. Many career opportunities are available to a lawyer.
7. The cable television company has recently installed lines to the suburbs.
8. That new book has been checked out and read by a dozen people this week.
9. Through the branches of the tree shone the light of the full moon.
10. The new highway will have been completed by January of next year.

Exercise 9 다음 각 문장에서 동사를 찾아 밑줄을 치시오.

1. Mittens *warm* the hands.
2. The smoke rose to the ceiling.
3. Those dormitories house the men.
4. Her laugh hurt my ears.
5. The will interests the lawyer.
6. His cries fell on deaf ears.
7. One can fell on the floor.
8. The experiments require live organs.
9. Secretaries book appointments.
10. Her dreams came true.

Exercise 10 다음 문장들에서 밑줄 친 단어의 역할을 확인하고, 명사인지 동사인지 말하시오.

1. In the desert the need for water is of primary importance. (명사)
2. Out of the darkness came a woman's cry for help.
3. On a dark night dreams can seem larger than life.
4. A safe place for a will is in a bank deposit box.
5. Coaches time exercises with a watch.
6. For a novice backpacker, an all-day climb on this mountain is strenuous.
7. After a day on the slopes, skiers warm their feet by the fire.
8. A rat mothers her young carefully during their first weeks.
9. At the last minute, a swift kick by one player tied the game.
10. For the engineering student recent studies are the most relevant.

Actual Test 1

다음 각 문장을 읽고 빈칸에는 알맞은 단어를 넣고, 밑줄 친 부분에서는 잘못된 부분을 찾으시오.

1. Like all other living creatures, _____.
   Ⓐ dying cells
   Ⓑ which cells die
   Ⓒ cells die
   Ⓓ the death of cells

2. Vitamin A, discovered in 1920, _____ first vitamin for which the molecular structure was established.
   Ⓐ the
   Ⓑ was the
   Ⓒ as the
   Ⓓ being the

3. Theatrical producer James Morris _____ the establishment of a professional repertory theater in America.
   Ⓐ who encouraged
   Ⓑ encouraged
   Ⓒ was encouraged
   Ⓓ who was encouraged

4. In 1960 Mary Jackson _____ her country as a United Nations delegates.
   Ⓐ served
   Ⓑ was served
   Ⓒ to serve
   Ⓓ serving

5. Boston, <u>the hub</u> New England, <u>it is</u> the <u>capital of</u> Massachusetts
            A   B   C
   and <u>the largest</u> city in the area.
       D

6. <u>Mixed</u> seeds, <u>such as</u> cracked corn, peanuts, and sunflower seeds, <u>is</u>
     A   B   C
   popular food for <u>winter birds</u>.
                     D

7. Unlike <u>most</u> capital cities, Washington <u>it was</u> constructed <u>specially</u> <u>to house</u>
           A   B   C   D
   government offices.

8. Borax, <u>usually</u> found in the desert, <u>being</u> useful <u>as</u> a water <u>softener</u> in
           A   B   C   D
   the laundry industry.

9. Modern buttons, unlike early ones, they are often mass-produced and
                                        A   B   C
   usually made of plastic.
          D

10. The letter 'A' probably it originated as a picture sign of a house.
                    A   B   C   D

11. Bats deterministic their position by using of echolocation, a system that
        A   B   C   D
    does not rely on sight.

12. Sixty-five percent of the Thai farmers although only ten percent of their
                              A   B   C
    land is under cultivation.
              D

13. In 1678, John Bunyan who published his masterpiece Pilgrim's Progress
                         A   B
    which was extremely popular for over 300 years.
                  C   D

14. Scientists know very little about the drug's long-term effects, since to
                    A   B
    having been on the market for only two years.
        C   D

Unit 2

문장의 종류

◀ 평서문(declarative sentence; active voice)

어떤 사실이나 의견을 단순히 있는 그대로 진술하는 문장이다.
진술문(declaration sentence)이라고도 한다.
긍정문(affirmative sentence) 또는 능동태(active voice) 문장이다.

> A day has twenty-four hours.
> Kind words are the music of the world.
> That candidate will surely be elected.
>
> 하루는 24시간이다. / 친절한 말은 세상에서 가장 아름다운 음악이다. / 저 후보는 반드시 선출될 것이다.

◀ 부정문(negative sentence)

일반부정문의 부정어 위치

1. be 동사
   have 동사 } +*not*/ *never* + (동사)
   일반조동사

   He is busy. → He is **not** busy.(/He's **not** busy./He **isn't** busy.)
   I have been there. → I **have never been** there.
   You should do that. → You **should not do** that./You **shouldn't do** that.

2. do동사 +not+일반동사

Basic Grammar for English Tests

They turn left here. → They **don't turn** left here.
He wants it. → He **doesn't want** it.
He wanted it. → He **didn't want** it.
They went there. → They **didn't go** there.

◀ 여러 가지 부정문형

1. 부사로 부정문을 만드는 경우

   * 주요 부정의미의 부사 (negative adverbs)
     1. hardly, scarcely, rarely, seldom, never, no, hardly ever, scarcely ever :
        거의 ~않다, 좀체 ~ 않다
     2. barely : 간신히 ~ 하다

   We **sometimes** see them nowadays. 우리는 요즘 그들을 가끔씩 보게 된다.
   → We **never** see them nowadays. 우리는 요즘 그들을 전혀 볼 수 없다.

   → We **hardly (ever) / scarcely (ever) / rarely** see them nowadays. 우리는 요즘 그들을 거의 볼 수 없다.

   Jane **barely** arrived on time.
   He **barely** escaped death.
   I **seldom** change my opinion.
   It **not seldom** happens that we have snow in March. (= often)
   There's **no** chalk in the drawer.
   John **rarely** comes to class on time.

   제인은 가까스로 정각에 도착하였다. / 그는 간신히 죽음을 모면하였다. / 나는 좀체 내 견해를 바꾸지 않는다. / 3월에 눈을 보는 것이 보기드문 일은 아니다. / 서랍에 분필이 없다. / 존이 정각에 등교하는 일은 거의 없다.

2. 기타 부정을 표현하는 부사

   She was **somehow** surprised. → She **wasn't in any way** surprised.
   → She was **in no way** surprised.
   He helped **to some extent**. → He **didn't** help **at all**.
   They've arrived already. → They **haven't** arrived **yet**.
   John is coming, **too**. → John **isn't** coming, **either**.
   They ate **too** much cakes. → They **didn't** eat **very** much.

그녀는 다소 놀랐다. → 그녀는 조금도 놀라지 않았다. / 그는 어느 정도 도왔다. → 그는 결코 돕지 않았다. / 그들은 벌써 도착하였다. → 그들은 아직 도착하지 않았다. / 존 역시 온다. → 존 역시 오지 않는다. / 그들은 케이크를 너무 많이 먹었다. → 그들은 그리 많이 먹지 않았다.

I understood **little** of his speech. (거의 ~않는)
She was **by no means** convinced by his arguments. (결코 ~않는)
We had **scarcely** started lunch **when** the doorbell rang. (하자마자 ~하다)

나는 그의 연설을 거의 이해하지 못했다. / 그녀는 그의 주장을 결코 납득하지 못했다. / 우리가 점심을 시작하자마자 초인종이 울렸다.

3. 'no, not ~ any'로 만드는 경우:
   - 동사+no+명사
   - 조동사+not+동사+any+명사
   * 부정어의 위치를 주의해서 익힌다.

긍정문	부정문	
	'no' 나 'no 복합어'	'any' 나 'any 복합어'
I've **some** time.	I've **no** time.	I don't have **any** time.
I've **some** problem.	I've **no** problems.	I don't have **any** problems
I've seen **some** one/somebody.	I've seen **no** one/nobody.	I haven't seen **any** one/anybody.
I've bought **some** of them.	I've bought **none** of them.	I haven't bought **any** of them.
I've done **something** today.	I've done **nothing** today.	I haven't done **anything** today.
I've been **somewhere** today.	I've been **nowhere** today.	I haven't been **anywhere** today.

나에게 시간이 약간 있다. 나는 시간이 없다. / 나에게 문제가 좀 생겼다. 나는 아무런 문제가 없다. / 나는 어떤 사람을 보았다. 나는 아무도 보지 못했다. / 나는 그중에 약간을 샀다. 나는 그중에서 어느 것도 사지 않았다. / 나는 오늘 어떤 것을 하였다. 나는 오늘 아무것도 하지 않았다. / 나는 오늘 어디를 다녀왔다. 나는 오늘 아무데도 가지 않았다.

* 두 부정형은 같은 뜻이지만, 'no 부정문'이 'not~any 부정문'보다 부정의 뜻이 더 강하다.

4. 일반적으로 하나의 문장에 두 개의 부정어는 쓰지 않는다.

I can't get **any** eggs. / I can get **no** eggs.
I can **never(hardly)** get **any** information.
He **hardly never** takes a vacation himself. (x)
→ He **hardly ever** takes a vacation himself. (o)

나는 계란이 하나도 없다. / 나는 어떤 정보도 전혀 얻을 수 없다. / 그는 혼자서 휴가를 갖는 일이 거의 없다.

Exercise 1 다음 중에서 문법에 틀린 문장을 골라 바르게 고치시오.

1. have no money. (o)
2. I don't need no help. (x) → *I don't need any help.*
3. I didn't see nobody.

4. I can't never understand him.
5. I don't trust anyone.
6. He doesn't like neither coffee nor tea.
7. I can't hardly hear the radio.
8. There was nobody in his room.
9. We couldn't see nothing but sand in the desert.
10. Methods of horse training haven't changed at all in the last eight centuries.

Exercise 2 다음 글을 읽고 괄호에 가장 적당한 말을 고르시오.

A Yeti is supposed to be a strange creature that lives in Himalayas. Nearly (*everyone*/no one) has heard of Yeti, but (everyone/no one) has actually seen one. Recently, a party of climbers went up Mount Jaonli looking for Yetis. Unlike more famous mountains, Jaonli has (hardly ever/hardly never) been climbed. The party saw (no/nothing) Yetis (anywhere/nowhere). There was a moment's excitement one night when a climber heard a strange, two-note sound. He rushed out of his tent and asked his Tibetan guide, if he had heard (anything/something). "No, I heard (anything/nothing)," the guide replied. "But I just heard a strange sound," the climber said. "That was no Yeti," the guide laughed. "It was me, blowing my nose!"

◀ 의문문(questions, interrogative sentences)

Yes/No 의문문 : 'Yes/No 문장'의 대답을 요구하는 질문

Have you ever been to Egypt? — Yes, I have.
　　　　　　　　　　　　　　　　　No, I haven't.
Haven't you ever been there? — Yes, I have. (아뇨, 있습니다.)
　　　　　　　　　　　　　　　　　No, I haven't. (예, 없습니다.)
Does he like fish? — Yes, he does.
　　　　　　　　　　　No, he doesn't.
Doesn't he like fish? — Yes, he does. (아뇨, 좋아합니다.)
　　　　　　　　　　　　No, he doesn't. (예, 좋아하지 않습니다.)

1. 의문문의 형식

   (1) be동사, have, 일반조동사가 있는 문장

   > be 동사
   > Have 동사   } →주어+동사 … ?
   > 일반조동사

   I **am** late. → **Am** I late?
   He **was** going. → **Was he** going?
   He **has** won. → **Has he** won?
   She **can** swim. → **Can she** swim?
   It **will** rain. → **Will it** rain?

   (2) 일반동사만 있는 문장 : Do+주어+동사 … ?

   You **dance** well. → **Do** you **dance** well?
   She **works** well. → **Does** she **work** well?
   It **ran** fast. → **Did it run** fast?

긍정문	의문문
I'm working too hard.	Are you working too hard?
I've eaten too much.	Have you eaten too much?
You may stop now.	May I stop now?
I work too hard.	Do you work too hard?
I ate too much yesterday.	Did you eat too much yesterday?

2. Yes/No 의문문과 Yes/No 대답

   (1) be 동사

   Are you ready? —Yes, I am. / No, I'm not.
   Is he leaving? —Yes, he is. / No, he's not./he isn't.
   Were you ill? —Yes, we were. / No, we weren't.

   (2) have

   Have you finished? —Yes, I have. / No, I haven't.
   Has she left? —Yes, she has. / No, she hasn't.

   (3) do

   Do you like it? —Yes, I do. / No, I don't.
   Does it work? —Yes, it does. / No, it doesn't.
   Did you paint it? —Yes, I did. / No, I didn't.

Basic Grammar for English Tests

(4) 일반조동사

Can I see him? —Yes, you can. / No, you can't.

부정의문문(negative questions)과 Yes/No 대답

· Didn't you go to a party last night?
—Yes, I did. / No, I didn't. / No, I did not. (강조)
· Don't you remember that holiday we had in spain? (Yes를 기대) —Yes, I do.
· Can't you (really) ride a bicycle? (믿어지지 않고 놀람을 표시) —No, I can't.
· Won't you help me? = Please help me. (부탁)
—Oh, all right then. / No, I'm afraid I can't(/won't).
· Can't you shut the door behind you? (귀찮은 듯 불만 섞인 표현—대답은 기대하지 않음)
· Didn't he do well! (감탄)
· Isn't it hot in here!

· 어젯밤에 파티에 가질 않았나요? —아뇨, 갔어요. / 예, 가지 않았습니다. / 예, 결코 가지 않았습니다.
· 우리가 스페인에서 가졌던 그 휴일이 기억나지 않으세요? —아뇨, 기억나요.
· 당신은 (정말로) 자전거를 탈 줄 모르시나요? —예, 모릅니다.
· 저를 좀 도와주지 않겠어요? —아, 그래야죠. / 예, 제가 도움이 될는지요.
· 문 좀 닫고 다닐 수 없겠니?
· 그 사람 정말 잘했잖아요!
· 여긴 너무 덥잖아요!

부가의문문(tag questions)과 Yes/No 대답

1. 형태

동사분류	긍정 →	부정	부정 →	긍정
be 동사	I'm late, They are waiting, We were late,	aren't I? aren't they? weren't we?	I'm not late, He isn't leaving, I wasn't ill,	am I? is he? was I?
have	I've finished, He's left,	haven't I? hasn't he?	I haven't finished, He hasn't left,	have I? has he?
do	You have it, It works, You painted it,	don't you? doesn't it? didn't you?	You don't have it, It doesn't work, You didn't paint it,	do you? does it? did you?
일반조동사	I can see him,	can't I?	I can't see him,	can I?

* 부가의문문의 끝을 올려 읽으면 : 대답을 요구하는 표현
끝을 내려 읽으면 : 상대방의 말에 동의한다는 표현

2. 주의할 문장

  (1) 부정의미의 부사 no, seldom, hardly, rarely, scarcely, nothing 등이 주절에
      있는 경우 : 부정문으로 인정한다.

   Jerry **hardly** studied last night, **did he**?
   We **seldom** see photos of these animals, **do we**?
   She **scarcely** remembers the accident, **does she**?

   제리는 밤중에는 거의 공부하지 않지요, 그렇죠? / 우리는 이 동물들의 사진은 거의 볼 수가 없지요, 그렇죠? / 그녀는 그 사고를 거의 기억하지 못해요, 그렇죠?

  (2) 'I think that' 문형의 복문인 경우

   I suppose (that) you're not serious, **are you**?
   I don't think (that) he's serious, **is he**? (= I think he's not serious.)

   제 생각에 당신은 심각하지 않지요, 그렇죠? / 저는 그가 심각하다고 생각하지 않아요, 그렇죠?

  (3) 중문에서는 뒤 문장을 받는다.

   I'm reading English **and you're** writing French, **aren't you**?
   You're a teacher, **but your sister is** a student, **isn't she**?

   저는 영어를 읽고, 당신은 불어를 쓰고 있어요, 안 그래요? / 당신은 교사이지만, 당신의 누이는 학생이죠, 안 그래요?

  (4) 일반 복문에서는 주절을 받는다.

   We **arrived** there **after** the sun had set, **didn't we**?
   He's **not** a man **who** tells a lie, **is he**?

   우리는 해가 진 후에 그곳에 도착하였지요, 안 그래요? / 그는 거짓말을 할 남자가 아니지요, 그렇죠?

  (5) 주어가 대명사일 경우

   This(That) **is** your book, **isn't it**? (this/that의 부가대명사는 it)
   These(Those) **are** yours, **aren't they**? (these/those → they)

   이(저)것은 당신 책이지요, 안 그래요? / 이(저) 책들은 당신 거죠, 안 그래요?

  (6) 유도부사 There/Here로 시작하는 문장

   There'll be a rail strike tomorrow, **won't there**?

   내일 철도파업이 있을 거죠, 안 그래요?

  (7) ┌ it ← everything, something, nothing
       └ they ← everyone, everybody, someone, somebody, no one, nobody

   Everything is okay, **isn't it**?
   Nothing is wrong, **is it**?
   Everyone's ready to leave now, **aren't they**?
   Nobody's been told, **have they**?

ENGLISH FORUM — Basic Grammar for English Tests

모든 것이 정상입니다, 안 그래요? / 아무것도 잘못된 것은 없어요, 그렇죠? / 모든 사람들이 지금 떠나려고 해요, 안 그래요? / 아무도 듣지 못했어요, 그렇죠?

(8) Let's로 시작하는 '권유문'

Let's go home, **shall we**?

집에 가시지 않을래요?

(9) '당위성'의 뜻인 have to, ought to 등의 경우

You have to sign this document, **don't you**?
She ought to go by plane, **shouldn't she**? (oughtn't to는 발음하기가 어려워 같은 뜻인 shouldn't를 쓴다.)

당신은 이 서류에 서명하셔야 합니다, 안 그래요? / 그녀는 비행기로 가야해요, 안 그래요?

(10) 조동사, have동사, be동사

 a. 일반조동사 + 동사

They'd go with us, **wouldn't they**?

 b. had + p.p

We'd decided to open a joint account, **hadn't we**?

 c. have/has + p.p

She's been elected, **hasn't she**?

 d. 진행형

He's writing her another letter, **isn't he**?

그들은 우리와 함께 갈 것입니다, 안 그렇습니까? / 우리는 통합구좌를 개설할 생각이에요, 안 그래요? / 그녀가 선출되었어요, 안 그래요? / 그는 그녀에게 또 다른 편지를 쓰고 있는 거예요, 안 그래요?

(11) 기타

I am supposed to be here, **am I not**? (문법에 맞는 문장)
I am supposed to be here, **aren't I**? (회화체로 사용)

제가 여기 있기로 되어 있어요, 맞죠?

Exercise 3 다음 빈칸에 부가의문문을 만들어 넣으시오.

1. They're on holiday, *aren't they*?
2. Clara was at home, _____
3. You've finished, _____
4. Jane has gone out, _____
5. I always do the wrong thing, _____
6. You've never been to Paris, _____

7. Something is wrong with Jane today, _____
8. Nobody cheated on the exam, _____
9. Nothing went wrong while I was gone, _____
10. Everyone can learn how to swim, _____

의문사의문문(question-word questions : Wh-question)

1. 분류

   서술 : Jane went to her mother's by bus yesterday because the trains weren't running. 기차가 운행하지 않아서 어제 제인은 버스로 어머니에게 갔습니다.

의미	의문문	대답
시간	When did Jane go to her mother's?	Yesterday.
장소	Where did Jane go yesterday? Whose house did Jane go to?	To her mother's. Her mother's.
수단	How did she get there?	By bus.
이유	Why did she go by bus?	Because the trains weren't's running.
정보	What did Jane do yesterday?	She went to her mother's by bus.

2. 의문사의문문의 쓰임새

   (1) When (언제)

   When will you come? — Tomorrow morning.
   When will he arrive? — At 5.

   너는 언제 올거니? — 내일 아침에요. / 그는 언제 도착하지요? — 5시에요.

   (2) Where (어디)

   Where is he? — He's over there./Over there./There.
   Where are you **from**?/**Where** do you come **from**? — Spain.

   그 사람 어디에 있죠? — 저기 계십니다 / 어디 출신입니까?/어디서 오셨습니까? — 스페인에서요.

   (3) Who (누가) — 주어

   Who can answer that question? — I can.
   Who came to visit you? — Jane and Eric.

   누가 저 질문에 답하겠습니까? — 제가요. / 누가 당신을 방문하였습니까? — 제인과 에릭입니다.

Basic Grammar for English Tests

(4) Whom (누구를)

whom은 실제 회화체에서는 잘 쓰지 않는다. 그러나 '전치사+의문사' 표현에는 whom으로 쓴다.

Who(m) are you visiting?—My relatives.
Who(m) should I talk to? = **To whom** should I talk? (문어체)—The secretary.

누구를 방문하는 것입니까?—제 친척들입니다. / 저는 누구에게 이야기해야 하죠?—비서입니다.

(5) Whose (누구의)

Whose (key) is this?—It's mine.
Whose children are they?—The Bakers'.

이건 누구의 것(열쇠)입니까?—그건 제겁니다. / 그 애들은 누구집 아이들입니까?—베이커씨네 아이들입니다.

(6) What (무엇)

What made you angry?—His rudeness made me angry.
What went wrong?—Everything went wrong.
What's this **for**?—(It's for) peeling apples.
What did he talk **about**?—His vacation.
What kind(sort) of picture do you like best?
What kinds(sorts) of pictures do you like best?
What size shirt do you wear?—(Size) 100.
What's the height of Everest? = What height is Everest?
What's John **like**?—He's kind and friendly.
What's the weather **like** today? = What's it like today?—It's hot and humid.
What does John **look like**?—He's tall and thin.

당신을 화나게 한 것이 무엇입니까?—그의 무례함이 저를 화나게 만들었습니다. / 무엇이 잘못되었죠?—모든 것이 잘못되었습니다. / 이것은 무엇에 쓰는 것이죠?—사과를 깎는 것입니다. / 그 사람이 무슨 이야기를 했습니까?—자기의 휴가에 대해서 입니다. / 어떤 그림을 가장 좋아하십니까? / 어떤 종류의 그림들을 가장 좋아하십니까? / 당신은 셔츠를 어느 치수로 입나요?—100호입니다. / 에베레스트산의 높이는 얼마죠? = 에베레스트산은 얼마나 높죠? / 존은 어떤 사람입니까?—친절하고 우호적입니다. / 오늘 날씨는 어떻습니까? = 오늘은 날씨가 어때요?—덥고, 습합니다. / 존은 어떻게 생겼습니까?—키가 크고 야위었습니다.

(7) Which (어느-)

⎡ Which is the cheaper/the cheapest?
⎣ Which is the longest river in the world: the Amazon or the Nile?

⎡ **Which countries** did he visit?—Peru and Chile.
⎣ **What countries** did he visit?

어느 것이 더 쌉니까? / 가장 쌉니까? / 어느 것이 세계에서 가장 긴 강입니까? 아마존과 나일강 중에서. / 어느 나라들을 방문하였습니까?—페루와 칠레입니다. / 어떤 나라들을 방문하였습니까?

(8) How (어떻게)

How did you come to school?—By bus.
How many people are invited?

34 | Part 1 구문편

How much does this cost?

학교에는 어떻게 왔어요?—버스로요. / 몇 사람이나 초대 됩니까? / 이것은 비용이 얼마나 듭니까?

* How+형용사/부사 …?

　How old are you?—Sixteen.
　How cold is it?—It is ten degrees below zero.
　How far is it to Seoul?—50 miles. (거리)

몇 살입니까?—16살입니다. / 얼마나 춥죠?—영하 10도입니다. / 학교까지는 얼마나 멀죠?—50마일입니다.

* How+부사 … ?

　How often do you visit your mother?—Once a week. (빈도)
　How well do you know him?—Not very well. (정도)
　How long have you been here?—Two years. (시간)
　How long ago did Bach live?—300 years ago. (시간)
　How quickly can you do it for me?—In two days. (시간)
　How soon can you get here?—In ten minutes. (시간)
　How fast were you driving?—50 miles an hour. (시간)

어머니께는 얼마나 자주 찾아뵙습니까?—일주일에 한 번입니다. / 그 사람을 얼마나 잘 아시나요?—그리 잘 알지는 못합니다. / 여기 온 지는 얼마나 되었습니까?—2년요. / 바하는 얼마 전에 살았습니까?—300년 전이요. / 그것을 얼마나 빨리 해주실 수 있으세요?—이틀 안에요. / 여기에는 얼마나 빨리 오실 수 있습니까?—10분 안에요. / 얼마나 빨리 운전하셨습니까?—시속 50마일요.

(9) Why (왜)

　Why did he leave so early?—Because he's ill.
　I'm not going to work today.—Why not?
　Why don't you change it?
　Why not wait till the winter sales to buy a new coat?
　Let's eat out tonight.—Yes, why not?
　Why can't you shut up?

그는 왜 그렇게 일찍 떠났죠?—아파서요. / 오늘 저는 출근하지 않을 것입니다.—왜 그래요? / 그것을 바꾸지 않겠어요? / 새 코트를 사려면 겨울세일까지 기다리시는 것이 어때요? / 오늘밤 외식하실까요?—예, 좋지요! / 입 좀 다물지 못하겠니?

◀ 명령문(imperative sentence, commands)

일반 명령

흔히 주어를 생략한다.
인칭, 시제에 상관없이 원형동사를 쓴다.

Basic Grammar for English Tests

1. 경고

   Look out! / There's a bus! / Don't panic!
   주의해! / 버스가 있다! / 겁 먹지 마!

2. 지시

   Take the 2nd turning on the left and then turn right.
   Turn to the right at the river and keep straight on.
   왼쪽에서 두 번째 회전을 하고, 다음에 우회전하시오. / 강에서 우회전하고서 똑바로 가시오.

3. 설명

   Use a moderate oven and bake for 20 minutes.
   적절한 오븐을 사용하여 20분간 구우시오.

4. 금지

   Keep off the grass! / Do not feed the animals!
   잔디를 밟지 마시오! / 동물들에게 먹이를 주지 마시오!

5. 충고 (always, never 등으로 시작)

   Always answer when you're spoken to!
   Never speak to strangers!
   Behave yourself.
   누가 말을 걸면 항상 대답을 하라! / 낯선 사람들에게는 말을 걸지 마라! / 점잖게 굴어라.

6. 초대

   Come and have dinner with us soon.
   Come inside and meet my daughter.
   곧 오셔서 저희들과 같이 저녁식사를 하십시오. / 들어오셔서 제 딸을 만나 보세요.

7. 제공

   Help yourself. / Have a biscuit. / Enjoy yourself.
   드시지요. / 비스켓 드세요. / 맛있게 드세요.

8. 거친 표현

   Shut up! / Push off!
   입 다물어! / 너 죽어!

9. 간청

   Spare a penny, sir, for a starving man.
   한푼 줍쇼, 선생님, 배고픈 사람입니다.

10. 조건

    일반명령문, and/or + S + V ... (… 하라, 그러면/그렇지 않으면 … 할 것이다.)

    Be diligent, **and**(= if you are diligent) you will succeed.
    Come right away, **or**(= if you don't come right away) you will be late.
    부지런히 일하시오, 그러면 성공할 것입니다. / 당장 오시오, 그렇지 않으면 지각할 것입니다.

11. 1인칭과 3인칭 명령문은 Let로 시작

    Let me have a book.
    Let each man decide for himself.
    책 한 권 가질게요. / 각자 스스로 결정하게 하오.

12. 부정형

    Open the door. → **Don't open** the door.
    Let's talk about it. → **Let's not talk** about it.
    Let someone open the door. → **Don't let anyone open** the door.
    문을 열어라. → 문을 열지 마라. / 그 문제를 이야기해보자. → 그 문제는 이야기하지 말자. / 누군가 문을 열게 하라. → 누구도 문을 열게 하지 마라.

강한 명령

부가의문문을 붙이는 경우에 생략된 주어가 2인칭임을 알 수 있다.

Come in, **will you?**(/won't you?)
Take a seat, **will you?**(/won't you?)
Don't tell anyone I told you, **will you?**
Wait here, **will you?**
들어오시겠어요? / 자리에 앉으시겠어요? / 내가 네게 말한 것을 누구에게도 말하지 마, 알겠지? / 여기서 기다리시겠어요?

◀ 감탄문(exclamations)

What … !, How … !

1. 기본표현

    What a pretty girl she is!
    How old you are!
    그 애는 참 예쁜 여자야! / 이제 다 컸구나!

Basic Grammar for English Tests

2. What+관사+명사! : 주어+동사가 생략된 경우

What a feeling!
What a surprise!
What a lot of trouble!

오, 이 느낌! / 아이구 깜짝이야! / 아이구 골치야!

부정사와 함께

What a thing to say!
What a way to behave!
How kind of him to help us!

어쩜 그런 말을 하지! / 어쩜 저런 식으로 행동하지! / 우리를 도와주다니 그분은 어쩜 그렇게 친절도 하시지!

◀ 수동문 (passive voice)

수동태의 형태 : 목적어(주절)+be+p.p.+by+주어(목적격)

	능동	수동
현재	She helps me.	I am helped by her.
현재진행	She is helping me.	I am being helped by her.
현재완료	She has helped me.	I have been helped by her.
과거	She helped me.	I was helped by her.
과거진행	She was helping me.	I was being helped by her.
과거완료	She had helped me.	I had been helped by her.
미래	She will help me.	I will be helped by her.
is going to	She is going to help me.	I am going to be helped by her.
미래완료	She will have helped me.	I will have been helped by her.

주의할 수동의 형태

1. 조동사의 수동태

   (1) 조동사+be+p.p.

   Tom **will be invited** to the picnic.
   Children **should be taught** to respect their elders.
   May I be excused from class?

   톰이 소풍에 초대될 것입니다. / 어린이들은 어른들을 공경하도록 가르쳐야 합니다. / 화장실에 가도 되겠습니까?

(2) 조동사+have been+p.p.

The letter **should have been sent** last week.
This house **must have been built** over 200 years ago.

편지는 지난 주에 부쳐졌어야 해요. / 이 집은 200년도 더 전에 건축된 것이 틀림없어요.

2. 자동사와 타동사

Someone **found** this wallet in the street. → This wallet **was found** in the street.
The door **opened**.
The door **was opened**.

어떤 사람이 거리에서 이 지갑을 발견했습니다. → 이 지갑은 거리에서 발견되었습니다. / 문이 (저절로) 열렸습니다. / 문이 (누군가에 의해) 열렸습니다.

3. 상태의 수동태

I locked the door five minutes ago.
→ The door **was locked** by me five minutes ago. (행위)
→ Now the door **is locked**. (상태)
Ann **broke** the window.
→ The window **was broken** by Ann. (행위)
→ Now the window **is broken**. (상태)

나는 5분 전에 문을 잠갔다. → 문은 5분 전에 나에 의해 잠겼다. → 지금 문은 잠겨 있다.
앤이 창문을 깼습니다. → 창문은 앤에 의해 깨어졌습니다. → 지금 창문이 깨어져 있습니다.

4. 진행형의 수동태

They **are interviewing** her now. → She **is being interviewed** now.
They **may be interviewing** her at this very moment.
→ She **may be being interviewed** at this very moment.

그들이 지금 그녀를 면담하고 있다. → 그녀는 지금 면담 받고 있다. / 그들은 바로 이 순간 그녀를 면담하고 있다. → 그녀는 바로 이 순간 면담 받고 있을지도 모른다.

5. 숙어형태 : 흔히 수동태로 쓰인다.

A gust of wind **blew** the tent down. → Our tent **was blown down**.
We have done away with the old rules.
→ The old rules **have been done away with**.
I **am interested** in Korean music.
He **is satisfied** with his job.
I **was surprised** at his sudden death.
Ann **is married** to Alex (상태)
Shakespeare **is known** to everybody.
I **am finished** with my work. = I **am done** with my work.

Basic Grammar for English Tests

I **was born** in 1980.
You**'re not obliged to** work overtime if you don't want to.

한 줄기 바람이 텐트를 무너뜨렸다. → 우리 천막이 바람에 무너졌다. / 우리는 오래된 규칙들을 폐지하였다. → 오래된 규칙들이 폐지되었다. / 저는 한국음악에 흥미가 있습니다. / 그는 자기 일에 만족합니다. / 저는 그의 갑작스러운 죽음에 깜짝 놀랐습니다. / 앤은 알렉스와 결혼하였습니다. / 셰익스피어는 모든 사람에게 알려져 있습니다. / 저는 일을 끝마쳤습니다. / 저는 1980년에 태어났습니다. / 당신은 원치 않으면 과외작업을 하지 않아도 됩니다.

6. 동명사와 부정사의 수동태

Most people don't like **being criticized**.
He hates **to be criticized**.
On/After being informed that her mother was seriously ill, she hurried back to England. (= When she was informed …)

대부분의 사람들은 비난받는 것을 좋아하지 않습니다. / 그는 비난받기를 싫어합니다. / 자기 어머니가 몹시 편찮으시다는 사실을 연락 받자마자, 그녀는 영국으로 서둘러 돌아갔습니다.

7. 수동의미를 지닌 행위동사

This surface **cleans** easily. (clean: 지워지다)
These clothes **wash** well. (wash: 씻기다)
This wine **is selling** quickly. (sell: 팔리다)
What's **showing** at the cinema this week? (show: 보여지다, 방영되다)
His novel **is reprinting** already. (reprint: 재인쇄되다)

이 표면은 청소가 쉽게 됩니다. / 이 옷들은 세탁이 잘 됩니다. / 이 와인은 금방 팔려 나갑니다. / 이번 주 극장에서 방영되는 것은 무엇입니까? / 그의 소설은 벌써 재판되고 있습니다.

8. 재귀동사와 수동태

What's the matter?—I've burnt(/cut/hurt …) myself.
*burn myself: 화상을 입다, cut myself: 칼에 베다, hurt myself: 다치다

I **was hurt** in a car crash last summer.
Jim was in a fight and **his shirt was torn** in the struggle.

무슨 일이죠?—화상을 입었습니다.(칼에 베었습니다./다쳤습니다.) / 저는 지난 여름 자동차 충돌사고로 다쳤습니다. / 짐은 싸움판에 끼어들었고, 그의 셔츠는 싸우다가 찢어졌습니다.

9. 명령문의 수동

> Let+목적어+수동태
> Don't let+목적어+수동태
> Let+목적어+not+수동태

Bring the man here. → Let the man be brought here.
Do it at once. → Let it be done at once.

Don't forget to water these plants. → Let it not be forgotten to water those plants.
Don't touch the furniture. → Don't let the furniture be touched.
→ Let the furniture not be touched.

그 사람을 이리 데려오시오. → 그 사람을 이리 오게 하시오. / 즉시 그렇게 하시오. → 즉시 그렇게 되도록 하시오. / 이 식물들에 물을 주는 것을 잊지 마시오. → 이 식물들에 물을 주는 것을 잊지 않도록 하시오. / 가구를 만지지 마시오. → 가구가 만져지지 않도록 하시오.

◀ 수동태의 기타 활용

1. 능동 표현보다 수동태가 더 적절한 표현인 경우

   (1) 능동 표현이 어색하고 수동 표현이 적절한 문장
   Rome **wasn't built** in a day.
   I don't know where I am. **I am lost**.
   I can't find my purse. **It is gone**.
   로마는 하루에 건설되지 않았다. / 제가 어디에 있는지 모르겠습니다. 길을 잃었습니다. / 제 지갑을 찾을 수가 없습니다.

   (2) 말하는 이의 확신을 뺄 경우
   The matter **will be dealt with** as soon as possible.
   Thousands of books **are published** every year and very few of them are noticed.
   Even those that **are reviewed** in the papers rarely reach large audiences.
   그 문제는 가능한 빨리 처리될 것입니다. / 매년 수천 권의 책이 출간되며, 그중 극소수만이 알려집니다. / 심지어 신문에 소개되는 책들도 독자대중에게까지 이르는 일이 드뭅니다.

   (3) 사건에 초점을 두는 경우
   Our roof **was damaged** in last night's storm.
   My car's been scratched!
   Thousands of beaches **were polluted**.
   간밤의 폭풍에 우리집 지붕이 파손되었다. / 제 자동차가 긁혔습니다. / 수많은 해변이 오염되었습니다.

   (4) 막연한 주어(one, someone, they, a person …)를 피할 때
   After my talk, **I was asked** to explain a point I had made.
   The form has to be signed in the presence of a witness.
   말을 마치자, 저는 제가 달한 요점을 설명해달라는 요청을 받았습니다. / 그 서류는 증인이 보는 데서 서명되어야 합니다.

2. by+행위자

   The window was broken **by** the boy who lives opposite.
   The window was broken **by** a stone.

Basic Grammar for English Tests

Who composed that piece? — It was composed **by** Mozart.
What destroyed the village? — It was destroyed **by** a bomb.

창문은 반대편에 사는 소년에 의해 깨어졌습니다. / 창문은 돌에 의해 깨어졌습니다. / 누가 그 곡을 작곡하였습니까?—모차르트에 의해 작곡되었습니다. / 무엇이 그 마을을 파괴하였습니까?—폭탄으로 파괴되었습니다.

cf. This bridge was built **in** 1816.(/**of** stone./**before** the war.)
During the World Cup our streets were filled **with** soccer fans.
The mountain is covered **with** snow.

이 다리는 1816년에(/돌로/전쟁 전에) 건설되었습니다. / 월드컵이 진행되는 동안 우리의 거리는 축구팬들로 가득 찼습니다. / 산은 눈에 덮여 있습니다.

3. get+p.p.

> arréstéd(체포되다) caught(잡히다) confúsed(혼동되다) deláyed(지연되다)
> divórced(이혼하다) dressed(옷을 입다) drowned(물에 빠지다) drunk(술 취하다)
> eléctéd(선출되다) engáged(약혼하다) hit(부딪히다) killed(죽다) lost(길을 잃다)
> married(결혼하다) stuck(얽매이다) tired(피곤하다) worried(걱정하다)

I **got dressed** as quickly as I could. (동작)
cf. He **is dressed** in the latest fashion.(상태)
I stopped working because I **got tired**.
They are **getting married** next month.
I **got worried** because he was two hours late.

저는 가능한 빨리 옷을 입었습니다. / 그는 최신 패션으로 옷을 입었습니다. / 저는 피곤해서 작업을 중단하였습니다. / 그들은 다음 달에 결혼을 할 것입니다. / 저는 그가 2시간이나 늦어서 걱정을 하였습니다.

4. 사실에 대한 확인이 필요할 때

> * 이 수동태에 쓰이는 동사 : 사유동사
> agrée(동의하다) allége(주장하다) assúme(가정하다) belíeve(믿다) consíder(고려하다)
> decíde(결심하다) discóver(발견하다) expéct(기대하다) féar(두려워하다) feel(느끼다)
> find(찾다) hope(희망하다) imágine(상상하다) know obsérve(관찰하다) prove(증명하다)
> repórt(보고하다) suggést(제안하다) say suppóse(상상하다) think understánd

(1) It+수동태+that절 …

He was a spy in World War II.
→ **It is said that** he was a spy in World War II.
It is said that there is plenty of oil off our coast.

그는 2차대전 때 간첩이었다. → 그는 2차대전 때 간첩이었다는 말이 있습니다. / 우리 해안 바깥에 많은 석유가 있다는 말이 있습니다.

(2) There+수동태+to be …

There is said to be plenty of oil off our coast.

There are known to be thousands of different species of beetles.
There is supposed to be a train at 12:30.

우리 해안 바깥에 많은 석유가 있다는 말이 있습니다. / 수천 종의 딱정벌레가 있는 것으로 알려져 있습니다. / 12시30분에 열차가 있는 것으로 되어 있습니다.

(3) 주어+수동태+to do …

He was a spy in World War II.
→ He is said to be a spy in World War II.
Tom was considered to be a genius even in his lifetime.
His therapy is believed to be very effective.
He is supposed to be at work at the moment.

그는 2차대전 때 간첩이었다. → 그는 2차대전 때 간첩이었다고 합니다. / 톰은 자기 일생 동안 천재로 살았으리라 생각됩니다. / 그의 치료법은 매우 효과가 있는 것으로 믿어집니다. / 그는 현재 작업중인 것으로 되어 있습니다.

Exercise 4 빈칸에 주어진 단어와 적당한 전치사를 사용하여 숙어형의 수동태 문장으로 완성하시오.

1. Carol *is interested in* ancient history. (interest)
2. Water _____ hydrogen and oxygen. (compose)
3. I _____ living here. (accustom)
4. Our son _____ dogs. (terrify)
5. Pat _____ her composition. (finish)
6. It's winter, and the ground _____ snow. (cover)
7. I _____ the progress I have made. (satisfy)
8. I _____ sitting here. (tire)
9. Your name is Mary Smith. _____ you _____ John Smith? (relate)
10. Mrs. Robinson works in an orphanage. she _____ her work. (dedicate)

Actual Test 2

다음 각 문장을 읽고 빈칸에는 알맞은 단어를 넣고, 밑줄 친 부분에서는 잘못된 부분을 찾으시오.

1. Catherine Jones _____ to support astronomical and astrophysical research until she was sixty-five years old.
   - Ⓐ began no
   - Ⓑ no beginning
   - Ⓒ did not begin
   - Ⓓ not begin

2. It was certain that _____ two fingerprints are identical.
   - Ⓐ nor
   - Ⓑ none
   - Ⓒ no
   - Ⓓ never

3. How much _____?
   - Ⓐ cost cellular phone calls
   - Ⓑ cellular phone calls cost
   - Ⓒ does cellular phone calls cost
   - Ⓓ do cellular phone calls cost

4. How much time _____ for you to prepare the final exam?
   - Ⓐ there is
   - Ⓑ is there
   - Ⓒ it is
   - Ⓓ is it

5. We had to read the twelfth chapter, _____?
   - Ⓐ didn't we
   - Ⓑ shouldn't we
   - Ⓒ don't we
   - Ⓓ weren't we

6. No, he is going to see you, _____ he?
   - Ⓐ weren't
   - Ⓑ doesn't
   - Ⓒ didn't
   - Ⓓ isn't

7. "I didn't pass the final exam." "_____ next time, and you will succeed."
   - Ⓐ Work hard
   - Ⓑ To work hard
   - Ⓒ Working hard
   - Ⓓ Hard-working

8. The American Red Cross _____ by Nancy Johnson.
   Ⓐ organized it
   Ⓑ was organized
   Ⓒ that was organized
   Ⓓ that it was organized

9. The distance from the Earth to the Mars _____ measured today by radar or by laser beams.
   Ⓐ is easy to
   Ⓑ can easily be
   Ⓒ easily being
   Ⓓ can be easy to

10. Much of the symbolism associated with tree is _____ and folklore.
    Ⓐ that is legend derived
    Ⓑ from derived legend that
    Ⓒ which legend derived
    Ⓓ derived from legend

11. One of the questions about the monolithic stone statues of Easter Island
                      A   B
    is "Why they were all made alike?"
           C   D

12. The Mars was once inhabited by plants and animals of which today there
             A   B   C
    is none living trace.
       D

13. I wouldn't want to ride a bus to office too, unless I lived too many miles
                  A   B   C   D
    away.

14. The shop manager insists that his staff use all of its vacation time, but he
                    A   B   C
    hardly never takes a vacation himself.
          D

15. Due to the newly invented vaccine, the liver disease has now been
            A   B   C
    disappeared.
       D

16. Jane Austin had liberal political opinions, which are reflection in her
                A   B   C
    stories and verse.
          D

17. This episode has described so often as to need no further cliches on
       A   B   C   D
    the subject here.

18. Emily Jones, a social worker and originator of the 'kitchen garden'
                           A   B
    movement, borned in Lebanon, Connecticut.
       C   D

19. The advantages of typing and editing by using computer are now being
                        A   B
    extending to all the written languages of the world.
       C   D

20. Woody Marshall was appointed to an associate justice of the United
                      A   B   C
    States Supreme Court in 1967.
                         D

Unit 3

단문

◀ 기본문형(basic sentence patterns)

문형 1 S + be + C(보어/부사어구)

This **is** a book. 이건 책입니다.
The total **was** a seventy-three. 합계는 73이었습니다.

Who **is** that? 저 사람 누구죠?
What age **is** she? 그녀는 몇 살이죠?

It **was** dark. 어두웠습니다.
Mary **is** charming. 메리는 매력적입니다.

She's in good health. 그녀는 건강이 좋습니다.
We **were** all out of breath. 우리는 모두 숨이 찼습니다.

Your friend's here. 자네 친구가 여기 있어.
The train **is** in. 열차가 들어와 있습니다.

cf. 감탄문형에서 here/there가 문두어 오는 경우

Here's your friend! 여기 자네 친구가 오는구먼!
There **are** the others! 저기 다른 것들도 있군요!
There it **is**! 바로 저기예요!

There **was** a large crowd. 대규모 군중이 있었습니다.
There is **no doubt** about it. 그것에 관해서는 아무런 의심이 없습니다.

Basic Grammar for English Tests

There **are three windows** in this room. 이 방에는 창문이 세 개 있습니다.
There **is a plan of the town** on page 23. 23쪽에 도시계획이 있습니다.

It's so nice **to sit** here with you. 당신과 여기 앉으니 참 좋아요.
It's a pity **to waste** them. 그것들을 버리다니 안됐습니다.

How nice (it is) **to sit** here with you! 당신과 함께 여기 앉으니 참 좋군요!
What a pity (it is) **to waste** them! 그것들을 버리다니 참 안됐습니다.

It's so nice **sitting** here with you. 당신과 함께 여기 앉으니 참 좋습니다.
It won't be much good **complaining** to them. 그들에게 불평하는 것이 그리 좋지는 않을 것입니다.

This house is **to let**. (= to be let) 이 집은 세놓습니다.
What's **to pay**? (= How much is there to pay?) 지급해야 될 돈이 얼마입니까?

It was hard **for** him **to live** on his small pension. 그는 자신의 적은 연금으로 살아가기가 어려웠습니다.
It will be quite all right **for** you **to leave** early. 당신은 일찍 떠나는 것이 아주 좋을 것입니다.

문형 2   S + Vi(자동사) + C(보어/부사어구)

We all **breathe, drink,** and **eat**. 우리 모두는 숨쉬고, 마시고, 먹습니다.
The moon **rose**. 달이 떴습니다.

There **followed** a long period of peace and prosperity. 오랜 평화와 번영의 시대가 이어졌습니다.

It wouldn't have **done to turn** down his request. 그의 요청을 묵살할 것이 참을 수 없었을지도 모릅니다.

They **had gone a long way**. 그들은 먼 길을 갔습니다.
He **jumped two meters**. 그는 2미터를 높이 뛰었습니다.

My hat **blew off**. 모자가 날아갔습니다.
They **ran all the way home**. (동작 ran—home) 그들은 집으로 내내 달려갔습니다.
I'll **stay at home** this evening. (상태 stay—at home) 저는 오늘 저녁에 집에 있을 것입니다.

> * 연결동사(linking verbs)
> appear, be, become, get, go, grow, prove, remain, seem, turn
> 이런 동사들은 형용사가 보어로 이어진다.

The leaves are **turning brown**. 나뭇잎들이 갈색으로 물들고 있습니다.
He's **growing old**. 그는 어른이 되어가고 있습니다.
The meat has **gone bad**. 고기가 상했습니다.
Children **become tired** quite easily. 어린이들은 아주 쉽게 지칩니다.

The small puppy couldn't **remain quiet** for very long. 어린 강아지는 그리 오래 가만히 있지 못합니다.
They **were sorry** to see us leave. 그들은 우리가 떠나는 것을 보고 안타까워 했습니다.
At last his story **proved false**. 드디어 그의 이야기가 거짓임이 드러났습니다.
Don't **get angry**. 화내지 마세요.

> * 감각동사(sense verbs)
> appear(시각), feel(촉각), look(시각), smell(후각), sound(청각), taste(미각)
> 이 동사들은 형용사가 보어로 이어진다.

The dinner **smells good**. 저녁식사 냄새가 좋군요.
Silk **feels soft** and **smooth**. 비단은 촉감이 부드럽고 매끄럽습니다.
This medicine **tastes horrible**. 이 약이 맛이 지독합니다.
Mary **feels bad** about her test grade. 메리는 자신의 시험성적에 대해 기분이 좋지 않습니다.
The soup **tastes good**. 수프 맛이 좋습니다.
Lucy will **look radiant** in her new dress. 루시가 새 드레스를 입은 것을 보면 눈이 부실 것입니다.
The music **sounded beautiful** to her ears. 그 음악이 그녀의 귀에는 아름답게 들렸습니다.
Everything **looks**(appears) **different**. 모든 것이 달라 보입니다.
I'm **feeling fine**. 저는 기분이 좋습니다.

> * 대개 '동사+형용사'가 관용적으로 짝이 된 경우
> hold tight, stand still, keep quiet, open wide

Please **keep quiet**. 조용히 하십시오.
Do **lie/sit/stand still**! 가만히 누워/앉아/서 있어!
The door **blew open/shut**. 문이 바람에 열렸다/닫혔다
Her dreams have **come true**. 그녀의 꿈은 실현되었습니다.

You **look tired**. 당신은 지쳐 보입니다.
He **appeared perplexed**. 그는 당황한 모습이었습니다.
How did they **become acquainted**? 그들이 어떻게 친해졌지요?

The children **came running** to meet us. 어린이들이 우리를 만나러 달려왔다.
Do you like to **go fishing**? 낚시 가는 것을 좋아하십니까?
She **went shopping** this afternoon. 그녀는 오늘 오후에 쇼핑하러 갔습니다.
We soon **got talking**. 우리는 곧 이야기를 주고받게 되었습니다.

He **died a millionaire**.(= He was a millionaire when he died.)
그는 백만장자로 죽었습니다. (= 사망할 당시 그는 백만장자였습니다.)
She will **make a good wife**. 그녀는 어진 아내가 될 것입니다.
You're not **looking yourself** today. 당신은 오늘 당신다워 보이지 않습니다.
On leaving school he **became a sailor**. 학교를 떠나자마자 그는 선원이 되었습니다.
Is it wise for a general to **turn politician**? 장군이 정치가로 변신하는 것이 현명한가요?

Basic Grammar for English Tests

Exercise 1 다음 문장이 바른 문장으로 성립하도록 괄호 안에서 알맞은 말을 고르시오.

1. Your cold sound (*terrible*/terribly).
2. The pianist plays very (good/well).
3. The food in the restaurant always tastes (good/well).
4. The campers remained (calm/calmly) despite the thunder-storm.
5. They became (sick/sickly) after eating the contaminated food.
6. Professor Andersen looked (quick/quickly) at the students' sketches.
7. John was working (diligent/diligently) on the project.
8. Paul protested (vehement/vehemently) about the new proposals.
9. Our neighbors appeared (relaxed/relaxedly) after their vacation.
10. The music sounded too (noisy/noisily) to be classical.
11. At the height of the season, the roses smelled (sweet/sweetly).
12. The child grew (silent/silently) when his father entered the room.
13. The water flowed (rapid/rapidly) over the falls.
14. When his team fumbled the ball, the coach shouted at them (angry/angrily).
15. After a rigorous training program, the boy could lift the weights (easy/easily).
16. At the mention of a test, the child turned (pale/palely).
17. The police checked out the man's story, and it proved (false/falsely).
18. Aluminum can be (easy/easily) bent.
19. Going (crazy/crazily) in their tiny apartment, the couple decided to move.
20. That bubbling soup smells very (good/well).

문형 3   S + Vi(자동사) + 전치사 + 명사어구

You can **rely on** my being discretion. 당신은 나의 판단을 믿어도 됩니다.
He **succeeded in** solving the problem. 그는 그 문제를 푸는 데 성공하였습니다.
What has **happened to** them? 그들에게 무슨 일이 일어났습니까?
We must **send for** a doctor. 우리는 의사를 불러와야 합니다.

They're **hoping for** the dispute **to be settled**. 그들은 분쟁이 해결되기를 원하고 있습니다.
(= They want the dispute to be settled.)
I'll **arrange for** a taxi **to meet** you at the station. 저는 역에서 당신을 만나려고 택시를 불렀습니다.

(= I'll order a taxi to meet you at the station.)
I **appealed to** the children **to make** less noise. 저는 아이들에게 조용히 하라고 간청하였습니다.
(= I begged the children to make less noise.)
She **pleaded with** me **to give up** the plan. 그녀는 제게 그 계획을 포기할 것을 촉구하였습니다.
(= She urged me to give up the plan.)

문형 4   S + Vi + C(to부정사구)

We **stopped to have** a rest. 우리는 쉬려고 걸음을 멈췄습니다.
He **got up to answer** the phone. 그는 전화를 받으려고 일어났습니다.

The drunken man **awoke to find** himself in a ditch.
(= He awoke and found … /= When he awoke he found …)
주정꾼은 잠에서 깨어나 자신이 도랑에 있는 것을 발견하였습니다.

The good old days have **gone never to return**.
(= The good old days have gone and will never return.)
좋았던 옛날은 가고 다시는 돌아오지 않을 것입니다.

They **agreed not to oppose** my plan. 그들은 제 계획에 반대하지 않기로 동의하였습니다.
(= They agreed to my plan.)
Harry **aims to become** a computer expert. 해리는 컴퓨터 전문가가 되기로 목표를 정하였습니다.
(= Harry aims at becoming a computer expert.)
We all **rejoiced to hear** of your success. 우리 모두는 당신의 성공소식을 듣고서 기뻐하였습니다.
(= We all rejoiced at the news of your success.)

He **seemed** (to be) surprised at the news. 그는 그 소식에 놀란 것 같았습니다.
This **seems** (to be) a serious matter. 이것은 심각한 문제인 것 같습니다.
This **appears** (to be) an important matter. 이것은 중요한 문제 같아 보입니다.

It **seems** a pity to waste them. 그것들을 낭비하는 것이 안타까워 보입니다.
It doesn't **seem** much good(/use) going on. 계속 진행하는 것이 그리 좋아/소용있어) 보이지 않습니다.

The baby **seems** to be asleep. 아기가 조는 것 같습니다.
My inquiries **appear** to have been resented. 제 질문들이 화나게 한 것 같군요.
She **happened** to be out when I called. 제가 전화했을 때 그녀는 마침 외출 중이었습니다.
We **chanced** to meet in the park that morning. 우리는 그 날 아침 공원에서 우연히 만났습니다.

John and I **are to meet** at the station at six o'clock. (약속)
존과 저는 6시에 역에서 만나기로 되어 있습니다.
At what time **am I to come**? (의도) 제가 몇 시에 올까요?
When **am I to ring** you up? (의도) 제가 언제 당신을 깨워드릴까요?

Basic Grammar for English Tests

문형 5   S + 조동사 + 동사원형

You **may leave** now. 당신은 지금 떠나셔도 됩니다.
Can you **come** early? 당신 일찍 오실 수 있나요?
You **had better start** at once. 당신은 즉시 출발을 하는 것이 좋겠소.
I **would rather** not **go**. 저는 차라리 가지 않겠어요.

문형 6   S + Vt(타동사) + O(목적어)

아래 타동사는 모두 수동태로 바뀔 수 있는 타동사들이다.

We all **enjoyed the** film. 우리 모두는 영화를 재미있게 보았습니다.
An idea **struck** me. 어떤 생각이 떠올랐습니다.
Have you ever **climbed** that mountain? 저 산을 등정하신 적이 있습니까?

아래 타동사는 수동태로 바뀔 수 없다.

He's **got** great charm. 그는 대단한 매력을 가졌습니다.
Have you **hurt** yourself? 다치셨습니까?
She **laughed** a merry laugh. (= She laughed merrily.) 그녀는 즐겁게 웃었습니다.

She **enjoys playing** tennis. 그녀는 테니스 치기를 즐깁니다.
I couldn't **help laughing**. 저는 웃지 않을 수 없었습니다.
Do you **mind waiting** a bit longer? 조금만 더 기다려 주시겠습니까?

> * '동명사'를 목적어로 취할 수 있는 타동사
>
> admít(인정하다), advíse, ádvocate(옹호하다), avóid, begín, begrúdge(시기하다), consíder, contémplate(숙고하다), contínue, defénd, defér(구별하다), dený(부인하다), describe, discontínue(중지하다), dislíke, enjóy, entáil(수반하다), excúse(용서하다), face(직면하다), fáncy(상상하다), fínish, forbíd(금지하다), forgét, grúdge(꺼리다), hate, can't help(~하지 않을 수 없다), imágine(상상하다), inténd(작정하다), invólve(수반하다), jústify(정당화하다), like, love, mean(의미하다), mind(꺼리다), miss(그리워하다), necéssitate(필요로 하다), postpóne(연기하다), prefér, prevént(방지하다), propóse, recáll(상기하다), recolléct(회상하다), recomménd(추천하다), regrét(후회하다), remémber, repórt, resíst, start, suggést(제의하다), try, understánd

아래 타동사는 '동명사'와 'to부정사' 둘 다 목적어로 취할 수 있으며, 두 가지 경우는 뜻이 달라진다.

She **likes swimming**. 그녀는 수영을 좋아합니다.
I **hate having** to refuse every time. 저는 언제나 거절해야 한다는 것이 싫습니다.
She can't **bear seeing** animals treated cruelly. 그녀는 동물들이 잔인하게 취급되는 것을 보는 것을 참지 못합니다.

* **'동명사'와 'to부정사' 둘 다 목적어로 취할 수 있는 타동사**
  comménce(시작하다), contínue, dread, endúre(참다), hate, inténd, like, love, prefér, regrét, start

의미 차이 비교

I **like swimming**. 저는 수영이 좋아요.
I don't **like to swim** in that cold lake. 저는 저렇게 차가운 호수에서 수영하고 싶지 않아요.
Would you **like to go** for a swim this afternoon? 오늘 오후에 수영하러 가시겠습니까?

They **prefer staying** indoors when the weather is cold.
날씨가 추울 때 그들은 차라리 실내에 있으려고 합니다.
Would you **prefer to stay** at home this evening? 오늘 저녁에 집에 계실래요?

He **began(/started) borrowing** money. 그가 돈을 꾸기 시작했습니다.
He **began(/started) to borrow** money. 그는 돈을 꾸러 출발하였습니다.

The garden **needs watering**. (= to be watered) 정원에 물을 주어야겠습니다.
My shoes **want mending**. (= need to be repaired) 제 신발은 수선해야 해요.

문형 7   S + Vt + (not) + O(to부정사구)

I **prefer** (not) **to start** early. 저는 일찍 출발하(지 않)는 것이 좋겠어요.
It's **begun/started to rain**. 비가 오기 시작했습니다.
He **pretended** not **to see** us. 그는 우리를 못본 척했습니다.
Would you **like to come** with me? 저와 같이 가시겠습니까?
Sorry, but **I forgot to post** them. 미안해요, 제가 그것들을 부치는 것을 깜빡했어요.

You'll **have to go**. 당신은 가야만 할 거예요.
You **ought** (not) **to complain**. 당신은 항의해야(하지 않아) 합니다.

* **'to부정사'를 목적어로 취하는 타동사**
  affórd(~ 할 여유가 있다), arránge(준비하다), attémpt, (can) béar(견디다), begín, bóther(성가시게 하다), céase(중지하다), chóose, cláim(청구하다), contínue, contríve(궁리하다), dáre(도전하다), decíde, declíne, desérve(~ 할 만하다), detérmine, dréad(두려워하다), endéavor(노력하다), expéct, fáil, forbéar(억제하다), forgét, háte, help, hésitate(망설이다), hope, inténd(작정하다), learn, like, long(고대하다), love, mánage(간신히 ~ 하다), mean(의미하다 : intend), need, omít(빼먹다), plan, prefér, presúme(도전하다 = vénture), preténd(~ 인 체하다), profés(자칭하다), prómise, propóse, réckon(추정하다), refúse, resólve(결심하다), seek(찾다), start, swéar(맹세하다 : promise, make an óath), thréaten(위협하다), tróuble (폐를 끼치다), undertáke(떠맡다), want, wish

Basic Grammar for English Tests

Exercise 2 다음 괄호 안에서 적당한 말을 골라 바른 문장으로 완성하시오.

1. The teacher decided (accepting/*to accept*) the paper.
2. They appreciate (to have/having) this information.
3. His father doesn't approve of his (going/to go) to Europe.
4. We found it very difficult (reaching/to reach) a decision.
5. Donna is interested in (to open/opening) a bar.
6. George has no intention of (to leave/leaving) the city now.
7. We are eager (to turn/turning) to school in the fall.
8. You would be better off (to buy/buying) this car.
9. She refused (to accept/accepting) the gift.
10. Mary regrets (to be/being) the one to have to tell him.

문형 8　S + Vt + 의문사(Wh-) + to부정사구

She couldn't **decide what to do** next. 그녀는 다음에 무엇을 해야 할지를 결정하지 못했습니다.
Have you **settled where to go** for your holidays? 휴일에 어디로 갈지 결정하셨어요?
I'll **ask/inquire how to do** it. 그것을 어떻게 하는지 물어봐야겠어요.
She didn't **know whether to laugh or to cry**. 그녀는 웃어야 할지, 울어야 할지 몰랐습니다.
How can you **tell which button to press**? 어느 단추를 누르는지 당신은 어떻게 아시나요?

> * '의문사+ **to do**'를 목적어로 받을 수 있는 타동사
>
> ask, consíder, debáte(논쟁하다), decíde, discóver, expláin, forgét, guéss, inquíre(문의하다), know, learn, obsérve(관찰하다), percéive(감지하다), remémber, see, settle(결정하다), tell(알다, 구별하다), think(= form an opínion about), understánd, wonder(궁금해 하다)

문형 9　S + Vt + IO(간접목적어) + DO(직접목적어)

Have they **paid you the money**? 그들이 당신에게 돈을 지불했습니까?
Won't you **tell us a story**? 저희들에게 이야기를 해주시지 않겠어요?
I'll **read you the letter**. 제가 편지를 읽어드릴게요.
He **ordered himself a bottle of champagne**. 그는 직접 샴페인 한 병을 주문하였습니다.
Will you **do me a favor**? 부탁 하나 들어주시겠습니까?
Will you please **call me a taxi**? (*cf*. She called him a fool.)
택시를 한 대 불러주시겠어요?(*cf*. 그녀는 나를 바보라고 했어요.)

특히 이 문형에 사용되는 동사를 수여동사라 한다.

The sun **gives** us the light. 태양은 우리에게 빛을 줍니다.
He **taught** me how to drive. 그는 제게 운전을 가르쳐주었습니다.
He **asked** me a favor. 그는 제게 부탁을 하나 했습니다.
She **sent** me a letter. 그녀는 제게 편지를 보냈습니다.
My father **brought** me a camera. 아버지가 제게 카메라를 사주셨어요.

The cow **provides us with milk**. (= The cow provides milk for us.)
소는 우리에게 우유를 제공합니다.
She **supplied the hungry with food**. (= She supplied food for the hungry.)
그녀는 배고픈 사람에게 음식을 제공하였습니다.
He **presented me with a watch**. (= He presented a watch to me.)
그는 제게 시계를 선물하였습니다.

I **showed** them how to do it. 저는 그들에게 그것을 어떻게 하는지 보여주었습니다.
Ask your teacher how to pronounce the word. 선생님께 그 단어를 어떻게 발음하는지 여쭤보렴.

이 문형에서 타동사와 두 목적어는 관용어구로 형성된 것들이라 간접목적어나 직접목적어로 구분하기 애매하다.

He **struck the door a heavy blow**. (= He struck the door heavily.)
그는 문을 세게 한 방 쳤습니다.
Give your hair a good brushing. (= Brush your hair well.) 머리를 잘 빗어라.
May I ask you a favor? (= May I ask a favor of you?) 부탁 하나 드릴까요?
I envy you your fine garden. (= I envy you. + I envy your fine garde.)
저는 당신의 훌륭한 정원이 부럽습니다.
He **took the dog a long walk**. (= He took the dog (out) for a long walk.)
그는 개를 장시간 산책시켜 주었습니다.

문형 10　S + Vt + DO(직접목적어) + 전치사 + IO(간접목적어)

She **read the letter to** all her friends. 그녀는 자기 모든 친구들에게 그 편지를 읽어주었습니다.
They **told the news to** everyone in the village. 그들은 그 소식을 마을에 있는 모든 사람들에게 말해주었습니다.
I've **sent presents to** most of my family. 저는 식구들 대부분에게 선물을 보냈습니다.

I've **bought some chocolate for** you. 내가 널 주려고 초콜릿을 좀 샀어.
She **made a new party dress for** her youngest daughter.
그녀는 자기 막내딸에게 새 파티드레스를 만들어주었습니다.
Won't you **play a Beethoven sonata for** me? 제게 베토벤 소나타를 연주해주시지 않겠어요?
Can you **cash this check for** me? 이 수표를 제게 현금으로 바꿔주실 수 있습니까?

Basic Grammar for English Tests

* 문형 9와 문형 10의 문장비교

1. She read me the letter. 그녀는 제게 편지를 읽어주었습니다.
   She read the letter to all her friends. 그녀는 편지를 자기 모든 친구들에게 읽어주었습니다.
2. He sold me his old car. 그는 제게 자기의 낡은 자동차를 팔았습니다.
   He sold his old car to one of his neighbors. 그는 자신의 낡은 자동차를 이웃에게 팔았습니다.
3. He still owes me a lot of money. 그는 내게 아직 빚이 많아요.
   He still owes a lot of money to the tax office. 그는 아직도 세무서에 내야할 돈이 많습니다.
4. They told her the news. 그들은 그녀에게 그 소식을 말해주었습니다.
   They told the news to everyone in the village.
   그들은 그 소식을 마을에 있는 모든 사람들에게 말해주었습니다.
5. I've sent Jane a present. 저는 제인에게 선물을 보냈습니다.
   I've sent presents to most of my family. 저는 식구들 대부분에게 선물을 보냈습니다.
6. I've bought you some chocolate. 내가 네게 초콜릿을 좀 사줬잖아.
   I've bought some chocolate for you. 내가 널 주려고 초콜릿을 좀 샀어.
7. She made herself a new dress. 그녀는 새 드레스를 직접 만들었습니다.
   She made a new party dress for her youngest daughter.
   그녀는 막내딸에게 새 파티드레스를 만들어주었습니다.
8. Please boil me an egg. 달걀을 삶아주세요.
   Please boil enough rice for ten people. 열 명이 먹을 충분한 밥을 지어주세요.
9. I'll get you what I can. 제가 할 수 있는 것을 마련해 드리겠습니다.
   I'll get what I can for you. 당신을 위해 제가 할 수 있는 것을 마련하겠습니다.
10. Will you do me a favor? 부탁을 하나 들어주시겠어요?
    Will you do a favor for a friend of mine? 제 친구를 위해 부탁을 하나 들어주시겠습니까?

문형 11   S + Vt + DO + 전치사 + 명사구/대명사구
S + Vt + 전치사 + 명사/대명사 + DO

숙어형으로 전치사와 짝을 지워 알아둔다.

We **congratulated** him **on** his success. 우리는 그의 성공을 축하해주었습니다.
He **spends** a lot of money **on** CDs. 그는 CD를 구입하는 데 많은 돈을 씁니다.
He **cleared** my mind **of** doubt. 그는 내 마음에 의구심을 씻어주었습니다.
What **prevents** you **from** coming earlier? 당신을 일찍 오지 못하게 한 것은 무엇인가요?
The accident **robbed** him **of** his sight. 사고가 그에게서 시력을 빼앗아 갔습니다.
She **reminds** me of my dead sister.
그녀는 나에게 죽은 내 여동생을 생각나게 합니다. (그녀를 보면 죽은 내 여동생이 생각납니다.)
They **accused** him of stealing the jewels. 그들은 보석을 훔친 혐의로 그를 기소하였습니다.
This will **relieve** you of your pain. 이것은 당신에게서 통증을 가시게 해줄 것입니다.
He **informed** me of her success. 그는 내게 그녀의 성공을 알려주었습니다.

He **spends on** books much more than he spends on clothes.
그는 옷에다 쓰는 것보다 책을 사는 데 훨씬 더 씁니다.
Add to the stew all the meat and vegetables. 고기와 채소를 몽땅 스튜요리에다 넣으시오.

문형 12 S + Vt + DO + 부사어구 / S + Vt + 부사어구 + DO

Please **put** the milk **in** the refrigerator. 우유를 냉장고에 넣어 두오.
The secretary **showed** me **into** the manager's office. 비서는 저를 부장의 방으로 안내하였습니다.
They **kept** the child **indoors**. 그들은 아이를 실내에 있게 하였습니다.
Take your coat **off**. 외투를 벗으시오.

Lock up your room. 방문을 잠궈라.
She **gave away** her old books. 그녀는 자신의 헌 책들을 내다 버렸습니다.
He **cleared away** the rubbish. 그는 쓰레기를 치웠습니다.
Don't **throw away** that hat. 저 모자를 버리지 마라.

목적어가 긴 경우
You'd better **take off** your wet overcoat and those muddy shoes.
젖은 외투와 흙묻은 신발을 벗는 것이 좋겠소.
Don't forget to **switch off** the lights in the rooms downstairs.
아래층 방에 있는 전등 끄는 것을 잊지마세요.
The mob **broke down** the doors guarding the main entrance.
시위대는 정문 출입구를 막고 있는 문을 부쉈습니다.

문형 13 S + Vt + DO + to부정사구 / S + Vt + DO + as/like/for전치사구

He **brought** his brother **to see** me. 그는 나를 만나러 자기 동생을 데려왔습니다.
They **gave** a party **to celebrate** their success. 그들은 자신들의 성공을 자축하기 위해 파티를 열었습니다.
I **sent** Tom **to buy** some fruit. 저는 톰을 보내 과일을 사오게 하였습니다.

He **began** his career **as** a teacher. 그는 자신의 경력을 교사로 시작하였습니다.
Can we **take** this document **as** proof of this guilt? 우리가 이 서류를 유죄증거로 채택할 수 있을까요?
She **mistook** me **for** my twin sister. 그녀는 나를 내 쌍둥이 여동생으로 착각하였습니다.

* 'as 전치사구'와 함께 쓰이는 동사

accépt~as… (~을 …로 받아들이다)	acknówledge~as … (~을 …로 인정하다)
class~as… (~을 …로 분류하다)	cháracterize~as … (~을 …로 특징짓다)
consíder~as… (~을 …로 고려하다)	describe~as… (~을 …로 묘사하다)
know~as… (~을 …로 알다)	récognize~as… (~을 …로 인식하다)
regárd~as… (~을 …로 간주하다)	take(= accept)~as… (~을 …로 생각하다)
treat~as… (~을 …로 취급하다)	use~as… (~을 …로 이용하다)

Basic Grammar for English Tests

문형 14 S + Vt + O + C

이 문형에서 보어(C)인 to부정사의 (의미상) 주어가 목적어(O)이므로 이 보어는 목적보어(OC)이다.

We can't **allow** them **to do** that. 우리는 그들에게 그 일을 하도록 허용할 수 없습니다.
His salary **enabled** him **to have** a holiday abroad.
그의 봉급은 그가 해외에서 휴일을 지내는 것을 가능케 하였습니다.
I have never **known** her **to tell** lies. 저는 그녀가 거짓말을 하는 것을 결코 몰랐습니다.

> ＊목적보어로 to부정사를 받는 타동사
>
> advíse, allów, ask, beg(간청하다), beséech(간청하다), bríbe(매수하다), cause(야기하다), chállenge(시도를 권하다), commánd(지휘하다), compél(강요하다), dáre(시도하다 = challenge), diréct(지시하다), drive(강요하다 = compel), empówer(권한을 주다), enáble(할 수 있게 하다), encóurage(격려하다), entítle(자격을 주다), expéct, forbíd(금지하다), fórce(강요하다), help, impél(재촉하다), incíte(고무시키다), indúce(유도하다), instrúct(가르치다), inténd(의도하다), invíte(초대하다), know, lead, mean(의미하다, 말하다 = intend), oblíge(강제하다), permít(허락하다), persuáde, press(압박하다 = úrge), requést, require, teach, tell, tempt(유혹하다), urge(촉구하다), warn(경고하다)

He **likes** his wife **to dress** colorfully. 그 사람은 자기 아내가 화려하게 옷을 입는 것을 좋아합니다.
Would you **prefer** me **not to come** tomorrow? 당신은 제가 내일 오지 않으면 좋겠습니까?
Will you **help** me **to carry** this box upstairs? 이 상자를 위층으로 운반하는 것을 좀 도와주시겠습니까?

a. I **want** you **to** try it again. (o) 저는 당신이 다시 한 번 시도해 보시기를 바랍니다.
   I want that you should try it again. (x)
b. I **warned** him **not to** smoke. (o) 저는 그에게 담배 피지 말라고 경고하였습니다.
   I warned that he should not smoke. (x)
c. I **hope that** you will succeed. (o) 저는 당신이 성공하기를 바랍니다.
   I hope you to succeed. (x)
d. She **said that** she was innocent. (o) 그녀는 자기가 결백하다고 말했습니다.
   She said to be innocent. (x)

문형 15 S + Vt + O + C(원형부정사)

> ＊지각동사(perceptive verbs) 중에 시각과 청각 관련 동사
>   feel, hear, nótice(알아차리다), obsérve(관찰하다), see, watch, listen to, look at

Did anyone **hear** John **leave** the house? 존이 집을 떠난다는 것을 누가 들은 사람이 있습니까?
We **felt** the house **shake**. 우리는 집이 흔들리는 것을 느꼈습니다.

I **saw** him **hit** the cat. 저는 그가 고양이를 때리는 것을 보았습니다.

> *사역동사(causative verbs) : bid, help, let, make, have

What **makes** you **think** so? 당신이 그렇게 생각하도록 만든 것은 무엇입니까?
We can't **let** the matter **rest** here. 우리는 그 문제를 여기서 쉬도록 할 수 없습니다.
Shall I **help** you **carry** that box upstairs? 저 상자를 위층으로 운반하는 것을 도와드릴까요?
We like to **have** our friends **visit** us on Sundays. 친구들이 일요일에 우리를 방문하도록 하고 싶어요.

문형 16 S + Vt + O + C(-ing)

> *이 문형에 쓰이는 지각동사는 시각, 청각에다 후각(smell)이 보태진다.
> feel, glimpse(얼핏보다), hear, notice, observe, percéive(감지하다), see, smell, watch, listen to, look at

They **saw** the thief **running** away. 그들은 도둑이 달아나고 있는 것을 보았습니다.
Can you **smell** something **burning**? 무엇인가 타는 냄새가 나요?
Did you **notice** anyone **standing** at the gate? 누가 정문에 서 있는 것을 아셨어요?
She could **feel** her heart **beating** wildly. 그녀는 자기의 심장이 심하게 뛰는 것을 느낄 수 있었습니다.

> *이 경우처럼 현재분사를 목적보어로 받는 타동사
> bring, catch(포착하다), depict(묘사하다), discover, draw, find, get, imagine, keep, leave, paint, send, set, show, start, take

I **found** him **dozing** under a tree. 저는 그가 나무 밑에서 졸고 있는 것을 발견하였습니다.
We mustn't **keep** them **waiting**. 우리는 그들을 계속해서 기다리게 해서는 안됩니다.
They **left** me **waiting** outside. 그들은 저를 밖에서 기다리게 내버려두었습니다.
This set me **thinking**. 이것은 저를 생각하도록 하였습니다.

I can't **understand** him(/his) **leaving** so suddenly. 저는 그가 그렇게 갑자기 떠나는 것을 이해할 수 없어요.
We'll fight to **prevent** these houses **being** torn down.
우리는 이 집들이 철거되는 것을 막으려고 싸웠습니다.
Do you **mind** my brothers **coming** with us? 제 형제들이 우리와 함께 가는 것이 괜찮으신지요?

문형 17   S + Vt + O + C(과거분사)

Have you ever **heard** a pop song **sung** in Japanese?
일본에서 팝송이 불러지는 것을 들어보신 적이 있습니까?
You must **make** yourself **respected**. 당신은 스스로를 존중받도록 해야 합니다.
They **found** themselves **stranded** at the airport.
그들은 자신들이 공항에서 꼼짝 못하게 되었다는 것을 알았습니다.

She's **had** her handbag **stolen**. 그녀는 자기 핸드백을 도둑맞았습니다.
Last week we **had** all our windows **broken** by hooligans.
지난 주에 불량배들이 우리집 유리창을 모두 깨뜨렸습니다.
She's **having** her eyes **tested**. 그녀는 눈을 검사받고 있습니다.

I must **have**(/**get**) my hair **cut**. 저는 이발을 해야겠어요.
You'll have to **get** that tooth **filled**. 당신은 그 이를 해넣어야 할 거예요.

Exercise 3   빈칸에 주어진 동사의 적당한 형태를 넣어 바른 문장으로 완성하시오.

1. The teacher made Jane _leave_ the room. (leave)
2. Tom had his car _repaired_ by a mechanic. (repair)
3. Jane got John _____ her paper. (type)
4. I made Jane _____ her friend on the telephone. (call)
5. We got our house _____ last week. (paint)
6. Dr. Andersen is having the students _____ a composition. (write)
7. Mark got his transcripts _____ to the university. (send)
8. Maria is getting her hair _____ tomorrow. (cut)
9. We will have to get the Dean _____ this form. (sign)
10. We have to help Janet _____ her keys. (find)

문형 18   S + Vt + O + OC(형용사)

We **painted** the ceiling **green**. 우리는 천장을 초록색으로 칠했습니다.
The Governor **set** the prisoners **free**. 주지사는 죄수들을 석방하였습니다.
She **dyed** her hair **green**. 그녀는 머리를 초록색으로 물들였습니다.
They **beat** the poor boy **black and blue**. 그들은 불쌍한 소년을 멍이 들도록 때렸습니다.
The barber has **cut** your hair **very short**. 이발사가 당신의 머리를 너무 짧게 잘랐습니다.
They **found** the birdcage **empty**. 그들은 새장이 비어있는 것을 발견하였습니다.
We **proved** him **wrong**. 우리는 그가 틀렸다는 것을 증명하였습니다.

> * 이 문형에 쓰이는 타동사
>
> bake(bake it hard), beat(때리다), color(색칠하다, color it red), cut, drive(drive someone mad : 누구를 미치게 하다), dye, eat(eat oneself sick), fill, find, get, hammer(망치로 치다), hold(= consider), keep, lay(lay the country waste : 시골을 황폐하게 하다), leave, lick, like, make, point, render(~하게 하다), see, set, sleep, wash, wipe(닦다), wish

문형 19 | S + Vt + O + OC(명사)

They **made**(/**declared**/**elected**/**appointed**) Newton **President of the Royal Society**. 그들은 뉴튼을 왕립학회의 회장으로 만들었(선언하였/선출하였/지명하였)습니다.
He **seduced** the girl but later **made** her **wife**. 그는 그 여자를 꾀었지만 나중에 아내로 만들었습니다.
They **named** the baby **Richard** but usually **call** him **Dick**.
그들은 아기를 리처드라 이름지었으나 흔히 그를 딕이라 부릅니다.
She has **dyed** her hair **a beautiful shade** of green. 그녀는 머리를 초록색의 아름다운 색조로 물들였습니다.

문형 20 | S + Vt + O + C

Most people **considered** him **(to be) innocent**. 대부분의 사람들은 그를 순수하다고 생각하였습니다.
They all **felt** the plan **to be unwise**. 그들 모두는 계획이 현명하지 않다고 느꼈습니다.
We **believe** it **to have been a mistake**. 우리는 그것이 실수였다고 믿고 있습니다.
Everyone **reported** him **to be the best man** for the job.
모두가 그를 그 일에 최적임자라고 보고하였습니다.

Do you **think it odd for**(/**of**) me **to live alone**? 당신은 제가 혼자 살아가는 것이 이상하다고 생각하십니까?
People no longer **consider it strange for** men **to let** their hair grow long.
사람들은 남자들이 머리를 길게 기르는 것을 더 이상 이상하다고 생각하지 않습니다.
Don't you **consider it wrong to cheat** in examinations?
시험에서 부정행위를 하는 것이 나쁘다고 생각하지 않습니까?

Actual Test 3

다음 각 문장을 읽고 빈칸에는 알맞은 단어를 넣고, 밑줄 친 부분에서는 잘못된 부분을 찾으시오.

1. George may _____, but we must go at once.
   Ⓐ stay lately
   Ⓑ stay a little
   Ⓒ have stayed very late
   Ⓓ stay late

2. Food prices last week increased only _____.
   Ⓐ slightly
   Ⓑ on a small scale
   Ⓒ small
   Ⓓ little

3. I like Brahms' music very much because his music sounds _____.
   Ⓐ sweet and soothing
   Ⓑ sweetly and soothingly
   Ⓒ sweetingly and soothingly
   Ⓓ sweetingly and soothing

4. All the people in this village have red hair. They all _____ each other.
   Ⓐ resemble as
   Ⓑ resemble with
   Ⓒ resemble
   Ⓓ resemble from

5. Returning to my house, _____.
   Ⓐ my watch was missing
   Ⓑ I found my watch disappeared
   Ⓒ I found my watch missing
   Ⓓ the watch was missed

6. X-rays can pass through objects and make _____ details that are otherwise impossible to see.
   Ⓐ it visible
   Ⓑ visibly
   Ⓒ visible
   Ⓓ they are visible

7. This morning, in a radio address, the president urged people _____ to the Red Cross.
   Ⓐ that we subscribed
   Ⓑ subscribe
   Ⓒ subscribing
   Ⓓ to subscribe

8. "What exactly did you see last night, Miss Lyon?" "Well, I saw _____."

   Ⓐ a bank being robbed with two men
   Ⓑ robbing a bank two men
   Ⓒ two men robbing a bank
   Ⓓ two men who rob a bank

9. James Oakley became <u>fame</u> as one of the world's most <u>accurate</u> shots with
                              A   B
   <u>a pistol</u>, a rifle, and <u>a shotgun</u>.
      C   D

10. <u>My reaction</u>, <u>I think</u>, <u>could have been called</u> <u>to be instinctive</u>.
        A   B   C   D

11. The computer <u>makes</u> <u>possibly</u> <u>a great leap</u> in <u>human proficiency</u>.
                       A   B   C   D

12. He <u>made</u> this cart <u>strongly enough</u> <u>to hold</u> five <u>adults</u>.
        A   B   C   D

13. An epigram is <u>generally</u> <u>defined to be</u> a bright <u>or</u> witty thought briefly
                      A   B   C
    <u>expressed</u>.
      D

14. <u>No bank</u> keeps <u>enough</u> cash <u>paying</u> all its depositors <u>in full</u> at one time.
      A   B   C   D

15. Like jazz, African-American quilts are lively and <u>spontaneously</u>, but
                                                  A
    <u>unlike jazz</u>, the quilts are <u>just now</u> starting <u>to be known</u>.
      B   C   D

16. <u>Some part</u> of the wall proved <u>obstinately</u>. The mason attacked the archway
       A   B
    at the side <u>to weaken</u> its <u>support</u>.
                  C   D

17. The <u>origin</u> of the moon is <u>interest</u> <u>not only</u> in itself <u>but also</u> as a part of
         A   B   C   D
    the larger genesis of the Earth and the Solar System.

18. In an adult human, <u>the skin</u> <u>weighs</u> about eight pounds and <u>covers it</u>
                              A   B   C
    thirty-nine <u>square feet</u>.
              D

19. Having spent his last penny for the butter, he was determined to eat
            A   B
    it all, even though it tasted bitterly to him.
              C   D

20. Since no ammonia fumes are detected, this theory does not seem credibly.
      A   B   C   D

Unit 4

중문

◀ **중문이란?**

둘 이상의 절(clause)이 서로에게 종속되지 않고 대등한 등위절 또는 상관절 관계로 서술된 문장.

중문의 종류

1. 등위접속사로 연결되는 경우

   He washed the car **and** polished it.
   Tom went to the movie, **but** Jane went to the circus.

   그는 자동차를 세차하고 윤을 냈습니다. / 톰은 영화를 보러 갔으나, 제인은 서커스를 보러 갔습니다.

2. 상관접속사로 연결되는 경우

   Both my mother **and** my sister are here.
   Not only will she make a contribution herself, **but** she will **also** ask her friends.

   어머니와 누이 두 분 다 여기 계십니다. / 그녀는 스스로 헌신할 뿐 아니라, 친구들에게도 요청을 합니다.

3. 접속부사로 연결되는 경우

   We fished all day; **however**, we didn't catch a thing.

   우리는 하루 종일 낚시를 했지만, 한 마리도 낚지 못했습니다.

4. Semi-colon(;)으로 연결되는 경우: but의 뜻이 들어 있다.
   We fished all day; we didn't catch a thing.

◀ 등위접속사(coordinating conjunctions)

1. 추가(addition/continuation) : and, and then — 순접

    Tom phoned. He left a message. (같은 주어)
    = Tom phoned **and** (he) left a message.
    Tom phoned. Frank answered. (다른 주어)
    = Tom phoned **and** Frank answered.
    It was raining hard, **and** there was a strong wind. (항상 문어체)
    = It was raining hard **and** there was a strong wind. (가끔 문어체)
    He washed the car **and** polished it. (행동의 추가)
    = He washed the car **and then** polished it. (행동의 순서)

    톰은 전화를 걸어 메시지를 남겼습니다. / 톰이 전화를 걸었고 프랭크가 받았습니다. / 비가 몹시 왔습니다. 그리고 거센 바람도 불었습니다. / 그는 자동차를 세차한 다음 윤을 냈습니다.

2. 대조(contrast) : but, yet — 역접

    He washed the car, **but** (he) didn't polish it.
    Jimmy fell off his bike, **but** (he) was unhurt.
    He did not study, **yet** he passed the exam.

    그는 자동차를 세차하였으나 윤을 내지는 않았습니다. / 지미는 자전거에서 넘어졌으나 다치지는 않았습니다. / 그는 공부를 하지 않았지만 시험에 붙었습니다.

3. 선택(choice) : or, nor

    You can park your car on the driveway **or** on the street.
    The keys are in the car **or** in your pocket.
    Many students do not like study for tests, **nor** do they like to write term papers.

    진입로나 차도에 자동차를 주차하셔도 됩니다. / 열쇠는 자동차 안이나 호주머니 안에 있습니다. / 많은 학생들이 시험 공부도 하지 않고 학기말 과제물도 작성하기 싫어합니다.

4. 조건

    Work hard, **or** you will fail.
    You'd better hurry, **or** (**else**) you'll be late.

    열심히 공부하거라, 그렇지 않으면 실패할 것이다. / 서두르는 게 좋겠어, 그렇지 않으면 늦을 거야.

5. 이유(reason) : for

    We rarely stay in hotels, **for** we can't afford it.
    The child hid behind his mother's skirt, **for** he was afraid of the dog.

    우리는 좀처럼 호텔에 묵지 않습니다. 왜냐하면, 그럴 형편이 못되기 때문입니다. / 어린이는 어머니 치마 뒤로 숨었습니다. 왜냐하면, 개가 무서워서였습니다.

6. 결과(result) : so

He couldn't find his pen, **so** he wrote in pencil.
He was tired, **so** he went to bed.

그는 펜을 찾을 수가 없었습니다. 그래서 그는 연필로 썼습니다. / 그는 지쳤습니다. 그래서 잠자리에 들었습니다.

7. 예를 들 때 : for example(= e.g.), for instance, and such as

There are many interesting places to visit in the city, **for example**, the botanical garden or the art museum.
I prefer to wear casual clothes, **such as** jeans and a sweatshirt.
Countries **such as** Brazil and Canada are big.
Such countries **as** Brazil and Canada are big.

그 시에는 가볼 만한 재미있는 곳이 많습니다. 예를 들면, 식물원이나 미술관이 있습니다. / 저는 평상복을 입기를 좋아합니다. 예를 들면, 청바지나 스웨터 같은 것들입니다. / 브라질이나 캐나다 같은 나라들은 큽니다. / 브라질이나 캐나다 같은 그런 나라들은 큽니다.

◀ 상관접속사(correlative conjunctions)

> * 종류: both~and, either~or, neither~nor, not only~but also(/as well/too), as well as, whether~or, so~as, not~but

He excels **not** in English, **but** in mathematics.
= He excels in mathematics, but not in English.
He has **neither** a pen **nor** paper.
Both Susie **and** Mark are working on the problem.
Either the outlet **or** the plugs need changing.
Neither my mother **nor** my sister is here.
Whether I vote **or** not is none of your business.
Not only he **but also** his parents are very kind to me.
= His parents **as well as** he are very kind to me.

그는 영어가 아니라 수학에 우수합니다. / 그는 펜도 종이도 없습니다. / 수지와 마크가 그 문제를 풀고 있습니다. / 콘센트와 플러그를 교체할 필요가 있습니다. / 어머니도 누이도 여기 안 계십니다. / 제가 투표를 할 것인가 말 것인가는 당신이 상관할 바가 아닙니다. / 그뿐만 아니라 그의 부모도 제게 매우 친절하십니다.

Basic Grammar for English Tests

◀ 접속부사(conjunctive adverbs or connecting adverbs)

1. 추가(addition)

   also, besides, furthermore, in addition, and moreover

2. 반대/대조(opposition/contrast)

   however, on the other hand, in contrast, and otherwise, nevertheless, in fact

3. 결과(result)

   anyhow, consequently, then, therefore, and thus

   Learn to speak more slowly; **otherwise**, no one can understand you.
   You seem to be certain of your facts; **however**, I do not agree.
   The politician spoke indistinctly; **besides**, she had no real facts.

   좀더 천천히 말하는 것을 배워라. 그렇지 않으면, 아무도 네 말을 알아듣지 못할 것이다. / 당신은 당신의 사실을 확신하는 것 같군요. 그러나 저는 동의할 수 없어요. / 그 정치인은 분명하지 않게 말을 합니다. 게다가 아무런 실제 진실도 없습니다.

Exercise 1 다음 글을 읽으면서 내용에 맞게 괄호에서 적당한 접속어를 고르시오.

> The customers at the amusement park were leaving (1) (*and*/but) the lights were going out. The last two people on dodgem cars paid (2) (and/so) left. The big wheel stopped (3) (for/and) the merry-go-round stopped (4) (as well/not only). The stalls closed down (5) (so/and) the stall-owners went home. At 2 a.m. four nightwatchmen walked round the park, (6) (but/so) there was no one to be seen. "I'm tired of walking round." one of them said, (7) ("yet/and) what can we do?" "We can (8) (or/either) play cards (9) (either/or) sit and talk." They were bored, (10) (so/for) there was nothing to do on this quiet warm night. "We can have a ride on the merry-go-round!" one of them cried. "That'll be fun!" Three of them jumped on merry-go-round horses (11) (yet/and) the fourth started the motor. Then he jumped on too (12) (and/but) round they went. They were having the time of their lives, (13) (but/so) suddenly realized there was no one to stop the machine. They weren't rescued till morning (14) (and/but) by then they felt very sick indeed!

Exercise 2 다음 빈칸에 적당한 상관접속어를 넣어 문장을 완성하시오.

1. Julia speaks *not only* Spanish but also French.
2. She bought the yellow sweater _____ the beige skirt.
3. They have houses _____ in the country and in the city.
4. He is not only industrious _____ ingenious.
5. Her children have American cousins _____ Spanish ones.
6. Their European tour includes _____ Germany and Austria but also Switzerland.
7. He bandaged the arm both tightly _____ quickly.
8. Clark not only practices law _____ teaches it.
9. Tom is a playwright _____ an actor.
10. The bride's bouquet included roses _____ orchids.

◀ 병렬구문(parallel structure)

병렬구문(parallelism)이란?

1. 두 개 이상의 어구(words or phrases)나 절이 등위접속사나 상관접속사로 연결된 구문에서 양쪽의 문장성분이나 구조가 같다.
2. 비교구문에서 둘 이상의 비교대상은 문장성분이나 구조가 같다.

The boss *and* his secretary are flying to Paris.
= *Both* the boss *and* his secretary are flying to Paris.
I met Jane and her husband. = I met *both* Jane *and* her husband.
I didn't meet *either* Jane *or* her husband. = I met *neither* Jane *nor* her husband.
The boss, *but not* his secretary, is flying to Paris.

사장과 비서는 파리로 날아가고 있습니다. / 저는 제인과 그의 남편을 만났습니다. / 저는 제인도 그의 남편도 만나지 못했습니다. / 비서가 아닌 사장이 파리로 날아가고 있습니다.

등위접속사로 연결된 구문

Steve, Joe, *and* Alice are coming to dinner. (주어)
The colors in that fabric are red, gold, black, *and* green. (형용사)
John Glenn has served his country as a pilot, an astronaut, *and* a senator. (명사)
That lazy student always takes a nap *or* watches television in the afternoon. (동사+목적어)

스티브와 조, 앨리스가 저녁식사에 옵니다. / 저 직물에 들어있는 색깔은 빨강, 황금, 검정, 초록색입니다. / 존 글렌은 비행기 조종사로, 우주인으로, 그리고 상원의원으로 조국에 봉사하였습니다. / 저 게으른 학생은 오후에 늘 낮잠을 자거나 아니면 텔레비전을 봅니다.

Basic Grammar for English Tests

- A student needs textbooks, notebooks, and he needs pens. (x)
- A student needs textbooks, notebooks, and pens. (o)

- Jane is young, enthusiastic, and she has talent. (x)
- Jane is young, enthusiastic, and talented. (o)

- We learned to read the passages and underlining the main ideas. (x)
- We learned to read the passages and (to) underline the main ideas. (o)

- Professor Baker enjoys teaching and to write. (x)
- Professor Baker enjoys teaching and writing. (o)

- A student who does well in exams attends class, reads the textbook, and he reviews the notes. (x)
- A student who does well in exams attends class, reads the textbook, and reviews the notes. (o)

- The students wanted to know what the calculus problems were and the due date. (x)
- The students wanted to know what the calculus problems were assigned and when the due date was. (o)

학생은 교과서와 공책, 펜이 필요합니다. / 제인은 젊고 열정적이고 재능이 있습니다. / 우리는 본문을 읽고 주제에 밑줄 치는 것을 배웠습니다. / 베이커 교수는 가르치는 것과 글쓰기를 좋아합니다. / 시험을 잘 보는 학생은 수업을 잘 듣고, 교과서를 읽고, 필기한 것을 다시 봅니다. / 학생들은 어떤 계산문제가 숙제인지, 마감일이 언제인지를 알려고 했습니다.

상관접속사로 연결된 경우

Robert excels *not only* **in mathematics** *but also* **in science**. (전치사구)
Paul Anka *not only* **plays the piano** *but also* **composes music**. (동사+목적어)
Beth plays **the guitar** *as well as* **the violin**. (목적어)
He writes **correctly** *as well as* **neatly**. (부사)
He is *both* **talented** *and* **handsome**. (형용사)
Many people are *neither* **concerned about pollutants** *nor* **worried about their future impact**. (동사+전치사구)

로버트는 수학뿐 아니라 과학에서도 뛰어납니다. / 폴 앵카는 피아노를 칠 뿐만 아니라 음악을 작곡하기도 합니다. / 베스는 바이올린뿐만 아니라 기타도 연주합니다. / 그는 깔끔할 뿐만 아니라 정확하게 글을 씁니다. / 그는 재능이 있을 뿐더러 잘 생기기까지 합니다. / 많은 사람들이 오염물질에 대해 염려하지 않을 뿐더러 미래에 끼치는 영향에 대해서도 걱정조차 하지 않는다.

- He is not only famous in Italy but also in Switzerland. (x)
- He is famous not only in Italy but also in Switzerland. (o)

- She didn't know whether to sell her books or kept for reference. (x)
- She didn't know whether to sell her books or to keep them for reference. (o)

- The students wanted to know what the calculus problems were and the due date. (x)
- The students wanted to know what the calculus problems were assigned and when the due date was. (o)

⎡ She has succeeded not because of her intelligence but because she works hard. (x)
⎣ She has succeeded not because she is intelligent but because she works hard. (o)

그는 이탈리아뿐 아니라 스위스에서도 유명합니다. / 그녀는 자기 책들을 팔 것인지 아니면 참고용으로 보관할 것인지를 모릅니다. / 학생들은 어떤 계산문제들이 숙제인지 그리고 마감일이 언제인지를 알고 싶어합니다. / 그녀는 똑똑해서가 아니라 열심히 일해서 성공하였습니다.

비교구문의 비교대상

⎡ *Making* friends is more rewarding than *to be* antisocial. (x)
⎣ **Making** friends is more rewarding than **being** antisocial. (o)

⎡ *The area of* Alaska is greater than *Texas*. (x)
⎣ **The area of** Alaska is greater than **that of** Texas. (o)

⎡ Alaska is larger than any state. (x)
⎣ Alaska is larger than any **other** state. (o)

⎡ John is taller than anyone in this class. (x)
⎣ John is taller than anyone **else** in this class. (o)

⎡ *Riding* a bicycle is *similar to the driving of* a car. (x)
⎣ **Riding** a bicycle is *similar* to **driving** a car. (o)

⎡ *Trying* to get used to foreign food seems so hard as *learn* a foreign language. (x)
⎣ **Trying** to get used to foreign food seems as hard as **learning** a foreign language. (o)

친구를 사귀는 것은 반사회적이 되는 것보다는 더 보람있습니다. / 알래스카 지역은 텍사스 지역보다 더 큽니다. / 알래스카는 다른 어떤 주보다 더 큽니다. / 존은 이 학급의 다른 학생들보다 더 큽니다. / 자전거를 타는 것은 자동차를 타는 것과 비슷합니다. / 외국음식에 익숙하려고 애쓰는 것은 외국어를 배우기만큼이나 힘든 것 같습니다.

Exercise 3 다음 문장을 읽고 잘못 기술된 부분을 고치오.

1. Benjamin Franklin was a writer, a scientist and politics. (politics → *a politician*)
2. Pele was a quick, skillful, and accuracy soccer player.
3. Among his vices are cigarettes, alcoholic, and drugs.
4. After a day at the lake, the children came home tired, sunburned, and hunger.
5. After dinner, Maria usually has a cup of coffee, a cup of tea, or wine.
6. This anthology of American literature contains poetic, short stories, and a novel.

7. A sentence can contain a series of two, third, or four items.
8. The motto of the French revolution was liberty, equal, and fraternity.
9. A good writer edits his work slowly, careful, and regularly.
10. On the English test, you should check each verb for agree, tense, and form.

Exercise 4 다음 두 문장 중 바른 문장을 고르시오.

1. a) A stream either can erode or deposit material as it flows.
   b) A stream can either erode or deposit material as it flows. (o)
2. a) Lichen both carries on photosynthesis and respiration.
   b) Lichen carries on both photosynthesis and respiration.
3. a) Climate influences soil formation not only through moisture and temperature but also through the vegetation it permits.
   b) Climate influences soil formation through not only moisture and temperature but also through the vegetation it permits.
4. a) Computer languages are classified as either high-level or as low-level.
   b) Computer languages are classified either as high-level or as low-level.
5. a) Erosion can occur either through the action of water or the action of wind.
   b) Erosion can occur through the action of either water or wind.
6. a) Edmund Haley not only published the first map of the winds but also contributed to knowledge of weather by relating winds to heat.
   b) Edmund Haley published not only the first map of the winds but also contributed to knowledge of weather by relating winds to heat.
7. a) Computer languages can be further classified as either problem-oriented or procedure-oriented.
   b) Computer languages can be further classified either as problem-oriented or procedure-oriented.
8. a) Lunar craters may have originated from either the collapse of volcanoes or from the impact of large meteorites.
   b) Lunar craters may have originated either from the collapse of volcanoes or from the impact of large meteorites.

Actual Test 4

다음 각 문장을 읽고 빈칸에는 알맞은 단어를 넣고, 밑줄 친 부분에서는 잘못된 부분을 찾으시오.

1. Collecting stamps was her favorite pastime, but _____.
   - Ⓐ she also enjoy music listening
   - Ⓑ listening to music also gave her great pleasure
   - Ⓒ also listening to music
   - Ⓓ to listen to music was enjoyed by her also

2. Nancy delayed her departure until morning, _____
   - Ⓐ being tired and afraid about driving at night
   - Ⓑ for fear of driving at night and tiredness
   - Ⓒ for she was tired and afraid to drive at night
   - Ⓓ being fearful to drive at night and being tired

3. The Rocky Mountain goat in America is not a true goat _____ a goat antelope.
   - Ⓐ and
   - Ⓑ but
   - Ⓒ any
   - Ⓓ yet

4. Pianist George Winston has won Grammy awards for his recordings of _____ Jazz and classical music.
   - Ⓐ also
   - Ⓑ together
   - Ⓒ the two
   - Ⓓ both

5. _____ their nests well but also build them well.
   - Ⓐ Not only American eagles protect
   - Ⓑ Protect not only American eagles
   - Ⓒ American eagles not only protect
   - Ⓓ Not only protect American eagles

6. Robert Frost went to Chicago, bought some books, and _____.
   - Ⓐ visiting his daughter
   - Ⓑ to visit his daughter
   - Ⓒ visited his daughter
   - Ⓓ visit his daughter

7. Mary wanted neither the assignment in London nor _____.
   Ⓐ the job in New York   Ⓑ did he want to go to New York
   Ⓒ to be sent to New York   Ⓓ at New York

8. Generally making friends is more rewarding _____.
   Ⓐ than to be antisocial
   Ⓑ than being antisocial
   Ⓒ than to be like an antisocial person
   Ⓓ than it is to be antisocial

9. Every night <u>the</u> watchman would lock the doors, <u>turning</u> on the <u>spot light</u>,
            A   B   C
   and <u>walk</u> around the building.
       D

10. To control quality and <u>making</u> decisions <u>about</u> manufacturing <u>are</u> <u>among</u>
                           A   B   C   D
    the many responsibilities of an industrial engineer.

11. To read a foreign literature and <u>being introduced</u> to a different culture <u>are</u>
                                     A   B   C
    two excellent reasons <u>for learning</u> a foreign language.
                          D

12. The <u>suggested</u> increase in the utility rate <u>was</u> neither a fair request <u>and not</u>
        A   B   C
    a practical <u>one</u>.
                D

13. The surgeon examined <u>the</u> patient <u>quickly</u>, <u>and then</u> <u>the operation</u>
                         A   B   C   D
    <u>was begun</u>.

14. The assistant-teacher did not know whether to report the student for
    <u>cheating</u> <u>or</u> <u>warning</u> <u>him</u> first.
    A   B   C   D

15. Please lend <u>me</u> <u>the</u> smallest, most <u>recently</u> published, and <u>less</u> expensive
                A   B   C   D
    dictionary that you have available.

16. In order to become a law in the United States, a bill must be passed not
    ___   _____
     A   B
    only by the Senate but also the House of Representative.
    ____   _____
     C   D

17. Because of its thick blackness and permanent, Indian ink is utilized
                    _____ _____   _____
                      A   B   C
    extensively by architects and engineers.
    _____
        D

18. The leaves of the yucca are usually point, stiff, and slim, with sawlike
                             ___   _____   ____ ____
                              A   B   C   D
    or fibrous edges.

19. The firemen were unable to determine exactly what caused the fire, when
                           _____   ____   ____
                                A   B   C
    they said that they would include the investigation.
                   _____
                          D

20. Neither Russia nor the United States have been able to find a mutually
                   ___   _____   _____
                    A   B   C
    satisfactory plan for gradual disarmament.
                 ____
                   D

Unit 5

복문

◀ 복문의 정의

복문은 하나의 주절(main clause)과 주절의 뜻을 보완하는 하나 이상의 종속절(dependent/subordinate clauses)로 구성된 복합문장이다.

복문의 형태

1. 주절과 종속절로 결합된 경우

   The alarm was rung *as soon as* the fire was discovered.
   (주절)　　　　　(종속접속사)　　(종속절)

   Who came to the party is no concern of yours.
   (종속접속사) (종속절) (주절)

   화재가 발견되자마자 비상벨이 울렸습니다. / 파티에 누가 왔느냐는 당신이 상관할 바가 아닙니다.

2. 주절이 부정사나 분사구문과 결합된 경우

   To get into University, you have to pass a number of examinations.
   Seeing the door open, the stranger entered the house.

   대학에 들어가기 위하여, 당신은 많은 시험을 통과해야 합니다. / 문이 열린 것을 보고서, 낯선 이들이 집으로 들어갔습니다.

Free trade agreements are always threatened (주절)
　　when individual countries protect their own markets (종속절)
　　　　by imposing duties on imported goods (분사어구)
　　　　　　to encourage their own industries. (부정사구)

자유무역협정은 늘 위협받고 있습니다. / 개별국가들이 자기 나라의 시장을 보호할 때 / 수입제품에 세금을 부과함으로써 / 자기 나라의 산업을 장려하기 위하여

3. 두 절의 주어가 같을 경우, 반복하지 않고 종속절에는 대명사가 온다.

The racing car went out of control before **it** hit the barrier.
When **she** got on the train, **Mrs. Tomkins** realized **she** had made a mistake.

경주자동차는 벽을 들이받기 전에 통제를 벗어났습니다. / 열차에 올라탔을 때, 톰킨스 부인은 자신이 실수했음을 깨달았습니다.

4. 중문과 복문이 결합된 경우

The racing car went out of control **and** hit the barrier several times **before** it came to a stop on a grassy bank.

강둑에 다다라 멈추기 전까지 경주자동차는 통제불능의 상태가 되었고, 몇 차례 벽을 들이받았습니다.

5. 주절과 종속절의 주어가 같을 경우, 주절에는 고유명사로 종속절에는 대명사로 쓰는 것이 일반적이다.

After she got married, Madeleine changed completely.
(After Madeleine got married, she changed completely.)

결혼을 한 뒤, 마들린은 완전히 변했습니다.

종속절의 종류

1. 명사절(noun clauses)

주절에 포함되어 주어, 목적어, 보어 등 명사 역할을 하는 종속절.

Who came to the party is no concern of yours. (주절의 주어)
Kim wished **that she could ride a horse**. (목적어)
He told me **that the match had been cancelled**. (목적어)
One serious problem is **that there is no running water**. (보어)
We judged people by **what they do**. (전치사의 목적어)
The doctor came to the conclusion **that the patient was out of danger**. (명사 the conclusion과 동격)

누가 파티에 왔느냐는 당신이 상관할 바가 아닙니다. / 킴은 자신이 말을 탈 수 있기를 바랬습니다. / 그는 제게 그 시합이 취소되었다고 말했습니다. / 한 가지 심각한 문제는 흐르는 물이 없다는 것입니다. / 우리는 직업으로 사람들을 판단했습니다. / 의사는 그 환자가 위험한 상태에서 벗어났다는 결론에 도달하였습니다.

2. 형용사절(관계사절, adjective/relative clauses)

명사를 수식하는 형용사 역할을 하는 종속절. 흔히 생략하기도 한다. 관계대명사절과 관계부사절이 있다.

The bat **that you have used** has been broken. (즈어 The bat를 수식하는 형용사)
Holiday resorts **which are very crowded** are not very pleas-ant. (주어 Holiday resorts를 수식)
He knows the reason **why I could not come**. (목적어 the reason을 수식)
The job has been given to the person **whom you recommended**. (목적어 the person을 수식)
She is a girl **I never could stand**. (보어 a girl을 수식하며, 관계대명사 whom이 생략되어 있다)

당신이 쓰던 방망이는 부러졌습니다. / 매우 붐비는 휴일의 유원지는 그리 즐겁지 않습니다. / 그는 제가 왜 올 수 없었는지 그 이유를 알고 있습니다. / 그 일자리는 자네가 추천한 그 사람에게 주어졌네. / 그녀는 제가 도저히 참을 수 없었던 그런 여자입니다.

3. 부사절(adverb clauses)

부사 역할을 하는 종속절.
주절의 문장구조에는 영향을 주지 않으면서 주절의 동사, 형용사, 부사를 수식하거나 그 의미를 보충하는 종속절.

(1) 시간(time) : when, before, while, since

When you row a boat, you *must keep* control of the oars. (When 절은 동사 must keep을 보충)

당신이 보트를 저을 때, 당신은 노를 잘 다루어야 합니다.

(2) 장소(place) : where, wherever

After *finding* a book **where** I had left it, I *hurried* back into the house. (where 절은 finding을, After 절은 hurried back을 수식함)

제가 그걸 두었던 곳에서 책을 찾은 뒤 저는 집으로 서둘러 돌아갔습니다.

(3) 원인(cause) : because, as, since

The train, three hours *late* **because** the locomotive had broken down, was full of angry passengers. (because 절은 late를 수식)

기관차가 고장나서 3시간이 늦었기 때문에, 열차는 성난 승객들로 가득찼습니다.

(4) 결과(result) : that, so that, so ~ that

We were so *hungry* **that** we ate stale crackers. (so~that 절은 hungry를 수식)

우리는 너무 배가 고파서 상한 크래커를 먹었습니다.

(5) 목적(purpose) : in order that, so that

> The students *worked* hard all day **so that** the gym would be ready for the dance. (so that 절은 worked를 수식)
>
> 체육관에서 무용을 할 준비가 되도록 학생들은 하루 종일 열심히 일을 하였습니다.

(6) 양보(concession) : though, although, even though

> **Although** he did not score, he *made the best play* of the game. (Although 절은 made를 수식)
>
> 그가 비록 점수는 내지 못했지만, 그는 시합에서 가장 멋진 경기를 펼쳤습니다.

(7) 정도 · 비교(degree · comparison) : than, as much as, as~as, just as

> Sally climbed *farther* **than** you did. (than 절은 farther를 수식)
>
> 샐리는 당신이 올랐던 것 보다 더 멀리 등정을 하였습니다.

(8) 조건(condition) : if, even if, unless, provided that …

> **Unless** you make the payment, service *will be cut off*. (Unless 절은 will be cut off를 수식)
>
> 당신이 지불을 하지 않으면, 서비스는 중단될 것입니다.

(9) 태도(manner) : as, as if

> She *kicked* the can **as if** it were a ball. (if 절이 kicked를 수식)
>
> 마치 그것이 공인 것처럼 그녀는 깡통을 찼습니다.

종속접속어(subordinate conjunctions)의 종류

	종속절	종속접속어
명사절	의문사	who(ever), whose, whom(ever), when(ever), where(ever), what(ever), which(ever), why, how(ever), how much(/many/often …)
	관계대명사	what
	접속사	that whether (or not), if
형용사절 (관계사절)	관계대명사 (relative pronoun)	사람 { who+동사 whose+명사 whom+(S+V) which that : 수식(한정)용법에만 쓰임
	관계부사 (relative adverbs)	when (시간) where (장소) why (이유) : 수식용법에만 쓰임

부사절	시간 (time)	when(ever), while, as, after, before, since, until/till, once, as soon as, as/so long as, the moment (that), by the time (that), every time (that), the first time (that), the last time (that)
	장소 (place)	where(ever), anywhere, everywhere
	태도/방법 (manner)	as, as if, as though, how, (in) the way (that), (in) the way in which, (in) the same way (as)
	원인 (cause)	because, since, as, as/so long as, now that, insomuch as
	결과 (result)	so+형용사/부사+that, such+a/an+명사구+that
	목적 (purpose)	so that ~ (can/may/will), in order that ~ (can/may/will), lest ~ (should), for fear (that)
	조건/가정 (condition)	if, only if, assuming (that), on condition (that), provided (that), providing (that), in case (that), in the event (that), as/so long as, unless
	양보 (concession)	although, though, even though, even if, much as, while, whereas, considering (that), 의문사+ever, however much(/badly/good …), no matter how(/where/when/who …)
	정도/비교 (degree/comparison)	as~as, not so/as~as, 비교급~than

Exercise **1** 다음을 읽고 주절과 종속절을 구별하시오.

1. it started to rain (주절)
2. after the runner fell down (종속절)
3. before the telephone was invented
4. which no one clearly understood
5. she left because of you
6. what you said to me
7. a singer performed after dinner
8. because the chicken was burned
9. she has been crying a lot
10. when you left town

Basic Grammar for English Tests

11. the cost of chicken has gone up
12. whom he saw at the theater
13. exercise promotes health
14. walking develops leg muscles
15. winning is not everything
16. that apples are very nutritious
17. while the choir was singing
18. if prices continue to climb
19. they arrived after the deadline
20. although there was ice on the road

Exercise 2 다음 중에서 문장을 가려내시오.

1. When the seasons change, many small animals change their colors. (o)
2. When winter approaches and the landscape turns white with snow. (x)
3. Nature has given different types of creatures different types of camouflage.
4. Camouflage which refers to an animal's ability to hide itself.
5. Because many insects and small lizards have no way to protect themselves.
6. Unless a camouflaged insect is seen against a contrasting background, it may be completely invisible.
7. A small insect needs camouflage so that its enemies cannot find it.
8. Although some fish can become almost transparent.
9. Many species of fish which protect themselves through camouflage.
10. Reef fish can escape an enemy by changing their appearance to match almost any background.

◀ 명사절(noun clauses)

주절에 포함되어 동사의 주어나 목적어, 보어, 전치사의 목적어 등 명사 구실을 하는 종속절.

의문사(question words)로 시작하는 명사절
의문문이 다른 문장의 종속절이 될 때는 〈의문사+주어+동사〉의 어순이 된다.

1. 주어 역할

   What he said surprised me. (What did he say?)
   What matters most is good health. (What matters most?)

   그가 말한 것이 저를 깜짝 놀라게 했습니다. (그이가 뭐랬죠?) / 가장 중요한 것은 건강입니다. (무엇이 가장 중요하죠?)

2. 보어 역할

   The question is **When he did it**.
   Is this **what you're looking for**?

   문제는 그가 언제 그렇게 했느냐 입니다. / 이것이 당신이 찾고 계신 것입니까?

3. 목적어 역할 – 간접의문문

   I wonder **when he did it**.
   Please tell me **what happened**. (What happened?)

   저는 그가 언제 그 일을 했는지 궁금해요. / 무슨 일인지 말씀해주세요. (무슨 일이세요?)

4. 전치사 뒤에

   It depends on **when he did it**.
   I'm interested in **when he did it**.

   그것은 그가 언제 그렇게 했느냐에 달려있습니다. / 저는 그가 언제 그렇게 했느냐에 관심이 있습니다.

   cf. 주절에 think, suppose, believe, imagine, guess, say 등의 동사가 있을 때는 의문사를 앞세운다.

   Who do you think **is going with me**?
   Where do you suppose **she is living**?

   누가 저와 함께 갈 거라고 생각하세요? / 그녀가 어디에 살고 있는지 아시겠어요?

의문사+ever

Whoever wants to come is welcome.
= **Anyone** who wants to come is welcome.

오고 싶은 사람은 누구든지 환영입니다.

He makes friends easily with **who(m)ever** he meets.
= He makes friends easily with **anyone who(m)** he meets.

그는 누구를 만나든지 쉽게 친구로 사귑니다.

He always says **whatever** comes into his mind.

Basic Grammar for English Tests

= He always says **anything that** comes into his mind.
그는 늘 생각나는 것이면 무엇이든지 말합니다.

There are four good programs on TV at eight o'clock.
We can watch **whichever program(/whichever one)** you pr-efer.
= We can watch **any of the four programs that** you prefer.
8시에 TV에는 좋은 프로그램이 4개가 있다. / 우리는 어느 것이든 당신이 좋아하는 프로그램을 시청할 수 있어요.

You may leave **whenever** you wish.
= You may leave at **any time that** you wish.
당신은 언제든지 원하는 시간에 떠날 수 있습니다.

She can go **wherever** she wants to go.
= She can go **anyplace that** she wants to go.
그녀는 어디든지 가고 싶은 곳에 갈 수 있습니다.

The students may dress **however** they please.
= The students may dress in **any way that** they please.
학생들은 어떤 식으로든 자기들이 좋아하는 대로 옷을 입을 수 있습니다.

Exercise 3 다음 문장들의 구조를 확인하고 의문사로 시작한 명사절의 역할을 확인하시오.

1. *Where the dog went* is a mystery. (주어)
2. My father doesn't know how much money I spent.
3. What you said hurt my feeling.
4. Harry knows how he did on the test.
5. What the reporter asked was not polite.
6. The babysitter knows what the children like to eat.
7. Where we spend our vacation is not far from here.
8. The advertisement doesn't say how much the car costs.
9. Even his parents don't know why he ran away from home.
10. The class will explore how children learn.
11. The tropics are where the study of biology really begins.
12. How I spent my summer vacation is a boring topic.
13. The pamphlet explains where students can get a library card.
14. The subject of the film is how dolphins communicate.
15. The officer asked where I lived.

관계대명사 what절

1. 선행사를 자체에 포함한 관계대명사

   the man who—, the thing which—, those which—, and all that—

   What is beautiful is not always good. (= The thing that is beautiful …)
   My teacher made me **what I am now**. (= the man that I am now.)
   I gave him **what money I had with me**. (= all the money that I had with me.)

   아름다운 것이 언제나 좋은 것은 아니다. / 우리 선생님께서 지금의 나를 만들어주셨습니다. / 저는 그에게 제가 지닌 돈을 모두 주었습니다.

2. 의문사 what와 비교

   I ask him **what he had found**. ('무엇'—의문사)
   I gave him **what I had found**. ('~것'—관계대명사)

   저는 그가 무엇을 찾았는지 물어보았습니다. / 저는 제가 찾은 것을 그에게 주었습니다.

3. 관용어구

   She is charmed by **what he is**, not by **what he has**.
   Air **is to** man **what** water **is to** fish.
   She is **what you call** a Venus.
   He is clever, and **what is better still**, very brave.
   What is worse, they fought fiercely with each other.
   What with heat and **what with** thirst, he fell down.

   그녀는 가진 것 때문이 아니라, 인격 때문에 매력이 있습니다. / 공기와 인간의 관계는 물과 물고기의 관계와 같다. / 그녀는 소위 비너스입니다. / 그는 똑똑한데다 금상첨화로, 매우 용감합니다. / 설상가상으로, 그들은 서로 맹렬하게 싸웠습니다. / 열이 나고 한편으로는 갈증도 나서 그는 쓰러지고 말았다.

접속사 that

흔히 생략하기도 한다

1. 주어 역할

   That the world is round is a fact.
   That she doesn't understand spoken English is obvious.

   세상이 둥글다는 것은 사실입니다. / 그녀가 구어체 영어를 이해하지 못한다는 것은 확실합니다.

2. 목적어 역할

   I think **(that) he is a good actor**.
   He boasted **(that) he was successful**.
   I agree **it was a mistake**.

Basic Grammar for English Tests

He complained **he had been underpaid**.

그는 좋은 배우라고 생각합니다. / 그는 자기가 성공했다고 자랑하였습니다. / 저는 그것이 실수였다는 데 동의합니다. / 그는 봉급을 적게 받았다고 불평을 하였습니다.

3. 보어 역할 : 보어 다음에 that은 흔히 생략하기도 한다.

The assumption is **that things will improve**.
I'm afraid **(that) we've sold out of tickets**.

그 가정은 모든 일이 나아질 거라는 것입니다. / 저는 우리가 표를 다 팔아버린 것을 유감으로 생각합니다.

4. 명사와 동격 (the fact = that S+V)

The fact that his proposal makes sense should be recognized.
The idea that everyone should be required to vote by law is something I agree with.
We must face *the fact* that we might lose our deposit.

그의 제안이 사리에 맞다는 사실이 인식되어야 합니다. / 모든 사람이 법에 따라 투표해야 한다는 생각은 제가 동의하는 바입니다. / 우리의 적립금을 잃을 수도 있다는 사실을 직시해야 합니다.

5. 가주어, 가목적어 ('It~that ~'구문)

It was a pity **that** you couldn't come.
It's strange **that** he should have said that.
It seems **(that)** you're not really interested.

당신이 올 수 없다는 것이 슬펐습니다. / 그가 그렇게 말했을 것이라는 것은 이상합니다. / 당신은 실제로 관심이 없는 것 같아요.

Exercise 4 다음은 접속사가 생략된 문장들입니다. 종속절을 찾아 밑줄을 치시오.

1. Ambitious students feel *hard work is ultimately rewarded*.
2. The pilot said his plane was in good condition.
3. The fire inspector stated the building lacked sufficient safety equipment.
4. Results of the garbage study reveal fifteen percent of the city's edible food is wasted.
5. Search parties reported they had found the lost hikers.
6. The chief of the police said his men have arrested a suspect.
7. The instruction booklet says the appliance should not be dropped in water.
8. Few believe the report is accurate.
9. The city council believes the planning committee has been heavily influenced by developers.
10. The upholsterer felt the old couch was not worth recovering.

가정법의 뜻으로 쓰이는 that절

1. 다음의 동사들은 가정의 that절을 동반한다.

   > advise, ask, command(명령하다), decide, decree(공표하다), demand(요구하다), insist(주장하다), instruct(가르치다), move(동의하다), order, persuade(설득하다), prefer, propose, recommend(추천하다), request, require, stipulate(요구하다), suggest, urge(촉구하다)

   S+(위의 동사)+that+S+ 원형동사 ...

   이때 that절의 동사는 항상 원형이어야 하는데, should를 동사 앞에 쓰기도 한다. 이 경우는 주로 영국영어이다

   I **suggested** that she **see** a doctor.
   The judge **insisted** that the jury **return** a verdict immediately.
   I **move** that we **adjourn** until this afternoon.

   저는 그녀에게 진찰을 받아보라고 제안했습니다. / 판사는 배심원들이 즉시 평결을 제출할 것을 주장하였습니다. / 저는 오늘 오후까지 우리가 휴회할 것을 동의합니다.

2. 다음의 형용사들 역시 가정의 'It~that 문형'을 만든다.

   > advised, essential(필수적인), important, imperative(오연한), mandatory(명령받은, 강제적인), necessary, obligatory(의무적인), proposed(제안된), recommended(추천 받은), required(요구되는), suggested(제안되는), urgent(긴급한), vital(활력이 넘치는)

   It+be+(위의 형용사)+that+S+ 원형동사 …

   이때 역시 that절의 동사는 원형이며, should가 동사 앞에 오기도 한다.

   It is **necessary** that he **find** the books.
   It has been **suggested** that he **forget** the election.
   It was **urgent** that she **leave** at once.
   It is **important** that they **be** told the truth.

   그가 책을 찾는 것은 필요한 일입니다. / 그가 선거를 잊어야 한다는 의견이 제기되었습니다. / 그녀가 즉시 떠나야 한다는 것은 긴급합니다. / 그들이 진실을 들어야 한다는 것은 중요합니다

Exercise 5 다음에서 틀린 문장을 찾아 틀린 부분을 바르게 고치시오.

1. The teacher demanded that the student left the room. (left → *leave*)
2. It was urgent that he called her immediately.
3. It was very important that we delay discussion.
4. She intends to move that the committee suspends discussion on this issue.

Basic Grammar for English Tests

5. The king decreed that the new laws took effect the following month.
6. I propose that you should stop this rally.
7. I advise you take the prerequisites before registering for this course.
8. His father prefers that he attends a different university.
9. The faculty stipulated that the rule be abolished.
10. She urged that we found another alternative.

접속사 whether/if ~(or not)

1. 주어

   Whether she comes or not is unimportant to me.
   Whether he has signed the contract (or not) doesn't matter.

   그녀가 올지 안 올지는 제게 중요하지 않습니다. / 그가 계약서에 서명했는지 안 했는지는 중요하지 않습니다.

2. 보어

   The question is **whether he has signed the contract**.

   문제는 그가 계약에 서명했느냐 입니다.

3. 목적어

   I don't know **whether she will come**.
   I wonder **if he needs help**.

   저는 그녀가 올지 모르겠습니다. / 저는 그가 도움이 필요한지 궁금합니다.

4. 전치사 뒤에

   I'm concerned about **whether he has signed the contract**.

   저는 그가 계약에 서명했는지를 염려하고 있습니다.

의문사+to do

I don't know **what I should do**. = I don't know **what to do**.
Please tell me **how I can get to the bus station**. = Please tell me **how to get to the bus station**.
Jim told us **where we could find it**. = Jim told us **where to find it**.

저는 제가 무엇을 해야 할지를 모르겠어요. / 버스정거장까지 어떻게 가야하는지 말씀해주세요. / 짐은 그것을 어디서 찾을지 우리에게 말해주었습니다.

Exercise 6 다음 문장들의 구조를 확인하고 명사절을 찾아 밑줄을 치시오. 접속사가 생략된 경우도 있다.

1. One archeologist thinks *<u>that human beings did not develop the idea of numbers until after 3100 B.C.</u>*
2. That Samuel Colt developed a practical handgun in 1836 has had a great influence on modern society.
3. Christians' belief that Jesus Christ rose from the dead is one of the bases of their religion.
4. The fact that he proved unreliable made them reluctant to employ him again.
5. Recent news articles have reported that fifty to eighty percent of all handguns are used for criminal purposes.
6. Why man sleeps has been the subject of much research.
7. There is a biologist at Boston University who believes that insects developed wings in order to collect solar heat.
8. What caused dinosaurs to disappear from the earth is still unknown.
9. Few people realize that there are only six landing strips in the world long enough for the space shuttle to land safely.
10. A computer program called 'Eliza' acts as a personal counselor and asks 'her clients' how they are feeling.

◀ 형용사절(관계사절 adjective/relative clauses)

형용사절/관계사절이란?

1. 명사(곧, 선행사—사람, 사물, 동물, 사건)를 수식하거나 서술하고 어떤 정보를 제공하는 형용사 역할을 하는 종속절이다.

2. 이때, 이 형용사절을 이끄는 종속접속사/관계사를 특히 관계대명사 또는 관계부사라 부른다.
   (1) 관계대명사(relative pronouns) : who, whose, whom, which, that
   (2) 관계부사(relative adverbs) : when, where, why

형용사절의 용법

1. 수식용법(한정용법, 제한용법) : 단순히 선행사를 수식하는 기능

   The government **which promises to cut taxes** will be popular.

   세금부담을 줄여주겠다는 정부는 인기가 좋을 것이다.(—막연한 정부)

2. 서술용법(계속용법) : 선행사에 관해 서술을 하거나 어떤 정보를 보태주는 기능을 하며 comma(,)로 연결된다.

The government, **which promises to cut taxes**, will be popular.
= The government—which promises to cut taxes—will be popular.
= The government (which promises to cut taxes) will be popular.

그 정부는 세금부담도 줄여주겠다고 하는데, 인기가 좋을 것이다.(→현재 대화에서 언급되고 있는 정부)

3. 관계대명사 who가 있는 두 가지 문장의 의미 비교

(1) We took some children on a picnic. The children, **who** wanted to play soccer, ran to an open field as soon as we arrived at the park.

(2) We took some children on a picnic. The children **who** wanted to play soccer ran to an open field as soon as we arrived at the park. The others played a different game.

⑴ 우리는 소풍 때 아이들을 데리고 갔습니다. 아이들은 축구를 하고 싶어했는데, 우리가 공원에 도착하자마자 곧장 운동장으로 달려갔습니다.
⑵ 우리는 소풍 때 아이들을 데리고 갔습니다. 축구를 하고 싶어하는 아이들은 우리가 공원에 도착하자마자 곧장 운동장으로 달려갔습니다. 다른 아이들은 다른 경기를 했습니다.

The man **who(m)** I met teaches chemistry.
The professor **who** teaches Chemistry 101 is an excellent lecturer.
Professor Wilson, **who** teaches Chemistry 101, is an excellent lecturer.
Korea, **which** is surrounded on three sides by water, is a peninsula.
Hawaii, **which** consists of eight principal islands, is a favorite vacation spot.

제가 만난 남자는 화학을 가르칩니다. / 화학개론 강좌를 가르치는 그 교수는 뛰어난 강사입니다. / 윌슨 교수는 화학개론을 가르치시는데, 뛰어난 강사입니다. / 한국은 삼면이 물로 둘러싸여 있는 반도입니다. / 하와이는 8개의 주요 섬으로 이루어진 누구나 좋아하는 휴가장소입니다.

관계대명사/관계부사의 형태

관계대명사	사람+who(주격)+V 사람+whom(목적격)+S+V 사람/사물+whose(소유격)+명사 사물/동물 + { which(주격)+V 　　　　　　 { which(목적격)+S+V 사람/동물/사물 + { that(주격)+V 　　　　　　　　{ that(목적격)+S+V } → 수식용법에만 쓰인다.
관계부사	시간+when 장소+where 이유+why → 수식용법에만 쓰인다.

관계대명사의 용법

1. 주격 관계대명사

    (1) 사람+who/that+V ...

    I thanked the woman. She helped me.
    → I thanked the woman **who(that)** helped me.
    He is the man **who(that)** lives next door.
    They are the women **who(that)** live next door.

    저는 저를 도와주신 그 여자분께 감사드립니다. / 그는 옆집에 사는 남자입니다. / 그들은 옆집에 사는 여자들입니다.

    (2) 사물/동물+which/that+V ...

    The book is mine. It is on the table.
    → The book **which(that)** is on the table is mine.
    These are the photos **which(that)** show my house.
    This is the cat **which(that)** caught the mouse.

    탁자 위에 있는 책은 제 것입니다. / 이것들은 우리 집을 보여주는 사진들입니다. / 이것은 그 생쥐를 잡은 고양이입니다.

2. 소유격 관계대명사 : 사람/사물+whose+명사

    I know the man. His bicycle was stolen.
    → I know the man **whose** bicycle was stolen.
    The student writes well. I read **her** composition.
    → The student **whose** composition I read writes well.
    The millionaire **whose** son ran away from home a week ago has made a public appeal.

    저는 자기 자전거를 도둑 맞은 남자를 알고 있습니다. / 제가 읽고 있는 글의 주인인 그 학생은 글을 잘 쓰는군요. / 자신의 아들이 일주일 전에 집을 나간 백만장자는 광고를 냈습니다.

    ∗ 전치사와 함께 쓸 때

    > He is the man **from whose** house the pictures were stolen.
    > = He is the man **whose** house the pictures were stolen **from**.
    > In 1980 he caught a serious illness **from whose** effects he still suffers.
    > = In 1980 he caught a serious illness the effects **of which** he still suffers **from**.
    >
    > 그는 자기 집의 그림을 도둑 맞은 사람입니다. / 1980년에 그는 심한 병을 앓았는데, 그 영향으로 아직도 고생을 합니다.

3. 목적격 관계대명사 : 흔히 생략된다.

    (1) 사람+who(m)/that+S+V ...

The man was Mr. Jones. I saw him.
→ The man **who(m)/that** I saw was Mr. Jones.
= The man I saw was Mr. Jones.
She is the woman **who(m)/that** I met on holiday.
= She is the woman I met on holiday.

제가 본 그 남자는 존스씨였습니다. / 그녀는 제가 휴일에 만난 여자입니다.

※ 전치사와 함께 쓰는 경우

> She is the woman. I told you **about her**. 그녀는 제가 당신에게 말했던 그 여자입니다.
> = She is the woman **about whom** I told you.
> = She is the woman **(who(m)/that)** I told you **about**.
> The person **to whom** I complained is the manager. 제가 불평을 했던 사람이 부장입니다.
> = The person **(who(m)/that)** I complained **to** is the manager.
> The hotel manager, **to whom** I complained about the service, refunded part of our bill. 호텔 매니저는 제가 서비스에 대해 의의를 제기했더니, 계산의 일부를 환불해주었습니다.
> = The hotel manager, **who(m)** I complained to about the service, refunded part of our bill.

(2) 사물/동물+which/that+S+V ...

The movie wasn't very good. We saw it last night.
= **The movie (which/that)** we saw last night wasn't very good.
This is **the photo** (which/that) I took.
These are **the cats (which/that)** I photographed.

어젯밤에 우리가 본 영화는 그리 좋지 않았습니다. / 이것이 제가 찍은 사진입니다. / 이것들이 제가 사진 찍은 고양이들입니다.

※ 전치사와 함께 쓰는 경우

> The music was good. We listened **to it** last night.
> → The music **to which** we listened last night was good.
> = The music (which/that) we listened **to** last night was good.
> This is the pan **in which** I boiled the milk.
> = This is the pan (which/that) I boiled the milk **in**.
> These are the cats I gave the milk **to**.
> 우리가 어젯밤에 들은 음악은 좋았습니다. / 이것이 제가 우유를 끓인 팬입니다. / 이것들이 제가 우유를 준 고양이들입니다.

4. 삽입절이 있는 경우

This is the actress **who** *his father claims* has seduced his son.

In the rain I saw a man **who** *I thought* was a detective.
This is the boy **who** *everyone thought* would be chosen the winner by the judges.

이 사람이 자기 아들을 유혹하였다고 그의 아버지가 주장하는 그 여배우입니다. / 빗속에서 저는 형사라고 생각되는 사람을 보았습니다. / 이 사람이 심사원들에 의해 우승자로 뽑힐 것으로 모두가 생각하는 그 남자입니다.

비교
- I picked up a man **who** I *thought* was honest. (주격)
- I picked up a man **whom** I thought to be honest. (목적격)

저는 정직하다고 생각되는 사람을 뽑았습니다. / 저는 제가 정직하다고 생각한 사람을 뽑았습니다.

관계부사의 용법

1. when (때, 시간)

    I'll never forget the day. I met you **then**(/**on that day**).
    → I'll never forget (the day) **when** I met you.
    = I'll never forget **the day on which** I met you.
    = I'll never forget **the day (that)** I met you.
    1994 was **the year in which** my first son was born.
    = 1994 was **(the year) when** my first son was born.

    저는 당신을 만난 그날을 잊지 못할 것입니다. / 1994년은 내 아들이 태어난 해입니다.

2. where (곳, 장소)

    The building is very old. He lives **there**(/**in that building**).
    → The building **where** he lives is very old.
    = The building **in which** he lives is very old.
    = The building **(which/that)** he lives **in** is very old.
    This is **the place where** I grew up.
    = This is **the place in which** I grew up.
    = This is **the place** I grew up **in**.

    그가 살고 있는 건물은 아주 오래되었습니다. / 여기가 제가 자란 곳입니다.

3. why (이유, 원인)

    That's **(the reason) why** he dislikes me.
    = That's **the reason for which** he dislikes me.
    Tell me **the reason why** you did it. (형용사절)
    = Tell me **why** you did it. ('명사절'이 더 일반적인 문형이다.)

    그것이 그가 나를 싫어하는 이유입니다. / 너가 왜 그랬는지 그 이유를 말해 봐.

Basic Grammar for English Tests

* 방법(the way)

That's not the way (in which) I do it.
That's the way the money goes!

그것은 제가 하는 방법이 아닙니다. / 그것은 돈으로 해결하는 식입니다!

관계대명사의 기타 중요 용법

1. 앞 문장 전체 또는 일부를 받는 관계사 which—서술용법

   Tom was late. **That** surprised me.
   → Tom was late, **which** surprised me.
   The elevator is out of order. **This** is too bad.
   → The elevator is out of order, **which** is too bad.
   She married Joe, **which** surprised everyone. (=and this fact)
   I may have to study late, **in which case** I'll telephone. (그럴 경우에는)

   톰이 게을러서 저는 놀랐습니다. / 엘리베이터가 고장나서 너무 나빴습니다. / 그녀는 조와 결혼을 하여 모든 사람을 놀라게 하였습니다. / 저는 늦게까지 공부를 할 수도 있는데, 그럴 경우에는 전화를 하겠습니다.

2. 선행사가 대명사인 경우

   There is **someone (whom)** I want you to meet.
   God bless this ship and **all who** sail in her.

   All that remains for me to do is to say goodbye. (not which)
   Everything that can be done has been done. (not which)
   Everything (that) he said was pure nonsense.
   Anybody who wants to come is welcome.
   I'll do **anything (that)** I can.

   He is **the only one who** knows the answer.
   Paula was **the only one** I knew at the party.
   It is **I who** am responsible.
   He who laughs last laughs best.
   Scholarships are available for **those who** need financial assistance.

   Bach is **the greatest composer that's(who's)** ever lived.
   Is this **the best that** you can do? (not which)
   He reads **the same** books **that** you read. (not which)
   Who that has read his great novels can forget his name?
   John is not the man **that** he was. (not who)
   My typewriter is not the machine **(that)** it was. (not which)

   제 생각에 당신이 만나봤으면 하는 사람이 있습니다. / 이 배와 이 배로 항해하는 모든 사람들에게 하나님의 은총이 있기를. / 제가 하도록 남겨진 일은 안녕이라고 말하는 것 뿐 입니다. / 할 수 있는 일은 모두 다 했습니다. / 그가 말한 것은 모두 넌센스입니다. / 오고 싶어하는 사람은

누구든지 환영입니다. / 저는 제가 할 수 있는 것이면 어떤 것이든 하겠습니다. / 그는 정답을 알고 있는 유일한 사람입니다. / 폴라는 파티에서 제가 아는 유일한 사람이었습니다. / 책임이 있는 사람은 바로 저입니다. / 마지막에 웃는 자가 가장 잘 웃는 것입니다. / 장학금은 재정보조를 필요로 하는 사람들에게 유용합니다 / 바하는 지금까지 살았던 가장 위대한 작곡가입니다. / 이것이 당신이 할 수 있는 최선입니까? / 그는 당신이 읽고 있는 것과 같은 책을 읽고 있습니다. / 그의 위대한 소설을 읽은 사람이라면 누가 그의 이름을 잊을 수 있겠습니까? / 존은 과거의 그가 아닙니다. / 저 타자기는 예전의 그 기계가 아닙니다.

3. 수량대명사(한정사)가 선행사인 경우 : 선행사+of+관계대명사

In my class there are 20 students, **most of whom** are from the East Asia.
Both players, **neither of whom** reached the final, played well.
The treasure, **some of which** has been discovered, has been sent to the British Museum.
The teachers discussed Jim, **one of whose** problems was poor study habits.

우리 학급에는 20명이 있는데 그들 대부분이 동아시아에서 왔습니다. / 두 선수는 아무도 골인지점에 닿지는 못했지만, 잘 뛰었습니다. / 그 보물은 일부가 발견되어서, 대영박물관에 보내졌습니다. / 선생님들은 짐과 의논하셨는데 그 문제 중 하나가 나쁜 공부습관이었습니다.

4. but가 관계대명사로 쓰이는 경우

There is no rule **but** has some exceptions. (= that ~ not)
= There is no rule **that** has **not** some exceptions.
There is no one **but** knows him.
= There is no one that doesn't know him.
= Who but knows him?
= Everybody knows him.

예외 없는 규정은 없습니다. / 그를 모르는 사람은 없습니다.

5. '주격관계대명사 + be'의 생략 → 형용사구로 전환

The girl **who is sitting next to me** is Mary. (형용사절)
= The girl **sitting next to me** is Mary. (형용사구)
The boy **who is playing the piano** is Ben.
= The boy **playing the piano** is Ben.
　cf. The boy (whom) I saw was Tom. (생략하지 못함)
The ideas (which are) **presented in that book** are interesting.
The books (that are) on **that shelf** are mine.

제 옆에 앉아있는 여자가 매리입니다. / 피아노를 치는 남자가 벤입니다. / 제가 본 남자는 톰이었습니다. / 그 책에 표현된 사상이 흥미롭습니다. / 저 서가의 책들은 제것입니다

(1) be동사가 없으면 동사가 -ing형으로 바뀐다.

English has an alphabet **that consists** of 26 letters.
= English has an alphabet **consisting** of 26 letters.
Anyone **who wants** to come with us is welcome.
= Anyone **wanting** to come with us is welcome.
Anyone **who wishes** to leave early may do so.

Basic Grammar for English Tests

= Anyone **wishing** to leave early may do so.

영어는 26자로 구성된 알파벳을 가지고 있습니다. / 우리와 함께 가려는 사람은 누구든지 환영입니다. / 일찍 떠나려는 사람은 누구든지 그렇게 해도 됩니다.

(2) 서술용법(, … ,)에서

George Washington, (**who was**) the first president of the United states, was a wealthy colonist and a general in the army.
Louisville, (which is) the largest city in Kentucky, was founded in 1778.

조지 워싱턴은 미국의 초대 대통령인데 부유한 식민지인이자 군대의 장군이었습니다. / 루이스빌은 켄터키에서 가장 큰 도시인데 1778년에 건설되었습니다.

Exercise 7 다음의 문장구조를 확인하고 주절과 형용사절을 구별하시오.

1. whom the doctors treated (형용사절)
2. whom did they visit (주절)
3. who failed the last exam (둘 다)
4. that one is an old photograph
5. which dog bit the child
6. that scientists recently discovered
7. which movie did he see
8. whose test had the teacher misplaced
9. whom they saw at the hotel
10. that the sailors threw overboard
11. those people have recently moved in
12. who babysits for the next-door neighbors
13. whose name he had forgotten
14. at what time did he leave
15. for which he carefully looked

Exercise 8 빈칸 뒤에 오는 절이 명사절이면 접속사 that을, 형용사절이면 관계대명사 which를 넣으시오.

1. a) the news _that_ Mount St. Helen erupted
   b) the news _which_ the magazine prints
2. a) the fact _____ handguns are dangerous
   b) the fact _____ the student had forgotten to mention
3. a) the claim _____ the senator made
   b) the claim _____ ginseng cures cancer

4. a) the belief _____ God exists
   b) the belief _____ the woman expressed
5. a) the proof _____ there is life on Mars
   b) the proof _____ the scientists were looking for
6. a) the statement _____ the man made
   b) the statement _____ dolphins can communicate
7. a) the hope _____ the man would survive
   b) the hope _____ the teacher expressed
8. a) the dream _____ Freud analyzed
   b) the dream _____ the world will remain at peace
9. a) the theory _____ there are black holes in the universe
   b) the theory _____ the psychologist explained
10. a) the argument _____ the man is innocent
    b) the argument _____ the lawyer used in court

Exercise 9 다음 문장구조를 확인하고 that절이 명사절이면 밑줄을 긋고, 형용사절이면 괄호를 치시오.

1. Newspapers reported the fact *that a major earthquake had occurred in Algeria*.
2. The beliefs (*that Moslems hold*) are based on the teachings of Mohammed.
3. The lawyer expressed his belief that his client was innocent.
4. The facts that the witness concealed would have saved the defendant from being convicted.
5. Searchers have given up hope that the hikers will be found before nightfall.
6. The newspaper frequently misquoted the statements that the governor made.
7. The jurors seemed unconvinced by the witness's statement that he had seen an armed man running from the house.
8. Several people overheard the argument that the couple had.
9. News that a ship had sunk off the Georgia coast reached the Coast Guard very quickly.
10. The hope that all students have is to pass their exams.

Basic Grammar for English Tests

◀ 부사절(adverb clauses)

부사절이란?

부사 역할을 하는 종속절.
주절의 문장구조에는 영향을 주지 않지만 주절의 동사, 형용사, 부사를 수식하거나 그 의미를 보충한다.

[시간] Tell him **as soon as he arrives**. (언제?)
[장소] You can sit **where you like**. (어디서?)
[태도] He spoke **as if he meant business**. (어떻게?)
[이유] He went to bed **because he felt ill**. (왜?)

그가 도착하거든 곧 그에게 말하시오. / 좋은 곳에 앉아도 됩니다. / 그는 마치 자기가 사업을 아는 것처럼 말하였습니다. / 그는 아파서 잠자리에 들었습니다.

시간을 나타내는 부사절

1. 시간의 부사절을 인도하는 종속접속사

> after, before, when(ever), everytime, while, as, once, since, as soon as, as/so long as, by the time that, the moment (that), till/until, the first time that, the last time that …

When I arrived, he was talking on the phone.
You didn't look very well **when** you got up this morning.
We stayed there **till** we finished our work.
I spent every summer on a farm **until** I was about twelve.
Everytime I see her, I say hello.
Whenever I have to write a paper, I don't know where to begin.
Once I start, the paper seems to write itself.
As soon as it stops raining, we will leave.
After she (had) graduated, she got a job.
An echo is a sound heard **after** it is reflected from an object.
I will leave **before** he comes.
I (had) left **before** he came.
While I was walking home, it began to rain.
As I was walking home, it began to rain.
By the time he comes, we will already have left.
I haven't seen him **since** he left this morning.
I will never speak to him again **as(/so) long as** I live.
The first time I went to New York, I went to an opera.

I saw two plays **the last time** I went to New York.
The next time I go to New York, I'm going to see a ballet.

제가 도착했을 때, 그는 전화통화를 하고 있었습니다. / 당신이 오늘 아침에 일어났을 때 아주 좋아 보이지 않았습니다. / 우리가 일을 마칠 때까지 우리는 그곳에 있었습니다. / 제가 거의 열두 살이 될 때까지 저는 농장에서 매년 여름을 보냈습니다. / 그녀를 볼 때마다 저는 인사를 합니다. / 제가 글을 써야할 때면, 저는 어디서부터 시작해야 할지를 모릅니다. / 일단 시작하면, 글은 저절로 써지는 것 같습니다. / 비가 그치자마자, 우리는 떠날 것입니다. / 졸업을 한 뒤에 그녀는 일자리를 잡았습니다. / 메아리는 물체로부터 반사된 뒤에 들리는 소리입니다. / 그가 오기 전에 저는 떠날 것입니다. / 그가 오기 전에 저는 떠났습니다. / 제가 집으로 걸어가는 동안 비가 오기 시작하였습니다. / 제가 집으로 걸어갈 때 비가 오기 시작하였습니다. / 그가 올 때까지는 우리는 이미 떠났을 것입니다. / 그가 오늘 아침 떠난 이후에 저는 그를 보지 못했습니다. / 살아있는 한 저는 다시는 그와 말을 하지 않겠습니다. / 제가 뉴욕에 처음 갔을 때, 저는 오페라에 갔습니다. / 뉴욕에 마지막으로 갔을 때 저는 연극을 두 편 보았습니다. / 다음 번에 뉴욕에 가면, 저는 발레를 볼 것입니다.

2. 주절이 미래시간을 언급할 때에도, 다음의 시간부사절에는 현재시제를 쓴다.

> [순수시간] after, before, when, as soon as, till/until,
> by the time (that), the moment (that)

The Owens **will move** to a new apartment **when their baby is born**.
I will try to finish this work **before you come**.
I will move as soon as I find a new house.
She **will call** you back **after she finishes dinner**.

오웬스씨네는 아기가 태어날 때에는 새 아파트로 이사를 갈 것입니다. / 저는 당신이 오기 전에 이 작업을 끝마치려고 애쓰겠습니다. / 저는 새 집을 찾자마자 곧 이사를 할 것입니다. / 그녀는 저녁식사를 끝내고 당신에게 다시 전화를 할 것입니다.

장소를 나타내는 부사절

> [장소 부사절을 인도하는 접속사] where(ver), anywhere, everywhere

You can't camp **where(/wherever/anywhere)** you like these days.
Consumers usually prefer to do business **wherever** credit cards are accepted.
Everywhere I shop, I use my credit cards.
I usually stop for lunch **anywhere** that is handy.

요즈음에는 여러분이 좋아하는 아무 곳에서나 야영할 수 없습니다. / 고객들은 늘 신용카드가 받아들여지는 곳에서 거래를 하려합니다. / 저는 어디서 쇼핑을 하든지, 신용카드를 사용합니다. / 저는 어디든 가까운 곳에 들러 점심을 먹습니다.

태도/방법을 나타내는 부사절

> [접속사] as, how, (in) the way (that/in which), (in) the same way (as),
> as if, as though

1. 방법 : as, how, (in) the way that(/in which), (in) the same way as

   Type this again **as** I showed you a moment ago. (= in the way I showed you)
   This steak is cooked just **how**(/the way that) I like it.

She is behaving **(in) the same way** her elder sister used to.

잠시 전에 내가 보여준 대로 이것을 다시 타자 치게. / 이 스테이크는 제가 좋아하는 방식 그대로 요리가 되요. / 그녀는 그녀의 언니가 하던 대로 행동을 해요.

2. 태도(manner) : as if, as though

I feel **as if(/as though)** I'm floating on air.
Lillian was trembling **as if(/as though)** she had seen a ghost.
She acted **as if** she were mad.

저는 마치 공중에 떠있는 것 같은 느낌이에요. / 릴리언은 마치 귀신을 본 것처럼 떨고 있었습니다. / 그녀는 마치 미친 것처럼 연기하였습니다.

이유(reason)를 나타내는 부사절

[접속사] because, since, as, as/so long as, now that, in that, seeing that, insomuch as

As(/Because/Since) there was very little support, the strike was not successful.
He went to bed **because** he was sleepy.
Since he's not interested in classical music, he decided not to go to the concert.
Now that the semester is finished, I'm going to rest a few days and then take a trip.
Seeing that it's raining, you had better stay indoors.

지원이 너무 적어서, 파업은 성공적이지 못했습니다. / 그는 졸려서 잠자리에 들었습니다. / 고전음악에 흥미가 없어서 그는 음악회에 가지 않기로 했습니다. / 학기가 끝나므로 저는 며칠 쉬고서 여행을 가려고 합니다. / 비가 오니까 너는 집 안에 있는 게 좋겠다.

원인-결과(cause-result)를 나타내는 부사절

1. 접속사 형태

so+형용사/부사+that
such+(a/an)+형용사+명사+that } 너무 ~해서, 그래서 ~하다

The coffee is **so hot that** I can't drink it. (형용사)
I'm **so hungry that** I could eat a horse. (형용사)
She speaks **so fast that** I can't understand her. (부사)
He walked **so quickly that** I couldn't keep up with him. (부사)
It was **such good coffee that** I had another cup. (불가산명사)
It was **such a foggy day that** we couldn't see the road. (가산명사)

They are **such beautiful pictures that** everyone will want one.
This is **such difficult homework that** I will never finish it.

커피가 너무 뜨거워 저는 마실 수가 없습니다. / 너무 배가 고파서 저는 말고기도 먹을 수 있겠어요. / 그녀는 너무 빨리 말을 해서 제가 알아들을 수 없어요. / 그는 너무 빨리 걸어가서 제가 그를 쫓아가지를 못했습니다. / 너무 좋은 커피라서 저는 한 잔 더 다 마셨습니다. / 너무 안개가 많이 낀 날이어서, 우리는 길을 볼 수 없었습니다. / 그것들은 너무도 아름다운 그림들이어서 모두가 하나를 원할 것입니다. / 이것은 너무 어려운 숙제여서 저는 도저히 끝내지 못할 거예요.

2. 단, 수량형용사(many, much, few, little)로 수식된 경우에는
   so+수량형용사+명사+that

   { so+many/few+가산명사+that
   { so+much/little+불가산명사+that

She made **so many mistakes that** she failed the exam.
She has **so much money that** she can buy whatever she wants.

그녀는 실수를 너무 많이 해서 시험에 실패를 했습니다. / 그녀는 돈이 너무 많아서 원하는 것은 무엇이든 살 수 있습니다.

Exercise 10 다음 문장이 성립하도록 괄호에서 알맞은 단어를 고르시오.

1. The sun shone (*so*/*such*) brightly that Maria had to put on her sunglasses.
2. Dean was (*so*/*such*) a powerful swimmer that he always won the races.
3. There are (*so*/*such*) few students registered that the class was canceled.
4. We had (*so*/*such*) wonderful memories of that place that we decided to return.
5. We had (*so*/*such*) good a time at the party that we hated to leave.
6. The benefit was (*so*/*such*) great a success that the promoters decided to repeat it.
7. It was (*so*/*such*) a nice day that we decided to go to the beach.
8. Jane looked (*so*/*such*) sick that the nurse told her to go home.
9. Those were (*so*/*such*) difficult assignments that we spent two weeks finishing them.
10. There were (*so*/*such*) many people on the bus that we decided to walk.

목적(purpose)을 나타내는 부사절

> 접속사 : so that ~ (can/may/will)
> in order that ~ (can/may/will)
> lest ~ (should)
> for fear (that)

1. so(/in order) that

    I turned off the TV **so that** my roommate **could** study in peace and quiet.
    Yesterday I took my umbrella **so that I wouldn't** get wet.
    I'll take my umbrella **so that I won't** get wet.
    = I'll take my umbrella **in order that I won't** get wet.
    = I'll take my umbrella **in order(/so as) not to** get wet.

    저는 동료가 조용하게 공부할 수 있도록 텔레비전을 껐습니다. / 어제 저는 비를 맞지 않으려고 우산을 가지고 갔습니다. / 비를 맞지 않기 위해 저는 우산을 가져갈 것입니다.

2. lest ~ should ... : ~하지 않도록

    She studied hard **lest** she **should** fail in the examination.
    We have a memorial service every year **lest** we **(should)** forget our debt to those who died in battle.
    I avoided mentioning the subject **lest** she be angry.

    그녀는 시험에 떨어지지 않도록 열심히 공부했습니다. / 우리는 전쟁에서 죽은 사람들에게 진 빚을 잊지 않도록 매년 현충행사를 가집니다. / 저는 그녀가 화날까봐 그 주제의 언급을 피했습니다.

3. for fear (that) : ~할까봐 걱정되어서, ~경우에 대비해서

    I bought the car at once **for fear (that)** he **might** change his mind.
    = I bought the car at once **in case** he changed his mind.

    저는 그가 마음을 바꿀까봐 곧장 자동차를 샀습니다.

결과절과 목적절의 so that 비교

We arrived early **so that**(/in order that) we **could**(/might/would/should) get good seats. (목적)
We arrived early, **so that** we got good seats. (결과)
= We arrived **so** early **that** we got good seats.

우리는 좋은 자리를 잡기 위해 일찍 도착하였습니다. / 우리는 일찍 도착해서 좋은 자리를 잡았습니다.

조건(condition)을 나타내는 부사절

1. 접속사

> if, only if, assuming (that), on condition (that), provided (that), providing (that), as(so) long as, unless, in the event (that), suppose/supposing (that), in case (that)

2. 여러 가지 조건절 표현

I'm taking a raincoat with me **in case** (that) I need it. (~경우에 대비해서: 주로 미래 관련 문장에 쓴다.)
저는 필요할 때를 대비해서 코트를 가져가겠습니다.

As(So) long as you return the book by Saturday, I will lend it to you with pleasure. (= only if : ~하는 한, ~하기만 한다면)
토요일까지만 책을 돌려주신다면, 저는 기꺼이 당신에게 그 책을 빌려드리겠습니다.

Suppose/Supposing (that) your friends knew how you're behaving here, what would they think? (= If ...)
Supposing I accepted this offer, what would you say?
당신이 여기서 어떻게 행동을 하는지를 당신 친구들이 안다면, 그들이 어떻게 생각하겠습니까? / 제가 이 제안을 받아들인다면 당신은 뭐라고 말하겠습니까?

He says he'll accept the position **on condition that** the salary is satisfactory. (= only if : ~하기만 한다면)
봉급이 만족스럽기만 하면 그 사람은 그 자리를 받아들이겠다고 말합니다.

Provided/Providing (that) no objection is raised, we shall hold the meeting here. (= only if ...)
I will consent, **provided (that)** all the others agree.
아무런 의의가 제기되지 않는다면, 우리는 여기서 정회할 것입니다. / 다른 사람들이 모두가 동의한다면 저는 따르겠습니다.

He is, **as it were**, a grown-up baby. (as it were: 말하자면) 그 사람은 말하자면, 애어른입니다.

양보(concession)를 나타내는 부사절

> [양보절을 이끄는 접속사]
> 1. 양보
> (1) 비록~일지라도 : although, though, even though
>   even if, much as, considering (that)
> (2) 아무리 ~해도 : however+형용사+S+V
>   의문사ever = no matter 의문사
> 2. 대조   ~인 반면 : while, whereas

Basic Grammar for English Tests

1. **Even though(/Although/Though)** it was cold, I went swimming.
   We intend to go to India, **even if** air fares go up again.
   Much as I'd like to help, there isn't a lot I can do.

   날씨가 추웠지만 저는 수영하러 갔습니다. / 항공요금이 다시 오른다해도 우리는 인도에 갈 작정입니다. / 제가 돕고 싶어해도 제가 할 수 있는 일은 많지 않습니다.

2. 의문사+ever

   However often I try, I cannot find the answer.
   (= Although I often try, …)
   However far it is, I intend to drive there tonight.
   No matter where you go, you can't escape from yourself.
   = **Wherever you go**, you can't escape from yourself.

   아무리 자주 애써봐도 정답을 찾을 수가 없습니다. / 그곳이 아무리 멀다해도 저는 오늘밤 그 곳에 갈 작정입니다. / 어디를 가든지 당신은 자신으로부터 벗어날 수 없어요.

3. 대조(opposition)

   Mary is rich, **whereas** John is poor.
   = Mary is rich, **while** John is poor.
   = John is poor, **while** Mary is rich.
   = **Whereas** Mary is rich, John is poor

   메리가 부자인 반면에 존은 가난합니다.

정도/비교(degree/comparison)를 나타내는 부사절

> [접속사]   as+형용사/부사+ as
>   not so(as) ~ as
>   비교급 ~ than

He is **as** quick in answering **as** his sister (is). (이때, as, than은 전치사이기도 하다.)
= He answers **as** quickly **as** his sister (does).
He is **not so(/as)** quick in answering **as** his sister (is).
His sister is **quicker than** he (is).
He moves **more slowly than** his sister (does).

그는 자기 누이처럼 대답을 빨리 합니다. / 그는 대답할 때 자기 누이만큼 빠르지 않습니다. / 그의 누이는 그보다 빠릅니다. / 그는 자기 누이보다 더 느리게 움직입니다.

부사절의 축약 : 종속절인 부사절의 '주어와 be동사'를 흔히 생략하여 문장을 간략하게 하기도 한다.

While (she was) **at college**, Jane wrote a novel.
If (it is) **possible**, please let me know by this evening.
Though (he was) **exhausted**, he went to bed very late.

대학에 있는 동안, 제인은 소설을 썼습니다. / 가능하다면 오늘 저녁까지 알려주십시오. / 녹초가 되었는데도 그는 매우 늦게 잠자리에 들었습니다.

Exercise 11 다음 문장들을 읽고 부사절을 찾으시오.

1. *Until cable television was invented*, many viewers could not get clear reception on their sets. (시간절)
2. Applications will be considered provided that their files are complete before the deadline.
3. Mr. Williamson will be leaving the firm soon whether or not he voluntarily turns in his resignation.
4. As water vapor cools, it changes from a gas to a liquid and finally to solid ice.
5. Because Neptune orbits the sun only once every 165 years, it has not yet completed a full revolution since it was discovered in 1946.
6. While vision is the dominant sense in sighted people, for the blind the sense of touch is the most important.
7. In the late 1800's the number of murders in the U.S. fell although the percentage of murders committed with handguns increased.
8. Unless the sewing machine is repaired by Monday, the costumes will not be ready in time for the first performance.
9. The weeds and tall grass in that yard make the house look as if it has been vacant for quite some time.
10. Stacy Pool will be closed for a week so that it can be repainted before the summer season begins.

Exercise 12 다음 각 종속절을 읽고 그 종류를 말하시오.

1. whom they visited last weekend (형용사절)
2. because the creek flooded (부사절)
3. what the people used to do (명사절)
4. whose language the researcher studied

Basic Grammar for English Tests

5. how much money the candidates spent
6. as long as it takes to learn them
7. when Europeans came to North America
8. which early settlers knew nothing about
9. who came to their rescue
10. how well he did on the last test
11. that he knew the answer to the question
12. that he talked to yesterday
13. if the students fail to do homework
14. until the deadline has passed
15. which was given to each applicant

Actual Test 5

다음 각 문장을 읽고 빈칸에는 알맞은 단어를 넣고, 밑줄 친 부분에서는 잘못된 부분을 찾아내시오.

1. _____ story of King Charles' rescue of Jane Lyon is authentic is now doubted by some historians.
   - Ⓐ The
   - Ⓑ In the
   - Ⓒ That the
   - Ⓓ Although the

2. I wonder how many years ago _____.
   - Ⓐ did your grandfather retire
   - Ⓑ your grandfather retired
   - Ⓒ has your grandfather retired
   - Ⓓ your grandfather has retired

3. _____ some of the mammals came to live in the sea is not known.
   - Ⓐ Which
   - Ⓑ Since
   - Ⓒ Although
   - Ⓓ How

4. _____ time and space have been to physics, liberty and equality have been and still are to democracy.
   - Ⓐ Since
   - Ⓑ That
   - Ⓒ How
   - Ⓓ What

5. _____ brings about happiness has utility, according to the theory of utilitarianism.
   - Ⓐ It
   - Ⓑ Whatever
   - Ⓒ Each
   - Ⓓ Why

6. Jane Lyon, who _____ from 1876 to 1945, founded Saint Paul College in Massachusetts.
   - Ⓐ she lived
   - Ⓑ living
   - Ⓒ did she live
   - Ⓓ lived

7. Tom Jones, _____ wrist and arm were hurt badly in the Second World War, nevertheless became an outstanding artist.
   - Ⓐ that
   - Ⓑ whose
   - Ⓒ for whom
   - Ⓓ of which

8. Croquet is a popular lawn sport _____ players hit wooden balls through wire arches called wickets.
   Ⓐ when
   Ⓑ which
   Ⓒ in when
   Ⓓ in which

9. Collecting coins was a hobby _____.
   Ⓐ which she found real pleasing to her
   Ⓑ pursuing which she got much pleasure
   Ⓒ that gave her a lot of pleasure doing
   Ⓓ that gave her a great deal of pleasure

10. The tea plant usually grows fast at low altitudes _____.
    Ⓐ where is the air warm
    Ⓑ the warm is where
    Ⓒ is where the warm air
    Ⓓ where the air is warm

11. _____ in history when great progress was made in relatively short periods of time.
    Ⓐ Moments
    Ⓑ Throughout moments
    Ⓒ Moments have been
    Ⓓ There have been moments

12. _____ she has created remarkable stage settings for the Martha Graham dance company, artist Ann Landers is more famous for her sculpture.
    Ⓐ But not
    Ⓑ Nevertheless
    Ⓒ In spite of
    Ⓓ Although

13. No matter how _____, it is not totally worthless.
    Ⓐ dry a desert may be
    Ⓑ a desert may be dry
    Ⓒ may a desert be dry
    Ⓓ a desert dry may be

14. Most People which live in a metropolitan area often have little feeling of
                   A   B   C
    political unity among themselves.
          D

15. The president announced the names of those whom were to be named to the cabinet.
                      A   B   C   D

16. The man <u>whom</u> they think did <u>it has</u> been taken to <u>his lawyer</u> for <u>counsel</u>.
     　　　　A　　　　　　　　B　　　　　　　　C　　　　　　D

17. He had trouble <u>finding out</u> <u>that</u> the capital city of the state <u>lay in</u> the coastal
     　　　　　　　A　　　　　B　　　　　　　　　　　　　　　C
    area or <u>in the mountains</u>.
    　　　　　　D

18. There <u>are</u> many organizations <u>which</u> only purpose <u>is</u> <u>to help</u> mentally
    　　　　A　　　　　　　　　　　B　　　　　　　　C　　D
    retarded children.

19. A boy <u>who</u> you must <u>meet right</u> away is Karl Harris, <u>the best</u> math student
    　　　　A　　　　　　B　　　　　　　　　　　　　　C
    <u>in our</u> dormitory.
    　　D

20. Mrs. Green, a member of the social committee for the <u>coming</u> year, <u>is</u> the
    　　　　　　　　　　　　　　　　　　　　　　　　　　　　A　　　　　　B
    <u>only</u> woman <u>which</u> has a car.
    　　C　　　　　　D

21. We <u>had been</u> in the country <u>not more than</u> three days <u>until</u> we found that we
    　　　　A　　　　　　　　　　　　　B　　　　　　　　　　C
    <u>needed</u> a guide.
    　　D

22. A measuring worm <u>can hold</u> <u>itself</u> straight <u>out</u> from a branch so <u>that looks</u>
    　　　　　　　　　　　A　　　　　B　　　　　　　C　　　　　　　　　　　D
    like a small twig.

23. The cost of a college education has risen as <u>rapidly</u> <u>during</u> the <u>past ten years</u>
    　　　　　　　　　　　　　　　　　　　　　　　A　　　　B　　　　　　C
    that it is now <u>beyond the reach</u> of many people.
    　　　　　　　　　　　　D

24. Mr. Park <u>has been</u> <u>at the center of</u> political power since <u>1962</u>, <u>where</u> he
    　　　　　　A　　　　　　B　　　　　　　　　　　　　　　　　　　　　　C
    <u>became</u> the leader of Republican Party.
    　　D

25. The Brooklyn Bridge <u>which</u> was <u>built by</u> John Roeblings who <u>completed</u>
    　　　　　　　　　　　A　　　　　　B　　　　　　　　　　　　　　　　C
    the <u>suspension</u> bridge.
    　　　　D

Unit 6

특수문형

◀ 분사

1. 분사(participles)란 형용사 역할을 하는 동사형태를 말한다.

2. 종류와 형태

	현재분사	완료형분사	과거분사
능동태	finding	having found	—
수동태	being found	having been found	found

3. 서술용법

   (1) 다른 동사와 함께 동사구를 형성하여 문장의 동사 역할을 하는 경우

   Hazel **was going** to the convention. (진행형)
   Randy **had talked** to the coach. (과거완료형)
   I **have finished** my essay. (현재완료형)

   헤이즐은 회의장에 가고 있었습니다. / 랜디는 감독과 이야기를 했습니다. / 저는 작문을 끝냈습니다.

   (2) 주격보어로서 상황표현을 나타낸다. (~하면서, ~한 채로)

   I stood **looking** at the picture.
   He sat **surrounded** by his children.

   저는 그림을 보면서 서 있었습니다. / 그는 아이들에 둘러싸여 앉아 있었습니다.

Basic Grammar for English Tests

(3) 목적격보어

I heard him **speaking** French. (he was speaking)
I don't like to see you **disappointed**. (you are disappointed)

저는 그가 불어를 말하는 것을 들었습니다. / 저는 당신이 실망하는 것을 보고 싶지 않아요.

4. 수식용법 : 명사를 수식하는 형용사 역할을 하는 경우

(1) 현재분사(-ing) : 명사가 분사의 의미(행위/상태)상 주어 또는 주체(subject)이다.

a **confusing** problem (= the problem which is confusing)
a **sleeping** baby (= the baby who is sleeping)
an **exciting** game (= the game which is exciting)
an **amusing** story (= the story which is amusing)

헛갈리는 문제 / 잠자는 아기 / 신나는 경기 / 재미난 이야기

(2) 과거분사(-ed) : 명사는 분사가 가진 의미(행위/상태)의 피동적인 객체 또는 대상(object)이다.

confused students (= the students who are confused)
fallen leaves (= the leaves which were fallen)
a **broken** window (= the window which was broken)
amused children (= the children who are amused)

헛갈린 학생들 / 떨어진 나뭇잎 / 깨진 유리창 / 흥겨운 어린이들

(3) 뒤에서 수식하는 경우 : 형용사절이 분사로 축약된 경우이다.

The student (who is) **sketching** the model is Kevin.
He has a little son (who is) **called** John.
He is a musician (who has) just **returned** from Italy.
Of those (who had been) **invited** only a few came to the party.

모델을 스케치하는 학생이 케빈입니다. / 그는 존이라고 하는 막내아들이 있습니다. / 그는 이탈리아에서 금방 돌아온 음악가입니다. / 초대받은 이들 중에 겨우 소수만이 파티에 왔습니다.

Exercise 1 다음 문장의 구조를 확인하면서 분사가 수식하는 명사를 찾아 화살표를 그리시오.

1. That *hanging basket* contains a rare species of fruit.
2. People suffering from a severe depression should seek help from a licensed psychologist.
3. A crying child is easily comforted by a few soothing words.
4. The homes destroyed by the hurricane will be restored by one of the city's wrecking crews during the coming weeks.
5. The number of vacation days provided by the school is adequate for most students.

6. Baked potatoes are frequently served with sour cream, grated cheese, and bits of fried bacon.
7. The old movies shown late at night are frequently better than movies produced in the last five years.
8. Badly torn clothes should be mended by an experienced tailor.
9. Volunteers recruited by the sheriff searched for the lost hikers for several exhausting days.
10. People walking in poorly lighted areas at night should be extremely careful.

Exercise 2 다음 문장들의 구조를 파악하고 잘못 표기된 분사를 찾아 바르게 고치시오.

1. The large jar filling with freshly-baked cookies was quickly emptied by the hungry children. (filling → *filled*)
2. Artificially-sweetened beverages are purchased by individuals trying to lose weight.
3. Television viewers boring with the reruns shown at the end of the season turn to public television for more interesting programs.
4. The verdict handed down by the jury surprised none of the lawyers involved in the case.
5. Household pets infected with fleas should be bathed weekly with a specially-prepared flea soap.
6. Publishing houses constantly receive manuscripts from aspired young writers.
7. Letters of recommendation received after the first of the month will not be reviewed by the recruiting officer assigning to your file.
8. A chimney filled with soot requires the services of a qualified chimneysweep.
9. Houseplants requiring constant attention are not suitable for working couples with little spare time.
10. Steamed vegetables retain more nutrients than boiling ones.

분사구문(participle constructions)이란?

중문이나 복문을 간략하게 하기 위하여 분사로 축약한 문형이다.

Basic Grammar for English Tests

1. 중문 → 분사구문 (상황)

   [단문]   He walked out of the room. He slammed the door behind him.
   [중문]   He walked out of the room **and slammed** the door behind him.
   [분사구문] He walked out of the room, **slamming** the door behind him.
                   She lay awake all night **and recalled** the events of the day.
                 → She lay awake all night, **recalling** the events of the day.

   그는 방을 걸어나갔습니다. 그는 문을 쾅 닫았습니다. / 그는 방을 나가서는 문을 쾅 닫았습니다. / 그는 문을 쾅 닫으며 방을 나갔습니다. / 그녀는 밤새 자지 않고 앉아, 그날의 일들을 회상하였습니다. → 그녀는 그날의 일들을 회상하며 밤새 자지 않고 있었습니다.

2. 복문 → 분사구문 : 부사절을 분사구로 축약한 문형

   [단문]   You want to order a vehicle. You have to pay a deposit.
   [복문]   **If you want to order** a vehicle, you have to pay a deposit.
   [부정사구문] **To order** a vehicle, you have to pay a deposit.
   [분사구문] **When ordering** a vehicle, you have to pay a deposit.

   당신은 자동차를 주문하기를 원합니다. 당신은 보증금을 지불해야 합니다. / 자동차를 주문하기를 원하신다면, 보증금을 지불해야 합니다. / 자동차를 주문하기 위해서는 보증금을 지불해야 합니다. / 자동차를 주문할 때는 보증금을 지불해야 합니다.

3. 복문 → 분사구문 : 형용사절(관계대명사절)을 분사로 축약한 문형

   [복문]   Who is that boy **who is wearing** a blue shirt?
   [분사구문] Who is that boy **wearing** a blue shirt?
                 The system **which is used** in this school is very successful.
                 The system **used** in this school is very successful.

   푸른 셔츠를 입고 있는 저 남자는 누구죠? / 이 학교에서 이용되는 체제는 매우 성공적입니다.

분사구문의 형식

1. 일반적으로 주절과 종속절(부사절)의 주어가 같을 경우에만 분사구문이 가능하다.

   While **I** was sitting in class, **I** fell asleep.
   = While sitting in class, I fell asleep.
   While **Ann** was sitting in class, **she** fell asleep.
   = While sitting in class, **Ann** fell asleep.

   수업을 하는 동안 저는 잠이 들었습니다. / 수업을 하는 동안 앤은 잠이 들었습니다.

2. 주어가 다른 경우는 일반적으로 분사구문이 불가능하다.

   While **the teacher** was lecturing to the class, **I** fell asleep.
   While **we** were walking home, **a frog** hopped across the road in front of us.

   선생님이 학급에서 강의를 하시는 동안, 저는 잠이 들었습니다. / 우리가 집으로 걸어가는 동안, 개구리 한 마리가 우리 앞으로 깡충깡충 길을 건너갔습니다.

3. 독립분사구분(absolute participial construction)

   (1) 주어가 서로 다를 경우에는 분사의 주어를 생략할 수 없다.

   As it was a bank holiday, **all the shop** were shut.
   = **It being** a bank holiday, **all the shops** were shut.
   As it was fine, **we** went for a walk.
   = **It being** fine, **we** went for a walk.
   After the sun had set we gave up looking for them.
   = **The sun having set**, we gave up looking for them.
   I was reading a book **and my wife was sewing** beside me.
   = I was reading a book, my wife sewing beside me. (동시상황)

   은행 휴일이라서, 모든 상점들이 문을 닫았습니다. / 날씨가 좋아서, 우리는 산책을 갔습니다. / 해가 진 후에 우리는 그들을 찾는 일을 포기했습니다. / 저는 책을 읽고, 아내는 제 옆에서 바느질을 하고 있었습니다.

   (2) 일반적인 사람(they, we …)이 주어인 경우 생략한다.

   - Generally/Broadly/Frankly/Strictly speaking
     : 일반적으로/광범위하게/솔직히/엄격히 말해서
   - Concerning~, Regarding~ : ~에 관해서
   - Considering~, Taking everything into account~ : ~를 고려할 때
   - Excepting~ : ~를 제외하고
   - Judging from~ : ~로 판단하건대

   Strictly speaking, he is not honest.
   = If we speak strictly, he is not honest.
   Judging from his appearance, he seems to be poor.

   엄밀히 말해서 그는 정직하지 않습니다. / 외모로 판단하건대, 그는 가난한 것 같습니다.

시간절

1. 현재완료형

   While I was walking to class, I ran into an old friend.
   = While walking to class, I ran into an old friend.
   Before I left for work, I ate breakfast.
   = Before **leaving** for work, I ate breakfast.
   Since **Mary came** to this country, **she** has made many friends.
   = Since **coming** to this country, **Mary** has made many friends.

   수업에 가는 동안, 저는 옛 친구를 우연히 만났습니다. / 회사로 떠나기 전에 저는 아침을 먹었습니다. / 메리가 이 나라에 온 뒤로, 그녀는 많은 친구들을 사귀었습니다.

Basic Grammar for English Tests

2. 과거완료형

   When it was viewed from a distance, the island looked like a cloud.
   = **Viewed** from a distance, the island looked like a cloud.

   멀리 떨어져서 보면, 그 섬은 마치 구름 같았습니다.

3. 완료분사형 : 시제가 앞선 경우

   After I **had finished** my essay, I turned it in.
   = **Having finished** my essay, I turned it in.

   작문을 끝낸 다음, 저는 그것을 제출하였습니다.

4. on/upon -ing : ~을 하자마자

   As soon as/when I reached the age of 21, I received my inheritance.
   = **On/Upon reaching** the age of 21, I received my inheritance.
   On finding the front door open, I became suspicious.
   On being informed the flight would be delayed we made other arrangements.

   스물한 살이 되자마자, 저는 유산을 물려받았습니다. / 앞문이 열린 것을 발견하자, 저는 의심스러워졌습니다. / 비행기가 연착된다는 통지를 받자마자, 우리는 다른 준비를 했습니다.

이유절

1. 현재분사형

   Because she was unable to afford a car, she bought a bicycle.
   = **Being unable** to afford a car, **she** bought a bicycle.
   = **Unable** to afford a car, **she** bought a bicycle.
   As I was anxious to please him, I bought him a nice present.
   = **Being anxious** to please him, I bought him a nice present.
   He is(was) so ill that he can't(couldn't) go back to work yet.
   = **Being so ill**, he can't(couldn't) go back to work yet.

   자동차를 살 여유가 없었기 때문에, 그녀는 자전거를 샀습니다. / 몹시도 그를 기쁘게 하고 싶어서, 저는 그에게 좋은 선물을 사주었습니다. / 그는 너무 아파서 아직 직장으로 돌아갈 수가 없(었)습니다.

   * 분사가 접속사와 도치된 경우 — 분사의 뜻을 강조하는 관용적 표현

   Standing as it does on the hill, my house commands a fine view.
   (= As it (really) stands on the hill, ⋯)
   I regard it as a special case, **occurring as it does** only once a year.
   (= ⋯ as it (really) occurs only once a year.)

   언덕 위에 서 있어서, 우리 집은 전망이 좋습니다. / 일년에 한 번씩 발생하므로, 저는 그것을 특별한 경우로 여깁니다.

2. 완료분사형

    As I had seen that movie before, I didn't want to go again.
    = **Having seen** that movie before, I didn't want to go again.
    He has(had) been ill for a very long time, so he needs(needed) more time to recover.
    = **Having been ill** for a very long time, he needs(needed) more time to recover.

    저는 전에 저 영화를 보았기 때문에, 저는 또 다시 가고 싶지 않았습니다. / 오랫동안 아팠기 때문에, 그는 회복하는 데 시간이 더 필요합니다.

조건절(가정)

1. 현재분사형

    If you are travelling north, you must change at Taejon.
    = **If travelling** north, you must change at Taejon.
    Unless you pay by credit card, please pay in cash.
    = **Unless paying** by credit card, please pay in cash.

    북쪽으로 여행하신다면, 당신은 대전에서 갈아타야 합니다. / 신용카드로 지불하지 않으신다면, 현찰로 내십시오.

2. 과거분사형

    If you are accepted for this position, you will be informed by May 5.
    = **If accepted** for this position, you will be informed by May 5.
    Unless it is changed, this law will make life difficult for farmers.
    = **Unless changed**, this law will make life difficult for farmers.

    당신이 이 자리를 받아들이신다면, 5월 5일까지 통지를 받을 것입니다. / 개정하지 않는 한, 이 법률은 농부들의 생활을 어렵게 만들 것입니다.

양보절

    While he admitted that he had received the stolen jewelry, he denied having taken part in the robbery.
    = **While admitting** that he had received the stolen jewelry, he denied having taken part in the robbery.
    Although it was built before the war, the engine is still in perfect order.
    = **Although built** before the war, the engine is still in perfect order.

    훔친 보석을 받았음은 인정해도, 그는 강도행각에 참가한 것은 부인했습니다. / 그 엔진은 전쟁 전에 만들어졌지만 아직도 완벽하게 움직인다.

Basic Grammar for English Tests

Exercise 3 다음 분사구문을 읽고 둘 중 바른 문장을 고르시오.

1. a) When applying for a parking sticker, the campus police require students to have proper identification.
   b) When applying for a parking sticker, students must show campus police proper identification. (o)
2. a) Increasing from 2.5 billion in 1950, the late 1970's saw the world's population reach 4.25 billion.
   b) Increasing from 2.5 billion in 1950, the population of the world reached 4.25 billion in the late 1970's.
3. a) Hoping to save taxpayers' money, biologists are experimenting with a weed-eating fish that can clean canals.
   b) Hoping to save taxpayers' money, a weed-eating fish that can clean canals is being studied by biologists.
4. a) Borrowing from nature's designs, new oil tankers designed by bio-medical engineers will be stable and fuel-efficient.
   b) Borrowing from nature's designs, engineers are designing stable and fuel-efficient oil tankers.
5. a) When renting an apartment, a lease is signed by the tenant.
   b) When renting an apartment, the tenant is asked to sign a lease.

Exercise 4 다음 중 분사구와 주절의 주어가 일치하는 바른 문장을 찾으시오.

1. Before winning the war for independent in 1965, Algeria lost many of its young men. (o)
2. Awarded in 1901, Sully-Prudhomme received the first Nobel Prize for literature. (x)
3. Decorated with intricate geometric designs, Moslem metal workers produce beautiful trays of copper, tin, and bronze.
4. After fleeing Mecca, the city of Medina was founded in 622 A. D. by Mohammed and his followers.
5. Located on an island in the Seine River, the Cathedral of Notre Dame is one of the most famous landmarks in Paris.
6. Although rejected as a cause of death for many years, miners' widows are now receiving compensation for black-lung disease.
7. After drinking as much water as it wants, it is possible for a camel to survive without water for up to two weeks.
8. When formed with copper, aluminum alloys are quite strong.
9. When placed in direct sunlight, plants tend to wilt.
10. Running home through the snow, her nose got extremely cold.

Actual Test 6

다음 각 문장을 읽고 빈칸에는 알맞은 단어를 넣고, 밑줄 친 부분에서는 잘못된 부분을 찾아내시오.

1. Baseball and American Football _____ played in America today are basically modifications of games that originated in England.
   - Ⓐ as
   - Ⓑ are
   - Ⓒ being
   - Ⓓ that

2. Dragonflies have compound eyes that consist of hundreds of lenses _____.
   - Ⓐ together they are joined
   - Ⓑ joined together
   - Ⓒ that when joined together
   - Ⓓ together are joined

3. Francis Johnson, _____ born in Ohio, lived and practiced law in Michigan.
   - Ⓐ was
   - Ⓑ he was
   - Ⓒ although
   - Ⓓ who he was

4. Hard hit by the financial crisis of 1937, _____.
   - Ⓐ Jane Lyon turned to writing for her livelihood
   - Ⓑ for her livelihood Jane Lyon turned to writing by
   - Ⓒ turned to writing for her livelihood by Jane Lyon
   - Ⓓ by writing for her livelihood turned Jane Lyon

5. _____ in all parts of the state, pines are the most common trees in Wisconsin.
   - Ⓐ Found
   - Ⓑ Finding them
   - Ⓒ To find them
   - Ⓓ They are found

6. While traveling in Europe, _____.
   - Ⓐ Jane Smith was stimulated by the social reform movement
   - Ⓑ it was the social reform movement that stimulated Jane Smith
   - Ⓒ the social reform movement stimulated Jane Smith
   - Ⓓ Jane Smith, stimulated by the social reform movement

7. The institution, founded in 1961 by Jesse Jackson, provides educational
   　　　　　　　　A　　　　　　　　　　　　　　　　　　　　　　　　　　B
   assistance to children live in economically depressed communities.
   　　A　　　　　　　　　　　C　　　　D

8. The average age of the Mediterranean olive trees grow today is three
   　　　　　A　　　　　　　　　　B　　　　　　　　　C　　　　　　　
   hundred years.
   　　　D

9. The first short story publish by Washington Irving was 'Rip-van Winkle'
   　　　A　　　　　　　　B　　　　　　　　　　　　　　　　　　C
   which appeared in 1829.
   　D

10. The electric furnace is used extensively to produce the high-quality steel
    　　　　　　A　　　　　　　B
    is required for the manufacture of steel alloys.
    　　C　　　　　D

11. Many abandoned parts of the hill, covering by vines and bushes, are
    　A　　　　　　　　　　　　　　　　B
    still easily traceable across cornfields or through orchards and thickets.
    　　　　C　　　　　　　　　　　　　　　D

12. Standing in the driveway, the church appeared to be much smaller than it
    　　　　A　　　　　　　　　　　　　　　B
    had seemed to us as children many years ago.
    　　C　　　　　D

13. Elizabeth Tailor, was known for her hard work to improve mental institutions,
    　　　　　　　　A　　　　　　　　　　　　　　　　B
    served as superintendent of nurses during the American Civil War.
    　C　　　　　　　　　　　　D

14. Wind and rain constantly hit against the surface of the Earth, broken large
    　　A　　　　　　　　　　　　　　　　　B　　　　　　　　　　C
    rocks into smaller and smaller particles.
    　　　　　　　　D

15. Founded in 1971 and employed an estimated 40,000 people, the
    　　　A　　　　　B
    organization has gained a reputation for brutality.
    　　　　　　C　　　　　　　　D

16. When saw near the horizon, the moon appears remarkably larger than
    　　　A　　B　　　　　　　　　　　　　　　C
    when viewed overhead.
    　　　　　　D

조건문/가정법(conditional sentences)

조건문/가정법이란?

실제는 그렇지 않은 어떤 일이나 상황을 가정하여 말하는 화법.
종속절인 조건절에서 가정을 제시하고 주절에서 결과를 말한다.

종속절—조건절 : 가정	주절—결과절
If the rain stop,	we'll able to go for a walk.
If the price of oil comes down,	more people will buy it.
(If I were you,)	I wouldn't go that way.
(If we had had the money,)	We could have had a good time.

*조건절이 없을 수도 있다.

비가 그치면, 우리는 산책을 나갈 수 있을 것입니다. / 석유가 내려가면, 더 많은 사람들이 구매할 것입니다. / 내가 너라면,) 나는 그 길을 가지는 않을 것입니다. / (우리가 돈이 있었다면,) 우리는 좋은 시간을 가졌을 것입니다.

가정법 현재

현재나 미래에 있을 일(사실)을 미리 가정하는 표현
If S+현재시제동사 … , S+will+동사원형 …

1. 기본형태 : 조건절 동사의 종류에 따라

[be동사]	If I **am** better tomorrow, I **will** get up.
[have동사]	If I **have** a headache, I **will** take an aspirin.
[현재]	If she **finishes** early, she **will** go home.
[현재진행]	If he **is standing** in the rain, he **will** catch cold.
[현재완료]	If she **has arrived** at the station, she **will** be here soon.
[완료진행]	If he **has been travelling** all night, he **will** need a rest.
[조동사 can/must]	If I **can afford** it, I **will** buy it.

내일 더 나아지면, 저는 일어날 거예요. / 두통이 있으면, 저는 아스피린을 먹을 것입니다. / 일찍 마치면, 그녀는 집에 갈 것입니다. / 빗속에 서 있으면, 그는 감기에 걸릴 것입니다. / 그녀가 역에 도착하면, 곧 여기로 올 것입니다. / 밤새 여행을 한다면, 그는 휴식이 필요할 것입니다. / 제가 여유가 있다면, 그것을 살 것입니다.

2. 결과절 조동사의 다양성

If it's fine tomorrow, she { can/could (자유로운 상태) / may/might (가능성) / should/ought to (권고성) / must (필요성) } go out.

If she **can't understand** it, she **must** phone me.
If she **has been waiting**, she **might phone** me.
If I **hear** from Tim, **I may be leaving** tonight.

내일 날씨가 좋으면, 그녀는 밖에 나갈 수 있을 것입니다. / 나갈지도 모르겠습니다. / 나가야 할 것입니다. / 나가야 합니다.
그녀가 그것을 이해하지 못한다면, 그녀는 분명 제게 전화를 할 것입니다. / 그녀가 기다리고 있다면, 제게 전화를 할지도 모릅니다. / 제가 팀에게서 소식을 들으면, 저는 오늘밤 떠날지도 모릅니다.

3. 주절(결과절)의 동사가 일반동사인 경우

> 일상적이거나 습관적인 행위나 상황표현
> If S+현재시제동사…, S+일반동사 현재형…

John **usually walks** to school if he **has** enough time.
If I **don't eat** breakfast, I **always get** hungry during class.
Water **freezes**(will freeze) if the temperature **goes** below zero.

시간이 충분히 있으면 존은 늘 학교까지 걸어갑니다. / 아침을 먹지 않으면, 저는 늘 수업 중에 배가 고픕니다. / 기온이 영하로 내려가면, 물이 얼게 됩니다.

4. 결과절이 명령문인 경우

> If S+(Sould)+V …, 명령문 : 공손한 요구나 제안을 할 때

If you (should) see him,
Should you see him,
If you (should) happen to see him,   please give him my regards.
Should you **happen to see him**,

If you should write to her, send her my love.
If you should go to England, go and see the British Museum.
If John should call, tell him I'll be back around five.
*If he **calls**, tell him I'll ring back.

그를 보시거든, 제 안부를 전해주십시오. / 그녀에게 편지를 쓰시거든, 제 사랑을 전해주십시오. / 영국에 가시거든, 대영박물관을 가보세요. / 존이 전화를 하거든, 제가 5시까지 돌아온다고 말씀주세요. / 그가 전화를 하거든, 제가 나중에 전화한다고 전해주세요.

5. 조건절 대신 쓰이는 명령문 : 명령문+등위접속사+결과절

명령문=조건절	등위접속어	결과절
Stop shouting	or	you'll wake up the neighbors.
Put that down	or else	I'll smack you.
Be there on time	otherwise	you'll create a bad impression.
Fail to pay	and	they'll cut off the electricity.

소리지르지 마라, 안 그러면, 이웃들을 다 깨우게 된다. / 그것을 내려놓아라, 안 그러면, 내가 너를 때려줄 것이다. / 정각에 가거라, 안 그러면, 너는 나쁜 인상을 줄 것이다. / 납부하지 못하면, 그들이 전기를 끊어버릴 것입니다.

Provide the materials **and** we'll do the job.
= If you provide the materials, we'll do the job.
Tell us what to do **and** we'll get on with it.
= If you tell us what to do, we'll get on with it.
Stop eating sweets, **or** you won't get any dinner.
= If you don't stop eating sweets, you won't get any dinner.
Take a taxi, **otherwise** you'll miss your train.
= If you don't take taxi, you'll miss your train.

자료를 제공하십시오, 그러면 우리가 그 일을 하겠습니다. / 무엇을 해야할지를 말해주시면, 우리가 그것을 진행하겠습니다. / 단것을 먹지 마라, 안 그러면, 저녁을 먹지 못할 거야. / 택시를 타세요, 안 그러면, 기차를 놓칠 것입니다.

가정법 과거

> 현재나 미래의 불가능하거나 사실이 아닌 상황을 가정하는 표현
> If S+과거시제동사 … , S+would+동사원형 …

1. 기본 형태

   [be동사]   If I **were** taller, I **would become** a policeman.
   [have동사] If he **had** any money, he'd **leave** home.
   [일반동사] If you **took** a taxi, you'd **get** there quicker.
   [could]   If you **could** see me now, you'd **laugh** your head off.

   키만 좀더 크다면, 저는 경찰이 될 것입니다. / 돈만 좀 있으면, 그는 집을 떠날 것입니다. / 택시를 잡으시면, 더 빨리 그곳에 도착할 것입니다. / 지금 저를 보시면, 자지러지게 웃을 것입니다.

2. 조건절의 동사가 be동사인 경우 반드시 were

   > If S+were … , S+would/should …

   (1) 전혀 불가능한, 완전히 상상의 가정

   If I **were** a bird, I'd be able to fly to you.
   If I **were** the Queen of Sheba, you'd be King Solomon.

   내가 새라면, 너에게 날아갈 수 있을 텐데. / 내가 시바 여왕이라면, 너는 솔로몬 왕이야.

   (2) **If I were you / If I were in your position** (내가 너라면)

   If I **were** you(/in your position), I'd accept their offer.
   If I **were** Jane(/in Jane's position), I'd walk out on him.

Basic Grammar for English Tests

If I **were** you, I would accept their invitation.

내가 너라면, 그들의 제안을 받아들이겠네. / 내가 제인이라면, 나는 그에게로 걸어가겠다. / 내가 너라면, 나는 그들의 초대를 받아들이겠어.

(3) **If it were not for / Were it not for** (~가 없다면) = But for, Without

If it weren't for your help, I would still be homeless.
Were it not for your help, I would still be homeless.

당신의 도움이 없다면, 저는 아직 집도 없을 것입니다.

3. 결과절 조동사의 다양성

If he **were** here, he **could** help us. (능력)
If he **were** here, he **might** help us. (가능성)
If he **failed**, he **ought to(/should)** try again. (의무)

그가 여기 있으면, 우리를 도와줄 수 있을 것입니다. / 그가 여기 있으면, 우리를 도와줄 것입니다. / 그가 실패를 하면, 그는 재도전해야 합니다.

If he **could get** the facts, he **might tell** us what to do.
If she **were** here now, she **could be** helping us.

그가 사실을 알 수 있으면, 우리에게 무엇을 해야 할지를 말할 것입니다. / 그녀가 지금 여기 있다면, 우리를 도울 수 있을 것입니다.

4. 공손한 제의를 할 때 : If S+were to …

If I **were to** ask, would you help me?
If you **were to** ask him, he might help you.

제가 요청을 한다면, 저를 도와주시겠습니까? / 당신이 그에게 요청을 한다면 그가 당신을 도울 것입니다.

5. 진행형인 경우

If it **were not raining** right now, I **would go** for a walk.
= It is raining right now, so I will not go for a walk.
If I **were living** in Chile, I **would be** working at a bank.
= I **am not living** in Chile. I am not working at a bank.

지금 비가 오지 않으면, 저는 산책을 갈 것입니다. / 칠레에 살고 있다면, 저는 은행에서 일을 할 것입니다.

가정법 과거완료

> 과거에 전혀 불가능했거나 사실이 아니었던 상황을 가정하는 표현
> If S+had p.p. …, S+would have p.p. …

1. 기본형태

[be동사]   If I **had been** taller, I would have joined the police force.

[have동사]　　　If I **had had** any sense, I would have kept quiet about it.
[과거완료]　　　If we **had gone** by car, we would have saved time.
[완료진행]　　　If I **had been trying** harder, I would have succeeded.
[could have]　　If I **could have stopped**, there wouldn't have been an accident.

키가 더 컸다면, 저는 경찰대에 지원했을 것입니다. / 생각이 있었다면, 저는 그것에 대해 조용히 있었을 것입니다. / 자동차로 갔다면, 우리는 시간을 절약할 수 있었을 것입니다. / 제가 더 열심히 노력했다면, 저는 성공하였을 것입니다. / 제가 멈출 수만 있었다면, 사고는 없었을 것입니다.

2. If I had been you / If I had been in your position (내가 너였다면)

　　If I had been you(/in your position), I'd have accepted their offer.
　　If I had been Jane, I'd have walked out on him years ago.

　　내가 너였다면, 나는 그들의 제안을 받아들였겠. / 내가 제인이었다면, 나는 몇 년 전에 그에게로 갔을 것이다.

3. If it hadn't been for / Had it not been for (~이 없었다면) = But for, Without

　　If it hadn't been for the rain, we would have had a good harvest.
　　If it had not been for your help, I must have failed.

　　비가 오지 않았다면, 우리는 좋은 수확을 얻었을 것입니다. / 당신의 도움이 없었다면, 저는 실패하였을 것입니다.

4. 다양한 결과절의 조동사

　　If he had been here yesterday, he **could have told** us. (능력)
　　If he had been here yesterday, he **might have told** us. (가능성)
　　If he had received a present, he **should have thanked** her. (의무)

　　그가 어제 여기 있었다면, 우리에게 말을 할 수 있었을 것입니다. / 그가 어제 여기 있었다면, 우리에게 말을 했을지도 모릅니다. / 그가 선물을 받았더라면, 그녀에게 분명 고마워했을 것입니다.

If를 생략할 경우 : 도치(동사+주어) — 주로 2, 3형식

　　Were I you, I wouldn't do that. (= If I were you)
　　Had I known, I would have told you. (= If I had known)
　　Should anyone call, please take a message. (= If anyone should call)

　　내가 너라면, 나는 그렇게 하지 않았을 것이다. / 내가 알았더라면, 나는 너에게 말했을 것이다. / 누가 전화를 하면, 메시지를 받아두세요.

기타 조건절 표현

1. 부정형 : if~not = unless

　　If you don't change your mind, I won't be able to help you.
　　= **Unless** you change your mind, I won't be able to help you.

You will fail **unless** you work harder.

당신 마음이 바뀌지 않는다면, 저는 당신을 도울 수 없을 겁니다. / 열심히 일하지 않으면, 당신은 실패할 것입니다.

2. if 대신 쓰이는 조건절 접속어

They'll lend us their flat **on** (the) **condition** (that) we look after it. (= if)

Providing (that) / **Provided (that)** / **As(/So) long as** } you clear your desk by this evening, you can have tomorrow off.

Suppose (that) / **Supposing (that)** } we miss the train, what shall we do?

What if / **Say** } he gets home before us and can't get in? What will he do then?

우리가 돌본다면, 그들은 우리에게 아파트를 빌려줄 것입니다. / 오늘 저녁까지 책상을 청소한다면, 내일은 쉴 수 있어. / 열차를 놓친다면, 우리는 어떻게 하지? / 그가 우리보다 앞서 집에 도착해서 들어간다면? 그때 그는 어떻게 할까?

3. 전치사구가 조건절을 대신하는 경우

With luck, we'll be there by tomorrow. (= if we're lucky,)
To hear him talk, you'd think he was Prime Minister.
(= if you could hear him talk,)
But for his pension, he would starve. (= if he didn't have,)
Without your help, I couldn't have done it. (= if you hadn't helped,)
In different circumstances, I would have said yes.
(= if circumstances had been different,)

운이 좋으면, 우리는 내일까지 그곳에 갈 것입니다. / 그가 말하는 것을 들으면, 그가 국무총리라고 생각할 것입니다. / 자기 연금이 없다면, 그는 굶어죽을 것입니다. / 너의 도움이 없었다면, 나는 그것을 하지 못했을 것이다. / 다른 상황이었다면, 저는 승낙했을 것입니다.

'wish' 조건문 : 말하는 이의 소망을 표현

1. 미래형

> 실제는 그렇지 않을 것이지만 미래에 어떤 행위를 하거나 일이 있기를 원함
> S+wish+(that)+S+would/could do/were -ing

I wish (that) she **would tell** me. (= In truth, she will not tell me.)
I wish he **were going to be** here. (= In truth, he isn't going to be here.)
I wish she **could come** tomorrow. (= In truth, she can't come tomorrow.)

그녀가 내게 말해주면 좋겠어. / 그가 여기 온다면 좋겠어. / 그녀가 내일 올 수 있으면 좋겠어.

2. 현재형

> 현재 그렇지 않은 사실을 소망하는 표현
> S+wish+(that)+S+과거동사

I wish **I knew** French. (= In truth, I don't know French.)
I wish it **weren't raining** right now. (= In truth, it is raining right now.)
I wish I **could speak** Japanese. (= In truth, I can't speak Japanese.)
cf. **If only** I knew French!

내가 불어를 안다면 좋겠어. / 지금 당장 비가 오지 않았으면 좋겠어. / 내가 일본어를 할 수 있다면 좋겠어. / 내가 불어만 안다면!

3. 과거형

> 과거 그렇지 않은 사실에 대한 유감표현
> S+wish+(that)+S+had p.p./could have p.p.

I wish John **had come**. (= In truth, John didn't come.)
I wish Mary **could have come**. (= In truth, Mary couldn't come.)
⎡ I wish I **had been** at the meeting.
⎢ (= I am sorry I was not at the meeting.)
⎣ I **wished** I **were** a boy. (= I was sorry I was not a boy.)

존이 왔더라면 좋았을 텐데. / 메리가 올 수 있었다면 좋았을 텐데. / 내가 회의에 참석했더라면 좋았을 것을. / 내가 소년이라면 좋았을 것을.

if ~ will/would ··· : 주어의 의지를 강조

If you **will(/would/could) wait** a moment, I'll fetch the money.
If he **will(/would/could) only try** harder, I'm sure he'd do well.
If you **will(/would) follow** me, I'll show you the way.
If you **won't stop** smoking, you can only expect to have a bad health.
If it **will suit** you, I'll change the date of our meeting.

잠시 기다리시겠다면, 제가 돈을 가져오겠습니다. / 그가 열심히 노력한다면, 저는 그가 잘 할 것이라고 확신합니다. / 당신이 저를 따라오신다면, 제가 길을 알려드리겠습니다. / 당신이 담배를 끊지 않는다면, 건강이 나빠지는 것을 예측할 수 있을 거예요. / 그것이 당신에게 맞는다면, 저는 만날 날을 바꾸겠습니다.

혼합시제 형식

If I **had eaten** breakfast several hours ago, I **would not be** hungry now.
= I did not eat breakfast several hours ago, so I am hungry now.
If he **were** a good student, he **would have studied** for the test.

= He is not a good student. He did not study for the test yesterday.
If I **am** as clever as you think, **I should have been** rich **by now**.
If I **had had** your advantages, **I'd be** better off now.

몇 시간 전에 아침을 먹었다면, 지금 제가 배고프지는 않을 것입니다. / 그가 좋은 학생이라면, 시험 공부를 했을 것입니다. / 제가 당신이 생각하는 만큼 똑똑하다면, 저는 지금쯤 부자가 되었을 것입니다. / 제가 당신의 이점을 가졌더라면, 저는 지금 부유할 것입니다.

Exercise 5 다음 빈칸의 괄호에 주어진 단어를 적당히 고쳐 조건문을 완성하시오.

1. Henry talks to his dog as if it *understood* him. (understand)
2. He would give you the money if he _____ it. (have)
3. I wish they _____ making so much noise so that I could concentrate. (stop)
4. She would call you immediately if she _____ help. (need)
5. Had they arrived at the sale early, they _____ a better selection. (find)
6. We hope that you _____ the party last night. (enjoy)
7. If you have enough time, please _____ the chair before you leave. (paint)
8. We could go for a drive if today _____ Saturday. (be)
9. If she wins the prize, it will be because she _____ very well. (write)
10. Mike wished that the editors _____ him to copy some of their material. (permit)

Actual Test 7

다음 각 문장을 읽고 빈칸에는 알맞은 단어를 넣고, 밑줄 친 부분에서는 잘못된 부분을 찾아내시오.

1. I'd get the book for you _____ I could remember who last borrowed it.
   - Ⓐ except that
   - Ⓑ if only
   - Ⓒ on condition that
   - Ⓓ considering whether

2. If you hadn't gone with George to the party last night, _____.
   - Ⓐ you would meet Tom already
   - Ⓑ you won't have missed Tom
   - Ⓒ you will have met Tom
   - Ⓓ you would have met Tom

3. If she'd let me know the time, _____ to meet her.
   - Ⓐ I'll be glad
   - Ⓑ I'd be glad
   - Ⓒ I've been glad
   - Ⓓ I'd have been glad

4. If I _____ her advice then, I should be happier now.
   - Ⓐ have accepted
   - Ⓑ did not accept
   - Ⓒ had accepted
   - Ⓓ accepted

5. I _____ Professor Miller had taught me this equation.
   - Ⓐ believe
   - Ⓑ wish
   - Ⓒ deeply think
   - Ⓓ am guessing

6. I have made some mistake again. I wish I _____ mistake every day.
   - Ⓐ don't make
   - Ⓑ haven't made
   - Ⓒ wouldn't have made
   - Ⓓ didn't make

7. I'd rather you _____ anything about it for a while.
   - Ⓐ do
   - Ⓑ didn't do
   - Ⓒ don't
   - Ⓓ didn't

8. I would wear the white dress save it _____ a stain in the front.
   - Ⓐ had
   - Ⓑ has
   - Ⓒ would have
   - Ⓓ has not

9. If John were to resign and if Harry were to be elected to take his place,
   　　　　A　　B　　　　　　　　　　　C
   we would have had more strong leadership.
   　　　　D

10. If John would have tried harder to reach the opposite shore, we would not
   　　　　　A　　　　　B　　　　　　　　C
   have had to pick him up in the boat.
   　　　D

11. If the ozone gases of the atmosphere did not filter out the ultraviolet rays
   　　　　　　　　　　　　　　　　　　　A
   of the sun, life, as we know it, would not have developed on earth.
   　　　　　　　　B　　　　C　　　　　　　　　　　　　　D

12. If jane had wanted to pass his exams, she would have study much harder
   　　　　　A　　　　　　　　　　　　　　　　　B　　　　　C　　D
   for them.

13. If the policeman would have arrived earlier, he would have seen the
   　　　　　　　A　　　　　　　B　　　　　　　C
   traffic accident.
   　　　D

14. If you have learned the speed reading, you would be a better reader today.
   　　　A　　　　　　　　B　　　　　　　C　　　　　　D

15. If you saw the amount of food she ate for breakfast this morning, you
   　　　　A　　　　　　　　　　　　　　B
   would understand why she has grown so fat.
   　　　　　C　　　　D

16. I wish I knew you were arriving today. I would have met you at the airport.
   　　　A　　　　B　　　　　　　　C　　　　　　D

17. She looked like she had been in some strange land where age advanced at
   　　　　A　　　　　　B　　　　　　　　C
   a double pace.
   　　　D

18. Jane has a curious expression on her face as though she was smiling
   　　　　　A　　　　　B　　　　　　　　　　　C
   about something that amused her.
   　　　　　　　　　　　D

19. I would go to visit that beautiful mountain, but I couldn't get in touch with
   　　　　　　　A　　　　　　　　B　　　　C　　　　D
   you while I am now in Chicago.

◀ 비교문형(comparisons)

동등비교(equal comparisons) : 원급비교

> as+형용사/부사+as
> the same+명사+as
> as { many/few + 가산명사 / much/little + 불가산명사 } + as
> not so(/as)+형용사/부사+as

1. > S+V+as+형용사/부사+as+(대)명사/S+(V)

   He is **not so(/as) tall as** his father. (형용사)
   His car runs **as fast as** a race car. (부사)
   My book is **as interesting as** yours. (형용사)

   그는 자기 아버지만큼 크지는 않다. / 그의 자동차는 레이스카만큼 빨리 달립니다. / 제 책도 당신 책만큼 재미있습니다.

2. > S+V+the same+ 명사+as+(대)명사/S+(V)

   My house is **the same** height **as** his.
   These trees are **the same as** those.

   우리 집은 그의 집과 같은 높이입니다. / 이 나무들은 저것들과 같습니다.

3. > S+V+as { many/few+가산명사 / much/little+불가산명사 } as+(대)명사/S+(V)

   He earns **as much** money **as** his brother.
   They have **as few** classes **as** we.

   그는 자기 형만큼이나 많은 돈을 법니다. / 그들은 우리처럼 수업이 거의 없습니다.

차등비교(unequal comparisons) : 비교급 비교

> 형용사/부사의 비교급+than
> far/more/still/yet+형용사/부사의 비교급+than
> more/fewer/less+명사+than
> the 비교급+of the two+명사

Basic Grammar for English Tests

1.
> S+V+형용사/부사의 비교급+than+(대)명사/S+(V)

John's grades are **higher than** his sister's. (형용사)
This chair is **more comfortable than** the other. (형용사)
This year's exhibit is **less impressive than** last year's. (형용사)
He speaks Spanish **more fluently than** I. (부사)
He visits his family **less frequently than** she does. (부사)
He acts **worse** now **than** ever before. (부사)

존의 성적은 자기 누이의 성적보다 더 높습니다. / 이 의자는 다른 것보다 더 편안합니다. / 올해의 전시는 작년 것보다 덜 인상적입니다. / 그는 나보다 스페인어를 더 유창하게 합니다. / 그는 그녀보다는 덜 자주 가족을 찾아봅니다. / 그는 과거보다 현재 더 나쁘게 행동합니다.

2.
> S+V+(by) far/more/still/yet+형용사/부사의 비교급+than+(대)명사/S+(V)

Harry's watch is **far more expensive than** mine.
That movie we saw last night was **still more interesting than** the one on TV.
A watermelon is **much sweeter than** a melon.
He speaks English **yet more rapidly than** he does Spanish.

해리의 시계는 제것보다 훨씬 더 비쌉니다. / 우리가 어젯밤에 본 그 영화는 텔레비전에 방영되는 것보다 훨씬 더 재미있습니다. / 수박이 멜론보다 훨씬 더 달아요. / 그는 스페인어보다 영어를 훨씬 더 빨리 말합니다.

3.
> S+V+ { more/fewer+가산명사 / more/less+불가산명사 } +than+(대)명사/S+(V)

I have **more books** than she.
February has **fewer days than** March.
He has **less time** now **than he had** before.

나는 그녀보다 책을 더 많이 가지고 있습니다. / 2월은 3월보다 날이 더 적어요. / 그는 전보다 지금 시간이 더 없습니다.

4.
> S+V+the 비교급+of the two+명사
> Of the two+명사, S+V+the 비교급

Harvey is **the smarter of the two** boys.
Of the two shirts, this one is the prettier.

두 남자 중에서 하비가 더 똑똑합니다. / 셔츠 두 장 중에서 이게 더 예뻐요.

5.
> 주어의 특징이나 성향을 비교하는 문형
> S+V+more(/rather)+형용사+than+형용사

He is **more** wise **than** kind.
She is **more** shy **than** unfriendly.

그는 친절하다기보다는 현명합니다. / 그녀는 비우호적이라기보다는 수줍어합니다.

6. 비교대상의 격

I like him more than **she** (does).
I like him more than (I like) **her**.
Tom likes me better than **Harry**. (모호성)
Tom likes me better than he likes Harry.
Tom likes me better than Harry does.

저는 그를 그녀보다 더 좋아합니다. / 저는 그녀보다 그를 더 좋아합니다. / 톰은 해리보다 저를 더 좋아합니다. / 톰은 해리를 좋아하기보다는 나를 더 좋아합니다. / 톰은 나를 해리보다 더 좋아합니다.

최상급비교(superlative comparisons)

1. S+V+the 형용사/부사의 최상급+in+단수명사/of+복수명사

John is **the tallest** boy in the family.
Diana is **the shortest of the three** sisters.
That child behaves **the most carelessly of all**.
Bob plays **the most recklessly of all**.

존은 가족 중에서 가장 키가 큰 아이입니다. / 다이애나는 세 자매 중에서 가장 키가 작습니다. / 저 아이가 가장 부주의하게 행동합니다. / 밥이 가장 무모하게 경기를 합니다.

2. S+V+형용사/부사의 비교급+than { any other+단수명사 / anyone else / anything else

Henry is **noisier than any other** boy in the bus.
He is **smarter than anyone else** in his class.

헨리는 버스 안의 다른 어떤 남자보다 더 시끄럽습니다. / 그는 자기 학급의 어떤 다른 이보다 더 똑똑합니다.

3. 부정어 ~비교급 = 최상급 의미

Nothing can be **simpler than** this.
No period of life is **happier than** one's school days.
I have **never** seen **a more** beautiful sight **than** this.

이것보다 더 단순한 것은 아무것도 없습니다 / 인생의 어떤 기간도 학창시절보다 더 행복하지는 않습니다. / 저는 이보다 더 아름다운 광경은 본 적이 없습니다.

Basic Grammar for English Tests

4. 최상급의미의 동등비교 (원급)

He is **as** happy **as** (happy) **can be**. (= he is the happiest.)
He is **as poor as poor can be**. (= He is the poorest.)
No (other) mountain in the world is **so** high **as** Mt. Everest.

그는 행복할 수 있는 만큼 행복합니다. / 그는 가난할 만큼 가난합니다. / 세상의 어느 산도 에베레스트산만큼 높지는 않습니다.

* **Nothing** is **so** precious **as** health.
  = **Nothing** is **more** precious **than** health.
  = Health is **more** precious **than anything else**.
  = Health is **the most** precious **of all**.

어떤 것도 건강만큼 소중한 것은 없습니다. / = 어떤 것도 건강보다 더 소중한 것은 없습니다. / = 건강은 다른 어떤 것보다 더 소중합니다.
= 건강은 모든 것 중에 가장 소중합니다.

5. the를 붙이지 않는 경우

This is **a most** interesting book to me. (= a very)
She is **happiest** when she was young. (서술형)
Summer is **hottest** in July.

이것은 내게 아주 재미있는 책입니다. / 그녀는 젊었을 때 가장 행복했습니다. / 여름은 7월에 가장 덥습니다.

than 없이 비교급만 있는 문장의 예

You will understand it **easier** if you consult the dictionary.
He is **better** now.
He became **more and more** eloquent towards the end of his speech.
It seems that honest people are becoming **fewer and fewer** these days.

만일 당신이 사전을 찾으면 그것을 더 쉽게 이해할 것입니다. / 저는 지금 더 났습니다. / 그는 연설이 끝나가면서 점점 더 달변이 되었다. / 요즈음 정직한 사람들이 점점 더 적어지는 것 같습니다.

* **라틴어 비교급 + to**

This is much **inferior to** the one I bought last week.
I regard him as **superior to** other musicians.
She is **junior to** me. = She is **younger than** I.

이것은 내가 지난주에 산 것보다 훨씬 더 못하다. / 저는 그 사람을 다른 음악가들보다 우수하다고 여깁니다. / 그녀는 저보다 어립니다.

⎡ senior to (~보다 손위의 = older than)
⎣ junior to (~보다 손아래의 = younger than)

⎡ major to (~보다 다수의 = more than)
⎣ minor to (~보다 소수의 = less than)

- interior to (~보다 안쪽의 = inner than)
- exterior to (~보다 바깥쪽의 = outer than)
- anterior to (~보다 먼저의 = earlier than)
- posterior to (~보다 나중의 = later than)
- superior to (~보다 우수한 = better than)
- inferior to (~보다 열등한 = worse than)
- prior to (~보다 먼저 = before)
- prefer to (~보다 더 좋아하다 = like better)

The 비교급 ..., the 비교급 ...: ~하면 할수록 더~

The **longer** we stayed there, **the more** we liked the place.
The sooner you start, **the sooner** you'll finish.
The more he has, **the more** he wants.
The more, the better.
The sooner, the better.

우리가 그곳에 오래 있을수록, 그곳을 더 좋아할 것입니다. / 당신이 일찍 시작할수록, 일찍 끝내게 됩니다. / 많이 가질수록 더 많이 원합니다. / 많으면 많을수록 좋습니다. / 빠르면 빠를수록 좋습니다.

이중비교(double comparisons)

원급과 비교급이 섞인 혼합비교. 이때 if는 양보절(= even if)이다.

He is as sorry as, if not sorrier than, Polly.
= He is as sorry as Polly, if not sorrier.
He is as tall as, if not taller than, you.
= He is as tall as you, if not taller.

그는 폴리보다 더하지는 않더라도, 폴리만큼 딱합니다. / 그는 너보다 더 크지는 않더라도, 너만큼 키가 크다.

배수비교(multiple number comparisons)

S+V+배수+as { much+(불가산명사) / many+(가산명사) } as+(대)명사/S+(V)

Jane has **half as many CDs** now as I had last year.
You've made **just as many mistakes as** I have.
This encyclopedia costs **twice as much as** the other one.
I would gladly have paid **three times as much as** he asked.

Basic Grammar for English Tests

제인은 현재 지난해 제가 가진 CD의 절반을 가지고 있습니다. / 당신은 제가 한 꼭 그만큼의 실수를 했습니다. / 이 백과사전은 다른 것의 두 배나 값이 나갑니다. / 저는 그가 요구한 만큼의 세 배는 기꺼이 지불했을 것입니다.

비교의 논리성 : 비교하는 대상이 같아야 한다.

- His drawings are as perfect as his instructor. (x)
- His drawings are as perfect as his instructor's. (o)

- The climate in Florida is as mild as California. (x)
- The climate in Florida is as mild as **that of** California. (o)

- The salary of a professor is higher than a secretary. (x)
- The salary of a professor is higher than **that of** a secretary. (o)

- The duties of a policeman are more dangerous than a teacher. (x)
- The duties of a policeman are more dangerous than **those of** a teacher. (o)

- Our boat is larger than any in the fleet. (x)
- Our boat is larger than **any other** in the fleet. (o)

- Mary is smarter than anyone in her class. (x)
- Mary is smarter than **anyone else** in her class. (o)

그의 그림은 자기 선생님 그림만큼 완벽합니다. / 플로리다의 기후는 캘리포니아 기후만큼이나 온화합니다. / 교수의 봉급은 비서의 봉급보다 높습니다. / 경찰의 임무는 교사의 임무보다 더 위험합니다. / 우리 배는 함대의 다른 어느 배보다 더 큽니다. / 메리는 자기 학급의 다른 어느 아이보다도 똑똑합니다.

Exercise 6 다음 문장이 성립하도록 괄호에서 알맞은 단어를 고르시오.

1. Of the four dresses, I like the red one (better/*best*).
2. He is the (happier/happiest) person that we know.
3. Jane's car is (faster/fastest) than Dan's.
4. This is the (creamier/creamiest) ice cream I have had in a long time.
5. This poster is (colorfuler/more colorful) than the one in the hall.
6. Does Fred feel (weller/better) today than he did yesterday?
7. This vegetable soup tastes very (good/well).
8. While trying to balance the baskets on her head, the women walked (awkwarder/more awkwardly) than her daughter.
9. Jane is the (less/least) athletic of all the women.
10. My cat is the (prettier/prettiest) of the two.
11. This summary is (the better/the best) of the pair.
12. Your heritage is different (from/than) mine.
13. This painting is (less impressive/least impressive) than the one in the other gallery.

14. The colder the weather gets, (sicker/the sicker) I feel.
15. No sooner had he received the letter (when/than) he called Maria.
16. A mink coat costs (twice more than/twice as much as) a sable coat.
17. Jim has as (little/few) opportunities to play tennis as I.
18. That recipe calls for (many/much) more sugar than mine does.
19. The museum is the (farther/farthest) away of the three buildings.
20. George Washington is (famouser/more famous) than John Jay.

Exercise 7 다음 두 문장 중 비교문형의 논리가 바른 문장을 고르시오.

1. a) Alaska is larger than any state.
   b) Alaska is larger than any other state. (o)
2. a) John is taller than anyone in his class.
   b) John is taller than anyone else in his class.
3. a) The area of Alaska is greater than Texas.
   b) The area of Alaska is greater than that of Texas.
4. a) The rent for an efficiency apartment is much less than that for a one-bedroom apartment.
   b) The rent for an efficiency apartment is much less than for a one-bedroom apartment.
5. a) In our institution, morning classes are far more popular than the afternoon.
   b) In our institution, morning classes are far more popular than afternoon ones.
6. a) According to recent surveys, the CBS news programs have bigger audiences than NBC.
   b) According to recent surveys, the CBS news programs have bigger audiences than those of NBC.
7. a) The university's administration building is taller than any building on the campus.
   b) The university's administration building is taller than any other building on the campus.
8. a) Monkeys and apes are more intelligent than any animals except man.
   b) Monkeys and apes are more intelligent than any other animals except man.

Basic Grammar for English Tests

Exercise 8 다음 두 문장 중 이중비교의 문형으로 바른 문장을 고르시오.

1. a) Latex paint is as good as, if not better than, oil-based paint. (o)
   b) Latex paint is as good, if not better than, oil-based paint.
2. a) Rebuilding that worn-out carburetor will be as expensive, if not more expensive than, buying a new one.
   b) Rebuilding that worn-out carburetor will be as expensive as, if not more expensive than, buying a new one.
3. a) Her skill as a typist is equal or exceeds that of her predecessor.
   b) Her skill as a typist is equal to or exceeds that of her predecessor.
4. a) John Phillips received grades that were as high as, if not higher than, those of any other person in his class.
   b) John Phillips received grades that were as high, if not higher than, those of any other person in his class.
5. a) Track lighting is one of the most popular types, if not most popular type, of lighting on the market today.
   b) Track lighting is one of the most popular types, if not the most popular type, of lighting on the market today.
6. a) Even if they are on sale, these refrigerators are equal in price to, if not more expensive than, the ones at the other store.
   b) Even if they are on sale, these refrigerators are equal in price, if not more expensive than, the ones at the other store.
7. a) Low tar cigarettes are as dangerous as, if not more dangerous than, regular cigarettes.
   b) Low tar cigarettes are as dangerous, if not more dangerous than, regular cigarettes.
8. a) The warranty on the radial tires is as good, if not better than, that on the four-ply tires.
   b) The warranty on the radial tires is as good as, if not better than, that on the four-ply tires.

Actual Test 8

다음 각 문장을 읽고 빈칸에는 알맞은 단어를 넣고, 밑줄 친 부분에서는 잘못된 부분을 찾으시오.

1. Steam engines weigh _____ that produce the same amount of power.
   - Ⓐ less than piston turbines and
   - Ⓑ less than piston turbines
   - Ⓒ piston turbines are less than
   - Ⓓ in piston turbines less than

2. Liberal party tend to favor _____ do conservative party.
   - Ⓐ more than immediate social change
   - Ⓑ change more immediate than social
   - Ⓒ more immediate social change than
   - Ⓓ social change more than immediate

3. Sound moves _____ water.
   - Ⓐ faster through air than through
   - Ⓑ faster than through air and
   - Ⓒ through air faster and
   - Ⓓ where it is faster through air than through

4. The crowd was much larger _____.
   - Ⓐ than that at last year's baseball game
   - Ⓑ as it were
   - Ⓒ in such a way to be compared
   - Ⓓ than that at last years a baseball game

5. Of the two houses my wife prefers _____.
   - Ⓐ the most isolated one
   - Ⓑ the one isolated more
   - Ⓒ the more isolated one
   - Ⓓ the isolated one more

6. The higher the standard of living and the greater the national wealth, the _____.

   Ⓐ greater is the amount of gold is used
   Ⓑ greater amount of gold is used
   Ⓒ amount of gold is used is greater
   Ⓓ greater the amount of gold used

7. Few American cities have grown <u>as rapidly that</u> Los Angeles, which had
                                            A
   <u>1,610 inhabitants</u> in 1850 and <u>currently has</u> a population of <u>around 4 million</u>.
         B   C   D

8. <u>Exercising</u> is <u>as good as</u> a method as any <u>to lose</u> <u>unwanted</u> weight.
       A   B   C   D

9. Even the most <u>discriminating</u> gourmet will agree <u>that</u> food in the East is
                   A   B
   as <u>good</u> as <u>any</u> other region in the country.
       C   D

10. Last year the country <u>had</u> fewer imports <u>as</u> it did the year <u>before last</u> <u>due to</u>
                            A   B   C   D
    the economic crisis.

11. She took down the <u>largest</u> of the two dictionaries and <u>began</u> to <u>research</u> for
                      A   B   C
    the word she <u>had</u> misspelled.
                  D

12. <u>No other</u> skill is more important <u>for</u> a student <u>to master</u> <u>as that</u> of
     A   B   C   D
    writing well.

13. O'Hare Airport in Chicago <u>handles</u> <u>more freight</u> and mail <u>than</u> <u>any another</u>
                                        A   B   C   D
    airport in the United States.

14. There are <u>a number of areas</u> in north Pennsylvania that are <u>more wilder than</u>
                        A   B
    any other <u>Eastern area</u> <u>outside the Smokies</u>.
                C   D

15. Of all his <u>outdoor</u> activities, John likes fishing <u>best of all</u>, but <u>he</u> doesn't
              A   B   C
    enjoy <u>cleaning</u> the fishing rods afterwards.
           D

16. Nobody speaks <u>more clearly</u> than <u>him</u>, but his writing is <u>frequently</u> difficult
                           A   B   C
    to <u>understand</u>.
       D

17. The philosopher's influence <u>over</u> people's minds became <u>still greater</u> <u>after</u>
                                 A   B   C
    his death than <u>his life</u>.
                    D

18. The songs of Michael Jackson are very popular <u>among young people</u>, <u>who</u>
                                                  A
    <u>regard</u> him as <u>more superior</u> to <u>other musicians</u>.
       B   C   D

19. <u>The price</u> of gold on the <u>world</u> market has <u>been rising</u> <u>highest</u> everyday.
         A   B   C   D

20. The more complex a subject <u>becomes</u>, the <u>better necessary</u> it is to <u>break it</u>
                                 A   B   C
    up into a number of parts <u>which</u> the reader can understand.
                              D

21. The <u>more</u> I attempted to explain <u>my</u> mistake, the <u>worst</u> my story <u>sounded</u>.
          A   B   C   D

22. <u>Artificial</u> rubies have the <u>same</u> <u>hard</u> and composition as the <u>real</u> ones.
        A   B   C   D

◀ 주어-동사의 도치 (inversion of subject-verb)

영어 문장의 기본구조는 '주어+동사'의 순서이며, 주어는 항상 동사 앞에 놓인다.
그러나 의문문처럼 몇 가지 경우 예외적으로 주어, 동사의 위치가 바뀌는 경우가 있다.
대부분 부사가 강조되어 문두에 온다.

유도부사 There/Here는 주어 자리에 온다.

There is no basis for this complaint.
There are few excuses that teachers will accept.
Here comes the bus!
Here are the most common rules for writing.
Here is a cup of tea for you.

이런 불평에는 아무런 근거가 없어요. / 선생님들이 받아들이실 변명이 거의 없습니다. / 여기 버스가 와요! / 글쓰기를 위한 가장 일반적인 규칙들이 있습니다. / 커피 여기 있습니다.

cf. 주어가 대명사인 경우에는 도치되지 않는다.
· Here it comes. (여기 그것이 옵니다.)
  There she goes. (저기 그녀가 가네요.) ⎫ 위치를 강조
  There she is. (저기 그녀가 있군요.) ⎭
· Here you are. (여기 있습니다.) — 제공의 뜻을 강조

부사를 강조하여 문두에 둘 때

Down came the rain and **up** went the umbrellas.
Then came a sudden change. (= A sudden change came then.)
On and on went the soldiers. (= The soldiers went on and on.)

비가 내려 우산들을 썼습니다. / 그때 갑작스런 변화가 찾아왔습니다. / 줄곧 병사들이 갔습니다.

'Only'로 시작하는 (특히 시간표현의) 문장에서

Only after her mother died, **did she** know loneliness.
Only after it became dark **did they** take a rest.
Only once was John late to class.

어머니가 돌아가신 후에야 그녀는 외로움을 느꼈습니다. / 어두워진 뒤에야 그들은 휴식을 취했습니다. / 존은 딱 한 번 수업에 지각을 하였습니다.

전치사구 (특히 위치표현)를 문두에 둘 때

On the corner stood a police officer.
At the top of the hill stood the tiny chapel.
In the distance could be seen the purple mountains.

모퉁이에 경찰관이 서 있었습니다. / 언덕 위에 작은 교회가 서 있었습니다. / 멀리 보랏빛 산이 보였습니다.

* **주어가 대명사인 경우는 도치되지 않는다.**

   At the top of the hill it stood out against the sky.
   언덕 위에 그것은 하늘을 배경으로 드러나 보였습니다.

'부정'의 뜻을 지닌 부사가 문두에 올 때

> few, little, hardly, seldom, rarely, barely, scarcely, never, not only, at no time(결코 ~ 않은), on no account(결코 ~ 않은), not till/until, no sooner(~ 하자마자), never before

Not only did they go but they also stayed until the end.
No sooner had we started out for California, **than** it started to rain.
Never before in similar circumstances **had a British Prime Minister** refused to step down.
Not until 1940's did the television broadcasting begin.
Little did I realize how important the meeting was.

그들은 갔을 뿐만 아니라 끝까지 남아 있었습니다 / 우리가 캘리포니아로 출발을 하자마자 비가 오기 시작하였습니다. / 영국수상이 하야를 거절했던 비슷한 상황이 전에는 결코 없었습니다. / 텔레비전 방송이 시작된 것은 1940년대 이후였습니다. / 그 회의가 얼마나 중요한지 저는 거의 깨닫지를 못했습니다.

보어 'so-, such-' 등이 문두에 올 때

So great was her love for her children that she sacrificed everything for them.
Such was his strength that he could bend iron bars.

아이들에 대한 그녀의 사랑은 아주 대단해서 그녀는 그들을 위해 모든 것을 희생합니다. / 그의 힘은 대단해서 쇠막대도 구부릴 수 있었습니다.

조건절 접속사(if, unless ⋯)가 생략될 때

Were he to ask her, she would surely help him. (= If he asked her ⋯)
Should he ask her, she would surely help him. (= If he asked her ⋯)
Had he known, he would have come. (= If he had known, he would ⋯)

그녀에게 요청하였다면, 그녀는 당연히 그를 도왔을 것입니다. / 그가 알았더라면, 그는 왔을 것입니다.

Basic Grammar for English Tests

Exercise 9   다음 중 어순이 잘못된 문장을 찾아 고치시오.

1. Such behavior is not permitted in this classroom. (o)
2. So tired the boy was that he fell asleep almost immediately. (the boy was → *was the boy*)
3. Little do teenagers realize how much they have to learn.
4. Few and far between the gas stations are on this stretch of road.
5. So old the book was that its pages had turned yellow.
6. Little the boy realizes how sick he is.
7. So perfect was the foreigner's accent that everyone thought he was a native speaker.
8. Few were the nights that he went to bed before midnight.
9. Such crimes are punished by death in that country.
10. So great her love was that she sacrificed everything for her children.

Actual Test 9

다음 각 문장을 읽고 빈칸에는 알맞은 단어를 넣고, 밑줄 친 부분에서는 잘못된 부분을 찾으시오.

1. Out of the basic factors of elementary algebra _____ used today and the concept of an algebraic structure.

    Ⓐ the algebra of abstract evolution
    Ⓑ evolution of the abstract algebra
    Ⓒ the abstract algebra evolved
    Ⓓ evolved the abstract algebra

2. The magnetic compass does not operate well near the magnetic poles, nor _____ near the geographic poles.

    Ⓐ does the marine gyrocompass
    Ⓑ with the marine gyrocompass
    Ⓒ the marine gyrocompass does
    Ⓓ the marine gyrocompass operates

3. Never before in similar circumstances _____.

    Ⓐ a state governor had refused to step down
    Ⓑ did a state governor have refused to step down
    Ⓒ a state governor did have refused to step down
    Ⓓ had a state governor refused to step down

4. Rarely _____ for more than a few seconds once they enter the Earth's atmosphere.

    Ⓐ while meteors burn
    Ⓑ meteors that burn
    Ⓒ do meteors burn
    Ⓓ burn meteors

5. _____ at carrying her message through tight plots and contemporary characters that by 1950 her book had sold some one million copies.

    Ⓐ So successful, Grace Miller
    Ⓑ So successful was Grace Miller
    Ⓒ Grace Miller, so successful
    Ⓓ Because Grace Miller was so successful

6. Seldom children are under the age of thirteen permitted to register for
   　　　A　　　　B　　　　　　　C　　　　　　　　　　　　　D
   classes at this institute.

7. Not until a baby kangaroo is six months old it begins to live outside its
   　A　　　　　　　　　　　B　　　　　　　　C
   mother's pouch.
   　　D

8. Only after a baby seal is pushed into the sea by its mother it will learn
   　　　　　　　　　　　　A　　　　　　　　B　　　　　　　C
   how to swim.
   　　C

9. Such were the predominant land life throughout the Jurasic Period.
   　　　A　　　　　B　　　　　　　　C　　　　　　　D

10. Within the Alamo was two hundred and fifty men, more than two thirds
    　　　　　　　　A　　　　　　　　　　　　　　　　　　　　　　B
    of whom had recently migrated from near-by states.
    　　　　　　　　　　　　C　　　　　　　D

11. No sooner his luggage had been loaded than the truck started off.
    　　　　　A　　　　　　　　B　　　　　　　　　　C　　D

12. Rarely meteors blaze for more than a few moments once they enter the
    　　A　　　　　　　B　　　　　　　　　　　　C　　D
    Earth's atmosphere.

13. The magnetic compass does not operate well near the magnetic
    　　　　　　　　　　A　　　　　　　B
    poles nor the marine compass near the geographic poles.
    　　C　　　　　　　　　　　D

14. So great the force is exerted by tornadoes that they have been known to
    　A　　　　B　　　　　　　　　　　　　　　　　　C
    lift the trains off their tracks.
    　　　　　　　D

15. Only in the early twentieth century dreams were first scrutinized.
    　A　　　　　　　　　　　　　　B　　　　C　　　D

◀ 부가동의문(additional agreements)

어떤 사람이나 사물에 대한 진술에 일치하는 상황을 덧붙여 동의를 표하는 문형.
be, have, do 및 일부 조동사가 대동사로 쓰인다.

진술에 대한 '일치'와 '동의'를 표현

John can speak French	and I can, too. / and so can I.
John can't speak French	and I can't, either. / and neither(/nor) can I.
John speaks French	and I do, too. / and so do I.
John doesn't speak French	and I don't, either. / and neither(/nor) do I.

존이 불어를 말할 수 있는데, 저도 그래요. / 존은 불어를 말할 수 없는데, 저도 마찬가지예요. / 존이 불어를 말하는데, 저도 그래요. / 존은 불어를 말하지 못하는데, 저도 마찬가지예요.

＊ 앞뒤 문장의 화자가 다른 경우

John can speak French.	I can, too. / So can I.
John can't speak French.	I can't, either. / Neither(/nor) can I.
John speaks French.	I do, too. / So do I.
John desn't speak French.	I don't, either. / Nither(/nor) do I.

존이 불어를 말할 수 있어요. 저도 그래요. / 존은 불어를 말할 수 없어요. 저도 마찬가지예요. / 존이 불어를 말합니다. 저도 그래요. / 존은 불어를 말하지 못합니다. 저도 마찬가지예요.

상대방의 진술에 대해 '놀람'을 겸한 '공감' 표시

She's going to help us. — So she is!
John retires soon. — So she does!
I've got a new car. — So has John.
John's got a new car. — So he has!
Laura looks just like her uncle. — So she does!
I've got something in my eye. — So you have!

그녀는 우리를 도와줄 것입니다.-그렇군요! / 존은 곧 사직할 것입니다.-그렇군요! / 저는 새 차가 생겼습니다.-존도 그렇습니다. / 존은 새 차가 생겼습니다.-정말이군요! / 로라는 꼭 자기 삼촌 같아요.-정말 그렇군요! / 제 눈에 무엇이 들어갔습니다.-정말이군요!

Exercise 10 다음 빈칸에 적당한 말을 넣으시오.

1. Rose likes to fly, and her brother _does_ too.
2. They will leave at noon, and I _____ too.
3. He has an early appointment, and so _____ I.
4. She has already written her composition, and so _____ her friends.
5. Their plane is arriving at nine o'clock, and so _____ mine.

Unit 6 특수문형 | 147

Actual Test 10

다음 각 문장을 읽고 빈칸에는 알맞은 단어를 넣고, 밑줄 친 부분에서는 잘못된 부분을 찾아내시오.

1. "The Jones watch television all day long." "_____ do the Millers."
   Ⓐ So
   Ⓑ Either
   Ⓒ Neither
   Ⓓ Also

2. George went to the concert, _____.
   Ⓐ and his brother did, either
   Ⓑ but his brother went there also
   Ⓒ such went also his brother
   Ⓓ and so did his brother

3. "Tom can't leave until tomorrow." "I know. _____."
   Ⓐ I can't too
   Ⓑ I can too
   Ⓒ Neither can I
   Ⓓ I can't either

4. "Jane is not a graduate student." "No, _____."
   Ⓐ I wasn't, either
   Ⓑ either wasn't I
   Ⓒ I was not, neither
   Ⓓ neither I was

5. The Jones watch television all the time. So the Bushes do.
      A   B   C   D

6. George went to the movie, and did so his brother.
        A   B C D

7. Sally is studying law at the university, and so does John.
       A B   C   D

8. She isn't driving to the convention in June, and neither they are.
       A   B   C   D

9. I'd met Jane several times before. So would I.
     A   B C   D

10. George was not a college student. No, I wasn't, neither.
          A   B C   D

Unit 7

일치

◀ 주어-동사 수(number)의 일치

복수의미를 가진 단수대명사 — 단수동사

everyone	someone	anyone	no one	each
everybody	somebody	anybody	nobody	either
everything	something	anything	nothing	neither

Everything in the house **was** destroyed by the fire.
Everyone was required to write a composition.
Neither of these books **is** very new.
Neither of the reporters **was** allowed to interview the players.

집 안의 모든 것이 화재로 파괴되었습니다. / 모든 사람이 작문하기를 요구받았습니다. / 이 책들 중 어떤 것도 아주 새로운 것은 아닙니다. / 어떤 기자도 선수들의 인터뷰가 허용되지 않았습니다.

단수취급

Each student and teacher **has** a locker.
Every man, woman, and child **was** given a free ticket.

학생들과 선생님들은 각자 (옷)장이 있습니다. / 모든 남자, 여자, 어린이는 무료입장권이 주어졌습니다.

가주어 it와 형용사절

It **was** the dogs which **awakened** me.
It **is** his grades that **worry** him.

저를 잠 깨운 것은 개들이었습니다. / 그를 걱정하게 만드는 것은 성적이었습니다.

Basic Grammar for English Tests

전치사구는 있어도 없는 것과 같다

The man *together with his children* **is** leaving soon.
John *but not Mike* **has** gone to play soccer at the park.
Everyone *except him* **has** a book.
The teacher *along with her students* **is** viewing a film.

아이들을 데리고 있는 남자는 곧 떠날 것입니다. / 마이크가 아니라 존이 공원에 축구하러 갔습니다. / 그를 제외하고 모두 책을 한 권 가지고 있습니다. / 학생들과 함께 선생님이 영화를 보고 계십니다.

유도부사 here, there, where 등이 이끄는 문장에서 동사는 다음에 오는 명사를 주어로 하여 영향을 받는다

Here **are the results** of the experiments.
There **are no dogs** in this neighborhood.
Where **has everyone** gone?

실험의 결과가 나왔습니다. / 우리 이웃에는 개가 없습니다. / 모두 어디 갔습니까?

Exercise 1 다음 문장의 주어와 동사를 확인하고 틀린 부분을 고치시오.

1. Each fruit and vegetable were originally grown. (were → *was*)
2. Everyone have to arrive at 8:30 in the morning.
3. It were the children who broke the windows.
4. Everything in the house are for sale.
5. Every student want to pass the entrance exam.
6. There has never been so many joggers in the race.
7. A box of books as well as a large suitcase are under the bed.
8. The president together with his assistants have left for New York.
9. Here are the music as well as the words to the song.
10. Everyone in the two classes speak English very well.

Exercise 2 다음 각 문장에 적당한 동사를 괄호에서 고르시오.

1. There (isn't/*aren't*) any letters in the mail for you today.
2. There (isn't/aren't) any mail for you today.
3. There (is/are) over 600,000 kinds of insects in the world.
4. How many kinds of birds (is/are) there in the world?
5. Why (isn't/aren't) there a hospital close to those villages?

주어가 and, both~and 로 연결되는 경우 ―복수동사

A red Hyundai **and** a blue Ford **are** parked outside.
Both tigers **and** elephants **are** becoming extinct.

빨간 현대 자동차와 푸른 색 포드 자동차가 밖에 세워져 있습니다. / 호랑이와 코끼리는 멸종되어갑니다.

several, many, both, few 등 복수단어는 복수동사를 취한다

Both are going to attend the University of Texas.
Only a few have passed the exam.
Several of the fish **appear** to be dying.
When the bell rang, **a few were** still working on the test.

둘 다 텍사스대학에 가려고 합니다. / 겨우 몇 사람만이 시험에 합격하였습니다. / 물고기 몇 마리가 죽어가고 있는 것 같습니다. / 종이 울렸을 때, 몇 사람이 아직 시험을 치고 있었습니다.

복수형 명사 ―복수동사

> 의복 : trousers, pants, jeans, sunglasses
> 연장 : scissors, pliers, tweezers(핀셋, 족집게)
> 추상명사 : riches, thanks, means(수단)

His pants are still at the cleaners.
Your thanks are enough for me.
The scissors are in the bottom drawer.
That pair of pants **is** dirty.
A word of thanks **is** enough.

그의 바지는 아직 세탁소에 있습니다. / 당신의 감사는 제게 충분합니다. / 가위가 맨 아래 서랍에 있습니다. / 저 바지는 더럽습니다. / 감사의 말 한 마디면 충분합니다.

상관접속사로 연결된 병렬구조의 복수주어에서 동사는 가까이 있는 주어와 일치한다

Neither the students *nor* the teacher **is** allowed to smoke.
Either the teacher *or* the students **have** your books.
Not only the nurses *but also* the doctor **is** coming soon.

학생들도 선생님도 담배 피우는 것은 허용되지 않습니다. / 선생님이나 학생들이 당신 책을 가지고 있습니다. / 간호사뿐 아니라 의사도 곧 올 것입니다.

Basic Grammar for English Tests

다음의 주어들은 이어지는 전치사의 목적어인 명사의 수(number)와 일치한다

none, all, some, any, majority, most, half

All *of the book* has been burned.
All *of the books* have been thrown away.
All *of the money* is in bank.

그 책이 몽땅 타버렸습니다. / 그 책들이 몽땅 내버려졌습니다. / 그 돈이 모두 은행에 있습니다.

{ a number of (= many) — 복수동사
  the number of — 단수동사 }

A number of students were missing from class.
The number of Mexican students in class is small.

많은 학생들이 수업을 빼먹었습니다. / 학급에서 멕시코 학생들의 수는 적습니다.

Exercise 3 다음 문장의 구조를 확인하고 주어와 일치하는 동사를 고르시오.

1. Few (is/*are*) strong enough to finish the race.
2. There (is/are) a pair of sunglasses lying on the floor.
3. Both my good trousers and my old jeans (is/are) at the laundry.
4. Many of you (is/are) going to pass the entrance examination.
5. There (is/are) several books on the top shelf of the bookcase.
6. Neither the doctor nor the nurses (is/are) here.
7. The number of nurses in the city (is/are) very large.
8. All of the nurses (is/are) very good.
9. All of the medicine (is/are) gone.
10. Some of the water (is/are) used for irrigation.
11. Most of the money (is/are) counterfeit.
12. Not only the money but also the jewels (is/are) locked up in the safe.
13. Neither the jewels nor the money (is/are) mine.
14. All of the cookies (is/are) gone.
15. Half of the furniture (is/are) in the truck.

형태는 복수지만 단수동사로 받는 경우

시간(time), 돈(money), 무게(weight), 부피(volume) 등을 표현하는 단위의 합계

Two weeks is enough time for a nice vacation.

Five hundred dollars is required as a down payment.
Ten extra pounds is a lot to lose in a week.
Twenty gallons of gasoline **costs** a lot of money.

2주일은 멋진 휴가를 보내기에 충분한 시간입니다. / 첫 할부금으로 500달러가 필요합니다. / 10파운드는 일주일에 빼기로는 많습니다. / 휘발유 20갤런은 돈이 많이 듭니다.

형태는 복수지만 뜻은 단수인 명사는 단수동사로 받는다

학문이름 : mathemátics, phýsics, económics, statístics(통계학), cívics(시민론)
질병이름 : méasles(홍역), mumps(이하선염), hérpes(포진)
추상명사 : news, éthics(윤리), pólitics(정치)

Mathematics is a difficult subject.
The news was very good.

수학은 어려운 학문입니다. / 그 뉴스는 아주 좋습니다.

책, 영화의 제목은 복수형태일지라도 단수동사를 받는다

The New York **Times is** a good newspaper.
Star Wars **was** a good movies.

뉴욕타임스는 훌륭한 신문입니다. / 스타워즈는 훌륭한 영화입니다.

Exercise 4 다음 문장의 구조를 확인하고 주어와 일치하는 동사를 고르시오.

1. German measles (cause/*causes*) red spots on the chest and arms.
2. News of the peace talks (has/have) not yet reached the island.
3. Politics usually (attract/attracts) ambitious individuals.
4. There (was/were) extra copies of The New York Times in all the offices.
5. Two weeks (is/are) ample time for a camping trip to the state park.
6. According to the champion, one hundred pounds (is/are) easy to lift.
7. Two thousand dollars (is/are) a lot of him to pay for tuition.
8. Both mathematics and physics (is/are) interesting.
9. Jaws, a movie about sharks, (was/were) seen by a record number of people.
10. Despite the development of a vaccine, measles (is/are) still a serious danger to adult victims.

집합명사는 단수동사로, 그 구성원들인 경우는 복수동사로 받는다

> audience, class, committee, crew(승무원), faculty(교수단), family, police, press(언론), team

That class has its final test on Friday.
The class are working on **their** individual projects today.
The crew are asleep in **their** bunks down in the hold of the ship.
The family are fighting among **themselves** constantly.
The press are requested to show **their** credentials to the guard.

저 학급은 금요일에 기말 시험이 있습니다. / 그 학급은 오늘 각자의 프로젝트를 작업하고 있습니다. / 승무원들은 배의 선창 아래 각자 침상에서 잠을 자고 있습니다. / 식구들은 늘 자기들끼리 싸우고 있습니다. / 기자들은 경비에게 증명서를 보여야 합니다.

단수·복수형이 같은 단어

수식하는 대명사나 한정사의 수(number)에 따라 동사의 수가 결정된다.

> sheep, deer, species(종), series(연속물)

That species is rare. / **Those species are** common.
That deer is young. / **Those deer are** old.
All sheep are dipped in the spring to kill the parasites.

그 종은 드뭅니다. / 그 종들은 흔합니다. / 저 사슴은 어립니다. / 저 사슴들은 늙었습니다. / 모든 양들은 기생충을 잡으려고 샘에 몸을 적시게 됩니다.

hinese, French, English … { 외국어 — 단수동사
그 나라 사람 — 복수동사 }

French is a Roman language. / **The French are** romantic.
English is spoken in the U.S. / **The English love** tea.

불어는 라틴어입니다. / 프랑스인들은 낭만적입니다. / 영어는 미국에서 사용됩니다. / 영국인들은 차를 좋아합니다.

그리스어, 라틴어가 어원인 명사의 복수형을 주의할 것

- 그리스어
  básis [béisis] /báses [béisi:z], crísis [kráisis] /críses [kráisi:z] (위기),
  critérion [kraitíəriən] /critéria [kraitíəriə] (기준),
  phenómenon [finómənən] /phenómena [finómənə]

- 라틴어
  álga [ǽlgə] /álgae [ǽldʒi:] (바닷말), alúmnus [əlʌ́mnəs] /alúmni [əlʌ́mnai] (동창),
  dátum /dáta, médium /média, índex [índeks] /índices [índisi:z] (색인),
  appéndix [əpéndiks] /appéndices [əpéndəsi:z] (부록), rádius [réidiəs] /rádii [réidiai] (반경)

The algae in the pool **are** hard to remove.
The radius of the circle **is** two inches.
These bacteria are being studied by university scientists.
The criteria for promotion **are** clearly stated.
The appendices are usually found at the back of a book.

수영장의 바닷말은 제거하기 힘들어요. / 그 원의 반지름은 2인치입니다. / 이 박테리아들은 대학의 과학자들이 연구하고 였습니다. / 승진의 기준이 분명하게 기술됩니다. / 부록은 항상 책의 뒤쪽에서 찾을 수 있습니다.

Exercise 5 다음 각 문장의 주어와 일치하는 동사를 괄호에서 그르시오.

1. The extent of Jane's knowledge on various complex subjects (*astounds*/astound) me.
2. The subjects you will be studying in this course (is/are) listed in the syllabus.
3. Massachusetts and Connecticut (is/are) located in New England.
4. Only the black widow spider, of all the spiders in the United States, (has/have) caused death among human beings.
5. Oranges, tomatoes, fresh strawberries, cabbage, and green lettuce (is/are) rich in vitamin C.
6. The teacher and the student (agrees/agree) on that point.
7. Almost every professor and student at the university (approves/approve) of the choice of Dr. Brown as the new president.
8. Each girl and boy in the sixth-grade class (has/have) to do a science project.
9. Making pies and cakes (is/are) Mrs. Reed's specialty.
10. Getting to know students from all over the world (is/are) one of the best parts of my job.

◀ 대명사 격(form)의 일치

주격(subject form)

1. 주절이나 종속절의 주어

    He left his books in the classroom. (주절)
    John talked to the man **who** was standing near him. (형용사절)
    After **he** left, I went to bed. (부사절)
    I know **who** broke the window. (명사절)

그는 교실에 책을 두고 왔습니다. / 존은 자기 옆에 서 있는 남자와 이야기를 했습니다. / 그가 떠난 후, 저는 잠자리에 들었습니다. / 저는 누가 창문을 깼는지 알아요.

2. be동사의 보어

It's **I**(me).
It must have been **they** who left the message.
It was **we** who forgot to do our homework.

저예요. / 메시지를 남긴 것은 분명 그들이었습니다. / 우리의 숙제를 잊어버린 것은 우리들이었습니다.

3. 두개의 절에서 주어가 비교구문으로 비교될 때

She is taller than **he** (is). (이때, than은 전치사이기도 하다.)
They have more money than **we** (have).

그녀는 그이보다 키가 큽니다. / 그들은 우리보다 돈을 더 많이 가지고 있습니다.

목적격(object form)

1. 문장의 목적어

That policeman is watching **me**. (직접목적어)
The student **whom** I advised is Algerian. (형용사절 — 직접목적어)
If I send **him** a letter, he will be happy. (부사절 — 간접목적어)

저 경찰관이 저를 감시하고 있습니다. / 제가 충고를 한 학생은 알제리인입니다. / 제가 그에게 편지를 보낸다면, 그는 기뻐할 것입니다.

2. 전치사의 목적어

Everyone **except her** took the test.
Between you and **me**, I didn't like that party.
Bill won't go to the party **without her**.

그녀를 제외한 모두가 시험을 쳤습니다. / 당신과 나 가운데, 나는 저 파티를 좋아하지 않습니다. / 빌은 그녀 없이는 파티에 가지 않을 것입니다.

3. 두 개의 절에서 목적어가 비교구문으로 비교될 때

The teacher likes **you** better than (she likes) **me**. (than은 전치사이기도 하다.)
The child responds **to her** more readily than (to) **him**.
Our parents worry **about my brother** more than **about me**.

선생님은 나보다는 너를 더 좋아해. / 그 아이는 그이보다 그녀를 더 반깁니다. / 우리 부모님은 나보다 오빠를 더 걱정하셔.

Exercise **6** 다음 문장의 대명사의 격을 확인하고 틀린 것을 고치시오.

1. It was I whom called you last night. (whom → *who*)
2. It is true that I am taller than him.
3. It must have been him whom the police arrested.
4. If you were me, would you lend him the money?
5. My teacher thinks that I am more intelligent than him.
6. The men whom live across the street make a lot of noise.
7. No one knows what happened except you, Harry, and I.
8. It must have been him whom we saw at the movie.
9. This is a good picture of he.
10. I think that the teacher knows whom took these photographs.

소유격(possessive adjective form)

1. 명사를 수식하며 소유를 표시

   I lost **my wallet** in the park.
   The boy **whose dog** is lost is sad.
   Everyone did **his best** on the homework.

   저는 공원에서 지갑을 잃어버렸습니다. / 개를 잃어버린 아이가 슬퍼합니다. / 모두가 숙제를 하는 데 최선을 다했습니다.

2. 대명사가 동명사를 수식할 경우

   I appreciate **your helping** me.
   Her singing will calm the baby.
   The music teacher knows **whose playing** is the best.

   저를 도와주신 데 감사를 드립니다. / 그녀의 노래는 아기를 진정시킬 것입니다. / 음악선생님은 누구의 연주가 최고인지 알고 계십니다.

소유대명사(possessive pronoun form)

1. 주어, 목적어, 보어 역할

   Your coat is new, but **mine** isn't.
   I forgot my book so I borrowed **hers**.
   Everyone likes your singing but not **theirs**.
   I don't know **whose** that is.

   당신의 코트는 새것이지만, 제것은 아닙니다. / 저는 제 책을 잊어버리고 와서 그녀의 책을 빌렸습니다. / 모두가 당신의 노래를 좋아하지만, 그들의 노래는 아닙니다. / 저는 저것이 누구 것인지 모릅니다.

Basic Grammar for English Tests

2. 전치사 뒤에서

Marianne is a good friend **of mine**.
I found an old composition **of yours** in the file.
Some friends **of hers** are visiting Austin this week.

마리안은 저의 훌륭한 친구입니다. / 저는 파일에서 당신의 옛날 작문을 찾았습니다. / 그녀의 몇몇 친구들이 이번 주에 오스틴을 방문합니다.

3. 비교구문으로 비교되는 경우

His car can go faster than **yours**.
Lynn's house is larger than **mine**.

그의 자동차는 당신 차보다 더 빨리 갈 수 있습니다. / 린의 집은 제 집보다 더 큽니다.

재귀대명사(reflexive pronoun form)의 일치

1. 강조하려는 주어, 목적어와 성(gender) 일치

I always do the dishes **myself**.
You may burn **yourself** with those matches.
He is always talking to **himself**.
You cannot expect **a baby** to take care of **itself**.

저는 늘 직접 설거지를 합니다. / 너는 그 성냥불에 델 수도 있어. / 그는 늘 혼자 중얼거립니다. / 당신은 아기가 혼자 놀 수 있다고 기대하면 안돼요.

2. **by oneself** (= alone, without help)

Young children cannot get dressed **by themselves**.
After a busy day, he likes to be **by himself**.
We prefer living **by ourselves**.

어린이들은 스스로 옷을 입을 수 없습니다. / 바쁜 하루를 보낸 뒤에, 그는 혼자 있기를 좋아합니다. / 우리는 홀로 사는 것을 좋아합니다.

Exercise **7**   다음 문장에서 대명사의 격(form)을 확인하고 틀린 부분을 고치시오.

1. You will have to go alone unless you can wait until I finish me lunch. (me → *my*)
2. The student whom forgot his books is going to be unhappy tonight.
3. Our teacher doesn't like us speaking Spanish in class.
4. Your cat is much larger than me.
5. George brought a friend of him to class yesterday.
6. Bill forgot to bring his pencil to class so he borrowed me.

7. If I can do my homework, you should certainly be able to do your.
8. His son often gets hisself in trouble.
9. My brother and I usually drive ourself to work.
10. Both of you can help yourself more by working than by wasting time.

Exercise 8 다음 문장의 구조를 확인하고 괄호에 들어갈 적당한 대명사를 고르시오.

1. The director will hire the person (who/whom) has the best credentials.
2. No one except (she/her) brought a lunch.
3. The first ones in line were Nancy, Jim, and (he/him).
4. (Who/Whom) did you visit in Austin?
5. With (who/whom) is Bryan talking?
6. His shoes are much newer than (her/hers).
7. They offered their seats to you and (I/me).
8. It was (she/her) that asked the question.
9. No one was surprised at (him/his) winning the contest.
10. There should be no secrets between you and (he/him).
11. (Who/Whom) was it that asked that question?
12. Only (he/him) forgot about the test.
13. Beverly is a good friend of (me/mine).
14. She wants to know (who/whom) is giving the party.
15. The picnic won't be any fun without you and (they/them).
16. I can't figure out (who/whom) is on the phone.
17. John did all the homework by (him/himself).
18. This is a picture of Scott, his sister, and (I/me).
19. Everyone but (he/him) did well on the test.
20. If you were (I/me), where would you go for vacation?

◀ 대명사 수(number), 성(gender)의 일치

and, both ~and 로 연결되는 주어 – 복수대명사

Both John *and* Mary are returning to **their** class.
John *and* I are returning to **our** class.

존과 메리 둘 다 수업에 복귀합니다. / 존과 나는 수업에 복귀합니다.

Basic Grammar for English Tests

한정사로 시작하는 대명사는 단수대명사(he, his, she, it, its …)로 받는다

	-body	-one	-thing
some-	somebody	someone	something
any-	anybody	anyone	anything
no-	nobody	no one	nothing
every-	everybody	everyone	everything

Everyone must do **his** homework.
He never puts **anything** back in **its** place.
Anyone who wishes can bring **her** husband to the party.
You can tell from the blood on the bench that **someone** on the football team hurt **himself**.

모두가 자기 숙제를 해야 합니다. / 그는 결코 어떤 것도 제자리에 갖다놓지 않습니다. / 원하는 사람은 누구나 남편을 파티에 데려올 수 있습니다. / 축구팀의 누군가가 다쳤다는 것을 벤치에 묻은 피를 통해 알 수 있습니다.

상관접속사

{ either ~ or ~
  neither ~ nor ~
  not only ~ but also ~ 로 연결될 경우,
가까이 있는 대명사의 수(number)나 성(gender)에 일치한다.

Either the students *or* the teacher will give you **his** book.
Neither the dog *nor* the cats have on **their** collars.
Not only the players *but also* the coach has on **his** uniform.

학생들이나 선생님이 자신의 책을 네게 주실 거야. / 개도 고양이들도 목걸이를 착용하고 있지 않습니다. / 선수들뿐 아니라 감독도 자기 유니폼을 입고 있습니다.

집합명사인 경우는 단수/복수대명사 모두 받을 수 있다

The **team is** preparing for **its** big game.
The **team are** going to **their** homes now.
The **committee is** issuing **its** report tomorrow
The **crew has** to clean **its** boat.

그 팀은 큰 경기를 준비하고 있습니다. / 팀원들은 지금 자기 집으로 가고 있습니다. / 위원회는 내일 자체보고서를 발표합니다. / 승무원은 자기 배를 청소해야 합니다.

Exercise 9 다음 문장의 대명사가 일치하는지 확인하고 틀린 것을 고치시오.

1. Everyone in the American literature class will receive their textbooks tomorrow. (their → *his*)
2. Somebody put their cigarette out in the sink.
3. The queen and her daughter spend much of her free time on horseback.
4. My brother and I will spend my weekend at the lake.
5. It is surprising that no one turned in their paper on time.
6. Neither of the boys has had their hair cut lately.
7. The family has sold their summer home.
8. No one realized that both Bill and Tom had visited his families recently.
9. Either Martin or Jones will give their report next.
10. The faculty has cancelled their monthly meeting.

◀ 관계대명사의 일치

선행사-관계대명사 일치

- who, whom : 선행사가 사람일 때
- which : 선행사가 사물, 동물, 집합명사인 경우
- that, whose : 모든 명사

선행사는 명사다

The class was long which no one liked. (x)
→ No one liked the length of the class. (o)
The weather was too hot which spoiled the picnic. (x)
Everyone enjoyed the concert which was held in the park. (o)

아무도 그 등급의 길이를 좋아하지 않았습니다. / 모든 사람들이 공원에서 열린 음악회를 즐겼습니다.

Exercise 10 다음 문장의 관계대명사가 틀린 것을 찾아 고치시오.

1. The river which divides Texas and Mexico is the Rio Grande. (c)
2. A friend recommended the doctor which is treating my son. (which → *who*)

3. The beautician who does her hair is very good.
4. The Senator which introduced the bill was defeated in the last election.
5. Tigers who live in Africa are endangered.
6. The artist whose works are on display is a native Texan.
7. Someone stole the antique shop which had been left unlocked.
8. The cassette player that Phyllis borrowed was mine.
9. The rain whom the crops needed never came.
10. The advantages of which he spoke are numerous.

Actual Test 11

다음 각 문장을 읽고 빈칸에는 알맞은 단어를 넣고, 밑줄 친 부분에서는 잘못된 부분을 찾아내시오.

1. The schedule of these lectures _____ by the lecture committee.
   - Ⓐ announces
   - Ⓑ have been announced
   - Ⓒ announced
   - Ⓓ has been announced

2. Here _____ the last piece of cake and the last spoonful of ice cream.
   - Ⓐ we go
   - Ⓑ goes
   - Ⓒ go
   - Ⓓ are losing

3. Where to find her and how to find her _____ to us.
   - Ⓐ is not known
   - Ⓑ are not known
   - Ⓒ not known
   - Ⓓ has not known

4. The ability to hide <u>themselves</u> by camouflage <u>enable</u> some <u>otherwise</u>
                                 A   B   C
   defenseless animals <u>to survive</u>.
                    D

5. The most famous alumnus of the school <u>were</u> invited <u>to take part</u> in the
                                             A   B
   graduation ceremony and <u>related</u> activities scheduled <u>for late May</u>.
                                   C   D

6. <u>At present</u>, advertising <u>is</u> one of the <u>most strictly</u> regulated <u>industry</u> in America.
       A   B   C   D

7. The <u>Smith family</u> have <u>been</u> living in a <u>tiny</u> apartment since they <u>move</u>
          A   B   C   D
   to town last January.

8. Over the <u>last few</u> years medical researchers <u>have searching</u> for a <u>means</u>
             A   B   C
   <u>to control</u> the flu virus.
      D

9. <u>For some time now</u>, television <u>advertising</u> <u>is</u> tightly <u>controlled</u> by the
      A   B   C   D
   National Advertising Committee.

10. If one does not have respect for <u>himself</u>, <u>you</u> cannot expect <u>others</u> to
                                       A   B   C
    respect <u>him</u>.
           D

11. What happened <u>at New York</u> <u>in 1980</u> <u>were</u> the result of the president's
　　　　　　　　　　　A　　　　　B　　　C

    order to <u>invade</u> Cambodia.
　　　　　　　　D

12. Those of us <u>who</u> belong to the National Association for Foreign Student
　　　　　　　　A

    Affairs <u>should have</u> <u>their</u> membership renewed <u>in March</u>.
　　　　　　　B　　　　　　C　　　　　　　　　　　　　D

13. Neither my traveler's checks nor the money that my father <u>sent</u> me <u>are</u>
　　　　　　　　　　　　　　　　　　　　　　　　　　　A　　　　B

    sufficient <u>to pay</u> <u>for the tickets</u>.
　　　　　　　C　　　　D

14. There <u>have been</u> <u>little</u> rain in the last <u>two-weak</u> period <u>because of</u> a
　　　　　A　　　　　B　　　　　　　　C　　　　　　　D

    high pressure area over most of the state.

15. Everyone <u>who</u> <u>takes</u> the examination will receive <u>their</u> score reports
　　　　　　A　　B　　　　　　　　　　　　　　　C

    <u>in three weeks</u>.
　　　　D

16. He <u>strongly objected</u> <u>to</u> the eagle being chosen as the national bird
　　　　A　　　　　　　　　B

    <u>because of</u> <u>their</u> predatory nature.
　　　　C　　　　　D

17. Few airports in the United States <u>is</u> as modern <u>as</u> <u>that</u> <u>of</u> New York.
　　　　　　　　　　　　　　　　　A　　　　　　　B　C　D

18. Not one <u>in a thousand</u> seeds <u>develop</u> <u>into</u> a healthy plant, <u>even under</u>
　　　　　A　　　　　　　　B　　　C　　　　　　　　　D

    laboratory conditions.

19. Neither of the two alternatives that <u>had been planned</u> <u>at the last meeting</u>
　　　　　　　　　　　　　　　　　　　A　　　　　　　　　B

    <u>were</u> acceptable <u>to</u> the executive committee.
　　C　　　　　　　D

20. It is surprising that there <u>were</u> not a serious objection to <u>their changing</u> the
　　A　　　　　　　　　　　B　　　　　　　　　　　　　　　　C

    rules for the chess tournament without <u>consulting</u> the officials.
　　　　　　　　　　　　　　　　　　　　　　　　D

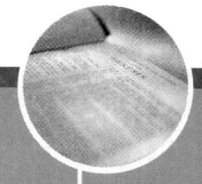

ENGLISH FORUM

Basic Grammar for English Tests

Part II

Word Classes 품사편

- **Unit 8** 명사
- **Unit 9** 관사
- **Unit 10** 대명사
- **Unit 11** 한정사와 수량표시
- **Unit 12** 형용사
- **Unit 13** 부사
- **Unit 14** 전치사
- **Unit 15** 동사
- **Unit 16** 조동사
- **Unit 17** 부정사와 동명사

Unit 8

명사

◀ 명사의 종류

```
1. 고유명사 : English, India, the Thames ...
                    ┌ 불가산명사 ┬ 구체명사/물질명사 : clothing, bread, water
                    │              └ 추상명사 : beauty, courage, death
2. 보통명사 ┤
                    └ 가산명사   ┬ 구체명사 : a book, two chairs
                                   └ 추상명사 : an idea, experiences
3. 집합명사 : audience, class, family, committee
```

고유명사(proper noun)

1. 특정한 사람이나 사물, 장소를 가리키는 이름.

2. 셀 수 없는 명사(불가산명사 : uncount noun)이므로 원칙적으로 복수를 할 수 없고, 관사(a, the)가 붙지 않는다.

[사람이름]	Andrew, John Smith, Mr. Andrew Smith, President Kennedy
[가족, 친척 명칭]	Mom, Dad, Auntie, Uncle Fred
[지리이름]	Asia, India, Wisconsin, East Asia
[장소이름]	Madison Square, Wall Street, Western Avenue
[요일, 공휴일, 월, 계절 이름]	Monday, Easter(부활절), Christmas, April, Spring

Basic Grammar for English Tests

3. 장소 이름이나 건물, 하천, 신문 이름 등에는 관사 the가 붙기도 한다.

  [지리]   the Arctic(북극), the Middle East, the Equator(적도)
  [산맥]   the Alps, the Rocky Mountains
  [바다, 하천] the Pacific Ocean, the Mississippi River
  [사막]   the Sahara Desert
  [신문]   the New York Times, the Munhwa Ilbo

보통명사(common noun)

  ┌ 가산명사(count noun) : 수를 셀 수 있는 명사
  └ 불가산명사(non-count noun) : 수를 셀 수 없는 명사

1. 가산명사

   (1) 관사 a/an이 붙는다.

   (2) 숫자나 수량형용사 many, few, a few 등을 사용하여 정확한 수량을 표현할 수 있다.
       a bank, an envelope
       How many stamps? - Four stamps.

2. 불가산명사

   (1) 관사 a/an이 붙지 않는다.

   (2) 정확히 셀 수 없으나, 수량형용사 much, little, a little 등으로 용량 표현이 가능하다.
       Sugar is expensive.
       How much meat? - A little meat.

3. 불가산명사의 종류

   (1) 총칭명사

       baggage(화물), clothing(의복), equipment(장비), food(식품), fruit(과일),
       furniture(가구), garbage(쓰레기), hardware(철물), jewelry(보석), junk(쓰레기),
       luggage(화물), machinery(기계류), mail(우편물/미국), postage(우편/영국),
       makeup(화장), money(돈)/cash(현금)/change(잔돈), scenery(경치), time(시간)

   (2) 물질명사(material noun)

       [액체] blood, coffee, gasoline(gas), milk, oil, soup, tea, water
       [고체] bread, butter, cheese, cotton, glass, gold, ice, iron, paper, silver,
              soap, wood, wool
       [기체] air, nitrogen(질소), oxygen(산소), pollution(공해), smoke, smog, steam

[입자] chalk, corn, dust, flour(밀가루), grass, hair, pepper(후추), rice, salt, sand, sugar

구체명사(Concrete Nouns)와 추상명사(Abstract Nouns)

구체명사 ┌ 셀 수 있는 구체명사(Countable Concrete Nouns)
         └ 셀 수 없는 구체명사(Uncountable Concrete Nouns)

추상명사 ┌ 셀 수 있는 추상명사(Countable Abstract Nouns)
         └ 셀 수 없는 추상명사(Uncountable Concrete Nouns)

1. 셀 수 있는 구체명사

   [사람이나 사물의 이름]   a girl, a hose, a bottle, a desk
   [집단 이름]   an army(군대), a crowd(군중), a herd(짐승무리)
   [측정단위]   a kilo, a liter, a mile, a pound
   [전체의 부분(조수사)]   a bit, a piece, a slice

2. 셀 수 없는 구체명사

   [총칭명사]
   [물질명사]
   [행위]   dancing, driving, eating, studying, shopping, swimming
   [여가활동]   baseball, camping, chess, poker, soccer, tennis
   [언어]   Arabic(아랍어), Chinese, English, Spanish
   [학문분야]   chemistry(화학), engineering(기계공학), history, literature, psychology(심리학)
   [자연현상]   darkness, electricity, fog, heat, humidity, light, rain, snow, sunshine, thunder, wind
   [지리]   countryside(시골), seaside(바닷가)

3. 셀 수 있는 추상명사 : 관사(a/an)나 수(number)가 붙는다.

   an example, an idea, a hope, an origin, a proposal(제안), a remark(언급), a situation(상황), a statement(진술)

4. 셀 수 없는 추상명사

   abuse, advice, anger, assistance, beauty, business, capital(money), conduct, courage, damage, education, energy, evidence, fun, grammar, happiness, harm(피해), health, help, homework, honesty, housework, news, importance, information, knowledge, leisure, laughter(웃음), luck, music, peace, poetry, pride, produce, proof(증거), recreation, safety,

Basic Grammar for English Tests

scenery(장면), significance(중요성), sleep, space, strength(힘), stupidity(어리석음), time, travel, trouble, truth, vocabulary, violence(폭력), wealth, work

불가산명사가 가산명사로 쓰이는 경우

전체를 가리키는 총칭명사와 그 특정한 일부를 가리킬 경우

총칭명사 - 불가산명사	부분명사 - 가산명사
Education should be free. Light travels faster than sound. Noise is a kind of pollution. Oil is produced in the North Sea. Knowledge is power.	A good education is expensive. I need a light by my bed. Try not to make a noise. The North Sea produces a light oil. Foreign students should get a good knowledge of English.

교육은 자유로워야 합니다. / 훌륭한 교육은 비용이 많이 듭니다. // 빛은 소리보다 더 빨리 여행합니다. / 제 침대 옆에 전등이 필요합니다. // 소음은 일종의 공해입니다. / 떠들지 않도록 해. // 석유는 북해에서 생산됩니다. / 북해는 경유를 생산합니다. // 지식은 힘입니다. / 유학생들은 영어를 잘 알아야 합니다.

cf. clothing은 단수, clothes는 복수

불가산명사의 부분을 표현하는 조수사

a bar of chocolate, a cake of soap, a loaf of bread
a piece of furniture, a piece of jewelry, a cup of tea
a slice of meat, a glass of water, a bottle/pack of milk
a can/mug of beer, a piece/sheet of paper

Exercise 1 다음 글을 읽고, 빈칸에 필요하면 한정사 a, some을 골라 넣으시오.

  (1) wine is not cheap and   (2) good wine can cost a lot of money these days. Mr. Brown,   (3) New York wine merchant, recently lost   (4) bottle of wine worth $70,000. It was   (5) 1784 chateau Margaux which had once belonged to Thomas Jefferson, the third president of America. Mr. Brown took the bottle to   (6) wine testing and put it on   (7) table. The bottle was made of   (8) dark glass and a waiter didn't notice it. He hit it with   (9) tray, making   (10) large hole in it. Most of the wine was lost, but Mr. Brown was able to taste   (11) of it. He said it was "not very good", but the loss of the bottle was described as " (12) terrible tragedy".

◀ 명사의 수(number) - 단수/복수

규칙형 -s: 일반적인 대부분 명사의 복수형

cakes, forks, tapes, shirts, months, friends, hands, roads, bags, dogs, legs, bells, tables, walls, arms, dreams, names, lessons, pens, spoons, songs, chairs, doors, workers, eyes, ways, windows, mouths, truths

규칙형 -es

1. -oes

    potatoes, echoes, heroes, tomatoes

2. -os

    kangaroos, radios, studios, videos, zoos, photos, pianos

3. -f/-fe → -ves

    half→halves, knife → knives, leaf→leaves, life→lives, self→selves(자신), shelf→shelves(선반), thief→thieves, wife→wives, wolf→wolves

    * dwarf→dwarfs/dwarves(난쟁이), scarf→scarfs/scarves
    * 예외 : handkerchief→handkerchiefs(손수건), cliff→cliffs(벼랑)
      belief→beliefs(믿음), roof→roofs(지붕)

[iz]로 발음되는 경우

axes(도끼), boxes, bridges, buses, noises, noses, houses, oranges, pages, classes, bushes(덤불), dishes, matches(성냥), speeches(연설), taxes(세금)

1. 자음+y → -ies

    country→countries, baby→babies, strawberry→strawberries

    * **단, 고유명사인 경우는 그대로 -ys : Kennedys, Januarys, Harrys**

      Have you met the Kennedys?
      The last four Januarys have been very cold.
      케네디가 사람들을 만나도셨어요? / 최근 4년간 1월에 매우 추웠습니다.

2. 모음+y → -ys : days, keys, boys, guys, toys

    There are three James and two Harrys in our family.
    우리 가족 중에는 제임스가 셋 해리스가 둘 있습니다.

Basic Grammar for English Tests

불규칙한 복수형

Watch your p's and q's.
the 1990s/1990's, VIPs/VIP's(=Very Important Persons)

_{p자와 q자를 주의하십시오. / 1990년대, 귀빈들}

1. 철자가 바뀌는 경우

   brother→brethren/brothers, child→children, foot→feet, goose→geese, louse→lice, mouse→mice, tooth→teeth(치아), ox→oxen, man/woman→woman/women, penny→pence/pennies, policeman/policewoman→policemen/policewomen

2. 단수·복수의 형태가 같은 경우

   craft(공예품), deer, fish, means(수단), salmon(연어), series(연재물), sheep, species(종), trout(송어)

   ∗ **국명과 국민**

   the Chinese→a Chinese, the Vietnamese→a Vietnamese, the Swiss→a Swiss

집합명사(collective nouns) : 단수/복수 역할을 모두 한다.

1. audience, class, club, committee, company, council, couple, crew, crowd, family, gang, government, group, jury, staff(중역), team, union(노조)

   ⎡ What will you be doing while the family is/are on holiday?
   ⎣ Many families are in need of help.

   ⎡ The present government, which hasn't been in power long, is trying to control inflation.
   ⎣ The government, who are looking for a quick victory, are calling for a general election soon.

   The company is/are going to employ six staff.
   The jury is/are trying to decide now.
   The committee is/are meeting now.

   _{가족들이 휴가 중일 때 당신은 뭘 하실 건가요? / 많은 가족들이 도움을 필요로 하고 있습니다. / 현 정부는 정권을 잡은지 오래되지 않았는데, 인플레이션을 잡느라 애쓰고 있습니다. / 그 정부는 신속한 승리를 원하고 있어, 곧 총선을 할 것을 요구하고 있습니다. / 그 회사는 중역을 여섯 사람 채용하려 합니다. / 배심원은 지금 결정하려 합니다. / 위원회는 지금 회의중입니다.}

2. the majority(다수파), the minority(소수파), the public(대중), the youth(젊은이들)

⎡ Give the public what it wants/they want.
⎣ The youth of today is/are better off than we used to be.

* Youth is the time for action; age is the time for repose.

대중에게 그들이 원하는 것을 주시오. / 오늘날의 젊은이들은 우리 때보다 부유합니다. / 청춘은 행동의 시기이나, 노년은 휴식의 시기입니다.

3. cattle(소떼), the military(군대), people(사람들)/peoples(민족들), the police

⎡ Some people are never satisfied.
⎣ The police/The military have surrounded the building.

* There are too many peoples.
  The peoples of the Arab World have a common language.

어떤 사람들은 결코 만족을 하지 않습니다. / 경찰이/군대가 건물을 에워쌌습니다. / 민족들이 아주 많이 있습니다. / 아랍세계의 민족들은 공통어를 가지고 있습니다.

형태는 복수지만 단수동사를 받는 경우

[뉴스]　　　news
[게임]　　　billiards(당구), darts(다트), dominoes(도미노), checkers(서양장기)
[도시이름]　Athens(아테네), Brussels(브루셀), Naples(나폴리)

The news on TV is always depressing.
Billiards is becoming more and more popular.
Athens has grown rapidly in the past decade.

텔레비전의 뉴스는 언제나 침울합니다. / 당구는 점점 인기를 더해갑니다. / 아테네는 과거 10년간 급속히 성장하였습니다.

-ics로 끝나는 학문이름들도 단수

athletics(체육), linguistics(언어학), mathematics(수학 maths), physics(물리학), politics(정치학)

Mathematics is a compulsory subject at school. 수학은 학교에서 필수과목입니다.

* 단수/복수 양쪽을 취하는 경우

acoustics(음향학), economics(경제학), ethics(윤리학), phonetics(음성학), statistics(통계학)

Basic Grammar for English Tests

Statistics is a branch of economics.
Your statistics are unreliable.

Acoustics is a branch of physics.
The acoustics in the Festival Hall are extremely good.

통계학은 경제학의 한 분야입니다. / 당신의 통계는 믿을 수가 없어요. / 음향학은 물리학의 한 분야입니다. / 축제회관의 음향은 아주 좋습니다.

질병이름은 단수/복수 둘 다 취한다

measles(홍역), mumps(볼거리), herpes(포진)

German measles is a dangerous disease for pregnant women.
Mumps are/is fairly rare in adults.

독일홍역은 임산부들에게는 위험한 질병입니다. / 볼거리는 어른들에게는 꽤 드뭅니다.

보통명사-집합명사 둘 다 되는 단어

barracks(병영막사), crossraods(교차로), headquaters(본부), means(수단), kennels(개집), series(연재물), species(종), works(공장=factory)

This species of moth is rare.
There are thousands of species of butterflies.

All means have been used to get him to change his mind.
One means is still to be tried.

이런 종의 나방은 드뭅니다. / 나비는 수천 종이 있습니다. / 그의 마음을 바꾸는데 모든 수단이 이용되었습니다. / 한가지 방법이 아직 남아있습니다.

짝을 이루는 사물 - 복수

boots, glasses(안경=spectacles), jeans, pants, scissors(가위), shears(큰 가위), shoes, shorts(반바지), skates, skies(스키), slippers, socks, stockings, trousers

My trousers are torn.
I bought a pair of shorts and two pairs of trousers yesterday.

내 바지가 찢어졌습니다. / 저는 어제 반바지 한 벌과 바지 두 벌을 샀습니다.

* 복수형 명사 - 복수취급

belongings(소유물), brains(인재), clothes, congratulations, earnings(소득), goods(제품), manners(풍속), means, remains(재고), riches(부), stairs(계단), thanks

All my belongings are in this bag.
Were those clothes expensive?

제 소유물은 몽땅 이 가방 안에 있습니다. / 저 옷들은 비쌉니까?

단수/복수형의 뜻이 다른 경우

air(공기)/airs(태도), ash(재)/ashes(유골), contént(내용)/cóntents(목차), custom(관습)/customs(세관), damage(손상)/damages(배상금), drawer(서랍)/drawers(속바지), glass(유리)/glasses(안경/미국), manner(태도)/manners(풍속), minute(분)/minutes(회의록), pain(고통)/pains(수고), scale(규모)/scales(저울), saving(절약)/savings(저축), spectacle(광경)/spectacles(안경/영국), work(일)/works(공장)

외래어 복수형

album/albums, genius/geniuses(천재), focus/foci(초점), agenda/agendas(안건), antenna/antennae/antennas(안테나), formula/formulae/formulas(공식), index/indices/indexes(찾아보기), appendix/appendices/appendixes(부록), aluminum/alumina, bacterium/bacteria, curriculum/curricula(교육과정), datum/data(데이터), medium/media/mediums(매체), crisis/crises(위기), memorendum/memorenda(메모), phenomenon/phenomena(현상), analysis/analyses(분석), basis/bases(기본), oasis/oases(오아시스)

복합어의 복수형

boyfriends, flower shops, matchboxes(성냥), frying pans(후라이팬), onlookers, lookers-on(구경꾼), passers-by(행인), breakdowns(고장), forget-me-nots(물망초), grown-ups(어른), attorney general / attorneys general (검찰총장/미 법무장관)

고유명사의 복수형

The Phillips are coming to dinner.
There are three Janes and two Harrys in our family.
We've had two very cold Januarys in a row.

필립스씨 가족이 저녁식사에 옵니다. / 우리 식구 중에는 제인이 셋, 해리스가 둘 있습니다. / 2년 연속 1월이 추웠습니다.

Basic Grammar for English Tests

수(number)에 의한 복수형

1. dozen(12)/dozens of(수십의), hundred/hundreds of(수백의), thousand/thousands of(수천의)

    two dozen eggs, three hundred men, ten thousand dollars
    Hundreds of people are going to the demonstration.
    Thousands of dollars have been spent on the new hospital.
    I said it was a secret but she's told dozens of people.

    달걀 24개 / 3,000명의 남자들 / 1만 파운드 / 수백 명이 시위에 가고 있습니다. / 수천 달러의 돈이 새 병원에 쓰여졌습니다. / 제가 그건 비밀이라고 했건만, 그녀는 수십 명에게 말했습니다.

2. 복수명사 전체가 한 단위인 경우 - 단수

    Three weeks is a long time to wait for an answer.
    Two hundred dollars is a lot to spend on a dress.
    Forty miles is a long way to walk in a day.

    3주일은 대답을 기다리기에 오랜 시간입니다. / 2백 달러는 옷을 사는데 쓰기에는 많은 돈입니다. / 40마일은 하루에 걷기에는 먼 길입니다.

3. and로 연결되는 복합어 - 단수

    bacon and egg (베이컨과 달걀), bread and butter (빵과 버터)
    cheese and wine (치즈와 와인), fish and chips (생선튀김과 감자칩)
    lemon and oil (레몬과 오일), sausage(s) and mash (소시지와 으깬 감자)

    Bacon and egg is a popular food in America.
    Bacon and egg make a good food.

    베이컨과 달걀이 미국에서는 인기 있는 식사입니다. / 베이컨과 달걀은 좋은 식품이 됩니다.

Exercise 2 다음 문장의 주어-동사가 일치하도록 괄호에 적당한 말을 고르시오.

1. All governments (is/*are*) trying to control crime.
2. There (is/are) vermin in this restaurant.
3. The military (has/have) occupied the house.
4. The police (is/are) interested in this case.
5. A lot of people (has/have) signed the petition.
6. The acoustics in this room (is/are) very good.
7. (Is/Are) there any kennels in this area?
8. The statistics in this report (is/are) inaccurate.
9. (Is/Are) there any statistics for road accidents?
10. Many species of moth (has/have) disappeared.

11. This species (has/have) green and white spots.
12. Our works (has/have) a good dormitory.
13. My maths (has/have) got worse and worse!
14. There (is/are) crossroads every mile.
15. Where (is/are) the scissors?

◀ 명사의 성(gender)

명사에는 문법적인 성(gender, sex) 구별이 있다.
종류 ┌ 남성명사(masculine noun)
　　　├ 여성명사(feminine noun)
　　　└ 중성명사(neuter noun)

	명사의 예	대명사 구분
사람	man, actor, king ... woman, actress, queen ... guest, student, teacher ...	he she he/she
동물	bull/cow ...	it
사물	chair, table ...	it

남성명사와 여성명사가 완전히 다른 경우 : he/she

boy/girl, brother/sister, bridegroom/bride, father/mother, uncle/aunt, gentleman/lady, grandfather/grandmother, grandson/granddaughter, hero/heroine, husband/wife, king/queen, landlord(집주인)/landlady(여주인), male(남성)/female(여성), man/woman, nephew/niece, sir/madam, son/daughter

동물의 암수(♂/♀)가 구분된 경우 : it

bull(숫소)/cow(암소), cock(rooster)/hen(닭), dog/bitch(개), gander/goose(거위), pig/sow(돼지), ram/ewe(양), stallion/mare(말)

-ess를 붙여 여성명사를 만드는 경우 : he/she

actor/actress, god/goddess, heir(상속인)/heiress(상속녀), host/hostess, prince/princess, steward(승무원)/stewardess(여승무원), waiter/waitress

Basic Grammar for English Tests

남성명사에 man/he/male, 여성명사에 woman/she를 붙여 구분하는 경우

(1) 사람

policeman/policewoman, postman(mailman)/postwoman(mailwoman), horseman/horsewoman(승마기수), salesman/saleswoman(판매원)

(2) 동물

he-goat/she-goat (염소), wolf/she-wolf (늑대)

(3) 관념상 성이 어느 한쪽으로 고정된 경우

male model/model (모델), male nurse/nurse (간호사), judge/woman judge (판사), wrestler/woman wrestler (레슬링선수)

성 구분이 없으므로 대명사로 구분하는 명사

adult, artist, child, cook, cousin, darling, dear, doctor, enemy, foreigner, friend, guest, journalist, lawyer, manager, musician, neighbor, owner, parent, passenger, person, scientist, singer, speaker, stranger, student, teacher, tourist, visiter, writer

My neighbor is always telling us about his/her famous son.
제 이웃은 늘 유명한 자기 아들 이야기를 합니다.

Exercise 3 다음 문장이 성립하도록 빈칸에 알맞은 대명사를 넣으시오.

1. Jane is a fine musician. _She_ plays in the Philharmonic.
2. My lawyer told me _____ would ring me when he had the information I wanted.
3. Your visitor left _____ glasses behind when he came here yesterday.
4. Professor Johnson is a brilliant scientist. _____ should be given the Nobel Prize for her work.
5. Mrs. Lyon, our English teacher, really knows _____ grammar!
6. The artist, Rembrandt, painted several pictures of _____ wife.
7. How would you describe her? - Well, _____ is a student of about 18.
8. How do you know this passport belongs to a woman? - The owner has _____ photo in it.
9. My daughter works as a journalist and _____ has been very successful.
10. You don't know _____ so you should begin your letter 'Dear Madam'.

◀ 명사의 격변화(the genitive - the possessive form)

-'s/-s' 소유격

- a child's dream, the dog's kennel, Frank's new job
- an actress's career, a waitress's job
- children's games, the men's club, sheep's wool
- boys' school, girls' school, Ladies' College
- James's house, Charles's address, Doris's party

cf. (1) 이름이 s로 끝나는 경우

　　Mr. Jones'(s) car, Keats' works(키이츠의 작품), Socrates' death,
　　Jesus' Disciples(예수의 열두 제자), Venus' beauty(비너스의 아름다움)

(2) 복합명사의 소유격

　　My sister-in-law's father is a pilot. 사돈은 비행기 조종사이십니다.

(3) 집단소유격

　　John and Mary's bank balance (존과 메리의 은행잔고)
　　Scott and Karl's race (스콧과 칼의 경주)

of-소유격

the book of the film, the shade of a tree (나무그늘)
the bottom (/top/side/inside), of the box (상자의 밑/위/옆/안)
the cost of living (생활비), the price of success (성공의 가치)

이중소유격(double genitive)

this son of mine, a friend of yours, a cousin of hers
a friend of my father's (= one of my father's friends)
a play of Shakespeare's (= one of Shakespeare's plays)

cf. ┌ This is a picture of my father. (아버지께서 그리신 그림)
　　└ This is a picture of my father's. (아버지께서 소장하고 계신 그림 중의 하나)

Actual Test 12

다음 각 문장을 읽고 빈칸에는 알맞은 단어를 넣고, 밑줄 친 부분에서는 잘못된 부분을 찾아내시오.

1. Acoustics _____ one of the oldest of the natural sciences.
   - Ⓐ it is
   - Ⓑ is
   - Ⓒ as
   - Ⓓ being

2. Deer _____ the only animals with antlers in the world.
   - Ⓐ also
   - Ⓑ is
   - Ⓒ are
   - Ⓓ being

3. I saw _____ at the shopping center.
   - Ⓐ my sister's boyfriend
   - Ⓑ boyfriend of my sister
   - Ⓒ my sister boyfriend
   - Ⓓ a boyfriend of my sister's

4. Her apartment is within _____ from my house.
   - Ⓐ a stone's throw
   - Ⓑ a throw of a stone
   - Ⓒ stone's throw
   - Ⓓ the stone's throw

5. I am going to the _____.
   - Ⓐ books store
   - Ⓑ book's store
   - Ⓒ book store
   - Ⓓ books' store

6. Roger Brown is one of the most successful _____ in the United States.
   - Ⓐ newspaper reporter
   - Ⓑ newspaper's reporters
   - Ⓒ newspaper's reporter
   - Ⓓ newspaper reporters

7. A Republican, _____, from 1946 to 1958.
   - Ⓐ Ann Landers was mayor of Austin, Texas
   - Ⓑ and mayor of Austin, Texas, Ann Landers
   - Ⓒ mayor of Austin, Texas, Ann Landers was
   - Ⓓ Ann Landers, mayor of Austin, Texas

8. Dr. Bell received a patent in 1888 for the ideas of using light to relay sound
               A   B   C   D
   via a telephone.

9. Pioneer man in the West had more opportunities to work than they had had
        A   B   C   D
   in the East.

10. Fireworks, which started century ago in China, were brought to Europe by
                 A   B   C   D
    Marco Polo.

11. Predators and parasites share a basic characteristics: they both survive at
                                                A   B
    the expense of others.
        C   D

12. It is difficult to classify mathematics as simply an art or a science because
                 A   B
    they include elements of both.
        C   D

13. It was during the 1930's that the friendship between Hemingway and
                        A   B
    Fitzgerald reached their highest point.
                C   D

14. The manufacturing of transportation equipments ranks as California's
                    A   B   C
    principal industry.
         D

15. People are generally interested in seeing a famous movie star just as
            A   B   C
    they are in real life.
      D

16. A scientist bases its study on hypotheses that have been checked through
                 A   B   C
    careful experimentation.
      D

17. Jane's and John's car broke down again, but luckly they knew how to fix it.
         A   B   C   D

18. Members of the party were surprised by Clinton winning the election
                      A   B   C
    so easily.
     D

Unit 9

관사

◀ 부정관사 : a/an

a/an과 발음 : 철자에 관계없이 발음에 따라 자음 앞에서 a를, 모음(a, e, i, o, u)앞에서는 an을 붙인다.

> an umbrella / a uniform, an usual case / a union,
> a year, a university, a Europe / an eye, an ear,
> a hall/an heir, an honest man, an honor, an hour

a/an의 활용

1. 보통명사를 총칭해서 말할 경우

    A cat is a domestic animal. (= Cats are domestic animals.)
    A clever politician never promises too much.
    (= Clever politicians never promise too much.)
    고양이는 가축입니다. / 똑똑한 정치인은 너무 많은 것을 약속하지 않습니다.

2. 보통명사를 분류해서 말할 때

    (1) [국적] He's a French / an American.
        [직업] She's a doctor. He's an electrician.
        [종교] She's a Catholic. He's an Anglican.
              그녀는 천주교인입니다. 그는 성공회교인입니다.
        [정치] He's a Socialist. / She's a Republican.
              그는 사회주의자입니다. 그녀는 공화주의자입니다.

(2) [물건] It's a bottle-opener.
　　[곤충] It's a beetle.
　　[식물] It's a tree.

(3) 좀더 세분할 때 : kind/sort/type of
　　kind/sort/type of - 단수취급,
　　kinds/sorts/types of - 복수취급

　　This kind of flower is easy to grow.
　　This kind of roses is rare.
　　These kinds of trees are easy to grow.

3. 고유명사 앞에 a/an을 붙이는 경우

(1) 가족의 일원 : He's a Kennedy. (케네디 가문의 한 사람)
(2) 문학·예술작품 : It's a Picasso. (피카소 작품)
　　　　　　　　　It's a Shakespeare play. (셰익스피어 연극)
　　　　　　　　　It's a Rembrandt. (렘브란트 작품)
(3) 같은 특성 : an Edison (에디슨 같은 사람)
(4) 막연한 사람(Mr., Mrs., Miss 앞에서) :A Mrs. Jones is waiting to see you.
　　　　　　　　　　　　　　　　　　　(존스부인이라는 사람)

건강이나 질병을 말할 때 **a/an**을 붙이기도 하고 무관사로 쓰기도 한다

1. a/an이 붙는 경우

　　a cold, a headache, a sore throat, a broken leg

　I've got a headache/a cold.

2. a/an을 생략해도 되는 경우

　　catch (a) cold (감기 걸리다), have (an) earache (귀가 아프다),
　　have (a) backache/stomachache/toothache (등이/배가/치아가 아프다)

　I've had (a) toothache all night. 밤새 치통에 시달렸어요.

3. 복수형 질병에는 무관사 : measles(홍역), mumps(볼거리)
　My children are in bed with mumps. 우리 애들이 볼거리로 누워있어요.

4. 셀 수 없는 명사인 일반적인 질병에도 무관사 : flu(독감), gout(통풍), hepatitis(간염) …

I was in bed with flu for ten days.

cf. 단, 정관사 the는 flu, measles, mumps 등과 같이 쓴다.

He's got the flu/the measles/the mumps.

◀ 정관사 : the

the는 알고 있는 어떤 것을 가리킬 때, 단수/복수 보통명사, 불가산명사 등에 붙여 쓴다.

a/an과 the의 비교

어떤 단수 명사를 처음 지칭할 대는 a/an을 붙이고, 다음 재차 지칭할 때는 the를 붙인다.

I watched a car as it came up our road. The car stopped outside our house and a man got out. The man was carrying a case in his hand. With the case in his hand, the man looked like a salesman.

자동차 한 대가 집 근처 도로에 다가오는 것이 보였어요. 그 차가 우리 집 앞에 섰고, 한 남자가 내렸습니다. 그 남자는 손에 가방을 들고 있었습니다. 손에 가방을 든 것으로 보아 그 남자는 세일즈맨 같아 보였어요.

집단을 분류할 때 : the

1. the+국적명사 : 그 국민집단 전체를 가리킨다.

   the Egyptians, the Russians, the Americans, the Koreans, the Mexicans, the Germans, the Greeks, the British, the Dutch, the French, the English, the Spanish

   The Japanese admire the traditions of the Koreans. 일본인들은 한국인들의 전통을 존경합니다.

2. the+복수명사 : 그 집단 전체

   The Europeans are a long way from political unity. 유럽인들은 정치적인 단일체와는 거리가 멉니다.

3. the+집합명사/복수보통명사 : the police, the public 등은 특정집단 사람들을 지칭한다.

   This new increase in fares won't please the public.
   이번 새로운 요금인상은 대중들을 실망시킬 것입니다.

수식 받는 특정한 말에 the를 붙인다

문맥이나 상황, 문법적으로 한정(수식)을 받는 말에는 the를 붙인다.

1. 앞에 나온 말을 다시 쓸 때

    We stopped at a small village. The village was very pretty.
    우리는 어느 작은 마을에 도착했는데, 그 마을은 아주 예뻤습니다.

2. the 명사 of -

    The freedom of the individual is worth fighting for.
    The life of Napoleon was very stormy.
    개인의 자유는 쟁취할 가치가 있습니다. / 나폴레옹의 인생은 아주 폭풍 같았습니다.

3. 구(phrase)나 절(clause)로 수식 받는 경우

    The family (you're looking for) no longer lives here.
    The letters on the shelf are for you.
    (당신이 찾고 있는) 가족은 여기 더 이상 살지 않습니다. / 책장에 놓인 편지들이 당신에게 온 것들입니다.

4. 문맥의 상황으로 보아 한정된 명사

    [사람] Who's at the door? - It's the postman. 문간에 있는 사람이 누구지? 우체부야.
    [장소] Where's Jenny? - She's gone to the butcher's.
    　　　　　　　　　　　　 She's at the supermarket/in the garden.
    　　　　　　　　　　　　 He's gone to the cinema.
    　　　　　　　　　　　　 the doctor's, the mountains, the seaside, the bank ...
    [유일한 곳] the earth, the sea, the sky, the sun, the moon, the planets
    　　　　　　the solar system (태양계), the galaxy (은하계), the universe (우주),
    [물질명사] Pass me the salt, please.
    [전체의 일부분 지칭]
    　　사람의 신체부위 : the body, the brain, the head, the heart, the lungs,
    　　　　　　　　　　 the mind, the stomach, the veins ..
    　　　　　　　　　　 look in the face (얼굴을 바라보다)
    　　　　　　　　　　 strike one on the head (머리를 때리다)
    　　　　　　　　　　 pat one on the back (등을 두드리다)
    　　방의 부분 : the ceiling, the door, the floor ...
    　　사물의 부위 : the back/the front, the center
    　　　　　　　　 the inside/the outside, the top/the bottom ...

특정한 것을 지칭할 때

(1) 조직이나 단체 : the United Nations, the Boy Scouts (무관사 : Congress, Parliament)

(2) 선박이나 열차, 항공기 이름 : the Titanic, the Discovery, the Mayflower

(3) 공공기관 : the police, the government, the Army, the White House

(4) 책이나 영화 제목 : *The Odyssey, the Sound and the Fury, the Great Gatsby*

(5) 기후 : the climate, the weather, the temperature

(6) 역사적 사건 : the French Revolution, the Civil War

(7) 직책 : the president, the director

(8) 정당 : the Democratic Party, the Republican Party

(9) 신문 : *The Economist, The Times, The New York Times*

시간을 표현할 때

1. 시간의 추이 : the beginning, the middle, the end, the first/last, the next, the following day, the present, the past, the future …

   In the past, people had fewer expectations.
   과거에 사람들은 기대가 아주 적었다.

2. 하루중의 시간변화 : in the morning, in the afternoon, in the evening

   We spent the day at home. 우리는 낮에 집에 있었습니다.
   In the evening, we went out. 저녁에 우리는 외출했어요.
   cf. 무관사: at down(새벽에), at night

3. 날짜의 정식표기 (흔히 서수는 the를 요구한다.)

   the 24th of May, the 4th of July

4. 특정한 시간표현 : all the while (내내), at the moment (현재), for the time being (당분간), in the end (결국) …

   I'm afraid Mr. Jones can't speak to you at the moment.
   존스씨가 지금 당신에게 말을 못하는 것이 안타깝습니다.

Basic Grammar for English Tests

Exercise 1 다음 각 문장에서 관사가 필요한 빈칸에 a/an이나 the를 골라 넣으시오.

1. *An/The* individual has every right to expect personal freedom. *The* freedom of *the* individual is something worth fighting for.
2. Who's at _____ door? It's _____ postman.
3. When you go out, would you please go to _____ supermarket and get some butter?
4. I've got _____ appointment this afternoon. I've got to go to _____ doctor's.
5. We went to _____ theater last night and saw *Hamlet*. It's _____ wonderful play.
6. We prefer to spend our holidays in _____ country, _____ mountains or by _____ sea.
7. This is the front room. _____ ceiling and _____ walls need decorating, but _____ floor is in good order. We'll probably cover it with _____ carpet.
8. _____ history of _____ world is _____ history of _____ war.
9. They're building _____ new supermarket in _____ center of our town.
10. Where's your mother at _____ moment? I think she's in _____ kitchen.

◀ 무관사인 경우

복수보통명사

[사람]	Women are fighting for their rights.
[장소]	Museums are closed on Mondays.
[식품]	Beans contains a lot of fiber.
[직업]	Doctors always support each other.
[국적]	Italians make delicious ice-cream.
[동물]	Cats do not like cold weather.
[곤충]	Ants are found in all parts of the world.
[식물]	Trees don't grow in the Antarctic.
[상품]	Watches have become very accurate.

여자들은 그들의 권리를 위해 투쟁하고 있습니다. / 박물관들은 월요일에 닫힙니다. / 콩은 섬유질을 많이 함유하고 있습니다. / 의사들은 언제나 서로 돕습니다. / 이탈리아인은 맛있는 아이스크림을 만듭니다. / 고양이는 추운 날씨를 좋아하지 않습니다. / 개미는 세계 모든 곳에서 발견됩니다. / 남극에서는 나무가 자라지 않습니다. / 시계는 매우 정확하게 되었습니다.

단수 취급하는 불가산명사

[음식]	I like butter.
[음료수]	Water must be pure if it is to be drunk.
[물질]	Oil is essential for the manufacture of plastic.
[돈]	Money makes the world go round.
[색깔]	Red is my favorite color.
[동명사]	Smoking is bad for the health.
[활동]	Business has been improving steadily this year.
[운동경기]	Football is played all over the world.
[추상명사]	Life is short; art is long.
[정치이념]	Capitalism is a by-product of free enterprise.
[언어]	English is a world language.

버터를 좋아해요. / 물은 식수가 되려면 순수해야 합니다. / 석유는 플라스틱 제조에 필수입니다. / 돈은 세상을 돌게 합니다. / 빨간색은 내가 제일 좋아하는 색이다. / 흡연은 건강에 해롭습니다. / 올해는 사업이 꾸준히 향상되었습니다. / 축구는 전 세계에서 행해집니다. / 인생은 짧고, 예술은 길다. / 자본주의는 자유기업의 산물입니다. / 영어는 세계어입니다.

고유명사

1. 사람 이름

   Elizabeth was my mother's name.
   These tools are made by Johnson and Son.

   엘리자베스는 우리 어머니 이름이야. / 이 공구들은 존슨부자가 만들었습니다.

2. 요일, 월, 계절, 공휴일 이름

   Mondays are always difficult. Monday is always a difficult day.
   June is my favorite month.
   Spring is a lovely season.
   Christmas is the time for family reunions.

   월요일은 언제나 힘듭니다. 월요일은 언제나 힘든 날입니다. / 6월은 내가 제일 좋아하는 달이야. / 봄은 아름다운 계절입니다. / 성탄절은 가족재회의 시간입니다.

3. 유명작가나 작품을 가리킬 때 : Brahms, Keats, Leonardo, Rembrandt

   Bach gives me a lot of pleasure.
   Chaucer is very entertaining.

   바하 음악은 제게 많은 즐거움을 줍니다. / 초서 작품은 아주 재미있습니다.

4. 잡지명 : *Life, Newsweek, Time*

5. 학문이나 그와 관련한 명칭 : Art, Biology, Chemistry, Geography, History, Physics ...

기타 무관사의 예

1. 밤낮을 나타내는 시간의 명사. 흔히 전치사 at, by, after, before 등과 같이 쓰인다.

   at dawn / at day break (새벽에)
   at sunrise / at sunset/at noon / at night / at dusk / at midnight
   by day / by night, before morning,
   at/by/before/after 4 O'clock …

2. 식사 : breakfast, lunch, tea, dinner, supper

   Let's have breakfast. 아침 먹읍시다.
   John is at lunch. 존은 점심 중입니다.
   Dinner is served. 저녁식사가 나옵니다.

   cf. The breakfast I ordered still hasn't arrived.
   　　That was a very nice dinner.
   　　제가 주문한 아침이 아직 나오지 않았습니다. / 아주 멋진 저녁이었습니다.

3. 보통명사가 '본래의 목적'으로 쓰일 때

   bed, church, class, college, court, hospital, market, prison
   school, sea, town, university, work …

   He is in bed.
   He was sent to prison for four years. 그는 4년간 교도소에 보내졌습니다.
   The children went to school early this morning. 아이들은 오늘 아침 일찍 등교했습니다.

   cf. Your bag is under the bed. 네 가방은 침대 아래 있어.
   　　There is a meeting at the school at 6. 6시에 학교에서 회의가 있어요.
   cf. cathedral, factory, office 등은 관사를 쓴다.

4. 운송수단 : by bus, by bicycle, by bike, by boat, by bus, by car, by coach,
   by land, by plane, by sea, by ship, by train, by tube, on foot …

   We travelled all over Europe by bus. 우리는 버스로 유럽전역을 여행했습니다.

   cf. 수식을 받는 경우
   　　I came here on the local bus. 저는 시외버스를 타고 여기 왔습니다.
   　　You won't go far on that old bike. 저 낡은 자전거로는 멀리 못 갑니다.

5. 관용표현

   · arm in arm, bumper to bumper (자동차가 꼬리를 문 모양), face to face,
   from top to bottom (머리부터 발끝까지), hand in hand, side by side …

· at home, by sea, by mistake, at hand ...

6. 짝을 이루는 두 명사가 and로 연결된 경우

   day and night, father and son, husband and wife, light and dark
   young and old, pen and ink, sun and moon, body and soul
   east and west, knife and fork,

고유명사는 무관사가 일반적인데, 지명을 나타내는 경우는 the를 붙이기도 한다

bay, canal, channel, gulf, kingdom, ocean, republic, river, sea, strait, union ...

	무관사	정관사
지리학적 지명	Central Asia, Upper Austria, Outer Mongolia	the Arctic, the Equator (적도), the Middle East, the North Pole, the West
호수	Lake Michigan, Lake Erie, Lake Huron, Lake Ontario	
대양, 바다, 강		the Pacific Ocean, the Caspian Sea, the Nile (the River Nile), the Mississippi River, the Suez Canal
사막		the Gobi Desert, the Kalahari Desert, the Sahara Desert,
반도, 군도, 해협, 산맥	Everest, Christmas Island, Easter Island, Mont Blanc (몽블랑산맥)	the Korean Peninsular, the Bahamas (바하마군도), the Philippines (필리핀-섬으로 된 나라), the Magelan Strait (마젤란해협), the English Channel (영국해협), the Rocky Mountains, the Alps (알프스산맥)
나라이름	대부분의 국명어는 무관사 Turkey, Germany	연합국, 연방국가 이름과 몇몇 국가 the UK(the United Kingdom), the USA(the United States of America, the Vatican, the Netherlands, the Argentine, the Philippines

Basic Grammar for English Tests

a/an, the, 무관사의 비교

1. 대표단수

   The cobra is dangerous.
   = Cobras are dangerous.
   A cobra is very poisonous snake.

   코브라는 위험합니다. / 코브라는 독이 강한 뱀입니다.

2. 약자(abbreviations) 앞에서

   I've just bought an LP. (= a Long Playing record 구식음반)
   She is an M.A. (= Master of Arts 예술학 석사)
   I listen to the news on the BBC. (= the British Broadcasting Corporation)
   We are members of UNESCO. (= the United Nations Educational, Scientific and Cultural Organization 유네스코)
   CO_2 stands for Carbon Dioxide. CO_2는 이산화탄소를 나타낸다.
   Planes use radar. (= RAdio Detection And Ranging)

Exercise 2 다음 각 문장의 빈칸에 관사가 필요하면 a/an 또는 the를 넣으시오.

1. We must be home before _____ midnight.
2. We reached the village before _____ sunset.
3. _____ lunch I ordered was burnt.
4. Let's have _____ breakfast on the terrace.
5. Do you always have _____ tea at four?
6. We've come here to see _____ sunset.
7. I had _____ nice lunch at the Rits.
8. I'm really tired and I'm going to _____ bed.
9. Your shoes are under _____ bed.
10. We've bought _____ lovely new bed.
11. We took some photos outside _____ church.
12. We always go to _____ church on Sunday.
13. Have you ever worked in _____ factory?
14. Susan's in _____ class at the moment.
15. My father went to _____ sea when he was 14.
16. When do you hope to go to _____ university?
17. How long will she be in _____ hospital?
18. There's a strike at _____ hospital.
19. When do you get home from _____ office?
20. I don't know much about _____ life of _____ Napoleon.

Actual Test 13

다음 각 문장을 읽고 빈칸에는 알맞은 단어를 넣고, 밑줄 친 부분에서는 잘못된 부분을 찾으시오.

1. Jane always looks her best in _____ of red color.
   - Ⓐ dress
   - Ⓑ a dress
   - Ⓒ that dress
   - Ⓓ the dress

2. William Phillip, _____ United States senator from Minnesota, helped found the Republican party in 1860's.
   - Ⓐ was a
   - Ⓑ a
   - Ⓒ who, as a
   - Ⓓ who was as a

3. Usually the workers in this company are paid _____.
   - Ⓐ by an hour
   - Ⓑ by the hour
   - Ⓒ by a hour
   - Ⓓ by hours

4. _____ found four-leaf clover is usually considered a lucky sign.
   - Ⓐ It is rarely
   - Ⓑ Rarely
   - Ⓒ The rarely
   - Ⓓ Despite its being rarely

5. The stronger _____ magnetic field, the higher the voltage produced by a generator.
   - Ⓐ that the
   - Ⓑ is the
   - Ⓒ that the
   - Ⓓ the

6. <u>At birth</u> blue whales are twenty to thirty feet in length and <u>gain weight</u> at
      A   B
   the rate of three hundred pounds <u>the day</u> during the nursing <u>period</u>.
                                            C   D

7. A watt is <u>an</u> <u>unit</u> <u>of power</u> equal to one joule <u>a second</u>.
           A   B   C   D

8. I held an opinion that <u>a honest</u> man who married and <u>brought up</u> a family
                                      A   B
   did more service than <u>he</u> who remained <u>single</u> and only talked of thepopulation.
                              C   D

9. Dacktyloscopy, the study(A) of fingerprints, is providing(B) medical researchers(C) with clue(D) to the discovery of Alzheimer's disease.

10. Some scientists insist that the newborn infant is remarkably(A) capable organism from the moment(B) it(C) begins to breathe(D).

11. Famous physicists from all over(A) the world came(B) to America to celebrate(C) a(D) centennial of Einstein's birth.

12. Though the dust lay(A) heavy on the floor, it was evident that an(B) old house must once(C) have been a(D) great mansion.

13. Since beginning(A) of photography, inventors have tried(B) to make(C) photographs that reproduce natural(D) colors.

14. At end(A) of the Civil War the United States was ready to restart(B) with aroaring surge(C) the westward expansion which had been stopped for four(D) years.

15. People's earliest(A) effort at(B) understanding the structure of universe(C) took the form of myths(D).

16. New Orleans, which is in the Louisiana(A), is a large port(B) at the entrance of(C) the Mississippi River(D).

17. Gatherings of(A) more than(B) three persons were forbidden supposedly in the name of(C) the law and order(D).

18. After the church(A) the women(B) stood together in the churchyard(C) saying he(D) must be crazy.

Unit 10

대명사

◀ 인칭대명사

I think, therefore I am.
Are you ready, Jane?
John is here. He can't stay long.
If you see Jane please give her this message.
The windows are dirty. I must wash them.
I love swimming. It keeps me fit.
There's a knock at the door. Who is it? - It's the postman.
It's a lovely baby. Is it a boy or a girl?
Let's go, shall we?
Our curtains look dirty. They need a good wash.

◀ One

1. 부정대명사로서 일반사람(everyone/anyone)을 받는다.

   One should obey one's/his/her parents.
   One should take care of one's/his/her health.
   One should give oneself/himself/herself a holiday from time to time.

   * 일반사람을 you로 표현하기도 한다. You should obey your parents.

2. 사람이나 사물 등 보통명사(가산명사)를 대신하여 쓴다.

Have you seen **this dictionary**?
- Is that **the one** that was published recently?
Have you met **our American neighbors**?
- Are they **the ones** who moved here recently?

3. one을 쓸 수 없는 경우

(1) 불가산명사를 대신하여 쓸 수는 없다.

I like red **wine** better than white.
I like red wine better than white one. (x)

(2) 수사와 함께는 쓰지 못한다.

He has three **cars** and I have two.
He has three cars and I have two ones. (x)

(3) 기타

This bed is **my own**.
This bed is my own one. (x)
He has two sisters; **the elder** is more beautiful than the younger.
He has two sisters; the elder one is more beautiful than the younger one. (x)

◀ It

1. 비인칭 주어

[시간]	It's 8 o'clock.(시각) **It's** Tuesday.(요일) **It's** May 25.(날짜)
	It takes half an hour to get to work. 회사까지 1시간 걸립니다.
[날씨]	It's hot. **It's** raining. **It** rains a lot here.
[기온]	It's 37° Centigrade.
[거리]	It's 25 miles from Boston.
[조수]	It's high tide at 11:44. 11시 44분에 만조입니다.
[환경]	It's noisy in here.
[현재상황]	Isn't **it** awful! Isn't **it** a shame!
[since와 함께]	It's three years **since** we last met.
[It says]	**It says** there was a big fire in this hotel.

2. 가주어

   It is easy **to learn English**. (= **To learn English** is easy.)
   It is no use **crying over spilt milk**. (= **Crying over spilt milk** is no use.)
   It is certain **that he will come here**. (= **That he will come here** is certain.)
   It doesn't matter **when we arrive**. (= **When we arrive** doesn't matter.)

3. 가목적어

   Tim finds **it** difficult **to concentrate**.
   Jane thinks **it** funny **that I've taken up yoga**.
   You will find **it** pleasant **talking with her**.

   팀은 집중이 어렵다는 것을 알았습니다. / 제인은 제가 요가를 시작한 것이 흥미롭다 합니다. / 그녀와 이야기하는 것이 즐겁다는 걸 알게 될 것입니다.

4. It ~ that/who/whom 강조구문

   Helen phoned John last night.
   - It was **Helen who** phoned John last night.
   - It was **John who(m)** Helen phoned last night.
   - It was **last night that** Helen phoned Jack.

5. 소유격 : 소유형용사/소유대명사

   (1) 소유격

   [**소유형용사**] : my, your, his, her, its, one's, our, your, their
   　　　　　　　Jane amused **her** son. The cat drank **its** milk.
   [**소유대명사**] : mine, yours, his, hers, ours, yours(복수), theirs
   　　　　　　　That book is **mine**.

   (2) 이중소유격

   He is **your friend**. - He is **a friend of yours**.
   He is **my father's friend**. - He is **a friend of my father's**.

   (3) one's own/of one's own : 소유관계를 강조할 때

   I have **my own room**. - I have **a room of my own**.
   I have **my very own room**. - I have **a room of my very own**.

6. 신체 부위를 가리킬 때

   She cleaned **her teeth**.
   I hurt **my finger**.

Basic Grammar for English Tests

* the를 쓰는 경우

He **hit me in the face**.
He hit me in my face. (x)
A bee **stung her on the nose**. 벌이 그녀의 코를 쏘았습니다.
A bee stung her on her nose. (x)

◀ 재귀대명사(Reflexive Pronouns)

1. 분류

	1인칭	2인칭	3인칭
단수	myself	yourself	himself, herself, itself, oneself
복수	ourselves	yourselves	themselves

2. 일반적인 용법 : 명사를 강조한다.

I **myself** heard the explosion quite clearly.
You heard the explosion **yourself**.
The engine itself is all right, but the lights are badly damaged.
Tom's all right **himself**, but his wife is badly hurt.

제가 직접 폭발음을 아주 똑똑히 들었습니다. / 당신은 폭발음을 직접 들었어요. / 엔진 자체는 좋은데 라이트가 부서졌어요. / 톰 자신은 괜찮은데 그의 아내가 심하게 다쳤습니다.

3. 재귀대명사와 함께 쓰는 동사

absent, avail, accustom, pride, cut, dry, enjoy, hurt, introduce, kill

absent oneself from (= be absent from) 결석/불참하다
avail oneself of (= make use of) 이용하다
accustom oneself to (= get accustomed to) 익숙해지다
pride oneself on (= be proud of = take pride in) 자랑스러워하다

The soldier **absented himself** with leave for three weeks.
I cut myself shaving this morning. (not cut me)
She **killed herself**. (= commit suicide)

그 병사는 3일간의 휴가로 불참하였습니다. / 오늘 아침에 면도하다가 (얼굴을) 베었습니다. / 그녀는 자살하였습니다.

4. 일반동사의 목적어로 쓰이는 경우

   I got such a shock when **I saw myself** in the mirror.
   The boss **gave himself** a rise. (= gave a rise to himself)
   Help **yourself**! Make **yourself** at home! Don't upset **yourself**!

   거울에 비친 제 모습을 보고 충격을 받았습니다. / 사장은 스스로 재기하였습니다. / 많이 드세요! 편히 쉬세요! 흥분하지 마세요!

5. 전치사의 목적어로 쓰이는 경우

   Look after **yourself**!
   Strictly between **ourselves**, do you think she's sane?
   In **itself**, his illness is nothing to worry about.

   몸조심하세요! / 우리끼리 말인데, 그녀가 정상이라고 생각하세요? / 본질적으로, 그의 병은 걱정할 게 아닙니다.

   of itself (저절로)
   by oneself (= alone, unaided 혼자서)
   She made the dress by herself.(= without help 혼자 힘으로)
   She lives by herself.(= alone 홀로)
   for oneself (= unaided 홀로 힘으로)
   beside oneself (= insane 미친)

◀ 지시형용사/지시대명사(Demonstrative Adjectives and Pronouns)

1. 지시형용사로 쓰이는 경우와 지시대명사로 쓰이는 경우와 비교

지시형용사	지시대명사
I don't like **this** coat. I don't like **this** one.	I don't like **this**.
I found **this** wallet. I know **this** girl.	I found **this**.
Who are **these** people? Who are **those** people? (/men/women/children)	What's **this**/**that**? What are **these**/**those**? Who's **this**/**that**?

2. 지시대명사를 대신 받는 대명사 : it, they, he, she

   Is **this**/**that** yours? - Yes, it is.
   Are **these**/**those** yours? - Yes, they are.

This is Mrs. Jones. - She is in charge here.
That is Mr. Jones. - He is in charge here.

3. 지시사 this/that, these/those의 일반용법

(1) 소개할 때

This is Mrs. Brown.
This is Tom Smith, and this is Jane Mills.
This is Mr. and Mrs. Jones. (부부)

(2) 전화통화

This is Tom here. Is that you, Jane?

(3) 시간관계

[현재] I'll see you this afternoon.
These days life is hard for old people. 요즘 생활은 노인들이 살기에 힘들어요.

[과거] I was born in 1935. In those days there was no TV.
At that time my father was a miner.

(4) 비교구문에서 비교대상을 가리킨다 : that, those

It cost a lot more than that.
The area of the USA is larger than that of Brazil.
Tom's essays are better than those of the other boy.

(5) this - that (후자 - 전자)

Work and play are both necessary to health; this gives us recreation, and that gives us energy.

일과 놀이는 둘 다 건강에 필요한데, 후자는 우리에게 오락을 주고 전자는 에너지를 줍니다.

(6) 정도(degree)를 표시하는 지시부사

Does it really cost this/that much?
I can't walk this/that far! Let's get a taxi!

비용이 이렇게나/그렇게나 많이 들어요? / 저는 이렇게/그렇게 멀리 걸을 수 없어요! 택시를 타요!

◀ 부정대명사(Indefinite Pronoun)

1. 부정대명사의 종류

종류	-one	-body	-thing
1. every-	everyone	everybody	everything
2. some-	someone	somebody	something
3. any-	anyone	anybody	anything
4. no-	no one	nobody	nothing

5. each   6. either   7 neither

※ 모두 단수동사와 단수대명사를 가져온다.

Everyone knows what **he** has to do, doesn't **he**?
Everybody who has not bought a ticket should be in this line.
Something was under the house.
Somebody left **his book** on the desk.
Anybody who has lost **his ticket** should report to the desk.
Nobody works harder than John does.
None of the boys is here.
If **either** of you takes a vacation now, we will not be able to finish the work.
Each of the boys has **his own** bicycle.

2. 부정대명사의 용법

   (1) **some-**
      (긍정문에서) I met **someone** you know last night.
      (권유, 제안) Would you like **something** to drink?

   (2) **any-**
      (부정문) There is not **anyone** who can help you.
      (대답이 불확실한 의문문에서) Is there **anyone** here who's a doctor?

   (3) **no-** (not와 함께 쓰지 않는다)
      There's no one here at the moment.
      (= There's not anyone here at the moment.)

   (4) 부정대명사(-thing)와 형용사, 부정사의 관계 - 대개 뒤에서 수식한다.
      This is **something** special.
      This isn't **anything** important.

Basic Grammar for English Tests

* Money is **everything** to her. (모든 것, 가장 중요한 것)
  He always thinks **something** of himself. (상당한 것, 중요한 것)
  She was a humble **nothing** a few years ago. (중요하지 않은 것)
  돈은 그녀에서 모든 것입니다. / 그는 항상 자신을 대단하게 생각합니다. / 그녀는 몇 년 전만 해도 그저 그런 사람이었습니다.

Exercise 1 다음 각 문장이 완성되도록 괄호에서 적당한 대명사를 고르시오.

1. I go to school with (he/*him*) every day.
2. We like (our/ours) new car very much.
3. The dog bit (she/her) on the leg.
4. John (he/himself) went to the meeting.
5. You'll stick (you/your/yourself) with the pins if you are not careful.
6. Mary and (I/me) would rather go to the movies.
7. Everyone has to do (their/his) own research.
8. Just between you and (I/me), I don't like this food.
9. Monday is a holiday for (we/us) teachers.
10. (Her/Hers) car does not go as fast as (our/ours).

Exercise 2 다음 각 문장의 빈칸에 들어갈 적당한 부정대명사를 아래에서 골라 넣으시오.

> anything/anyone, nothing, anything, nobody/no one, somebody/someone, something

1. There's *nothing* in the clothes basket. It's empty.
2. Is there _____ in the clothes basket? - No, it's empty.
3. I've tried phoning, but every time I phone there's _____ in.
4. I've prepared _____ for dinner which you'll like very much.
5. I've never met _____ who is as obstinate as you are.
6. Would you like _____ to start with before you order the main course?
7. I know _____ who can help you.
8. He sat at the table, but he didn't have _____ to eat.
9. Is there _____ here who can speak Korean?
10. Does _____ want a second helping?

Actual Test 14

다음 각 문장을 읽고 빈칸에는 알맞은 단어를 넣고, 밑줄 친 부분에서는 잘못된 부분을 찾으시오.

1. I know of no other woman in the club who is as kindhearted as _____.
   - Ⓐ she
   - Ⓑ her
   - Ⓒ his
   - Ⓓ herself

2. Mr. Brown will take the party of students to the station and make sure that _____.
   - Ⓐ all of them have their tickets
   - Ⓑ she have her tickets
   - Ⓒ you all have your tickets
   - Ⓓ all of them have his tickets

3. When heat travels by conduction, _____ moves through a material without carrying any of the substance with it.
   - Ⓐ what it
   - Ⓑ which
   - Ⓒ it
   - Ⓓ and

4. _____ that the creation of the sun, the planets, and other stars began with the condensation of a space gas cloud.
   - Ⓐ Believing
   - Ⓑ To believe
   - Ⓒ The belief
   - Ⓓ It is believed

5. Tape recordings, CD and computers have made _____ to store date conveniently and accurately.
   - Ⓐ easier
   - Ⓑ it easier
   - Ⓒ easier than
   - Ⓓ it is easier

6. The tenor in the opera last night is a favorite _____.
   - Ⓐ to me
   - Ⓑ to mine
   - Ⓒ of mine
   - Ⓓ of me

7. Unlike the budgets of other nations, _____ focuses chiefly on expenditures.
   - Ⓐ and the United States
   - Ⓑ that of the United States
   - Ⓒ the United States, which
   - Ⓓ which the United States

8. Undoubtedly, it was he, not me, who recommended that the ceremony be
   A   B   C   D
   cancelled.

9. No administrator or visitor can enter a classroom unless they are invited
   A   B   C   D
   by the teacher.

10. Even the best of drivers can have an accident if you are very tired and
    A   B   C
    driving conditions are bad.
    D

11. George Miller, a physician, became known for him work in the field of
                   A   B   C   D
    dermatology.

12. The field of guidance and counseling was still in its infancy in 1928 when
                                A   B   C
    Sarah Hatcher entered them.
                         D

13. The vanilla vine stretch out tiny rootlets by which the vine attaches oneself
                    A   B   C   D
    to trees.

14. No one who will not try to help the other people develop his abilities
    A   B   C
    deserves to have friends.
    D

15. Charles the Conqueror built the Tower of London to protect himself from
                          A   B
    them he had conquered.
    C   D

16. For them interested in nature, the club gives hikes and overnight camping
        A   B   C
    each week during the summer.
              D

17. No one is allowed on the building except employees and them who have a
    A   B   C
    valid identification card.
    D

Unit 11

한정사와 수량표시

◀ 한정사(Determiners)

흔히 명사 앞에 붙어서 수량을 표시하는 어휘

한정사의 종류

1. 부정대명사, 부정형용사

   > all, another, any, both, certain, each, either, enough, every
   > half, last, neither, next, no, other, own, same, some, such, whole ...

   There are **some** dogs in the garden.
   There were **no** eggs in the shop.

2. 수량형용사(Quantifiers)

   > few, least, less, little, many, more, most, much, plenty, several ...

   Please give me **some more** of these.
   There is **little** water in this pond.

한정사의 역할

1. 한정사+복수명사

   > both, a couple of, dozens/hundreds of, (a) few, fewer,

> the fewest, a/the majority of, (not) many, a minority of,
> a number of, several, two/three...

We have **fewer** students majoring in maths than in English.
We've had **a lot of** answers.
I'll lend you **some of these** books.
I'll lend you **a few of my** books.

2. 한정사+단수명사

> all (of) the, another, any (of the), each, either, every,
> half (of) the, most of the, neither, no, none of the, one,
> the only, the other, some (of the), the whole (of the) ...

(1) 항상 단수를 받으며 가산명사와 함께 쓴다.

One student was late to class.
Each student has his schedule.
Every student has his own schedule.
Every student has a schedule.

(2) **One of the students was** late to class.
Each (one) of the students has his schedule.
Everyone of the students has his own schedule.
(= All of the students ...)
Everyone of the students has a schedule.

3. 한정사+복수명사/불가산명사(공통)

(1) 종류

> some (of the), any (of the), all (the), hardly any, enough,
> half (of) the, a lot of, lots of, more, most (of the), no, none of the,
> the other, part of the, plenty of, the rest of the ...

There **aren't any cars** on the road at the moment.
There **isn't any traffic** on the road at the moment.
지금 거리에는 자동차가 없습니다. / 지금 거리에는 통행이 없습니다.

(2) 수량 표시어

> a lot of, lots of, plenty of

- **A lot of students** missed my lecture yesterday.
- **A lot of the students** who missed my lecture yesterday want to borrowed my notes.

- **None of the/this milk** can be used.
- **Part of this food** will be for supper.

- **The rest of this food** will be for supper.
- **Put the rest of those biscuits** in the tin.

Exercise 1 다음 각 문장의 괄호에서 적당한 한정사를 골라 문장을 완성하시오.

1. We have imported (*fewer*/less) videos this year than last year.
2. There has been (fewer/less) demand for videos this year than last year.
3. (A lot of/Much) vehicles have just been recalled because of a design fault.
4. (A lot of/Many) effort has been put into this project.
5. There isn't (much/many) hope of finding the wreck.
6. There aren't (much/many) dictionaries that can compare with this one.
7. (Most/Most of the) book was written by someone else.
8. (Most/Most of) magazines carry advertisements.
9. (Most/Most of) metal is liable to rust.
10. I'd like (a few/a little) milk in this coffee, please.
11. This room needs (a few/a little) pictures to brighten it up.
12. (A good deal of/Several) businesses have gone bankrupt this year.
13. There aren't (any/some) chocolates left!
14. There isn't (any/some) time to waste.
15. We've had (enough/hardly any) trouble with this machine already.
16. There have been (a good deal of/hardly any) accidents on this corner this year.
17. We can't accept the estimates. (Either/Neither) estimate is low enough.
18. (Both/Neither) examples prove that I am right.
19. There have been (no/any) changes in the new edition.
20. There has been (no/any) change in the new edition.

some, any, no/none의 용법 비교

1. some

    (1) 특별히 수량이 표시되지 않은 명사에 쓴다.

    There are **some letters** for you.
    There's **some bread** in the basket.

    (2) 긍정문에서 수량표시

    There are **some eggs** in the fridge.
    There is **some milk** in the fridge.

    (3) 권유 : yes를 기대하는 의문문에서
    Would you like **some (more) coffee**?

    (4) some = certain, same
    Some people have no manners.

2. any

    (1) 대답이 불확실한 의문문에서
    Would you like **any sugar**? - I have some, thank you.

    (2) 부정문에서, 흔히 not를 동반한다.
    We haven't got **any shirts** in your size.
    There isn't **any milk** in the fridge.

3. no : 흔히 명사를 부정하기 위해 그 앞에 쓴다.
    none : 스스로 대명사다.

    (1) 단수와 복수 가리지 않는다.

    There **aren't any buses** after midnight.
    There **are no buses** after midnight.

    (2) not와 no, never는 함께 쓰지 않는다.

    I could get no information.(o)
    I couldn't get no information.(x)

Exercise **2** 다음 각 문장이 바르게 성립하도록 괄호에서 적당한 한정사를 고르시오.

1. There are (*some*/any) eggs in that basket.
2. He's 89, but there's still (some/any) life in him.
3. Get (some/any) meat and salad for the weekend.
4. Some people don't eat (some/any) meat.
5. You won't find (some/any) biscuits in that tin.
6. Get (some/any) bread while you're out.
7. You need to earn (some/any) money.
8. There isn't (some/any) news of him.
9. Are there any more potatoes? - Yes, there are (some/any) potatoes in the dish.
10. May I have (some/any) more tea? - Yes, of course.

much와 many의 용법 비교

much는 불가산명사를 수식하고, many는 가산명사를 수식한다.

1. 긍정문에서 **Much** has been done to improve conditions of work.
   Many teachers dislike marking piles of exercise books.

2. 부정문에서 I haven't **much time**.
   There aren't **many pandas** in china.

3. 의문문에서 Is there **much milk**?
   Have you had **many inquiries**?

4. 'not so much (A) as (B)'의 비교구문

   It's not so much a bedroom, more a studio. (~라기 보다는 차라리)
   It's not so much that the dislikes his parents, as that(/but that) he wants to set up on his own. (~한다기 보다는 오히려)

a lot of/lots of 용법

1. 가산명사, 불가산명사, 단수/복수 명사에 모두 쓰인다.

   I've got a lot of (/lots of) time.
   I've got a lot of (/lots of) books.

Basic Grammar for English Tests

2. 수식 받는 명사의 수에 영향을 받는다.

There **has** been **a lot of** (/lots of / plenty of) **gossip** about her.
There **have** been **a lot of** (/lots of / plenty of) **inquiries**.

few-fewer-the fewest의 용법 : 셀 수 있는 복수명사에 쓴다.

1. few : 부정적 의미
   a few : 긍정적 의미

   Jane has had **very few opportunities** to practise her English. (= hardly any at all ~)
   The police would like to ask him **a few questions**. (= some, a small number ~)

   제인은 영어를 연습할 기회가 아주 적었습니다. / 경찰은 그에게 몇 가지 질문을 하고 싶었습니다.

2. 다른 수식어와 함께 쓰는 경우

   How many do you want? - **Just a few** please. (= a limited number, not many)
   There are **only a few** seats left. (= very few, hardly any)

   얼마나 원하세요? - 약간만요. / 남아 있는 좌석이 아주 적었습니다.

3. fewer — the fewest

   Fewer/The fewest videos were sold this year than last.

   올해는 작년보다 비디오가 더 적게 팔렸습니다.

little-less-the least의 용법 : 불가산명사나 단수명사 수식

1. little은 부정 의미

   He has **very little** hope of winning this race. (= hardly any at all)
   We climbed all day but made **little** progress. (= not as much as was expected)

   그는 이 경주에서 우승할 가망이 거의 없습니다. / 우리는 하루종일 등반을 했으나 진전이 거의 없었습니다.

2. a little은 긍정 의미

   I'd like **a little** time to think about it please. (= some, a small quantity ~)

   그 점에 대해 생각할 시간을 좀 주세요.

3. less — the least

Less oil was produced this year than last.
Less and less people can afford to go abroad for their holidays.
Political programs on TV attract **the least viewers**.

올해는 작년보다 석유가 덜 생산되었어요. / 휴일에 해외에 나갈 수 있는 사람들이 점점 더 적어져요. / TV의 정치프로그램은 사람들에게 거의 매력을 주지 못해요.

enough의 용법

가산명사/불가산명사를 모두 수식하고, 긍정/부정/의문문 도두에 쓰인다.

1. Have we got **enough books** to read while we are on holiday?
   Have we got **enough food** in the house to last the next few days?

   휴일에 읽을 책은 충분히 가져왔나요? / 남은 며칠을 버틸 수 있는 음식이 집에 충분히 있나요?

2. Is there **enough** hot water for me to take a bath? (양)
   Is **the water hot enough** for me to take a bath? (정도)

   제가 목욕할 수 있을 더운물이 충분히 있나요? / 물이 제가 목욕할 수 있을 만큼 충분히 더운가요?

Exercise 3 아래에서 적당한 한정사를 골라 빈칸에 넣어 각 문장을 완성하시오.

> few, a few, little, a little

1. There are very *few* scholarships for students in this university.
2. I'm sorry, but I'm going to have to ask you for _____ more time to pay this bill.
3. If you don't hurry, we'll miss our train. There's _____ time to spare.
4. It's a difficult text. I've had to look up quite _____ words in the dictionary.
5. I can't spare any of these catalogues. There are only _____ left.
6. I can't let you use much of this perfume. There's only _____ in the bottle.
7. If what you say is true, there is _____ we can do about it.

◀ 전치한정사(Predeterminers)

명사를 수식하는 다른 어떤 한정사보다 앞에 오는 한정사들을 말한다.

All, both, and half

both, all, half는 모두 복수명사를 수식한다.
all, half는 불가산명사나 단수명사를 수식하기도 한다.

1. Both ('둘'- 수)

    Both books are expensive.
    Both the/my/these books are expensive.
    Both of the/my/these books are expensive.
    Both of us left early. (= We both left early.)

2. All (명사 전체의 수량)

    All books are expensive.
    All the/my/these books are expensive.
    All of the/my/these books are expensive.
    All (of the) bread was fresh.
    All (of the) country was against it.
    All of them left early. (= They all left early.)

3. Half (복수명사/불가산명사)

    Half the(/my/these) eggs are rotten.
    Half of the(/my/these) eggs are rotten.
    Half (of) the country was against it.
    Half (of) the bottles are empty. (= Half of them are not empty.)

none of과 neither of : all과 both의 부정어

All the girls left early. ↔ None of the girls left early.
Both the girls left early. ↔ Neither of the girls left early.

all과 whole의 비교

all my business : my whole business
all my life : my whole life
all the time : the whole time
all my hair, all the money : the whole situation, the whole story

1. 둘 다 흔히 추상명사와 함께 쓰지만 가끔 단수보통명사와 함께도 쓴다.

   He ate all the loaf by myself. = He ate the whole loaf by myself.

2. 시간의 명사와 함께

   I waited all (the) week for him to answer.
   = I waited the whole week for him to answer.

3. 복수명사와 함께

   All forests in North Africa were destroyed during Roman times.
   (= every single one of them ~)
   Whole forests in North Africa were destroyed during Roman times.
   (= entire areas of forest ~)

all과 every

all은 스스로 명사로 쓰일 수 있으나, every는 반드시 명사를 수식한다.

1. I've read all the books. (= this whole collection : 전체 집합)
   She's used all the butter. (= the whole amount : 전체 양)
   I've read every book in the library. (= every single one : 개체나 개별 집단)

2. 흔히 every는 시간의 명사와 같이 쓰인다.

   every day, every week, every third day, every six week, every other day ...

   I work **every other day**: Monday, Wednesday and Friday. (격일로)
   Monica spent **all day** with us. (= one whole day 종일)
   Monica spent **every day** with us while she was here on holiday. (매일)

every와 each

둘 이상의 특정한 셀 수 있는 명사를 수식한다.
단수를 받는다.
each는 개별 명사를 각각 언급한다.

1. **Every child enjoys** Christmas.
   Almost every building was damaged in the earthquake.
   I answer **every single letter** I receive.
   Not every house on the island has electricity. (each 앞에는 not를 붙이지 않는다.)

Basic Grammar for English Tests

모든 어린이들이 성탄절을 즐거워합니다. / 거의 모든 건물이 지진으로 파괴되었습니다. / 저는 받은 모든 편지에 각각 답장을 씁니다. / 섬에 있는 모든 집에 전기가 들어가는 것은 아닙니다.

2. Each child in the school was questioned.
   Every/Each time I wash the car it rains.
   Each of us is responsible for **his/our** actions.
   Give the delivery men $5 **each**.

   학교의 어린이들은 각자 질문을 받았습니다. / 세차할 때마다 비가 옵니다. / 우리 각자는 자신의 행위에 책임이 있습니다. / 배달원들에게 5달러씩 주세요.

Exercise 4 다음 각 문장에 적당한 한정사를 괄호에서 고르시오.

1. Nearly (each/*every*) home in the country has television.
2. Here is something for (each/every) of you.
3. Not (each/every) students is capable of learning English.
4. Our motoring organization will give you (each/every) assistance if you break down.
5. The admission ticket cost us $7 (each/every).
6. They seem to be repairing (each/every) road in the country.
7. They are (each/every) fortunate to have such a good start in life.
8. They both did well and they will (each/every) receive prizes.
9. You've been given (each/every) opportunity to do well in this company.
10. I've phoned him twice, but he's been out on (each/every) occasion.

another, others, the other, the others의 용법 비교

'another, others'는 무한정이고 'the other, the others'는 한정적이다.

1. I need **another three driving lessons** before my test.
   There must be **another way** of solving the problem; that can be the only way.
   There must be **other ways** of solving problem.

2. This seat is free; **the other seat** is taken.
   These seats are free; **the other seats** are taken.

3. 특정한 것을 선택하거나 구분할 때

I don't like **this shirt**. ⎡ Can I try **the other one** please?
　　　　　　　　　　　　 ⎣ Can I try **another** (one)?
I'll take **these shirts** but leave **the others**.
One has buttons and **the other** hasn't.
Some people enjoy exercise, **others** don't.

each other와 one another

each other는 두 사람을, one another는 둘 이상일 경우에 쓰는 차이가 있으나, 흔히 일상적으로는 구분 없이 쓰기도 한다.

Karen and Dave are deeply in love with **each other**/one another.
Those two are always copying **each other's**/one another's homework.
카렌과 데이브는 서로 깊이 사랑하고 있습니다. / 저 둘은 항상 서로의 숙제를 베끼고 있습니다

either와 neither

1. ⎡ either(= one or the other : 이것 아니면 저것 - 둘을 따로따로 생각)
   ⎣ neither(= not one and not the other : 이것도 아니고 저것도 아님)

   Do you want an appointment at 9 or at 10?
   - **Either time** is difficult. / **Neither time** is convenient.

2. either ~ or와 neither ~ nor

   You can have **either** this one **or** that one.
   Neither this house **nor** the house next door has central heating.

수량형용사의 수와 동사의 일치

1. 명사의 수에 맞춘다

   Most of **us have** experienced sorrow in **our lives**.
   Most of our **steel is** imported.
   Neither of **us is/are** happy about the situation.
   None of my **friends has/have** been invited to the party.

2. 동사와 가까이 있는 명사를 따른다.

   Neither my brother nor **my sister is** red-haired
   Neither my brother nor **my sisters are** red-haired.

Basic Grammar for English Tests

Neither my brothers nor **my sister is** red-haired.
Neither James nor **I am** interested.

수의 표현

1. 서수와 기수의 표현

   The **first three** cars are Korean made.
   It's the fifth of October/October the fifth/October 5.
   19th century = the nineteenth century
   World War II = World War Two = the Second World War
   Vol. III = volume three = the third volume
   Lesson 5 = Lesson Five = the Sixth Lesson
   page 25 = page twenty-five = the twenty-fifth page
   Act IV = Act Four = the Fourth Act
   Henry 5 = Henry the fifth

2. 명사가 형용사 역할을 할 때는 단수 취급한다.

   a five-dollar bill (5달러 지폐)
   a six year old boy (6살 난 소년)
   the two three-hour periods (3시간 짜리 2회)
   a three-hundred-**year**-old three (300년 된 나무)
   cf. The tree is about the three hundred **years** old.

3. 복수로 표현된 복합명사가 단일개념일 때는 단수 취급한다.

   Five years *is* a long time.
   Ten dollars *is* all I have.
   cf. **Six months** *have* passed since I saw you last year.

Exercise 5 다음 각 문장의 빈칸에 들어갈 말을 아래에서 골라 넣으시오.

> another, other, the next, the other, others

1. John came to see me <u>*the other*</u> day. It was last Friday, I think.
2. I met two strangers on the way to work. One of them greeted me and _____ didn't.
3. Some people like to have the windows open all the time; _____ don't.

4. I can't see him today. I'll have to see him _____ day.
5. We spent the night in a small village and continued our journey _____ day.
6. Bill and _____ boy are playing in the yard. Jane and _____ girls are in the front room.
7. There must be _____ road that leads to the city center.
8. There must be _____ roads that lead to the city center.

Exercise 6 다음 문장의 괄호에서 적당한 말을 고르시오.

1. When shall we meet: at 7 or at 7:30? - I don't mind. (*Either*/Neither) time is convenient for me.
2. You can't use those screwdrivers. (Either/Neither) of them is suitable for the job.
3. I don't know who's on the phone. It's (either/neither) your mother or your aunt.
4. I met John a year ago, but I've (either/neither) seen him nor heard from him since.
5. Say what you like about those two applicants. I don't like (either/neither) of them!
6. I know you sent us two letters, but we have received (either/neither) of them.

[참고] 한정사의 수식어순

형용사 역할 : 가산명사 수식

주어		명사	동사	보어
한정사				
관사	first	단수명사	단수동사	
The	second next last	house car desk	.s	small. large. old. new.
지시형용사 소유격	This/That My/Your/John's			
	서수	기수	복수명사	복수동사	
The	first second next last	two three	houses cars desks	are	

Unit 11 한정사와 수량표시 | 219

Basic Grammar for English Tests

(*ex*) The second car is new.
　　　The last house is large.
　　　The first two houses are old.

대명사 역할 : 가산명사 수식

주어				동사	보어
(한정사)		(대명사)		(단수)	
One Each The first The second … Neither	of	them		is	bad.
All Both		these those		(복수)	
Several Two or Three None The first/next/last two or these three Few / A few A large/small number Some / Half Many / Most A lot / Lots		한정사	복수명사	are	
		the these those my/his John's	eggs		

대명사 역할 : 불가산명사 수식

주어				동사	보어
한정사		대명사			
All/Not all Most Some Half None Enough/Not enough Much/Not much A great(good) deal Little/A little A lot/Lots	of	it this that		is	fertile.
		한정사	복수명사		
		the this/that our/their … Mr. Green's	farm land		

가산명사에 more를 덧붙이는 경우

주어	동사	보어 또는 목적어		명사	장소부사
		한정사			
There are We have		plenty of a lot of A large(/good) number of enough		books	in the room.
		some several We have a few/few two or three many no	(more)		
		a lot/lots plenty			

불가산명사에 more를 덧붙이는 경우

주어	동사	보어 또는 목적어		명사	장소부사
		한정사			
There is We have		some, (not) much no, a little	(more)	tea coffee bread sugar meat salt	in the store room.
		a great/good deal a lot/lots plenty	more		
		a lot of a large quantity/amount of plenty of (not) enough			

Basic Grammar for English Tests

Exercise 7 다음 각 문장에서 알맞은 한정사를 고르시오.

1. He doesn't have (many/*much*) money.
2. I would like (a few/a little) salt on my vegetables.
3. She bought (that/those) cards last night.
4. There are (less/fewer) students in this room than in the next room.
5. There is (too much/too many) bad news on television tonight.
6. I do not want (these/this) water.
7. This is (too many/too much) information to learn.
8. A (few/little) people left early.
9. Would you like (less/fewer) coffee than this?
10. This jacket costs (too much/too many).

Exercise 8 다음 각 문장이 바르게 성립하도록 괄호에서 알맞은 동사를 고르시오.

1. Some of the fruit in this bowl (*is*/are) rotten.
2. Some of the apples in that bowl (is/are) rotten.
3. Half of the students in the class (is/are) from Arabic-speaking countries.
4. Half of this money (belongs/belong) to you.
5. A lot of the students in the class (is/are) from Southeast Asia.
6. A lot of clothing in those stories (is/are) on sale this week.
7. One of the chief materials in bones and teeth (is/are) calcium.
8. (Does/Do) all of the children have their books?
9. (Does/Do) all of this homework have to be finished by tomorrow?
10. (Does/Do) any of you know the answer to that question?

Actual Test 15

다음 각 문장을 읽고 빈칸에는 알맞은 단어를 넣고, 밑줄 친 부분에서는 잘못된 부분을 찾으시오.

1. Jane has never interested in what _____ has to say.
   - Ⓐ no one else
   - Ⓑ anyone else
   - Ⓒ somebody else
   - Ⓓ nobody else

2. In the United States Senate, _____, regardless of population, equally has one senator.
   - Ⓐ each state
   - Ⓑ where each state
   - Ⓒ each state that is
   - Ⓓ for each state

3. Amy and Laura were such close friends that they frequently exchanged gifts with _____.
   - Ⓐ each one
   - Ⓑ each other
   - Ⓒ the other
   - Ⓓ one another

4. _____ other big cats, leopards climb trees well.
   - Ⓐ The most unlike
   - Ⓑ They are unlike most
   - Ⓒ Unlike the most
   - Ⓓ Unlike most

5. I think Bush didn't win the election. He certainly didn't. _____ the people in the country voted for his opponent.
   - Ⓐ Almost all of
   - Ⓑ Most all of
   - Ⓒ Most of all
   - Ⓓ Almost the whole of

6. Glass that has been tempered may be up to _____.
   - Ⓐ five times as hard as normal glass
   - Ⓑ as hard as normal glass five times
   - Ⓒ hard as normal glass times five
   - Ⓓ normal glass as hard as five times

7. The final exam will be on the first half of the textbook. This means we'll have to finish _____.
   - Ⓐ fifteenth chapter
   - Ⓑ fifteen chapter
   - Ⓒ chapter fifteen
   - Ⓓ chapter fifteenth

8. _____ have ever had a more lucky chance at the Museum of Modern Art in New York than David Lawrence did.
   Ⓐ Few artists
   Ⓑ The few artists
   Ⓒ The artists are few
   Ⓓ Few are the artists

9. Because he has bought a large apartment, he will have to buy _____ furniture also.
   Ⓐ many
   Ⓑ a lot of
   Ⓒ a few
   Ⓓ quite a few

10. Within a few minutes, _____ jubilant Koreans poured in the streets.
    Ⓐ ten thousands
    Ⓑ ten thousand of
    Ⓒ tens of thousands of
    Ⓓ tens of thousand of

11. I bought _____ at the discount shop today.
    Ⓐ Only a French bread leaf
    Ⓑ A French bread loaf only
    Ⓒ Only a loaf of French bread
    Ⓓ A loaf of French bread only

12. <u>Nearly</u> half of the <u>ancient</u> meteor craters <u>has been</u> found in central and
       A   B   C
    <u>eastern</u> California.
       D

13. <u>All the day long</u> he did not once cause his wife <u>to worry</u> or be afraid,
          A   B
    except when he shot some <u>unsuspecting</u> animal <u>with</u> his gun.
                                  C   D

14. <u>Some the</u> large <u>paper-making</u> machines can produce more than three
        A   B
    million <u>pounds</u> of paper in <u>a single day</u>.
              C   D

15. There has been <u>hardly no sign</u> of agreement <u>as yet</u> <u>between</u> the management
                         A   B   C
    and the union <u>in their dispute</u> over wages and working conditions.
                         D

16. <u>Many other</u> such points included in <u>evaluating</u> a test <u>are discussed</u> in
         A   B   C
    <u>the Chapter 6</u>.
         D

17. He has only a seven-days vacation during the year despite the fact
       A   B   C
    that other workers get more time off.
         D

18. Of the billions of stars in the galaxy, how much are stable enough
           A   B   C
    to create life on their planets?
                          D

19. There exist much to be learned about the various vegetables and their
          A   B   C
    value to humans and animals.
          D

20. The Department of Psychology has been criticized for not having much
                                  A   B   C
    required courses scheduled for this semester.
                              D

21. In general, tax returns must be filed annually, but in few cases they
        A   B   C
    must be submitted every six months.
                      D

22. According to a recent report, the number of sugar that Americans consume
          A   B   C
    does not vary greatly from year to year.
         D

23. In the 1950's more than three thousands interview of former slaves
                    A   B
    were conducted by members of the Federal Writers Project.
          C   D

24. Leading researchers are often the kinds of person who have enjoyed
            A   B   C
    intellectual challenges all their lives.
                           D

25. The valerian family includes more than 200 different kinds of perennial
                        A   B
    or annual herb and a few shrubs.
       C   D

Unit 12

형용사

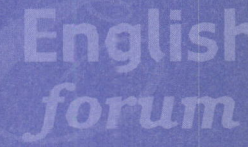

◀ 형용사의 용법

서술용법

1. 건강 : faint, ill, unwell, well ...

    What's the matter with Mr. Brown? - He's ill/unwell.
    He feels faint.
    How are you? - I'm very well thank you. I'm fine thanks.

2. 'a+동사'형 형용사

    afloat, afraid, alight, alike, alive, alone, ashamed, asleep, awake

    the **floating vessel** (표류중인 선박) → The vessel **is afloat**.
    the **frightened children** (겁에 질린 어린이들) → The children **are afraid**.
    the **burning buildings** (불타는 건물들) → The buildings **are alight**.
    all **living things** (모든 생명체) → Everything that **is alive**.
    It's a **live lobster**. (살아 있는 가재) → That lobster **is alive**.
    the **sleeping children** (잠자는 어린이들) → The children **are asleep**.
    in my **waking hours** (깨어있는 시간들) → when **I am awake**

    cf. · ashamed : shameful
         It was **a shameful act**. (행위를 강조) 그건 부끄러운 행동입니다.
         He should **be ashamed**. (사람을 강조) 그는 부끄러워해야 합니다.
       · alone(혼자) : lonely(외로운)
         You can be **alone** without being **lonely**. 너는 외로움을 타지 않고 혼자 있을 수 있어.

3. 감정과 반응

   contend, glad, pleased, sorry, upset

   I am very glad to meet you.
   She is contend. = She is a happy/contented woman.

4. 거리

   far, near (*cf.* the Far East 극동, the Near East 근동)

   Your hotel is **quite near** here.
   It **isn't far** from here.

5. 전치사가 붙는 형용사

   absent from, afraid of, anxious about(걱정하는),
   ashamed of(부끄러워하는), aware of(알아채는), careful of,
   content with(만족하는), different from, famous for, fond of(좋아하는),
   full of, interested in, obliged to(강제되는), pleased with, satisfied with,
   separate from(다른), sorry about, worried about(걱정하는)

   A capable person is one who manage well. 능력 있는 사람은 관리를 잘하는 사람이다.
   He **is capable of** managing well.

수식용법(Attributive Adjectives)

1. 완벽한 정도를 나타내는 형용사

   mere, out and out, sheer, utter

   What you say is **sheer/utter nonsense**. 네 말은 순전히 넌센스야.

2. 수식할 때 very의 뜻을 내포하는 형용사

   close, complete/perfect/total, pure, strong

   a close friend, a complete(/perfect/total) fool, a strong supporter
   What you say is pure nonsense.
   cf. **Pure** drinking water is best. This water is **pure**.

명사 앞뒤에서 모두 수식할 수 있는 형용사

1. 앞이든 뒤든 뜻이 변하지 않는 형용사 (-able, -ible)

available(유효한), eligible(적임의), imaginable(상상할 수 있는)

I doubt whether we can complete our contract in the **time available**.(= in the available time) 유효한 시간 내에 우리 계약을 완수할 수 있을지는 의심이 됩니다.

2. 수식하는 위치에 따라 뜻이 다른 경우

concerned, involved, present, proper, responsible

- The **concerned**(= worried) **doctor** rang for an ambulance.
- The **doctor concerned**(= responsible) is off duty today.

- It was a very **involved**(= complicated) **explanation**.
- The **boy involved**(= connected with this) has left.

- **Present employees**(= those currently employed) number 3,000.
- **Employees present**(= those here now) should vote on the issue.

- It was a **proper**(= correct) **question**.
- The **question proper**(= itself) has not been answered.

- Jane is a **responsible girl**.(= She has a sense of duty.)
- The **girl responsible**(= who can be blamed) was expelled.

걱정스런 의사는 앰뷸런스를 불렀습니다. / 담당의사는 오늘 휴무입니다. / 그것은 아주 복잡한 설명이었습니다. / 연루된 그 소년은 떠났습니다. / 현재 직원들은 3000명이 이릅니다. / 출근한 직원들은 그 문제에 투표해야 합니다. / 그것은 맞는 문제입니다. / 그 문제 자체는 답이 나오지 않았습니다. / 제인은 책임감 있는 여자입니다. / 책임이 있는 그 여자는 쫓겨났습니다.

명사 역할을 하는 형용사

1. the+형용사 = 집합명사 (복수동사를 받는다)

the blind, the dead, the deaf, the dumb, the elderly,
the guilty, the handicapped, the healthy, the homeless,
the injured, the innocent, the living, the old, the poor,
the rich, the sick, the unemployed, the young …

The rich are not always happy.
You can always judge a society by the way **the old are** cared for.

부자들이라고 해서 항상 행복한 것은 아닙니다. / 언제나 노인들이 보호받는 방식으로 사회를 평가할 수 있습니다.

2. the+형용사 = 추상명사 (단수동사를 받는다)

the true (진), the good (선), the beautiful (미), the supernatural (초자연),
the unexpected (예측불가능), the unknown (미상, 미확인)

The unknown is always something to be feared.

Basic Grammar for English Tests

The true, **the good**, and **the beautiful were** the ideals of the Greeks.
모르는 것은 언제나 두려운 것입니다. / 진선미는 그리스인들의 이상이었습니다.

형용사역할을 하는 명사 : 복합명사에서 명사를 수식하는 명사

a cotton shirt (= a shirt made of cotton 면셔츠)
a summer dress (= dress to be worn in summer 여름옷)
a gold watch (= a watch made of gold 금시계)
a plastic raincoat (= a raincoat made of plastic 비닐 레인코트)

형용사 역할을 하는 현재분사(-ing)와 과거분사(-ed)

1. This story **excites** me.

   → I am **excited** by it.
   → It is **exciting**.

   an exciting movie, frightening stories, interesting novels, boiling water
   a broken window, a frozen lake, a locked door, an aged parent
   a naked woman, a learned professor ...

   Gloria was quite **enchanting** to be with.
   (매혹적인 : She had an effect on other people.)
   Gloria was quite **enchanted**.
   (매혹된 : Someone/Something had an effect on her.)

2. '-ed/-ing' 짝을 이루는 단어들

   동사들의 분사가 되기 전의 행위의 '주체'(subject)나 '대상'(object)이 무엇인지를 알면 된다.
   '-ed'형태는 사람(동물)이 감정의 주체가 되고, '-ing'형태는 사람이 그 대상이 된다.

   alarmed : 놀란
   alarming : 놀라운, 걱정이 되는
   amused : 즐거운 기분이 된
   amusing : 즐겁게 하는
   appalled : 놀란, 질린
   appalling : 섬뜩하게 하는
   bewildered : 당황한
   bewildering : 당황케 하는
   confused : 당황한, 혼란된
   confusing : 혼란시키는

   amazed : 깜짝 놀란
   amazing : 놀랄 정도의, 굉장한
   annoyed : 귀찮아 속 타는
   annoying : 성가신, 귀찮게 하는
   astonished : 깜짝 놀란
   astonishing : 놀랄만한, 놀라운
   bored : 싫증난, 지루한
   boring : 지루하게 만드는
   depressed : 억압된
   depressing : 억누르는, 억압적인

- disgusted : 정떨어진, 질린
- disgusting : 정떨어지게 하는
- embarrassed : 난처해진
- embarrassing : 난처하게 하는
- exhausted : 다 써버린, 기운 빠진
- exhausting : 소도적인, 기운 빼는
- horrified : 겁에 질린
- horrifying : 소름끼치는, 무서운
- irritated : 화난, 약오른
- irritating : 화나게 하는
- pleased : 즐거운
- Pleasing : 즐거움을 주는
- satisfied : 만족한, 충족된
- satisfying : 만족할 만한
- surprised : 깜짝 놀란
- surprising : 놀랄만한, 의외의
- tired : 피로한, 지친
- tiring : 지루한, 지치게 하는

- distressed : 괴로운
- distressing : 괴롭히는, 비참한
- excited : 흥분된, 고무된
- exciting : 흥겨운, 흥분시키는
- frightened : 놀란, 겁에 질린
- frightening : 무서운, 굉장한
- interested : 흥거워하는, 이해관계 있는
- interesting : 흥미를 주는, 재미있는
- moved : 감동된
- moving : 감동을 주는
- relaxed : 느슨해진, 이완된, 편안해진
- relaxing : 편하게 하는, 느슨하게 하는
- shocked : 충격 받은, 놀란
- shocking : 충격적인, 놀라운
- terrified : 놀란, 겁먹은
- terrifying : 놀라게 하는, 겁주는
- worried : 난처한, 딱한
- worrying : 애태우는, 걱정시키는

cf. 뜻이 비슷한 경우

- delighted : 기쁜, (I am delighted to see you.)
- delightful : 즐거운, 기쁜
- impressed : 감격 받은
- impressive : 인상적인, 인상에 남는

Exercise 1 다음 각 문장이 성립하도록 괄호에서 알맞은 말을 골라라.

1. The (breaking/*broken*) dishes lay on the floor.
2. The (trembling/trembled) children were given a blanket for warmth.
3. Compassionate friends tried to console the (crying/cried) victims of the accident.
4. The (interesting/interested) tennis match caused a great deal of excitement.
5. When Jane noticed the (burning/burnt) building, she noticed the fire department immediately.
6. The (exciting/excited) passengers jumped into the lifeboats when notified that the ship was sinking.
7. The (smiling/smiled) Mona Lisa is on display in the Louvre in Paris.

8. The wind made such (frightening/frightened) noises that the children ran to their parents' room.
9. The (frightening/frightened) hostages only wanted to be left alone.
10. We saw the (advancing/advanced) army from across town.
11. Mrs. Harris's (approving/approved) smile let us know that our speeches were well done.
12. Our representative presented the (approving/approved) plan to the public.
13. The (blowing/blown) wind of the hurricane damaged the waterfront property.
14. We were going to see the movie at the Center Theater, but our friends told us it was a (boring/bored) movie.
15. Mary's (cleaning/cleaned) service comes every Wednesday.
16. The (cleaning/cleaned) shoes were placed in the sun to dry.
17. We found it difficult to get through the (closing/closed) door without a key.
18. As we entered the (crowding/crowded) room, I noticed my cousins.
19. Dr. Jameson told my brother to elevate his (aching/ached) foot.
20. The police towed away the (parking/parked) cars because they were blocking the entrance.

연결동사(Linking Verbs) 뒤에 보어로 오는 형용사

흔히 동사는 부사가 수식하는 것이 일반적이다. 그런데 '연결동사'는 주어와 보어(주격보어; 형용사)를 바로 연결시켜 준다. 이 동사들은 대부분의 동사들(동작동사 Active Verbs)과 달리 행위를 하지 않는 '상태동사'(Stative Verbs)다. 그래서 부사가 아니라 형용사의 수식을 받는다. '감각동사'(Sense Verbs) 역시 연결동사로 쓰인다.

1. 연결동사

   appear, be, become, feel, look, remain, seem, smell, sound, stay, taste

   Mary **feels bad** about her test grade.
   Children **become tired** quite easily.
   They **were sorry** to see us leave.
   The soup **tastes good**.

   메리는 자신의 성적에 기분이 나빴습니다. / 어린이들은 아주 쉽게 피곤해집니다. / 그들은 우리가 떠나는 것을 보고 아쉬워했습니다. / 수프는 맛이 좋습니다.

   cf. You **look well**. (well- 형용사) 좋아 보이네요.
   You **play well**. (well- 부사) 잘하시네요.

2. 동사+형용사와 결합 형태

   break loose, marry young, die young, die hard, keep silent, lie still, sit still, stand silent, live close to, remain open

   Many famous poets had **died young**.
   It's impossible for young children to **sit still**.
   The murder was not solved and the case **remains open**.
   The crowd **stood/was silent** at the end of the ceremony.

   많은 유명한 시인들이 일찍 죽었습니다. / 어린 아이들이 가만히 앉아 있는 것은 불가능합니다. / 살인은 해결되지 않고 사건은 미결로 남아 있습니다. / 군중들은 식이 끝났을 때 조용히 서/있었습니다

잘못 쓰기 쉬운 형용사들

1. **fat/thin** - 주로 사람, 동물을 수식
   a fat man/a thin woman, a fat cat/a thin cat

   thick/thin - 주로 사물을 수식
   a thick book/a thin book, thick material, thin material

2. **tall/short** - 사람의 신장 표현
   a tall man, a short woman

   tall/small - 건물, 산, 나무 등 규모 표현
   a tall building/mountain/tree
   a small building/mountain/tree

3. **high/low** - 목소리나 건물, 기타 사물의 높낮이 표현

   a high building/a low building, a high stool/a low stool,
   a high mountain, a low hill, a high voice/a low voice,
   a high note/a low note

4. **long/short** - 시간, 거리 및 기타 사물의 길이 표현

   a long skirt/a short skirt, a long time/a short time,
   a long walk/a short walk

5. **loud/soft** : hard/soft - 촉감 표현

   a loud/soft knock, a loud/soft thud,
   a hard/soft apple, a hard/soft mattress

Basic Grammar for English Tests

6. **old/young**(사람) : **old/new**(사람, 사물)

   an old/young man(/woman), a old/new handbag,
   an old/new house, a new boss, a new secretary, a new face

7. **large/big/great** (사람, 사물을 수식) ┌ large, big - 규모
                                                                                           └ great - 중요성

   a large/big man or woman, a large/big box,
   a great man, a great cathedral, a great idea

8. **small** - large/big 의 반대말로 사람이나 사물의 규모를 표현한다. 수식용법, 서술용법 모두 쓴다.

   a small boy, a small house
   My house is very small.

   little - 수식용법으로 쓸 때는 small 대신 쓸 수 있다.

   a little boy, a little house
   수량형용사 역할 - a little sugar
   특히, 사랑이나 연민의 느낌을 담은 표현에 사용 - my sweet little baby

Exercise 2 다음 각 문장에 알맞은 말을 괄호에서 골라라.

1. He behaved (nice/*nicely*).
2. The music sounds (nice/nicely).
3. The play ended (bad/badly).
4. This food smells (bad/badly).
5. Your cooking is (good/well).
6. You cook (good/well).
7. The train went (smooth/smoothly).
8. I've just shaved and my face feels (smooth/smoothly).

Exercise 3 다음 각 문장에서 형용사, 부사의 형태나 쓰임이 잘못된 것을 찾아 바로 잡으시오.

1. Since it is reusable, the space shuttle is least expensive than other spacecraft. (least → *less*)
2. At the end of the performance, the crowd left quick.
3. The bride was real polite to her new in-laws.
4. It was difficult to choose a good perfume because they all smelled sweetly.

5. After a considerable long wait, teachers were granted a pay increase.
6. Elephants will probable become extinct unless governments change existing laws.

◀ 형용사의 어순(word order)

다음은 흔히 쓰는 일반적인 형용사의 수식어순이다.

형용사 어순	명사 어순
일반성질 ←　　　　　　　　　→ 특수성질	
성질 - 크기 - 연령 - 모양 - 색깔 - 과거분사 - 기원·출처	재료 - 목적·용도 - 본명사
beautiful beautiful large beautiful large old beautiful large old round beautiful large old round brown beautiful large old round brown handmade beautiful large old round brown handmade French	cupboard kitchen cupboard wooden kitchen cupboard wooden kitchen cupboard wooden kitchen cupboard wooden kitchen cupboard wooden kitchen cupboard

〈주의〉
- 형용사의 수식어순은 매우 유동적이라서 말하는 사람의 의도나 강조에 따라 달라 질 수 있다. 그러므로 위의 표를 고정된 어순규칙으로 받아 들이지는 말기 바란다.
- '일반적인 성질'(general qualities)을 나타내는 형용사는 '특별한 성질'(particular qualities)의 형용사 보다 앞에 놓인다. 그러므로 그 성질이 특별할수록 명사와 가까이 자리잡는다.

◀ 형용사의 비교용법

모든 형용사가 다 비교급이나 최상급 형태를 가질 수 있는 것은 아니다.
'정도나 등급을 매길 수 있는 형용사'(gradable adjectives)만이 가능하다.
정도나 등급을 매길 수 없는 형용사는 '절대의미'(absolute meaning)를 가지고 있어서 비교급, 최상급 형태를 갖지 않는다.

* 정도나 등급을 매길 수 없는 형용사
　　complete, dead, daily main, medical, perfect, principal,
　　right, total, unique, wrong, yearly ……

Basic Grammar for English Tests

-er,-est형 : 일부 단어를 제외한 모든 '1음절 단어'

1. 종류

    (1) 형용사 + -er

    cold-colder-coldest, cool-cooler-coolest, great-greater-greatest, hard-harder-hardest, high-higher-highest, low-lower-lowest, short-shorter-shortest, small-smaller-smallest

    (2) 형용사의 끝 자음 하나 더 + -er

    big-bigger-biggest, fat-fatter-fattest, thin-thinner-thinnest, wet-wetter-wettest

    (3) -e로 끝나는 형용사 + -r

    fine-finer-finest, large-larger-largest, strange-stranger-strangest
    * late-later/latter-latest/last

    (4) y → i + -er

    busy-busier-busiest, early-earlier-earliest, easy-easier-easiest, funny-funnier-funniest, heavy-heavier-heaviest

    (5) 2음절 단어인 경우 : 아래의 형용사들은 more, most로 만들기도 한다.

    clever-cleverer-cleverest, common-commoner-commonest
    gentle-gentler-gentlest, narrow-narrower-narrowest
    simple-simpler-simplest

2. 비교급, 최상급이 불규칙변화를 하는 것들

일반형용사	good-better-best, bad-worse-worst far-father/further-farthest/furthest late-later/latter-latest/last old-older/elder-oldest/eldest
수량형용사	many/much-more-most little-less-least

* farther/further는 둘 다 '거리(distance)' 표현에 쓸 수 있다.
  London is five miles farther/further.
  further는 부가적인 뜻으로만 쓴다.(= in addition)
  There is no **further information**. (not farther)

more/less-, most/least- 형 : 흔히 2음절 이상인 형용사들

1. 종류

   (1) -er/more(/less), -est/most(/least) 두 경우 다 쓰는 것들

   clever, (un)common, gentle, handsome, (un)happy, narrow, (un)pleasant, quiet, shallow, simple, stupid, tired

   (2) more/less-, most/least- 형

   beautiful, careful, certain, comfortable, correct, dangerous, expensive, famous, foolish, frequent, important, modern, natural, necessary, normal, useful ...

   (3) -ing/-ed로 끝나는 분사형은 도두 more/less, most/least로 만든다.

   amused-more/less amused-most/least amused
   amusing-more/less amusing-most/least amusing
   annoyed-more/less annoyed-most/least annoyed
   annoying-more/less annoying-most/least annoying
   bored-more/less bored-most/least bored
   boring-more/less boring-most/least boring

한 사람이나 사물의 성질을 비교할 때는 음절에 관계없이 more(=rather)를 쓴다

He is **more/rather kind than wise**.
I think she is **more/rather shy than unfriendly**.

그는 현명하기보다는 오히려 친절합니다. / 저는 그녀가 비우호적이라기보다는 수줍어한다고 생각합니다.

여러 가지 중요 비교용법

1. than을 동반하여 비교

   이때 than은 전치사 뜨는 접속사 구실을 한다.

   - I know him **better than you**.
     ⎡ I know him better **than** you (know him). - than은 접속사
     ⎣ I know him better **than** (I know) you. - than은 전치사
   - My room is **cleaner than** the one next door.
     Driving is certainly less **tiring than** walking.
     February has **fewer** days **than** March.
     It's **pleasanter/more pleasant** today **than** it was yesterday.

     내방은 옆방보다 더 깨끗합니다. / 운전이 걷는 것보다 확실히 덜 피곤합니다. / 2월은 3월보다 날 수가 적습니다. / 어제보다 오늘이 더 즐겁습니다.

Basic Grammar for English Tests

than 없이 쓰는 비교급 : 대체로 비교의 내용이 분명한 경우

1. 묵시적으로 비교대상이 분명한 상황에서

   Which is **(the) longer** (of the two coats)?
   The grey coat is **(the) longer** (of the two coats).

   Which is **(the) cheaper** (of the two shirts)?
   The red shirt is **(the) cheaper**.

2. 비교대상이 둘인 경우

   Who is **smarter**, Brown and Jane?
   Brown is **the smarter of the two**.

3. 라틴어 비교급 : than 대신에 to를 쓴다.

   - prior to (= before ~앞에)
   - prefer ~ to … (= like better: …보다 ~을 더 좋아하다)

   exterior (= outer)   major (= more)   anterior (= earlier)
   interior (= inner)   minor (= less)   posterior (= later)

   senior (= older)   superior (= better)
   junior (= younger)   inferior (= worse)

점진비교 : 비교급 and 비교급(점점 더)

Jane is growing fast. She's getting **taller and taller**.
Computers are becoming **more and more** complicated.
Holiday flights are getting **less and less** expensive.

제인은 빨리 자랍니다. 그녀는 점점 커갑니다. / 컴퓨터는 점점 복잡해져갑니다 / 공휴일 항공료는 점점 싸집니다.

the 비교급…, the 비교급… (…하면 할수록)

대체로 앞뒤의 문장구조가 같다.

The more money you make, **the more** you spend.
The quicker a loan is repaid, **the less** it will cost.
The fewer seeds, **the fewer** plants.
The higher the tree, **the stronger** the wind.
The sooner, the better.
The more, the better.

돈은 많이 벌수록 더 씁니다. / 대부금은 빨리 갚을수록 적게 비용이 적습니다. / 씨가 적을수록 나무도 적습니다. (뿌린 대로 거둡니다.) / 나무가 높을수록 바람이 거셉니다. / 빠르면 빠를수록 더 좋다. / 많으면 많을수록 더 좋다.

비교급을 수식하는 표현(부사)들

a lot, lots, a little, rather, hardly, any, no, even, far, by far, (very) much, still

It's **much/far/a lot/a little** **colder** today **than** it was yesterday.
This is **much better than** that.
어제보다는 오늘 훨씬(/약간) 더 춥습니다. / 이것은 저것보다 훨씬 더 좋습니다.

부정어를 포함한 비교급의 관용표현

1. I have **no less than** $ 10,000. (= as much as) 1만 달러 정도는 가지고 있다.
   She **no less than** you is beautiful. 그녀도 당신 못지 않게 예쁘다.
   cf. Although John is indifferent to Alice, she likes him **no less** for it.
   (= none the less, not the less : 그래도 오히려)
2. She is **no less** rich **than** her sister. (as rich as) 언니 못지 않게 부자다.
   He was **no less** a person **than** the President. 다름 아닌 대통령 자신이었다.
   (= He was a person **no other than** the President.)
3. He has **not less than** 5 dollars. (= at least) 적어도 5 달러는 가지고 있다
   She is **not less** rich **than** her sister. 더 부자일망정 못하지 않다.
   (= She is as rich as, or richer than, her sister.)
4. We expect **nothing less than** an attack. (= only) 오직 공격만이 있으리라는 것쯤은 예상하고 있다.
5. I like her **none the less** for her faults. (= in spite of)
6. He has **no more than** 10 dollars. (= only) 10 달러밖에 없다.
7. I am **no more** mad **than** you are. 너와 마찬가지로 나는 미친 사람이 아니다.
   (= I am **not** mad **any more than** you (are). = You are not mad, nor am I.)
8. He has **not more than** five. (= at most) 기껏해야 다섯 또는 그 이하
9. A whale is **not** a fish **any more than** a horse is.
   (= A whale is **no more** a fish **than** a horse is.)
   말이 물고기가 아니듯이 고래는 물고기가 아니다.
10. He is **no better** than a begger. 그 사람은 거지 마찬가지다
11. He has **no better** right to the property than I have.
    나와 마찬가지로 그이도 그 물건에 대해 권리가 없다.
12. He is **not better** than a beggar. 그는 거지만도 못하다.
    He is **not better** than an engineer. 그는 고작 기술자에 불과하다.
    cf. It is **no bigger/smaller** than a fly. 그것은 파리보다 결코 크지/작지 않다.
13. I go there **no longer**. (= I don't go there **any longer**.) 더 이상 거기 가지 않는다.
14. It was **no other than** the king. (= the king himself) 그건 바로 왕 자신이었다.
    I can do **no other than** smile. (= cannot but) 웃을 수밖에 없었다.
15. I have **no other** friend **than** you. 당신 밖에는 다른 친구가 없다.
16. He is **none the wiser/better**. 조금도 나아지지 않고 여전히 모른다.

ENGLISH FORUM

Basic Grammar for English Tests

최상급의 비교용법

어느 한 사람이나 사물을 소속된 같은 집단 내에서 다른 여러 개체들과 비교할 때 최상급으로 표현하며, 앞에 the를 붙인다.

This is **the cleanest** room in this house.
This is **the worst** room in the hotel.
John is easily **the tallest** boy **in our class**.
Yesterday was **the hottest** day **of the year**.

Exercise 4 다음 각 문장에 알맞은 말을 괄호에서 고르시오. 둘 다 맞는 표현인 경우도 있습니다.

1. Is your house much (*farther/further*)?
2. Who is the (oldest/eldest) in the class?
3. Your driving is (worse/worst) than mine.
4. It's the (less/lesser) of two evils.
5. Have you heard the (last/latest) news?
6. We have no (farther/further) information.
7. Jane writes (good/well).
8. His (last/latest) words were: 'The end'.
9. This is the town's (oldest/eldest) house.
10. My apartment is (littler/smaller) than yours.
11. I've got (less/lesser) than you.
12. Jane is (older/elder) than I am.
13. This is the (more/most) expensive.
14. His English is (best/better) than mine.
15. It's the (best/better) in the shop.
16. It's the (farthest/furthest) point west.
17. It's the (oldest/eldest) tree in the country.
18. She's my (elder/older) sister.
19. I've got the (less/least)!
20. You've got the (more/most)!

Exercise 5 다음 각 문장이 성립하도록 괄호에서 알맞은 비교어를 고르시오.

1. Compared (to/*with*) children her own age, Jane is quite tall.
2. It is unlikely that he will do his (better/best) on the exam since he is sick.

3. Of all the children in the kindergarten, Charles is (more/the most) active.
4. The harder a person studies, the (more/most) he learns.
5. This test was much (less/least) difficult than the first one.
6. Of her two kicks, the second was definitely the (better/best).
7. The (faster/fastest) he ran, the more difficult it was for him to breathe.
8. The higher he climbed, the (less/least) oxygen there was to breathe.
9. History is (more easy/easier) for him than chemistry.
10. Her test score is superior (than/to) his.
11. The more she scolded the child, the (wilder/wildest) he became.
12. Taking calculus was the (worse/worst) experience in his life.

형용사의 기타 비교용법

1. 동급비교 : as ~ as

    John is as tall as Harry.
    John is as intelligent as Harry.

    [관용표현들]
    as clear as crystal, as cold as ice, as good as gold, as light as a feather, as old as the hills, as white as snow, as cool as a cucumber, as blind as a bat, as fat as a pig, as free as a bird, as hard as nails, as pretty as a picture, as quick as lightning ...

    How has Jimmy behaved himself? - He's been **(as) good as gold**.
    지미는 얼마나 점잖니? - 그 아이는 아주 착해.

2. 열등비교 : not as/so ~ as

    Mary is **not so/as** careful **as** Lucy.
    Judy is **not as/so** suitable for the job **as** me.(I am).
    He is **not such** a hard worker **as** his brother.
    메리는 루시만큼 조심스럽지 못해요. / 주디는 나만큼 그 일에 적합하지 않아요. / 그는 그의 형만큼 열심히 일하는 사람이 아니에요.

3. the same (as), similar (to) different (from) 등의 용법

    A and B are the same. = A is the same as B.
    C and D are similar. = C is similar to D.
    E and F are different. = E is different from F.

(1) the same as(= like)를 the same like, the same with 등으로 혼동하지 말 것

He's angry because my marks are **the same as** his.
It is almost **the same as** the one Joe has.
Mr. Kim bought **the same** kind of hair-dryer **as** yours.
cf. Those two dresses are the same.

그는 내 점수가 자기 것과 같아서 화났습니다. / 그것은 조가 가진 것과 아주 똑같습니다. / 미스터김은 자네 것과 같은 종류의 헤어드라이어를 샀어. / 저 두 드레스는 같아요.

(2) different from

Your car is different from mine.
We are quite different from each other.

자네 차는 내 것과 달라. / 우리는 서로 아주 다릅니다.

like/alike의 용법

like와 alike는 같은 뜻이나, 문장이 달라진다.

> This+be+like+that.
> This and that+be+alike.

(You have a blue pencil. I have a blue pencil.)
Your pencil is **like** my pencil. (like = similar to)
Your pencil and my pencil are **alike**. (alike = similar)
Our pencils are **alike**.

Exercise 6 각 문장에서 틀린 부분을 찾아 바르게 고치시오.

1. A rectangle is similar with a square. (with→*to*)
2. Jinho and Mina come from same country.
3. Girls and boys are different. Girls are different to boys.
4. My little brother is the same age with my cousin.
5. Wolves are similar with dogs.
6. Jane and Bill started to speak at same time.
7. You and I have similar books. Our books are like.
8. A town is alike city in some ways.
9. A motorcycle is alike a bicycle in some ways.
10. A dormitory and an apartment building are like in many ways.

Actual Test 16

다음 각 문장을 읽고 빈칸에는 알맞은 단어를 넣고, 밑줄 친 부분에서는 잘못된 부분을 찾으시오.

1. The bookstore at the corner did not prepare _____ textbooks for all students in our class.
   - Ⓐ plenty
   - Ⓑ enough
   - Ⓒ enough of
   - Ⓓ an many

2. That's not _____ the point that yours isn't a case of sour grapes.
   - Ⓐ enough for making
   - Ⓑ to make enough
   - Ⓒ enough to make
   - Ⓓ for making enough

3. The American dream does not come to those who fall _____.
   - Ⓐ sleeping
   - Ⓑ sleep
   - Ⓒ asleep
   - Ⓓ slept

4. I don't think that your computer is _____.
   - Ⓐ worthy the price
   - Ⓑ worth the price
   - Ⓒ worth of the price
   - Ⓓ worthy to buy

5. What percentage of the populace is aware that in _____ company the president hold only a small fraction of its shares?
   - Ⓐ a public typical
   - Ⓑ a typical public
   - Ⓒ typical a public
   - Ⓓ public typical a

6. Miami, Florida, is _____ in the United States.
   - Ⓐ city that is most southern
   - Ⓑ most southern cities
   - Ⓒ the southern of most cities
   - Ⓓ the southernmost city

7. California produces _____ any other state in the United States.
   - Ⓐ strawberries than more
   - Ⓑ than more strawberries
   - Ⓒ more strawberries than
   - Ⓓ more than strawberries

8. Scientists are <u>searching</u> for the <u>oldest</u> tree <u>lively</u> because it can tell <u>them</u> a
                       A   B   C   D
   great deal about many matters.

9. <u>During</u> dreams the human body is sleeping <u>but</u> the <u>thinking part</u> of the
      A   B   C
   brain is <u>awake wide</u>.
                 D

10. <u>Some</u> antibiotics <u>used in</u> the treatment of human disease are <u>like</u> only
       A   B   C
    in that they <u>are gained</u> from fungi and bacteria.
                      D

11. Afrikaans is <u>the only</u> language of European origin that <u>is not spoken</u>
                   A   B
    in Europe; it <u>has</u> Dutch roots but is <u>similar with</u> Flemish.
                  C   D

12. The human ribs are capable <u>to move</u> <u>so as</u> to allow space for the lungs
                                       A   B
    <u>to expand</u> <u>during breathing</u>.
        C   D

13. Now <u>many</u> doctors <u>have become</u> concerned <u>of</u> the <u>possible</u> long-term
           A   B   C   D
    effects of birth control pills.

14. Though Washington knew <u>their attitude</u>, he was <u>broad-minded</u> enough to
                                       A   B
    appoint <u>such</u> men to the important office because he was <u>convincing</u> of
             C   D
    their ability.

15. <u>During</u> the 1936 Olympic games, Jesse Owens <u>set</u> a <u>world new</u> record in
       A   B   C
    track and won <u>four gold</u> medals.
                    D

16. Women also played <u>a</u> large part <u>in</u> our great <u>first</u> <u>private</u> relief organization
                         A   B   C   D
    — the United States Sanitary Commission.

17. <u>As</u> every <u>other</u> nation, the United States <u>used to define</u> <u>its</u> unit of currency,
     A   B   C   D
    the dollar, according to the gold standard.

18. Rabbits and hares look much like and are usually mistaken for each other.
    　　　　　　　　　　　A　　　　B　　　　　　　　　　C　　　　　D

19. The scientists who are probably mostly interested in travels to the
    　　　　　　　　　A　　B　　　　　　C　　　　　　　D
    moon are geologists.

20. Microwave oven thermometers are much more costlier than other kinds of
    　　　　　　　　　　　　　　　A　　　　　　　B　　　　　C　　　D
    thermometers.

21. If you had taken my advice before doing your homework, you would
    　　　　A　　　　　　　　B
    have been able to do it more better.
    　　C　　　　　　　　　D

22. She was so disappointed that she angrily chose the worse movie she could
    　　　　　　　　　　　　　　　A　　　　　　　B
    find, in the hope that it might at least seem funny.
    　　　　C　　　　　D

23. Of all the Native American tribes, the Shawnee Indians were a most
    　A　　　　　　　　　B　　　　　　　　　　　　　　C　　D
    temporary.

24. Jupiter is the fifth planet from the Sun and the bigger planet of the
    　　　　　　　　　　　　　A　　　　　　　　B
    solar system, with a diameter about eleven times that of the Earth.
    　　　　　　　　　　　　　　C　　　　　　　　　D

25. Mercury is the most small planet in the solar system and the closest
    　　　　　　　A　　　　　B　　　　C
    to the Sun.
    D

Unit 13

부사

◀ 부사의 종류

1. 일반 부사

    (1) 행동양태의 부사
       (a) 부사의 대부분은 주로 -ly로 끝난다 : badly, happily, fortunately, patiently, usually ...
       (b) 형용사와 모양이 같은 부사 : fast, deep, late, long, hard ...
    (2) 장소의 부사 : here, there, away, abroad, somewhere ...
    (3) 시간의 부사 : then, once, late, already ...
    (4) 빈도 부사 : often, always ...
    (5) 정도의 부사 : quite, rather, far, enough ...
    (6) 강도의 부사 : very, indeed
    (7) 관심집중의 부사 : even, just
    (8) 관점의 부사 : perhaps
    (9) 연결어 : however, furthermore ...

2. 부사구 : 흔히 '전치사구' 형태로 되어 있다.

    in a hurry, in the garden, at the station, again and again, hardly at all, very much indeed, as a matter of fact, in that case

3. 전치사가 동사와 함께 하여 부사 역할을 할 경우

    The children have just **got in**. (=inward)
    Drink up your milk. (= completely)
    Put out your cigarettes. (= extinguish)

    어린이들이 금방 안으로 들어갔습니다. / 우유를 다 마셔라. / 담배 꺼라.

◀ 부사의 비교용법

모든 부사가 다 비교급이나 최상급 형태를 가질 수 있는 것은 아니다.
정도나 등급을 매길 수 있는 부사(Gradable Adverbs)만 가능하고, 그렇지 않은 부사는 '절대 의미'를 가지고 있어서 비교, 최상급 형태를 갖고 있지 않다.
daily, extremely, only, really, then, there, uniquely … 등은 비교, 최상급 형태를 가지지 않는 부사들이다.

종류

1. 형용사와 같은 모양의 부사 : 형용사와 같이 '-er/est'로 쓴다.

    big-bigger-biggest, cheap-cheaper-cheapest, clean-cleaner-cleanest, early-earlier-earliest, easy-easier-easiest, fast-faster-fastest, fine-finer-finest, hard-harder-hardest, high-higher-highest, kindly-kindlier-kindliest, long-longer-longest, low-lower-lowest, quick-quicker-quickest, slow-slower-slowest

2. '-ly'형의 행동양태 부사 : more/most 형

    badly-more badly-most badly, briefly-more briefly-most briefly, clearly-more clearly-most clearly, deeply-more deeply-most deeply, easily-more easily-most easily, sharply-more sharply-most sharply, quickly-more quickly-most quickly

3. 빈도부사 : more/most 형

    frequently-more frequently-most frequently, often-more often-most often, rarely-more rarely-most rarely, seldom-more seldom-most seldom

4. 비교급, 최상급이 불규칙 변화를 하는 부사

    far-farther/further-farthest/furthest, badly-worse-worst late-later-last, little-less-least well-better-best

    * **farther/further**는 둘 다 '거리(distance)' 표현에 사용하기도 한다.

    　　I drove ten miles farther/further than necessary.
    　　We learned, **further**, that he wasn't a qualified doctor. (= in addition)
    　　저는 필요한 것보다 10마일이나 더 갔습니다. / 게다가, 우리는 그가 자격 있는 의사가 아니라는 것도 알았습니다.

부사를 이용한 비교용법

1. 비교급 비교

   Dave drives **faster than** anyone I know.
   The rain cleared **more quickly than** I expected.
   The faster I type **the more** mistakes I make.
   It rained **more and more** heavily.

   데이브는 내가 아는 누구보다 운전을 빨리 합니다. / 예상보다 빨리 비가 개었습니다. / 저는 타이핑을 빨리 칠수록 실수가 많습니다. / 점점 비가 많이 내렸습니다.

2. 원급 비교

   Sylvia sings **as sweetly as** her sister.
   I can't swim **as well as** you (can).
   She can't jump (quite) **so high as** Billy (can).

   실비아는 자기 동생보다 노래를 더 잘합니다. / 나는 자네 만큼 수영을 못해. / 그녀는 빌 만큼 높이 뛰지 못합니다.

3. 최상급 비교

   I work **fastest** when I'm under pressure.
   Tom tries **the hardest of all the** boys in his class.
   Brown worked **harder than ever** (than anyone)
   Brown worked **the hardest**.

   저는 스트레스를 받으면 일을 빨리 합니다. / 톰은 자기 반의 모든 애들 가운데서 가장 열심히 노력합니다. / 브라운은 누구보다 더 열심히 집중하였습니다. / 브라운은 가장 열심히 집중하였습니다.

◀ 행동양태의 부사(Manner/How … ?)

형태 : 대부분 '-ly' 모양이다.

1. 형용사 + -ly형

   mad/madly, plain/plainly, sudden/suddenly,
   beautiful/beautifully, musical/musically, * full/fully

2. -y형용사 → -ily형

   busy/busily, funny/funnily * dry/dryly/drily, shy/shyly

3. 형용사 + -y형

   able/ably, nimble/nimbly, possible/possibly, due/duly, true/truly,
   * whole/wholly, extreme/extremely, tame/tamely

4. 형용사 + -ally형

   basic/basically, systematic/systematically

   cf. (1) 부사로도 쓰이는 '-ly형 형용사'(시간의 부사)
   daily, weekly, monthly, quarterly, yearly
   (2) early ┌ I hope to catch an **early** train.(형용사)
           └ I want to arrive **early**.(부사)

행동양태부사의 역할과 종류

1. 대부분의 양태부사는 '행위동사'(Active Verbs)를 수식하지만, '상태동사(Stative Verbs)'를 수식하는 것도 있다.

   I understand it **perfectly**.
   I know it **well**.
   I **hear** very **badly**.

2. 양태부사로 쓰이는 전치사구

   I came here **by bus**.
   She answered me **in a loud voice**.
   He left **in a hurry**.(= hurriedly)

3. '-ly'형 형용사 : 어미가 '-ly'인 단어가 모두 부사는 아니다.

   brotherly/sisterly, cowardly, elderly, friendly/unfriendly, heavenly, likely/unlikely, lively, lovely, manly/womanly, motherly/fatherly, sickly, silly, ugly ...

   Susan is a friendly woman. 수잔은 다정한 여인입니다.

4. 부사와 형용사의 형태나 의미가 같은 단어

   - A **fast** train is one that goes **fast**. 급행열차는 빨리 가는 것입니다.
     　(형용사)　　　　　　　　　　(부사)

   - I work **hard** because I enjoy **hard** work. 저는 힘든 일을 좋아하기 때문에 열심히 일합니다.
     　　(부사)　　　　　　　　(형용사)

   ┌ We had an **early** breakfast. (형용사)
   │ We had breakfast **early**. (부사)
   └ We had breakfast **earlier** than usual. (부사)
   우리는 이른 아침을 먹었습니다. / 우리는 아침을 일찍 먹었습니다. / 우리는 평소보다 더 일찍 아침을 먹었습니다.

We've had a **long** wait. (형용사)
Have you been waiting **long**? (부사)
I can't stay very **long**. (부사)

우리는 오래 기다렸습니다 / 얼마나 오래 기다렸어요? / 저는 아주 오래 기다리지는 못해요.

I want a **straight** answer to my question. (형용사)
Tell me **straight** what you think. (부사)
He has come **straight** from London. (부사)

저는 제 질문에 즉답을 원합니다. / 자네가 생각하는 것을 똑바로 말해주게. / 그는 런던에서 곧장 왔습니다.

단어	형용사로 쓰인 예	부사로 쓰인 예
all right	I'm all right.	You've done all right.
best	best clothes	do your best
better	a better book	speak better
big	a big house	talk big
cheap	a cheap suit	buy it cheap
clear	a clear sky	stand clear
close	The shops are close.	stay close
daily	a daily paper	They deliver daily.
deep	a deep hole	drink deep
early	an early train	arrive early
easy	an easy book	go easy
far	a far country	go far
fast	a fast driver	drive fast
firm	a firm belief	hold firm
hard	a hard worker	work hard
high	a high note	aim high
home	home cooking	go home
last	the last guest	come last
late	a late train	arrive late
long	long hair	Don't stay long.
loud	a loud noise	speak loud
quick	a quick worker	come quick
quiet	a quiet evening	sit quiet
right	the right answer	answer right
sharp	sharp eyes	look sharp
slow	a slow train	go slow
well	I am well.	do well
wrong	a wrong guess	answer wrong
yearly	a yearly visit (연례방문)	go there yearly

Basic Grammar for English Tests

5. 두 가지 모양을 가진 부사

   (1) 용법이 같은 경우
   - cheap(ly) : 값싸게

       That shopkeeper buys **cheap** but doesn't sell **cheap**.
       My wife buys her clothes **cheap(ly)**.

   - clean : 깨끗이, 완전히 = completely, absolutely
       I **clean** forgot to ask him about it. 그것을 그에게 질문할 것을 저는 깨끗이 잊었습니다.
       He kicked the ball **clean** over the roof. 그는 공을 차서 지붕위로 깨끗이 날렸습니다.
   - cleanly : This knife cuts very **cleanly**. (= sharply and neatly) 이 칼은 잘 듭니다

   - clear : (대체로 clean과 비슷한 뜻) = completely, = well away from, not touching
       The bullet went **clear** through the door. 탄환이 문을 완전히 뚫고 나갔습니다.
       The horse jumped **clear** of the hedge. (= without touching it)
       말이 울타리를 사뿐히 넘어 갔습니다.
   - clearly : He is **clearly** wrong / **clearly** in the wrong. 그는 완전히 잘못되었습니다.
       You must **clearly** understand that. 너는 그것을 완전히 이해해야 돼.
       He spoke loud(ly) and **clear(ly)**. 그는 큰소리고 또박또박 말했습니다.
       The moon shone **clear(ly)**. 달이 밝게 빛났습니다.

   - close : 가까이 = near
       Stay **close** to me. 내게 붙어 있어.
       He was following **close(ly)** behind. 그는 뒤에 바짝 붙어 따라왔습니다.
       This success brings us **closer** to final victory.
       이번 성공은 우리를 최후 승리에 더 가까지 데려다 줍니다.
   - closely : 뜻이 좀 다양하다.
       The prisoners were **closely** guarded. (= strictly) 죄수들은 엄격히 통제됩니다.
       Watch **closely** what I do. (= carefully) 내가 하는 것을 잘 보세요.
       He sent me a letter of two **closely** written pages. (깨알같이)
       그는 빽빽하게 두 장으로 쓴 편지를 제게 보내왔습니다.
       It was a **closely** contested election. (백중의, 막상막하의) 백중의 선거전이었습니다.
       * a close election: 백중의 선거전

   - dead : 완전히 = completely, absolutely
       go **dead** slow (= almost stopped) 아주 천천히 일하다, **dead** certain 아주 확실한,
       dead beat (= tired out, exhausted) 완전히 지친, **dead** drunk 완전히 취한
   - deadly : (형) **deadly** poison 치명적인 독약, the seven deadly sins 7가지 중대 죄악
             (부) **deadly** pale 죽을 것처럼 창백한, deadly dull 아주 둔한

   - fair (정정당당히) : play **fair**, fight **fair**
   - fairly (꽤; to a certain extent) : **fairly** good, **fairly** soon
       This book is **fairly** difficult. 이 책은 상당히 어렵습니다.

252 | Part 2 품사편

- false : play somebody **false** (누구를 속이다 = cheat or betray him)
- **falsely** : **falsely** accused (실수로) 잘못 기소된

- firm : 단단히, 굳게
  - Stand **firm**. 단단히 서있어
  - He holds **firm** to his belief. 그는 자신의 신념을 굳게 지킵니다.
- **firmly** : 단단히, 굳게, 단호하게
  - Fix the post **firmly** in the ground. 기둥을 땅에 단단히 고정시켜.
  - I had to speak **firmly** to him. 저는 그에게 단호하게 말해야 했습니다.

- loud(ly) : 시끄럽게, 큰 소리로
  - Don't talk so **loud**. 너무 큰소리로 말하지 마시오.
  - He spoke **loud**(ly) and clear(ly). 그는 크고 또렷하게 말했습니다.
  - He called **loudly** for help. 그는 큰소리로 도움을 청하였습니다.

- quick(ly) : Come **quick**(ly). - I need help. 빨리 와요. 도움이 필요해요.
  - I ran as **quick**(ly) as I could. 저는 가능한 빨리 달렸습니다.
  - The term passed **quickly**. 학기가 빨리 지나갔습니다.

- right : 곧, 즉시, 바로
  - It serves you **right**. 곧 가겠습니다.
  - He guessed/answered **right**. (= correctly) 그는 바로 맞혔어요.
  - Nothing goes **right** with me. 난 뭐 하나 제대로 되는 게 없어.
  - I'll come **right** away. (= at once) 곧 가겠습니다.
- **rightly** = correctly
  - He **rightly** guessed that ... ...을 그가 제대로 맞혔습니다.
  - I can't **rightly** recollect whether ... ...인지 제대로 기억할 수 없습니다.

- slow : 천천히 (흔히 go와 함께 쓴다.)
  - The workers decided to go **slow**. (= work slow) 노동자들은 태업하기로 결정하였습니다.
  - I told the driver to go **slower**/to go **more slowly**. 운전사에게 더 서행하자고 말했습니다.
- **slowly** : 천천히
  - How **slowly** the time passes! 시간이 참 늦게 가네!

- tight : 단단히, 꽉
  - Hold it **tight**. Hold **tight** to my hand. 그것을 꽉 잡아. 내 손을 꽉 잡아.
  - Screw the nuts up **tight**. 너트를 단단히 조여요.
  - The coat was made to fit **tight** round the waist. 코트가 허리에 꼭 끼도록 만들어졌어요.
  - We were packed **tight** in the bus. 우리는 만원버스에 올라탔습니다.
- **tightly** : 단단히, 꽉 (주로 과거분사와 함께 쓴다.)
  - The goods were **tightly** packed in the crate. 제품들은 상자에 꽉꽉 채워졌습니다.
  - The children sat with their hands **tightly** clasped. 어린이들은 두 손을 깍지낀 채 앉았습니다.

Basic Grammar for English Tests

(2) 뜻이 다른 경우

- deep : drink deep 과음하다
  Still waters run deep. 고요한 물이 깊다.
- deeply : deeply regret 철저히, 깊이 후회하다
  think deeply about a problem 문제를 깊이 생각하다

- direct : straight 똑바로, 곧장
  This train goes direct to New York. 이 열차는 뉴욕으로 곧장 갑니다.
  I shall communicate with you direct. 저는 당신과 직접 연락할 것입니다.
- directly : at once, immediately, very soon 곧, 즉시
  He left directly after breakfast. 그는 아침을 먹고 바로 떠났습니다.
  I'll be with you directly. 곧 당신에게 갈게.

- easy : Take it easy. (= Don't work too hard.) 잘 있어.
  Stand easy! 쉬어!   Go easy with the butter. 적당히 하게.
  Easier said than done. (= more easily) 말이 행동보다 쉽지.
- easily : He's not easily satisfied. 그는 쉽게 만족하지 않습니다.
  He won the race easily. (= with ease) 그는 쉽게 경주를 이겼습니다.

- flat : 전혀, 완전히
  The scheme **fell flat**. 계획이 완전히 실패했어요.
  His jokes all fell flat. 그의 농담은 전혀 들어 먹히지 않았습니다.
- flatly : 단호하게 = absolutely, in a downright way
  He flatly refused my request. 그는 제 요청을 단호하게 거절하였습니다.
  The suggestions were flatly opposed. 의견들이 단호하게 거부되었습니다.

- free : travel free 자유롭게
- freely : freely admit '기꺼이, 거리낌 없이'

- full : 꼭, 정면으로
  I hit him full in the face. 저는 그의 얼굴을 정면으로 쳤습니다.
- fully : 충분히, 완전히, 꼬박
  for fully three days and nights 꼬박 3일 밤낮동안
  I fully understand what you say. 난 자네가 하는 말을 완전히 이해해.

- hard : (열심히) I work hard and play hard. 난 열심히 일하고 열심히 논다.
- hardly : (거의 ~ 않다) I did hardly any work today. 저는 오늘 일을 거의 하지 않았습니다.

- high : 높이
  - aim high 목표를 높이다, fix one's hopes high 희망을 높은데 두다
  - hold one's head high 머리를 높이 쳐들다.
  - The sea was running high. 파도가 높이 칩니다.
  - Passions were running high. 열정이 대단합니다.
- highly : 대단히
  - highly amusing 대단히 고무된, highly paid 보수가 높은
  - a highly educated/intelligent woman 고등교육 받은/지적인 여자
  - speak/think highly of someone 누구를 높이 평가하다.
  - esteem someone highly 누구를 높이 존경하다.
- just : He has just finished the work. (이제 방금) 그는 일을 막 끝냈습니다.
  - I only just managed to catch the train. (겨우, 간신히) 저는 열차를 간신히 탔습니다.
  - He is just an ordinary man. (다만, 단지 = only) 그는 단지 평범한 남자입니다.
  - I'm just starving. (아주, 정말로 = very) 저는 아주 굶주렸습니다.
- justly : You should deal justly with him. (공정하게) 당신은 그를 공정하게 대해야 합니다.
  - He was justly punished. 그는 공정하게 처벌받았습니다.
- last : He arrived here last. (나중에, 최후에) 그는 여기 마지막으로 도착했습니다.
- lastly : Lastly, I think that he is right (= at last; 결국) 결국, 그가 옳다고 저는 생각합니다.
- late : We arrived an hour late. (뒤늦게 ↔ in time, early) 우리는 한시간 뒤늦게 도착했습니다.
  - He stayed up late last night. (밤늦도록) 그는 어젯밤 늦도록 안자고 있었습니다.
- lately : I haven't seen him lately. (최근 = recently) 저는 최근에 그를 보지 못했습니다.
  - It is only lately that I saw her. (최근) 제가 그녀를 본 것은 아주 최근이었습니다.
- near : go near, The station is quite near. (가까이) 역이 아주 가까이 있습니다.
- nearly : I nearly caught them. (거의 = almost) 저는 그들을 거의 잡았습니다
  - nearly escape death (겨우, 간신히) 간신히 죽음을 면하다
- pretty : 꽤 (= fairly, moderately)
  - I'm pretty well. 저는 건강이 꽤 좋습니다.
  - sit pretty 좋은 자리에 앉다, 출세하다
- prettily : smile prettily (곱게, 귀엽게 = attractively)
- real : We had a real good time. 우리는 '정말로' 좋은 시간을 가졌습니다.
- really : I really like him. 저는 '정말로/실제로' 그를 좋아합니다.
- rough : sleep rough '거칠게' 잠을 자다
- roughly : roughly twenty '대충/대략' 20정도

Basic Grammar for English Tests

- **sharp:** at six o'clock sharp 정각 6시 (정각 = punctually, exactly)
  - Look sharp! 조심해라!, 서둘러라! (= be quick!)
  - sing sharp '반음 높게' 노래 부르다
  - turn sharp left 갑자기 좌회전하다 (돌연, 갑자기 = abruptly)
- **sharply :** (= harshly, severely; 날카롭게, 호되게)
  - answer sharply 날카롭게 답하다, speak sharply to someone 누구에게 호되게 말하다,
  - a sharply pointed pencil 끝이 날카로운 연필

- **short :** (관용표현)
  - speak short 간단히 말하다 (= briefly),
  - stop short 갑자기 멈추다 (= suddenly),
  - cut short (행사나 회담 등을) 갑자기 중단하다,
  - run short 부족하다, 바닥나다
- **shortly :** in shorty afterward 잠시 후에 (= in a short time)
  - answer shortly 짤막하게 대답하다 (= briefly, curtly, abruptly)

- **strong :** still going strong 여전히 힘차게 일하는 (힘차게 = continuing vigorously)
  - go it strong 과장하다 (go = exaggerate)
- **strongly :** a strongly built man 건장한 남자
  - strongly oppose a measure 어떤 법안을 강하게 반대하다
  - strongly feel '격렬하게' 느끼다

- **sure :** (분명히, 확실히 = certainly)
  - I sure am late. 분명히 지각이다.
- **surely :** Will you go with us? - Surely! (물론!)
  - He will surely succeed. (확실히)

- **wide :** 'Open your mouth wide', said the dentist. (크게)
  - The windows were wide open/open wide. (활짝)
  - He was wide awake. 그는 잠이 완전히 깨었습니다.
  - Their views still wide apart. 그들의 견해는 여전히 '크게' 다릅니다.
  - We searched **far and wide** for the missing child. (널리)
  우리는 미아를 널리 찾았습니다.
- **widely :** '널리' (주로 과거분사와 함께 쓴다.)
  - widely scattered/known 널리 흩어진/알려진
  - He has travelled widely. 그는 널리 여행하였습니다.

Exercise 1 다음 각 문장이 성립하도록 괄호에서 알맞은 말을 골라라.

1. Jane plays the violin (good/*well*).
2. That is an (intense/intensely) novel.
3. The sun is shining (bright/brightly).
4. The girls speak (fluent/fluently) French.
5. The boys speak Japanese (fluent/fluently).
6. The table has a (smooth/smoothly) surface.
7. We must figure our income tax returns (accurate/accurately).
8. We don't like to drink (bitter/bitterly) tea.
9. The plane will arrive (soon/soonly).
10. He had an accident because he was driving too (fast/fastly).

Exercise 2 다음 각 문장이 성립하도록 괄호에서 적당한 부사를 골라라.

1. Farm workers have to work very (*hard*/hardly) during the harvest.
2. Farm workers earn (hard/hardly) enough money to pay their bills.
3. We've been receiving a lot of junk mail (late/lately).
4. The postman brings my mail so (late/lately) I rarely see it before I go to work.
5. I'm sure the boss thinks very (high/highly) of you.
6. If you want to succeed, you should aim (high/highly).
7. I don't think you were treated very (just/justly).
8. I've (just/justly) been offered a job in Mexico!
9. Please don't go too (near/nearly) the edge of the platform.
10. I (near/nearly) fell off the edge of the platform!

◀ 장소의 부사(Place/Where … ?)

장소부사의 역할

1. 주로 be, live, stay, work 등의 동사와 함께 쓰여 위치를 표현한다.

   Larry is in **Jamaica**.

2. 주로 go, come 등의 동사와 함께 쓰여 방향을 표현한다.

   Larry went by plane to Jamaica. (= Larry flew to Jamaica.)

Basic Grammar for English Tests

장소부사의 종류

1. abroad, ahead, anywhere/everywhere/nowhere/somewhere, ashore, away, back/backward/forward, here/there, left/right, north/south, upstairs/downstairs

2. 전치사로도 쓰이는 부사

    above, behind, below, beneath, underneath

3. 두 단어 짜리 - 장소를 강조

    down below, down there, up there, far ahead, far away, over here, over there

    She lives in a small house in a village outside Chicago.
    Inside it was nice and warm. Outside it was snowing heavily.
    그녀는 시카고 외곽의 한 마을에 작은 집에서 살았습니다. / 안에는 좋고 따뜻했으나, 밖은 눈이 몹시 내리고 있었습니다.

◀ 시간의 부사(Time/When … ?)

시간부사의 종류

1. 한정된 시간(definite time)을 표현하는 부사 - 시점

    yesterday, today, tomorrow, Monday …
    cf. **Tomorrow** is Tuesday, isn't it? (명사역할)

2. 무한시간(indefinite time)을 표현하는 부사 - 막연한 시간

    now, one day, soon, recently …

3. 기간(duration)을 표현하는 부사 : ago, all day, long …

한정된 시간(definite time)을 표현하는 부사

정확히 언제'(When exactly?)라는 '시점'(points of time)을 가리킨다.
주로 early/earlier, late/later 등의 수식을 받는다.
earlier today, late this evening …

무한시간(indefinite time)을 표현하는 부사

1. 종류

   afterward, already, another day, another time, at last, at once, early, eventually, formerly, immediately, just, late, lately, now, nowadays, once, one day, presently, recently, some day, soon, still, subsequently, suddenly, then, these days, ultimately, yet

2. yet와 already의 비교

   일반적으로 yet는 부정문과 의문문에, already는 긍정문에 쓴다.

   Did you see Jane **yet**? I **already** saw her.
   The new rule hasn't **yet** come into practice.
   Have you received her invitation **yet**? ('몰라서 '정보'를 구하려고 물을 때)
   Have you **already** received her invitation? ('확인'을 구하려는 의문문에서)
   제인 보았어요? 저는 벌써 봤습니다. / 새로운 규정이 아직 시행되지 않았습니다. / 그녀의 초대를 받았나요? / 그녀의 초대를 받았나요?

기간(duration)을 표현하는 부사

1. 종류 : ago, all (day) long, (not) any more/(not) any longer, no longer/no more

2. since와 ago의 비교

   (1) since : since+시점(since when?; '언제부터'라는 기간의 시작점을 표현한다.- 완료형 시제)
      I **haven't seen** Tom **since** January/last holiday.
      I **met** John last week. I **hadn't seen** him **since** 1984.

   (2) ago : 기간+ago(얼마 전, 언제 ; How long ago? When?)
      I **started** working at the gas station **seven months ago**.

3. for(for+기간 - 동안 ; how long?)

   ages, hours, days, weeks, months, years 등과 함께 쓴다.

   The Browns **lived** here **for five years**. (지금은 여기 살지 않는다.)
   The Browns **have lived** here **for five years**. (아직 여기 살고 있다.)
   I **haven't seen** him **for months**.

   * **since/for**의 용법구분

Basic Grammar for English Tests

4. from ~ to/till/until ~ : 제한된 시간

   The tourist seasons runs from June to/till October. 관광시즌이 6월에서 10월까지 계속됩니다.

5. by : till/until 용법차이

   (1) 'by+시점'까지 어떤 행위가 끝난다.
   I'll have left by Monday.
   I won't have left by Monday.

   (2) 'till/until+시점'까지는 어떤 행위나 상태가 지속된다. 흔히 지속성의 동사 stay, wait 등과 함께 쓴다.
   I'll stay here till/until Monday.
   I won't stay here till/until Monday.

6. during : 모든 기간을 나타내는 말에 쓸 수 있다.
   in : 단순한 기간에만 쓴다.
   throughout : 위의 두 전치사와 같은 용도로 쓴다. 특히 처음부터 끝까지 전 기간을 의미한다.

   ⎡ It was very hot during/in the summer.
   ⎣ He's phoned four times during/in the last half hour.

   ⎡ I posted it some time during the week. (during 대신 in을 쓰지 않는다.)
   ⎣ I didn't learn much during/in my teacher-training.

   ⎡ There were thunderstorms throughout/during/in July.
   ⎣ During/Throughout the whole winter she never saw a soul.
   　그녀는 겨우내 사람을 보지 못했습니다.

Exercise 3 다음 각 문장에 맞는 말을 괄호에서 골라라.

1. I'll wait (by/*till*) Monday before answering his letter.
2. I intend to stay in bed (by/till) 10 o'clock tomorrow morning.
3. Your suit will be ready (by/for) Friday.
4. I'm sure I will have left (by/for) Monday.
5. It was very hot (during/for) August.
6. I was sent abroad (during/in) my military service.
7. I tried to get a taxi (for/in) a whole hour.
8. I suddenly felt ill (during/for) my speech.
9. There was an accident (during/in) the race.
10. Can you hold your breath (for/in) two minutes?

◀ 빈도부사(Frequency/ How often?)

빈도의 정도에 따라 한정빈도(definite frequency)와 무한빈도(indefinite frequency)로 나눌 수 있다.

한정빈도(definite frequency)부사

빈도의 정도가 구체적이고 일정하게 규정된 경우

- once, twice, three times … several times(a day/week/month/year…)
- hourly, daily, weekly, monthly, yearly, annually
- every+시간 : every day/morning/afternoon/evening/night
  every week/month/year
  every other day, every third day
  every 3 days, every few days
- on Monday/Friday/weekdays …

무한빈도(indefinite frequency)부사

빈도의 정도를 막연히 정의하는 부사

1. 높다   always

   almost always, nearly always

   generally, normally, regularly, usually

   빈도   frequently, often

   sometimes, occasionally

   almost never, hardly ever, rarely, scarcely ever, seldom

   희박   not ~ ever, never

   I **hardly ever** see Brian these days.
   We only have dinner parties **very occasionally** these days.

2. 기타 무한빈도를 표현하는 부사
   - again and again, at times, every so often, from time to time, now and then
   - constantly, continually, continuously, repeatedly

◀ 정도부사 (Degree/ To what extent?)

종류와 역할

almost, altogether, barely, a bit, enough, fairly, hardly, nearly, quite, rather, somewhat, too

quite 용법 : 형용사, 부사, 동사, 명사를 모두 수식할 수 있다.

1. 형용사 수식

   The lecture was quite good. 강의는 아주 훌륭했습니다.
   The news is quite amazing. 뉴스는 아주 놀랍습니다.

2. 부사 수식

   He lectured quite well. 그는 강의를 아주 잘 했습니다.
   She plays quite amazingly. 그녀는 아주 놀라울 정도로 잘 놉니다.

3. 동사 수식

   I quite enjoy Japanese food. 저는 일본음식을 상당히 즐깁니다.
   I quite forgot to post your letter. 나는 네게 편지를 부칠 것을 까맣게 잊어버렸어.

4. 명사 수식 : quite+a(n)/the/some+명사

   It's quite some time since we wrote to each other.
   It's quite an interesting film. (= a quite interesting)
   It's quite the worst play I have ever seen.
   우리가 서로에게 편지한 지 아주 상당한 오래되었어. / 아주 재미있는 영화야. / 그건 내가 본 것 중에 최악의 연극이야.

fairly 용법 : 형용사와 부사를 수식

The lecture was **fairly good**. 강의는 꽤 훌륭했어요.
He lectured **fairly well**. 그는 강의를 꽤 잘 했어요.

rather 용법 : quite나 fairly보다 더 강하다.

I **rather like** raw fish. 저는 생선을 상당히 좋아합니다.
Frank is clever but **rather lazy**. 프랭크는 똑똑하지만 아주 게으릅니다.
Your results are **rather good** - better than I expected.
자네의 성적은 내가 예상한 것 보다 아주 좋아.

a (little) bit

He arrived **a bit**/a little/somewhat late. 그는 약간 늦게 도착했습니다.
You're **a bit**/a little/somewhat taller than Alice. 자네가 앨리스보다 조금 더 크다.

hardly

I've got so little time, I **hardly ever read** newspapers.
There's **hardly any** cheerful news in the papers.

저는 시간이 너무 없어서 신문을 거의 볼 수 없어요. / 신문에 재미난 뉴스가 거의 없어요.

빈도/정도부사의 강조와 문장의 어순 : 부사+조동사+주어+본동사

빈도부사를 강조하여 문두로 내면, 주어동사의 어순이 바뀐다.

Hardly does Jane remember the accident that took her sister's life.
← Jane hardly remembers the accident that took her sister's life.
Never have so many people been unemployed as today.
←So many people have never been unemployed as today.
Rarely does George forget to do his homework.
← George rarely forgets to do his homework.
Seldom does class let out early.
← Class seldom lets out early.
Only by hard work will we be able to accomplish this great task.
← We will be able to accomplish this great task only by hard work.

제인은 여동생의 생명을 앗아간 사고를 거의 기억하지 못합니다. / 오늘날처럼 이렇게 많은 사람들이 실업상태였던 적은 결코 없었습니다. / 조지는 숙제하는 것을 좀처럼 잊지 않습니다. / 수업이 일찍 끝나는 일은 좀처럼 없습니다. / 열심히 일해야만 이런 대작업을 완수할 수 있을 것입니다.

◀ 강도부사(intensifiers)

단어의 의미를 강화한다.

very

John has been **very ill**.
Bob is not a **very nice** person.

기타 강도부사

1. very much/so much

Byron is very much/so much admired in Greece.
I enjoyed your party very much/so much.

바이런은 그리스에서 대단히 존경받습니다. / 저는 댁의 파티가 아주 즐거웠습니다.

2. so/such

It was **such a nice party**! (= The party was so nice!)
It was **so important an occasion**, we couldn't miss it.

아주 멋진 파티였어요! / 그건 너무 중요한 사건이어서 잊을 수 없었어요.

3. very 대신 쓸 수 있는 jolly, pretty, dead

She's a **jolly good** player. (아주, 대단히)
The traffic is moving **pretty slowly**. (꽤)
You're **dead right**! The war did end on May 7, 1945. (완전히)

그녀는 아주 훌륭한 선수입니다. / 교통이 너무 서서히 움직입니다. / 자네 딱 맞아! 전쟁은 1945년 5월 7일에 끝났다.

* **dead의 여러 표현**

   dead certain (아주 확실한), dead drunk (완전히 취한),
   dead quiet (너무 조용한), dead right (딱 맞는), dead straight (똑바로),
   dead tired (완전히 지친), dead wrong (완전히 틀린)

4. indeed, not ~ at all

I enjoyed it **very much indeed**.
Mike doesn't enjoy classical music **(very much) at all**.

저는 그것이 정말로 아주 재미있었습니다. / 마이크는 고전음악이 전혀 재미없습니다.

very 대신 쓰는 '-ly'형 강도부사

(very = extremely, particularly, really, terribly)

Miss Brown is **extremely helpful**.
Billy works **really slowly**.
I'm **terribly confused** by all this information.
The information is **terribly confusing**.
Jane is a **particularly good** worker.
I **really appreciate** all you've done for me.

브라운양은 너무나 도움이 되는 분입니다. / 빌리는 정말 일을 느리게 합니다. / 저는 이 모든 정보에 너무나 혼란스럽습니다. / 그 정보는 너무도 헷갈립니다. / 제인은 특별히 훌륭한 직원입니다. / 당신이 제게 하신 모든 일에 저는 정말로 감사드립니다.

Actual Test 17

다음 각 문장을 읽고 빈칸에는 알맞은 단어를 넣고, 밑줄 친 부분에서는 잘못된 부분을 찾으시오.

1. The bowl-shaped form of the kettledrum _____ half of a huge eggshell.
   - Ⓐ looks rather like
   - Ⓑ looks like rather
   - Ⓒ that looks like rather
   - Ⓓ that looks rather like

2. American automobile production of the present time has been increased _____.
   - Ⓐ greatly
   - Ⓑ highly
   - Ⓒ on a large scale
   - Ⓓ infinitely

3. _____ west coast of the United States.
   - Ⓐ Tornadoes almost occur never
   - Ⓑ Tornadoes never almost occur
   - Ⓒ Never tornadoes almost occur
   - Ⓓ Tornadoes almost never occur

4. _____ superstitious beliefs about the mountains.
   - Ⓐ People have had long
   - Ⓑ People have long had
   - Ⓒ Have people long had
   - Ⓓ Long have had people

5. Mississippi has the finest agricultural land, but floods and poor drainage have _____ this area.
   - Ⓐ always problems in caused
   - Ⓑ caused always problems in
   - Ⓒ always caused problems in
   - Ⓓ caused problems in always

6. The life span of a goldfish is short, _____ five years.
   - Ⓐ more seldom than
   - Ⓑ more than seldom
   - Ⓒ seldom more than
   - Ⓓ seldom than more

7. The western part of the United States is changing _____.
   - Ⓐ with swiftness
   - Ⓑ rapidly
   - Ⓒ in fast ways
   - Ⓓ fastly

8. Mr. Jones did not get up until eight-thirty that morning, and he arrived at
          A   B   C
   the meeting late too much.
                   D

9. The mandarin, a musical instrument that has strings, was probably imitated
                               A   B
   from the lute, a many older instrument.
    C   D

10. Although aging usually improves some foods, fish must be handled prompt
      A
    and careful from the moment of the catch until final processing.
       B   C   D

11. Fog usually appears in many the same way that a cloud appears around a
                            A   B   C
    steaming kettle.
       D

12. Too much stress sometime causes the disc of a spinal vertebra to press
                      A   B   C
    on a nerve.
       D

13. As soon as I saw the smoke, I called the fire department, but they haven't
         A   B   C
    arrived already.
            D

14. The Verrazano-Narrows Bridge in New York only is fifty feet longer than
                                              A   B   C
    the Golden Gate Bridge in San Francisco.
             D

15. No matter how hard she is working, she will insist on the principle as
         A   B   C
    hardly as he can.
       D

16. The invitations to the party indicated that everyone should be dressed
           A   B   C
    formerly.
       D

17. The following night John returned quite lately from work to find his
          A   B   C
    mother lying unconscious beside the phone.
             D

18. Ordinary a tornado breaks up suddenly and dissipates less than five hours
       A   B
    after it has formed.
      C   D

Unit 14

전치사

◀ 전치사의 종류

1. 단일 전치사 (한 단어)

   about, after, at, before, between, by, for, from, in, of, off, on, to, under, up, with

2. -ing형 전치사

   concerning, considering excepting, excluding, including, regarding

3. 합성 전치사 (두 단어 이상)

   according to (~에 따르면), ahead of (~보다 앞서), along with (~와 함께),
   apart from (~은 별도로), as for (~에 대해 말하면), as from (~날로부터),
   as regards (~에 대해 말하면), as a result of (~의 결과로), as to (~에 관하여),
   as well as (~뿐아니라 ~도), away from (~과 떨어져), because of (~때문에),
   but for (~이 없다면, 없었다면), by means of (~에 의하여), due to (~때문에),
   except for (~을 제외하고), for the sake of (~을 위하여 = for the benefit of),
   from under <이중전치사>, in addition to (~뿐아니라 = as well as),
   in case of (~의 경우에), in charge of (~을 담당하여, 책임을 지고 있는),
   in common with (공통된), in comparison to/with (~와 비교하여),
   in connection with (~에 관련하여 = with reference to),
   in favor of (~을 의하여, 찬성하여), in front of (~앞에), in line with (~과 일치하여)
   in place of (~대신 = instead of), in view of (~라는 견지에서, ~때문에),
   in spite of (~에도 불구하고 = for all, notwithstanding)
   instead of (~대신), near to (거의 ~할 뻔하다), next to (~의 옆),

on account of (~때문에), on behalf of (~대신에),
out of (= from), owing to (~때문에), up to (~에게 달려있다),
regardless of (~에도 불구하고 = without regard to), together with (~와 함께),
with regard to (~에 관하여 = concerning, regarding, as to, as regards)

4. 전치사구의 특별역할

   문장에서 전치사구의 일반역할은 부사인데, 다음은 특별한 역할이다.

   (1) of+추상명사 = 형용사구

   He is a man **of wisdom**. (= He is a **wise** man.)
   She is a man **of importance**. (= She is an **important** man.)
   This is **of great use**. (= This book is **very useful**.)
   of no use = useless

   (2) 전치사+명사 = 부사구

   I made it **with ease**. (= easily)
   in haste = hastily
   by luck = luckily
   on purpose = intentionally
   to excess = excessively

   (3) 접속사 역할도 하는 전치사

   after, as, before, since, till/until - 종속접속사

   I haven't seen him **since** this morning. (전치사)
   I haven't seen him **since** he left this morning. (접속사)
   Let's have our meeting **after** lunch.
   Let's have our meeting **after** we have had lunch.

Exercise 1 다음 각 문장이 성립하도록 괄호에서 적당한 말을 골라라.

1. The invitation is for my husband and (I/*me*).
2. She gave these presents to (we/us).
3. Share this between yourselves and (they/them).
4. For (we/us), the older generation, there have been many changes in society.
5. The news came as quite a surprise to a person like (I/me).

Exercise 2 다음 글을 읽으며 전치사를 찾아 동그라미를 그리시오.

Animals live all over the world; on land, in water, and in the air. Some animals are common and well known, while others do not even look like animals. Many water animals look like plants growing on the rocks or in the sand beneath the water.

Plants and animals are different from each other in two important ways. First, plants can not move by their own power as animals can, and second, animals can not make their own food as plants do. There might be some doubt a sponge's being an animal, because a sponge can not move. The sponge, however, is an animal because it does not make its own food. It lives by feeding on small animals in the water. Because it can not move, the sponge does not fit the rule. Almost all other animals can move if they wish. Plants can make their food out of substances drawn in through their roots and leaves, but animals can not do this. Their food has to be ready-made in the form of plants or other animals.

◀ 장소를 표시하는 전치사

이동(movement)과 위치(position)

1. 이동을 표현하는 동사들(bring, drive, fly, get, go, move, pull, run, take, walk)과 함께 **to, into, onto, out of** 등의 전치사들이 이동방향을 표시한다.

   A bird **flew into** my bedroom this morning.
   I **drove out of** the car park.
   _{새 한 마리가 오늘 아침에 내 방으로 날아 들어왔습니다. / 저는 주차장에서 차를 몰고 나왔습니다.}

2. 위치를 표현하는 동사들(be동사, live, keep, meet, stay, stop, work, wait...)과 함께 **at, in, on** 등의 전치사들이 위치를 표시한다.

   The bird **perched on** the church tower.
   I **waited in** the hotel lobby.
   _{새는 교회첨탑에 앉았습니다. / 저는 호텔로비에서 기다렸습니다.}

Basic Grammar for English Tests

이동과 위치를 나타내는 중요 전치사 비교

이동방향/출발지 ----▶ 이동 ----▶ 이동 후의 위치
1. .... **to/from** a point　　　　　　　　　　......... **at** a point
Jim has gone **to**　⎡ The Grand Hotel　　　　　　　　　⎡ The Grand Hotel. Jim has come **from**　⎢ school　　　and now he's **at**　⎢ school. 　　　　　　　　　⎢ London Airport　　　　　　　　　⎢ London Airport. 　　　　　　　　　⎣ my brother's　　　　　　　　　　⎣ my brother's.
2. .... **to/from** a point　　　　　　　　　　......... **in** an area
Jim has gone **to**　⎡ the country　　　　　　　　　　⎡ the country. Jim has come **from**　⎢ Seoul　　　and now he's **in**　⎢ Seoul. 　　　　　　　　　⎣ bed　　　　　　　　　　　　　⎣ bed.
3. .... **to/from** a point .... **at** a point/**in** an area
Jim has gone **to**　⎡ the restaurant　　　　　　　　　⎡ the restaurant. Jim has come **from**　⎢ Seoul　　and now he's **at/in**　⎢ the hotel. 　　　　　　　　　⎣ bed　　　　　　　　　　　　　⎣ the bank.
4. .... **on(to)** a line/surface　　　　　　　　......... **on** a line/surface 　　　　　**off** a line/surface　　　　　　　　　　　**off** a line/surface
I put the pen **on(to)** the table　　　and now it is **on** the table. I put the pen **off** the table　　　　and now it is **off** the table. * Mr. Temple jumped **onto** the stage　and now he is **on** the stage.
5. .... **in(to)** an area/volume　　　　　　　　......... **in** an area/volume 　　　　　**out of** an area/volume　　　　　　　　　**out of** an area/volume
I have put the coin **into** my pocket and now it is **in** my pocket. * We walked **into** the park. (밖에서 안으로 이동) We walked **in** the park. (이미 안에 있으면서 걷는다.) We ran **out of** the building and then we were **out of** the building. * We were **outside** the building.

* get: We **get into** the house through the window.
　　　Now we have to **get out** (of the car).
　　우리는 창을 통해서 집으로 들어갔습니다. / 이제 우리는 (차에서) 내려야 합니다

장소를 표시하는 중요 전치사들

1. 이동(movement) : to, for, toward

    (1) to (방향, 도착지점)

    Their house is **to** the north of the park. (방위) 그들의 집은 공원에서 북쪽에 있습니다.
    Turn **to** the right. (방향) 우회전하시오.
    She got **to** London yesterday. (도착지) 그녀는 어제 런던에 도착하였습니다.
    She has been **to** the station. (공공장소) 그녀는 역에 갔습니다.

    (2) for (행선지/목적지)

    The train is bound **for** Busan. 열차는 부산행입니다.
    He left **for** Seoul. 그는 서울로 떠났습니다.

    (3) toward (막연한 방향)

    He ran **toward** the station.
    He went **toward** the west.

2. out of/outside

    (1) out of (↔ into)

    이동 : We ran **out of** the burning building.
    　　　 We got **into** the car in a hurry.
    위치 : Mr. Kim is **out of** the office. (= He is not in.)
    　　　 Mr. Kim is **in** his office. (= He is not out.)

    (2) outside (↔ inside) = out of

    이동 : We ran **outside** the burning building.
    　　　 We ran **inside** the burning building.
    위치 : She is **outside** the office.
    　　　 She is **inside** the office.

3. 위치(position) : at/in

    (1) at (한 지점)

    My car is **at** the cottage.
    I will meet you **at** the library.

    (2) in (지역)

    I work **in** Seoul, but live in the country.
    * Please watch TV **at a distance**! (떨어져서)

I saw the tree **in the distance**. (멀리 있는)
I have only seen the mountain **from a distance**. (먼데서)
* He lives **on/at** the corner of Tenth Avenue and 6th Street.(주소)

4. on/beneath (표면)

   There's a vase **on** the table.
   He hid the money **beneath** the carpet.

5. up/down

   We live **down** the street. (위치) 우리는 도로 아래쪽에 삽니다.
   His office is **up/down** the stairs. (위치) 그의 사무실은 계단 위/아래쪽에 있습니다.
   Let's climb **up** the hill, then climb **down**. (이동방향) 동산을 올랐다가 내려갑시다.
   The elevator moves **up and down** the building. (이동방향)
   엘리베이터가 건물 위아래로 이동합니다.

6. over/under : above/below

   The lamp was hanging **over** the window. (위치)
   My bedroom is **over/above** the kitchen. (위치)
   He isn't **over/above/more than** twenty. (수량)
   There are a lot of minerals **under** the sea. (위치)
   A ship passed by **under** the bridge. (이동방향)
   The moon is sinking **below** the horizon. (이동방향)

   램프가 창 위에 달려있었습니다. / 제방은 부엌 위에 있습니다. / 그는 20살이 안됩니다. / 바다 밑에는 수많은 광물이 있습니다. / 다리 밑으로 배가 한 척 지나갔습니다. / 달이 수평선 아래로 잠기고 있습니다.

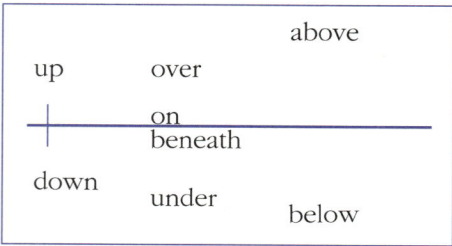

7. across/over/through(out)/along 비교

   (1) across/over : 공간(표면)을 건너는 의미, 횡단/교차

   The ship sailed **across** the Pacific.
   Children ran **over/across** the road without looking.
   There's a policeman **over/across** the road.

* Jane swam **across** the channel. (통과)
  They escaped by climbing **over** the wall. (이동위치)

  그 배는 태평양을 건너 항해를 했습니다. / 어린이들이 보지도 않고 길을 건너 달렸습니다. / 도로 건너편에 경찰이 있습니다. / 제인은 해협을 헤엄쳐 건넜습니다. / 그들은 벽을 타고 탈출하였습니다.

  (2) through/throughout (관통)

  The river flows **through** the city.
  We traveled **throughout** the country. (through보다 강조된 의미)

  강물이 도시를 관통해서 흐릅니다. / 우리는 전국을 여행하였습니다.

  (3) along : 선에 붙어서 이동

  We walked **along** the shore. 우리는 해안을 따라 걸었습니다.

8. (a)round/about

   (1) 운동방향이나 위치

   The moon moves **(a)round** the earth. 달이 지구 주위를 돕니다.
   Let's sit **(a)round** the fire. 불가에 앉읍시다.

   (2) approximately (대략)

   The telex was reserved (at) **(a)round/about** 8 o'clock.

   텔렉스가 8시쯤에 예약되었습니다.

   (3) 장소

   They were walking **about/around** the park. (여기저기)
   I lost my purse **about/around** here. (근처)

   그들은 공원을 거닐었습니다. / 저는 이 근처에서 지갑을 잃었습니다.

9. before/after (순서)

   You come **before/after** me in the race. 경주에서는 네가 내 앞/뒤에 왔어.
   Why don't you go **before/after** me? 내 앞/뒤에서 갈래요?

10. before/in front of (위치)

    I will wait **in front of** the shop. (not before) 저는 가게 앞에서 기다릴게요.
    There, **before/in front of** us, lay the desert. 저기 우리 앞에 사막이 있어요.

11. behind/at the back of (위치)

    There's a tree **behind** the house.
    There's a garden **at the back of** the house.

Basic Grammar for English Tests

12. by/near/on

    (1) by (옆에 (붙어) = next to, beside)

    I sat **by** the phone all morning. 저는 아침 내내 전화 옆에 앉아있었어요.

    (2) near (가까이 : by 보다는 조금 떨어져)

    We live **near** Chicago.

13. beside/besides

    (1) beside (옆 = next to)

    Come and sit **beside** me.

    (2) besides (= in addition to, as well as)

    There were many people there **besides** us. 우리말고도 거긴 많이 사람들이 있었습니다.

14. opposite (to) : 반대편

    There's a bank **opposite (to)** my office.

15. on/off : 접촉, 분리

    Turn the light **on(off)**. 전등을 켜/끄시오.

16. between/among : 가운데

    (1) between (둘 사이)

    I had a seat between two ladies.

    (2) among (셋 이상 사이)

    Birds are singing among the trees. 새들이 나무 사이에서 노래하고 있습니다.

    * between you and me, between ourselves: 우리끼리 얘기지만

이동방향과 위치표시의 비교

이동

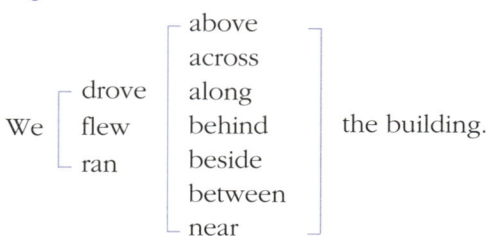

위치

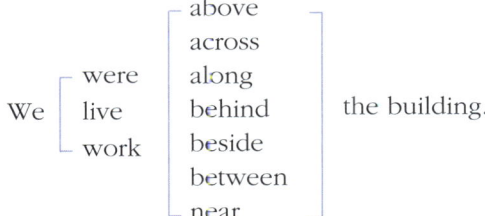

We went away/back/inside/outside/up/down. (이동)
We stayed away/back/inside/outside/up/down. (위치)
Where's Jim? I don't know. He went out. (이동)
Where's Jim? I don't know. He's out. (위치)

결국, 이동방향이나 위치를 표시하는 전치사가 각각 그 목적에만 고정되어 있는 것이 아니다. 동사의 성격에 따라 역할이 달라지는 융통성을 가지고 있다.

Exercise 3 다음 문장이 성립하도록 괄호에서 적당한 전치사를 골라라.

1. He's gone to the station. He's probably (*at*/in) the station now.
2. She's gone to school. She's probably (at/in) school now.
3. He flew from London. He's probably (at/in) Paris now.
4. He's gone into the garden. He's (at/in) the garden now.
5. She's gone to bed. She's (at/in) bed now.
6. He's gone to a dinner party. He's probably (at/in) the dinner now.
7. She's gone to a wedding. She's probably (at/in) the wedding now.
8. He's gone to the kitchen. He's probably (at/in) the kitchen now.
9. They've come out of the desert. They're probably (at/in) the jungle now.
10. They've gone to New York. They're probably (at/in) New York now.
11. She's gone to the waiting room. She's probably (at/in) the waiting room now.
12. He's been sent to prison. He's probably (at/in) prison now.
13. She's gone to the doctor's. She's probably (at/in) the doctor's now.
14. He's gone home. He's probably (at/in) home now.
15. She's gone to the old town. She's probably (at/in) the old town now.
16. They've sailed to the Pacific. They're probably (at/in) the Pacific now.
17. We live (at/in) 14 Woodland Avenue.
18. She was taken to hospital. She's (at/in) hospital now.

◀ 시간을 표시하는 전치사

전치사 at, on, in은 장소뿐만 아니라 시간을 표시하는 중요한 전치사이다. 이외에 during, for, from, since, till 등이 있다. approximately, (a)round, about 등이 수식하기도 한다.

The accident happened at approximately 5:30.
The accident happened (at) about(/around) 5:30.

at (시간 time)

What time do you arrive? - **Nine o'clock** in the morning.
At what time do you arrive? - **At nine o'clock** in the morning.

[정확한 시각]	at 10 o'clock, at 6:30 p.m. at 14 hundred hours
[식사시간]	at lunch time, at tea time, at dinner time
[하루구분의 시간 명사]	at dawn, at noon, at midnight, at night
[축제일]	at Christmas, at Easter, at Christmas-time
[나이]	at the age of 27, at 15
[time이 붙은 말]	at this time, at that time

on (날 day)

[요일]	on Monday, on Friday
[하루중의 시간 명사]	on Monday morning, on Friday evening
[날짜]	on June 1st, on 21st March
[요일+날짜]	on Monday, June 1st
[특별한 날이나 시간]	on that day, on that evening
[기념일]	on your birthday, on your wedding day
[축제일]	on Christmas day, on New Year's day

* 일상적으로 말할 때는 **on**을 생략해서 쓴다.
I'll see you Friday. See you June 21st.

in (연, 월 year, month)

흔히 기간을 표시하는 'during'과 같은 뜻이다.

[하루의 구분]	in the morning, in the evening
[월]	in March, in September
[연도]	in 1900, in 1984, 1993
[세기]	in the 19th century(1800-1899), in the 20th century(1900-1999)

[계절]	in (the) spring/Spring, in (the) Summer/spring in (the) Winter/winter
[축제일]	in Easter week
[기간]	in that time, in that age, in the holidays

시간의 경과 표시

1. in/within (~이내에 : before/after the end of -)

    I always eat my breakfast **in** ten minutes. (이내에)
    I finished the examination **in/within** an hour and a half. (이내에)
    * Father will be back **in** a few days. (후에 after the end of -)
    <small>저는 늘 아침을 10분 안에 다 먹습니다. / 저는 1시간30분 안에 시험을 끝냈습니다. / 아버지는 며칠 후에 돌아오십니다.</small>

2. after (~후에)

    Come and see me **after** work.
    He came back **after** a month.
    * Come and see me **after** you're finished. (접속사)

3. before (~전에)

    You should be there **before** 7 o'clock.

    * ┌ in time : 시간에 맞게
      └ on time : 정각에(= punctually)

    The teacher came **in time** to lecture us.
    The train, which was due at five o'clock, arrived **on time**.

    * ┌ on schedule = on time
      ├ ahead of schedule/time : 예정보다 빨리
      └ behind schedule : 예정보다 늦게

기간표시

1. for (구체적인 수치명사로 제시되는 기간)

    He stayed here **for** ten days.

2. during (지속되는 일정기간)

    during the night, during the war

    He stayed there **during** the vacation.

Basic Grammar for English Tests

3. through/throughout (내내, 처음부터 끝까지)

We camped there **through(out)** the summer.
He worked hard **through(out)** the vacation.

4. Over (초과하는 기간)

The patient won't live **over** a day. 그 환자는 하루를 넘겨 살지 못할 것입니다.

since (~이후; 계속되는 상황의 출발점, 완료시제와 함께 쓴다.)

Ten years have passed **since** his death. 그가 죽은 후 10년이 흘렀습니다.
(= It is ten years **since** he died. - 접속사)
He has lived here **since** 1950. 그는 1950년부터 여기 살았습니다.

till/until (동작, 상태의 지속)
by (동작의 완료)

I shall wait here **till** five. He didn't appear **till** six.
I shall come back **by** five. You must finish it **by** noon.
저는 5시까지 여기서 기다릴 겁니다. 그는 6시까지 나타나지 않았습니다. / 저는 5시까지 돌아올 것입니다. 당신은 정오까지 그것을 끝내야 합니다.

from ~ till/until/to ~ (제한된 시간)

I worked at my office **(from)** nine **to/till** five. 저는 9시부터 5시까지 사무실에서 일합니다.

Exercise 4 각 문장의 빈칸에 시간의 전치사 at/on/in 중에 가장 알맞은 것을 골라 넣으시오.

1. I'll meet you *at* 10:30 *on* Monday, June 14.
2. We're taking our holiday _____ July.
3. I always finish work early _____ Fridays.
4. Who knows what the world will be like _____ the year 2030?
5. You don't want anything to go wrong _____ your wedding day.
6. _____ the 19th century many children died before they were a year old.
7. We got up _____ dawn and reached the summit _____ noon.
8. _____ the age of 14 I realized I would never become a surgeon.
9. The birds don't find much to eat in our garden _____ winter.
10. What will you be doing _____ the holidays?
11. What will you be doing _____ New Year's Day?

12. The year was 1986. _____ that time I was working as a waiter.
13. We try to get away _____ Christmas time.
14. I'll see you _____ ten days' time.
15. They prepared a surprise for me at the office _____ my birthday.

◀ 기타 전치사

원인/이유/근거/목적을 표시하는 전치사

1. 원인/이유 : because of/on account of/owing to/due to

   I can't do the work [because of/on account of / owing to/due to] my illness.

   Because of the crisis in agriculture, farms are going bankrupt.
   (= On account of/owing to)

   * due to는 문두에 잘 쓰지 않는다.
     Our delay was **due to** heavy traffic. (= caused by; 서술적으로 쓸 수 있다.)

2. for의 용법

   He is the best man **for** the job. (목적)
   This tool is used **for** drilling holes. (용도)
   This is the train **for** New York. (목적지)
   Here is a gift **for** you. I've got news **for** you. (수여, 증여)
   I did it **for** the money. (이유)
   He's been away **for** several days. (기간)

3. according to (근거)

   According to the forecast, it will rain.
   According to my father, this is a very good car.

'양보'의 전치사 : in spite of/despite/(al)though/for all/with all/notwithstanding

It is still warm, **(al)though**/in spite of/despite/notwithstanding the drop in the temperature. (전치사) 기온이 떨어져도 여전히 따뜻합니다.

* It is still warm, **(al)though** the temperature has dropped. (접속사)
  For all her money, Mrs. Brown isn't happy. 돈이 많은데도 브라운부인은 행복하지 않습니다.
  With all this rain, there'll be a good crop. 이렇게 비가 많이 오지만, 수확은 좋을 것입니다.

예외 표시의 전치사 : but (for)/except (for)/excepting

Except/but for you everyone has helped. 당신을 빼고 모두가 도왔어요.
No one swam across the river **but** he. 그를 빼고는 아무도 강을 헤엄쳐 건너지 못했어요.
We go to school everyday **except** Sunday. 일요일을 빼고는 매일 학교에 갑니다.
Excepting Sundays the stores are open daily. 일요일만 빼고 가게들이 매일 영업합니다.

'주제에 대한 관심'을 표시하는 전치사 : on/about/over

어떤 주제에 대한 생각이나 의견을 표현할 때

1. **on** : 학구적 관심이나 연구

   Have you seen this article **on** the Antarctic? 남극에 관한 논문을 보셨나요?
   Dr. Johns is an authority **on** urban planning. 존스박사는 도시계획에 권위자입니다.

2. **about/over** : 평범한 관심

   I've read many book **about** animals. 저는 동물에 관한 책을 많이 읽었습니다.
   I've been worried **over** the result. 저는 결과를 걱정했습니다.

수단, 방편의 전치사 : by/with/without

1. **by** (수단, 편 = by means of)

   I usually go to school **by** bus. (교통수단)
   You can open this window **by** turning the key to the right. (방법)
   I'm paid **by** the hour/day/week. (단위)

   저는 늘 버스로 학교에 갑니다. / 열쇠를 오른쪽으로 돌리면 창을 열 수 있습니다. / 저는 시간/일/주당으로 급여를 받습니다. /

2. **with/without** (도구, 용도)

   It won't open **without** a bottle-opener.
   Someone broke the window **with** a stone.

   병따개 없이는 열리지 않습니다. / 누군가 돌로 창문을 깼습니다.

동반, 상황표현의 전치사 : with/without

1. 동반

   I went to the zoo **with** my sister.
   I can't manage **without** you.

   저는 여동생과 동물원에 갔습니다. / 저는 당신 없이는 못살아요.

2. 부대상황

He stood **with** his hand in his pockets.
We must get inside **without** waking her.
Don't speak **with** your mouth full.
He was standing **with** a hat on.

그는 주머니에 한 손을 넣고 서있었습니다. / 우리는 그녀를 깨우지 않고 안으로 들어갔습니다. / 입안에 먹을 것을 넣고 말하지 마라. / 그가 모자를 쓰고 서있었습니다.

분사를 동반하기도 한다.

With an eye bandaged, I couldn't write properly.
He walked **with** head bent.

한쪽 눈에 붕대를 하고서는 제대로 글을 쓸 수 없었습니다. / 그는 머리를 숙이고 걸었습니다.

소유의 전치사 : with/without/in/of

Who's the woman **with** the green umbrella? (소지)
I'm **without** any money.
He's a man **with** a big nose and red hair.
Who's the woman **in** the green blouse? (입은 상태)
He's a man **of** courage. (성격)

초록색 우산을 쓴 여자는 누구죠? / 저는 돈이 전혀 없습니다. / 그는 코가 크고 머리카락이 붉습니다. / 초록색 블라우스를 입은 여자는 누군가요? / 그는 용기 있는 사람입니다.

of/from/with

1. 재료, 원료

   My gloves are **made of** leather.
   Beer is **made from** hops.
   This sauce is **made with** fresh cream.

   장갑은 가죽으로 만듭니다. / 맥주는 호프로 만듭니다. / 이 양념은 신선한 크림으로 만듭니다.

2. 죽음의 원인

   He **died of** lung cancer. (질병)
   He **died from** the traffic accident. (질병 외 기타 원인)

   그는 폐암으로 죽었습니다. / 그는 교통사고로 죽었습니다.

like/as (비교/자격)

1. **like** (비교): ~와 같은, ~처럼 (= the same~ as)

Basic Grammar for English Tests

There's no one **like** you. 너 같은 사람은 없어.
It was **like** a dream. (= similar to) 꿈만 같았어요.

2. **as** (자격 : ～로서)

I work **as** a hotel receptionist. 저는 호텔안내원으로 일합니다.

instead (부사)/instead of

We eat margarine **instead of** butter. 우리는 버터대신 마가린을 먹습니다.

between/among (둘 사이/셋 이상)

What's the difference **between** these two watches? (차이)
Professor Webster is **among** the world's best authorities on Physics.

이 두 시계의 차이는 뭔가요? / 웹스터교수는 물리학의 세계 최고 권위자로 속합니다.

from (출신/출처)

Jane is **from** California. (출신)
We're **from** the council. (집단)
This line is **from** 'Hamlet'. (인용출처)
She's away **from** work. (거리감)
He died **from** a stroke. (원인)

제인은 캘리포니아 출신입니다. / 우리는 시의원들입니다. / 이 구절은 《햄릿》에 나옵니다. / 그녀는 직장을 떠났습니다. / 심장마비 그는 심장마비로 죽었습니다.

Actual Test 18

다음 각 문장을 읽고 빈칸에는 알맞은 단어를 넣고, 밑줄 친 부분에서는 잘못된 부분을 찾아내시오.

1. Edelweiss grow wild _____ most temperate regions of the world.
   - Ⓐ in
   - Ⓑ where
   - Ⓒ that
   - Ⓓ are in

2. _____ history the making of fine books has required much artistic skill and imagination.
   - Ⓐ The
   - Ⓑ It is the
   - Ⓒ Since the
   - Ⓓ Throughout

3. Coniferous trees first appeared on the Earth _____ the early Jurassic period, some 200 million years ago.
   - Ⓐ when
   - Ⓑ or
   - Ⓒ and
   - Ⓓ during

4. _____ left before the deadline, it doesn't seem likely that Tim will finish the report.
   - Ⓐ Although such a short time
   - Ⓑ It is such a short time
   - Ⓒ With so short time
   - Ⓓ With such a short time

5. I bought this carpet at that shopping center, but it's actually _____ Iran.
   - Ⓐ in
   - Ⓑ except
   - Ⓒ from
   - Ⓓ about

6. This conclusion has caused a strong controversy _____.
   - Ⓐ to the professors
   - Ⓑ among the professors
   - Ⓒ between the professors
   - Ⓓ with the professors involved

7. _____ one-celled organisms, nearly all animals have some kind of nervous system.
   - Ⓐ Some
   - Ⓑ The
   - Ⓒ Except for
   - Ⓓ Despite

8. We danced _____ the music of Dorothy Johnson's band at the club last night.

   Ⓐ to
   Ⓑ with
   Ⓒ in
   Ⓓ on

9. Cowboys in movies <u>never seem</u> <u>to have</u> any trouble drawing guns <u>out from</u>
             A   B   C
   <u>their</u> holsters.
    D

10. <u>Situated at</u> an altitude of 7,200 feet <u>over</u> sea level and only 30 degrees north
      A   B
    of the equator, Kagnew station occupies <u>a</u> unique <u>position in</u> the country.
                   C   D

11. Northern Michigan's Mackinac Island <u>is</u> situated <u>of</u> the mouth <u>of</u> the straits
                  A   B   C
    of Mackinac <u>in</u> Lake Huron.
         D

12. <u>After</u> a thorough inspection of the Babylonian <u>tables</u>, he predicted that
     A   B
    another eclipse of the sun <u>was due</u> <u>in</u> May 25, 650 B.C.
               C D

13. Doctors are not <u>familiar with</u> many incurable <u>diseases but</u> will be able
            A   B
    to <u>detect</u> tuberculosis or certain kinds of cancer <u>at the</u> near future.
      C   D

14. <u>Since</u> their high vitamin and low <u>calorie</u> content, tomatoes are <u>included</u> in
     A   B   C
    certain <u>diets</u>.
       D

15. All sewing was done <u>with</u> hand <u>until</u> the invention <u>of</u> the sewing machine
             A   B   C
    <u>in</u> the early twentieth century.
    D

16. It is <u>remarkable</u> <u>how much</u> we <u>can learn about</u> the structure and history of
        A   B   C
    the moon <u>by</u> a sample of lunar soil.
       D

17. Several <u>decades</u> ago <u>when</u> I was traveling in Europe, I <u>became</u> acquainted
        A   B   C
    with a man who had roamed the world in search <u>with</u> adventure.
                      D

18. My <u>neglect</u> to <u>extinguish</u> our campfire resulted <u>from</u> the destruction of
       A   B   C
    more than two hundred acres of <u>forest</u>.
                                      D

19. She wrote <u>at least</u> ten novels, but only two <u>from the ten</u> that <u>are now known</u>
              A   B   C
    were published <u>during her lifetime</u>.
                         D

20. <u>Besides to be</u> the state capital, Montgomery is <u>the center of</u> <u>agricultural trade</u>
         A   B   C
    and <u>the largest</u> cattle market of Alabama.
              D

21. In the opinion <u>with</u> most people, <u>a</u> teacher's status in a country will <u>usually</u>
                    A   B   C
    improve as he gets a <u>higher</u> salary.
                            D

22. Historian Janet Jones <u>campaigned</u> vigorously on <u>behalf</u> to <u>peace</u> and
                              A   B   C
    <u>equal rights</u> for women.
         D

23. The period <u>of</u> quarantine depends <u>to</u> the amount of time necessary <u>for</u>
                A   B   C
    protection <u>against</u> the spread of a particular disease.
                  D

24. <u>Opposite</u> to <u>ordinary</u> belief, the ostrich does not hide <u>its</u> head in the sand;
         A   B   C
    <u>when frightened</u>, it runs.
            D

Unit 15

동사

◀ 동사의 역할에 따른 분류

타동사 (Transitive Verbs; *vt.*)

주어의 행위를 완성하고, 상태를 서술하기 위한 목적어(대상; object - 명사나 대명사)를 필요로 한다. 목적어의 종류에 따라 다음과 같은 문형이 있다.

1. Jack **hit the ball**. (*vt.*+명사/대명사)
2. He **found that** the room was empty. (*vt.*+명사절)
3. Everybody **wishes to succeed** in life. (*vt.*+부정사/동명사)
4. She **took good care of the baby**. (동사구+목적어)
5. She **lived a** happy **life**. (*vt.*+동족목적어 = She lived happily.)
6. He **presented himself** at the meeting. (*vt.*+재귀대명사)
7. She **wiped off the table**. (*vt.*+대상목적어 = She wiped off the dust on the table.)

자동사 (Intransitive Verbs; *vi.*)

목적어를 가지지 않고도 주어의 행위나 상태를 표현하는 동사

He **ran** directly through the center of the forest.
She **walked** slowly down the street.
She **lived** to be ninety.

Basic Grammar for English Tests

* **자동사, 타동사 역할을 모두 하는 경우**

  We read the news with great care. (*vt.*)
  We read until late at night. (*vi.*)

  I won the first set. (*vt.*)
  I won easily. (*vi.*)

* **혼동하기 쉬운 타동사와 자동사**

타동사		자동사	
raise	Tom raised his head.	rise	The sun rises in the east.
set	I will set the book on the desk.	sit	I sit in the front row.
lay	I'm laying the book on the desk.	lie	He is lying on his bed.
hang	I hung my clothes in the closet. They hanged the criminal by the neck until he was dead.		

연결동사(Linking Verbs)

appear, be, become, feel, grow, look, prove, remain, seem, smell, sound, stand, taste, turn ...

1. 문장에서 주어와 뒤에 이어지는 보어인 명사(서술명사)/대명사(서술대명사)/형용사(서술형용사)의 관계를 표현하는(연결하는) 역할을 한다.

   That play **was** good.
   The director will **become** famous tomorrow.
   The student **seems** shy.
   Those bears **appear** coffee colored.

2. 이들 동사 뒤에 부사가 수식어로 오는 것으로 착각하지 말 것.

   Mary **feels** *bad* about her test grade.
   Children **become** *tired* quite easily.
   Lucy will **look** *radiant* in her new dress.
   They **were** *sorry* to see us leave.
   The flowers **smell** *sweet*.
   This soup **tastes** *good*.

3. 대부분 상태를 표현하는 동사들이다.

The sky looks cloudy this morning. (연결동사)
Bill looks at Mark as though he hates him. (행위동사)

The coffee tasted too sweet. (연결동사)
Betty cautiously tasted the steaming-hot soup. (행위동사)

The team did not feel bad about its defeat. (연결동사)
If you cannot see in the dark, try to feel your way along. (행위동사)

Exercise 1 다음 각 문장에서 알맞은 동사를 고르시오.

1. The Student (raised/rose) his hand in class.
2. Hot air (raises/rises).
3. Ann (set/sat) in a chair because she was tired.
4. I (set/sat) your dictionary on the table a few minutes ago.
5. Hens (lay/lie) eggs.
6. Al is (laying/lying) on the grass in the park right now.
7. Jane (laid/lay) the comb on top of the dresser a few minutes ago.
8. If you are tired, you should (lay/lie) down and take a nap.
9. San Francisco (lays/lies) to the north of Los Angeles.
10. We (hanged/hung) the picture on the wall.

Exercise 2 다음 각 문장이 성립하도록 괄호 안에서 알맞은 단어를 고르시오.

1. Your cold sounds (*terrible*/terribly).
2. The pianist plays very (good/well).
3. The food in the restaurant always tastes (good/well).
4. The camper remained (calm/calmly) despite the thunderstorm.
5. They became (sick/sickly) after eating the contaminated food.
6. Professor Baker looked (quick/quickly) at the student's sketches.
7. Peter was working (diligent/diligently) on the project.
8. Paul protested (vehement/vehemently) about the new proposals.
9. Our neighbors appeared (relaxed/relaxedly) after their vacation.
10. The music sounded too (noisy/noisily) to be classical.

◀ 주요 동사의 용법

Be 동사

1. be 명령문

    (1) be+명사

    a. 'be+명사'형 명령문

    Be a man! 남자답게 굴어라!
    Be your age! 나이 값을 해라!
    Be yourself. 너답게 굴어라. 정신차려라.
    Be an angel and fetch me my slippers please. 착하지~. 내 슬리퍼 좀 가져오너라.
    Don't be a clown! 천박하게 굴지마!
    Don't be a fool! 바보같이 굴지마!

    b. be = become

    Be a good girl at school. 학교에서는 얌전해야지.
    Be a better cook! 훌륭한 요리사가 되거라.

    (2) 'be+형용사'형 명령문

    Be quiet! 조용해!
    Be careful! 조심해!
    Be patient! 침착해라.
    Don't be long! 오래 끌지 마라.
    Don't be so impatient! 너무 조급하지 말게.
    Don't be careless! 정신 좀 차려라.
    Don't be silly! 바보처럼 굴지 마라.

    (3) 'be+p.p.'형 명령문

    Be seated! 앉으시오.
    Be prepared! 준비하시오.
    Be warned! 경고합니다.

2. have동사 대신 쓰는 경우

    I'm done with all that nonsense. (= have done, finished)
    I left my keys just there and next moment they were gone. (= had gone)
    Have you finished with the paper? - I'm nearly finished. (= have finished)

3. There be+한정사

   be 동사의 수(number)는 뒤에 오는 명사의 수에 지배받는다.

   There's **a letter** for you from Bill.
   There **are some changes** in the printed program.
   Are there **any lemons** in the fridge?
   There **are no volunteers** for a job like this!
   There **are seventeen people** coming to dinner.

4. be/become의 뜻으로 쓰이는 진행동사(progressive verbs)

   become, come, fall, go, get, grow, run, turn, wear

   (1) 진행동사+형용사

   It was gradually **growing dark**.
   As she waited to be served, she **became** very **impatient**.
   Old Mr. Parker **get tired** very easily since his operation.
   The milk in this jug has **gone bad**.
   The leaves are **turning yellow** early this year.
   My shoelaces have **come undone**.
   The river Thames **run dry** during the recent drought.

   날이 점점 어두워졌습니다. / 서빙을 기다리면서 그녀는 조급해졌습니다. / 연로하신 파커씨는 수술 뒤에 아주 쉽게 피로해집니다. / 이 병에 든 우유는 변했어요. / 나뭇잎이 올해건 일찍 물듭니다. / 신발 끈이 풀어졌습니다. / 템즈강이 최근의 가뭄으로 말랐습니다.

   (2) 진행동사(become, make)+명사

   The ugly frog **became** a handsome prince.
   Jim **became** a Buddist.
   I'm sure Lucy will **make** a good nurse one day. (= become)
   This piece of wood will **make** a very good shelf. (= become)

   못생긴 개구리는 멋진 왕자가 되었습니다. / 짐은 불자가 되었습니다. / 저는 루시가 언젠가 훌륭한 간호사가 되리라 확신합니다. / 이 나무 조각이 훌륭한 책장으로 만들어질 것입니다.

   (3) 진행동사(come, get, grow)+to do

   We didn't trust John at first, but we soon **grew to like** him.

   우리가 처음에는 존을 믿지 않았지만, 곧 그를 좋아하게 되었습니다.

Basic Grammar for English Tests

Exercise 3 각 문장의 빈칸에 be동사 대신 들어갈 가장 알맞은 동사를 넣어 문장을 완성하시오.

1. When I _grow_ old, I hope I'll have lots of grandchildren.
2. You must be very careful you don't _____ ill when you're travelling.
3. I think this milk _____ sour.
4. Food _____ bad very quickly in hot weather.
5. It hasn't rained for months and our local river _____ dry.
6. It's no good _____ impatient every time I ask you a question.
7. She always wanted to retire before the age of 40 and her dream _____ true.
8. I had to cut my trip short because I _____ ill.
9. Don't you _____ bored listening to political broadcasts?
10. Personally, I think he'll a _____ very good pilot.

본동사로서 Do의 역할

1. 대동사 do : 반복을 피하기 위해

   John works 16 hours a day. I don't know how he **does** it.
   Take the dog for a walk. - I've already **done** it.
   Did you finish the work? - Yes, I **did**.

2. do : 어떤 행위나 임무를 수행하는 뜻

   What are you doing? - I'm reading.
   I **did** a lot of work around the house today.

3. do+동명사

   I **did** all our **shopping** yesterday. (do shopping 쇼핑하다)
   I've **done the ironing**. (do ironing 다림질하다)
   I've **done the washing up**. (do the washing up 세탁하다)
   I **do** a lot of **swimming**. (= I swim a lot.)

4. 관용적인 표현

   What does he do? (= What work does he do for a living?: 직업)
   How do you do? (인사)
   That will do! (= That will be enough.: 그 정도면 될 거야!)

How many miles does it do to the gallon? (= go)
This simply won't do. (= It's unacceptable.: 마음에 들지 않는다.)
How did you do? (= How did you manage?: 어떻게 지내셨습니까?)
I could do with a drink. (= I would like a drink.: 술 마시고 싶다.)
It's got nothing to do with me. (= It doesn't concern me.: 관계없다.)
I can do without a car. (= manage without a car: ~없이 지내다.)
I was done! (= I was cheated.: 속았다! 당했다!)
Shall I do your room out? (= clean it: 청소하다)
You did me out of my share. (= cheated me: ~를 속이다. 사기 치다.)

사역동사(Causative Verbs)

1. 사역동사의 문형

    (1) 사역동사(make/have/let/get)+목적어+(원형)부정사

    I **made/had/let** my brother **carry** my suitcase.
    I **got** my brother **to carry** my suitcase.

    나는 동생에게 내 가방을 들게 했습니다.

    Sad movies **make** me **cry**.
    Jane **had** the waiter **bring** her some tea.
    My father **let** me **drive** his car.

    슬픈 영화는 나를 슬프게 해. / 제인은 웨이터에게 차를 가져오게 했습니다. / 아버지는 제게 차를 운전하게 하셨습니다.

    (2) 사역동사(have/get)+목적어+p.p.

    I **had/got** my watch **repaired** (by someone).
    We now **have** the problem **solved**.
    I refuse to **have** my house **used** as a hotel.
    I'm **having** her **taught** English.

    저는 시계를 수리하게 했습니다. / 우리는 이제 그 문제를 풀었습니다. / 저는 우리 집이 호텔로 사용되는 것을 거절합니다. / 저는 그녀에게 영어를 가르치고 있습니다.

    I finally **got** my roof **repaired**.
    I must **get** this car **serviced** soon.
    Get your hair **cut**!

    저는 결국 지붕을 고치도록 했습니다. / 저는 곧 이 차를 손봐야 할 것입니다. / 이발을 하도록 해!

    Why don't you **have** your hair **cut**? (제안)
    Why don't you **get** your hair **cut**? (명령조)

Basic Grammar for English Tests

Exercise 4 다음 각 문장의 빈칸에 주어진 단어를 문장에 맞는 형태로 넣으시오.

1. The teacher made John _leave_ the room. (leave)
2. Jane had her car _____ by a mechanic. (repair)
3. Ellen got Marvin _____ her paper. (type)
4. I made Jane _____ her friend on the telephone. (call)
5. We got our house _____ last week. (paint)
6. Dr. Brown is having the students _____ a composition. (write)
7. The policemen made the suspect _____ on the ground. (lie)
8. Mark got his transcripts _____ to the university. (send)
9. Maria is getting her hair _____ tomorrow. (cut)
10. We will have to get the Dean _____ this form. (sign)
11. The teacher let Al _____ the classroom. (leave)
12. Jane always has her car _____ by the same mechanic. (fix)
13. We have to help Sue _____ her keys. (find)

◀ 동사의 시제(Tenses)

시제의 분류

상태나 행위의 종료 여부에 따라 완료형(perfect tense)이 첨가되어 총 12시제로 분류된다.

구분	기본형	구분	기본형
현재	I work.	현재진행	I am working.
과거	I worked.	과거진행	I was working.
현재완료	I have worked.	현재완료진행	I have been working.
과거완료	I had worked.	과거완료진행	I had been working.
미래	I will work.	미래진행	I will be working.
미래완료	I will have worked.	미래완료진행	I will have been working.

과거(simple past)	현재(simple present)	미래(simple future)
It snowed yesterday. I studied last night.	The world is round. It snows in Alaska. I study everyday.	It will snow tomorrow. I will study tomorrow.
과거진행(past progressive)	현재진행(present progressive)	미래진행(future progressive)
I was studying when they came.	I am studying right now.	I will be studying when you came.

과거완료(past perfect)	현재완료(present perfect)	미래완료(future perfect)
I had already studied lesson 1 before I began to study lesson 2.	I have already studied lesson 1.	I will already have studied lesson 4 before I study lesson 5.
과거완료진행 (past perfect progressive)	현재완료진행 (present perfect progressive)	진행 미래완료진행 (future perfect progressive)
I had been studying for two hours before my friends came.	I have been studying for two hours.	I will have been studying for two hours by the time you arrive.

현재시제(Simple Present)

1. 시간적으로 현재상황을 표현할 때

   I have only a dollar right now.

2. 영원한 진리/불변의 사실을 진술할 때,
   과거/현재/미래에도 항상 엄연한 사실을 일반적으로 진술할 때

   Summer follows Spring
   Gases expand when heated.
   Twice two is four.
   Most animals kill only for food.
   The earth moves round the sun.
   The world is round.

3. 사실을 일반적으로 진술할 때

   Your sister speaks French well.
   John prefers films to stage plays.

4. 일상적이고 습관적인 행위를 표현할 때

   I get up at 7 o'clock. John smokes a lot.
   He always eats a sandwich for lunch.
   This magazine comes out once a week.

5. 과거나 미래와 관련된 사실을 인용할 때

   The newspaper **says** it's going to be cold today.

Basic Grammar for English Tests

I **hear** you're going to Italy soon.
My friends **tell** me that you've been unwell.

6. 감탄문으로 표현할 때

   Here he comes!
   Here comes the bus!
   There she goes!

7. 행사계획/시간표 : 시간적으로는 미래지만 현재형으로 쓴다.

   The concert begins at 7:30 and ends at 9:30.
   We leave tomorrow at 11:15 and arrive at 17:50.

8. 관심/선언의 의미

   I hope/assume/suppose/promise everything will be all right. 다 잘 되기를 바랍니다.
   I declare this exhibition open. 저는 이 전시회의 개막을 선언합니다.

9. 주어가 3인칭 단수형일 경우 : 동사+(e)s

   He works in the office.
   She studies in the library.

현재진행시제(present progressive) : be + -ing

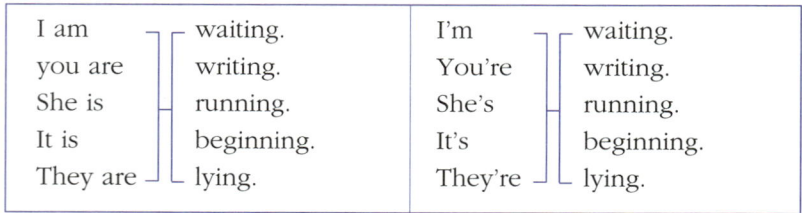

1. 현재진행형의 종류

   (1) 말하는 현재의 순간에 진행되고 있는 행위를 표현

   Someone is knocking at the door.
   He's working at the moment.
   John and Mary are talking on the phone.

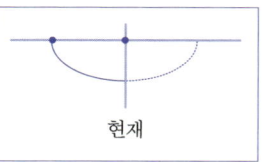

(2) 근황 표현

I'm taking five courses this semester. 저는 이번 학기에 5과목을 듣습니다.
John is trying to improve his work habits. 존은 자신의 근무습관을 개선하려고 합니다.
She is writing another book this year. 그녀는 올해 또 다른 책을 쓰고 있습니다.

(3) 반복되는 행위 표현

빈도부사 always constantly, continually, forever, perpetually, repeatedly 등과 함께

He's always complaining. 그는 항상 불평합니다.
You're forever finding fault with me! 너는 끝까지 나를 비난하는구나!

(4) 가까운 미래 표현

We're spending this summer in Australia.
He's arriving tomorrow morning on the 12:30 train.

2. 상태동사와 진행형

- He **appears** to be asleep. (상태동사/연결동사) 그는 졸리는 것 같아.
- The actor is **appearing** on the stage. (행위동사) 배우가 무대에 등장하고 있습니다.

- She **feels** better today. She is **feeling** better today. (자동사) 오늘은 좀 나아진 것 같아요.
- The cat's fur **feels** soft. (자동사) 고양이털은 부드러워요.
- Sue is **feeling** the cat's fur. (타동사) 수는 고양이털을 만져보고 있어요.

- I **find** that I was mistaken. (감지/판단) 내가 실수한 것 같아요.
- You're continually **finding** fault with me. (반복되는 행위) 넌 항상 나를 비난하는구나.
- We're **finding** out what really happened. (=discovering; 진행중인 행위) 우리는 실제로 어떤 일이 일어났는지 찾고 있습니다.

- He **has** a car. (상태) 그는 자동차를 가지고 있어요.
- I'm **having** a trouble. She is **having** a good time. (현재 상황) 제게 문제가 하나 있어요. 그녀는 즐거운 시간을 보내고 있어요.

- I **think** he is a kind man. (상태) 저는 그가 친절한 사람이라 생각합니다.
- We **are thinking** about this grammar. (진행중인 상황) 우리는 이 문법을 생각중입니다.

- She **looks** cold. I'll lend her my coat. (상태 - 연결동사) 그녀가 추워 보입니다.
- I'm **looking** out the window. (= out-looking; 진행중인 행위) 창 밖을 바라보고 있습니다.

- These flowers **smell** good. (상태 - 연결동사) 이 꽃들은 향기가 좋아요.
- Tess is **smelling** the roses. (진행중인 행위 - 타동사) 테스는 장미향을 맡고 있습니다.

- Do you **see** what I mean? (= understand; 상태동사) 내 말을 알아듣겠니?
- I'm **seeing** my lawyer this afternoon. (= paying a visit to 행위동사)
오늘 오후에 변호사를 만날 겁니다.

Basic Grammar for English Tests

- This food **tastes** good. (상태 - 자동사) 이 음식은 맛이 좋습니다.
- The chef **is tasting** the sauce. (진행중인 행위 - 타동사) 요리사가 양념을 맛보고 있습니다.

- A piano is heavy. It **weighs** a lot. (상태 - 자동사)
- The grocer **is weighing** the bananas. (진행중인 행위- 타동사)

피아노는 무거워요. 무게가 많이 나갑니다. / 과일상이 바나나를 달고 있습니다.

과거시제(Simple Past)

1. 완결된 행위 : 과거 (어느 특정한 시점에 시작되었거나 끝난) 행위나 상황을 표현한다.

    It rained yesterday.
    I bought a new car three days ago.

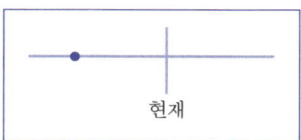

2. 과거사실/역사적 사실

    The first World War began in 1914. 첫 세계대전이 1914년에 시작되었습니다.

3. 과거의 습관적인 행위

    She took a shower every morning. 그녀는 매일 아침에 샤워를 했습니다.

4. 가까운 과거에 발생한 일

    Jimmy punched me in the stomach. 지미는 내 복부를 쳤습니다.

5. 사건 발생 순서대로 나열되는 경우

    I got out of the taxi, paid the fare, tipped the driver and dashed into the station.
    "I came, I saw, I conquered," Julius Caesar declared.

    저는 택시에서 내려, 요금을 내고, 운전사에게 팁을 주고, 역으로 달려갔습니다. / "왔노라, 보았노라, 정복했노라."고 시저가 선언하였습니다.

* 명백히 과거를 표현하는 부사와 함께 항상 과거형을 쓴다.

- I saw Jane yesterday.
- I met Robert ten years ago in Moscow.
- I played football everyday when I was a boy.

- I waited till he arrived.
- I met him when I was at college.
- I stood under a tree when it began to rain.
- When I dropped my cup, the coffee spoiled on my lap.

Exercise 5 각 문장에서 동사의 과거/과거분사형이 틀린 것이 있으면 찾아 바르게 고치시오.

1. After the bells had rang the students left the building.
2. A Japanese ship sank near the coast just after midnight.
3. Unfortunately, not everyone who tried out for the football team could be chose.
4. At his inauguration, the new President sworn to uphold the Constitution.
5. None of the dead woman's family knew what had become of her will.
6. The President always sends a delegation of government officials to meet important visitors.
7. The careless hiker was bit by a poisonous snake.
8. In the fall, my grandfather always climbed the nut trees and shaken off as many chestnuts as he could.
9. Individuals who have never ridden are advised to select one of the older horses.
10. Unlike adult dogs, puppies are feed twice a day.

과거진행시제(past progressive) : was/were+-ing

1. 단순히 과거에 진행되던 행위를 표현

   It was raining all night.
   At eight o'clock last night, I was studying.
   Last year at this time, I was attending school.

2. 과거 어느 때, 어떤 일이 일어나기 전에 또는 그와 동시에 시작된 상황이나 행위

   I met Jane when I was living in Hollywood.
   I was walking down the street when it began to rain.
   The sun was just setting as we reached home.

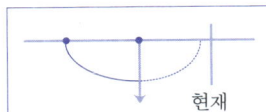

현재완료시제(present perfect) : have/has+p.p.

1. 현재완료와 단순 과거의 의미차이

   I've had lunch. (시간적으로 불과 얼마 전, 금방 먹었다)
   I had lunch. (시간이 나타나 있지 않아 분명치 않다. I had lunch an hour ago.가 더 명확한 문장이다.)

I've been here since February. (과거-현재; since February-now)
I'm here. (현재상황만 의미; only now)

I haven't seen him this morning. (말하고 있는 현재시간(아직 아침)까지)
I didn't see him this morning. (아침은 이미 지난 과거 시간이다.)

Have you ever flown in helicopter? (현재까지의 경험을 묻고 있다.)
When did you fly in helicopter? (정확히 과거 언제인지를 묻고 있다.)

2. 상황이 발생한 과거시간이 분명하지 않은 경우 : 정확한 시간은 중요하지 않고 결과가 중요하다.

 (1) They have moved into a new apartment.
   Have you ever visited Mexico?
   I've never seen snow.
   I've finished my work.

 (2) 최근 행위- 부사와 함께
   We've just finished breakfast.
   It has just struck twelve. 방금 12시를 쳤어요.
   He's recently arrived from New York.
   Have you seen that movie already?
   - I've already seen the movie.
   Have you passed your driving test yet?
   - I haven't passed my driving test yet.
   - I still haven't passed my driving test.

 (3) 반복적이고 습관적인 행위 - 정확한 시간은 중요하지 않다.
   She's attended classes regularly.
   I've met many people since I came here in June.

 (4) 현재까지 지속되는 행위나 상황 (so far, for, since ...)
   I've been here since 7 o'clock.
   I've known him for many years.

과거완료시제(past perfect) : had+p.p.

1. 대과거(과거보다 더 먼 과거)

   when, before, after, until, once, as soon as 등과 함께 쓴다.

   Sam **had left before** we **got** there.
   After the guests **had left**, I **went** to bed.

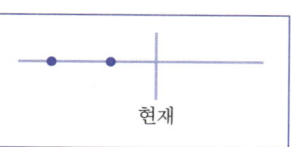

2. 이루지 못한 희망이나 소원 표현

   hope, expect, think/intend/mean, want, suppose

   We had hoped that you would be able to visit us.
   I hadn't expected that it was something important.

3. 단순 과거시제와 과거완료시제의 의미상 차이

   He had been born in the cottage and stayed there all his life. His children had grown up there; his wife had died there and now he lived there all alone.
   그는 그 오두막에서 태어나 거기서 평생을 살았습니다. 그의 아이들도 거기서 자랐습니다. 그런데그의 아내가 죽어서 이제 그는 그곳에서 혼자 살고 있었습니다.

현재완료진행(present perfect progressive) : have/has been + -ing

1. 과거 어느 시점에서 시작하여 현재까지 지속되는 경우를 표현
   - for, since, all morning, all day, all week 등과 함께 쓴다.

   It has been raining since early morning.
   It has been raining all day.
   The baby has been crying all morning.

   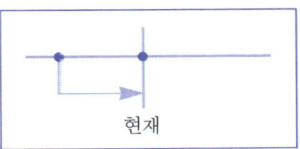

2. 최근에 진행중인 일반적인 행위를 표현할 때

   She has been taking violin lessons this year.
   He's been working late every evening this week.

과거완료진행시제(past perfect progressive) : had been + -ing

1. 과거 어느 시점에서 볼 때, 더 먼 과거(대과거)에서부터 발생하여 그 시점까지 계속 진행되던 행위나 상태를 강조한다.

   The police had been looking for the criminal for two years before they caught him.
   경찰은 그 범인을 잡기 전에 2년 간이나 그를 찾았습니다.

   Her eyes were red because she had been crying.
   그녀는 울어서 눈이 빨개졌습니다.

Basic Grammar for English Tests

2. 현재완료진행과 과거완료진행의 비교

   ⎡ She is very tired because she's been typing letters all day. (시점이 현재)
   ⎣ She was very tired because she'd been typing letter all day. (시점이 과거)

   ⎡ Her eyes are red because she has been crying.
   ⎣ Her eyes were red because she had been crying.

미래시제(simple future) : will/won't+동사원형

1. 단순미래(pure future) : 단순히 미래의 일을 진술하거나 예견할 때

   He will finish the work tomorrow.
   I shall be twenty next birthday.

2. 말하는 이의 의도나 의지가 깃든 표현

   I'll buy you a bicycle for your birthday. (약속)
   Shall we go for a swim tomorrow? (제안)
   Will you join us for dinner? (제안)
   If you start at once, you will arrive by six o'clock. (조건)

3. 계획된 행사

   The wedding will take place on June 27th.
   The reception will be at the Hilton Hotel.

4. 기타 미래표현 방법

   (1) 단순현재시제

      He leaves at 7:00 tomorrow.
      Classes begin next week.

   (2) be+-ing(현재진행시제)

      He's leaving at noon tomorrow. 그는 내일 정오에 떠납니다.
      It's going to rain tonight. 오늘밤에 비가 올 것입니다.

   (3) be+ to do(예정)

      I'm to see him tomorrow. 저는 내일 그를 만나게 됩니다.
      You're to deliver these flowers before 10. 이 꽃들을 10시전에 배달해주세요.

   (4) be due to do(예정)

      The plane is due to arrive from Seoul at 13:15.
      비행기는 1시15분에 서울에서 도착하기로 되어있습니다.

(5) be about to do/be on the point of -ing (막 ~하려하다.)

　　The race is about to start. 경주가 막 시작하려 합니다.
　　They're on the point of starting. 그들은 막 출발하려 합니다.

5. be going to의 미래표현

(1) I'm going to have a wonderful time. (미래= will) 저는 멋진 시간을 가질 것입니다.
　　I'm going to Chicago. (현재진행형) 저는 시카고에 갈 것입니다.

(2) 단순미래 대신 사용

　　It's going to rain. 비가 올 것입니다.
　　She's going to faint! 그녀는 곧 실신할 거요!
　　They're going to be married soon. 그들은 곧 결혼할 것입니다.

(3) 계획/의도 표현

　　I'm going to meet Jack at the library at seven. 나는 7시에 도서관에서 잭을 만날거야.
　　I'm going to buy a car. 나는 차를 살거야.

미래진행시제(future progressive) : will be+ -ing

1. 미래의 어느 시점에도 계속 진행되고 있을 행위나 상태를 표현

　　I will be studying when you come.
　　By this time tomorrow, I'll be lying on the beach.
　　I shall be playing tennis all afternoon.

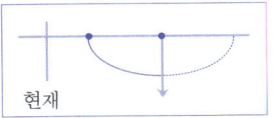

2. 약속, 계획

　　We shall be going to London next week.
　　We'll be spending the winter in Australia.

미래완료시제(future perfect) : will have p.p.

미래의 특정한 시점까지 완료되는 행위나 상태를 표현.

I will have retired by the year 2020.
I shall have finished this work by five o'clock.
By this time next year George will have taken his university degree.

2020년까지는 제가 은퇴하여 있을 것입니다. / 5시까지 이 작업을 마쳤을 것입니다. / 내년 이맘때면 조지는 대학학위를 받았을 것입니다.

미래완료진행시제(future perfect progressive) : will have been + -ing

미래의 특정한 시점에서 볼 때, 그 이전에 발생한 행위나 상태가 계속 진행되고있는 상황을 표현.

I will have been studying for two hours by the time you arrive.
당신이 도착할 때까지 2시간 동안 저는 공부하고 있을 겁니다.

By this time next week, I will have been working for this company for 24 years.
We will have been living here for twenty years by the end of the year.
다음 주 이맘때 되면 제가 이 회사에 24년 간 일해온 것이 될 것입니다.
연말까지면 우리가 여기 20년 간 살아온 것이 됩니다.

Actual Test 19

다음 각 문장을 읽고 빈칸에는 알맞은 단어를 넣고, 밑줄 친 부분에서는 잘못된 부분을 찾아내시오.

1. Igneous rock _____ from the cooling and solidification of molten rock from the eruption of volcano.
   - Ⓐ being originated
   - Ⓑ have originated
   - Ⓒ originates
   - Ⓓ originating

2. _____ to Chicago, her father has not heard from her.
   - Ⓐ Because she went
   - Ⓑ After she went
   - Ⓒ When she went
   - Ⓓ Since she went

3. Marble _____ as a material for sculpture since the time of the early Greeks.
   - Ⓐ has been used
   - Ⓑ being used
   - Ⓒ has used
   - Ⓓ used

4. The great Chicago fire in November 1926, _____ much of the city and left about 50,000 people homeless.
   - Ⓐ that it destroyed
   - Ⓑ that destroyed
   - Ⓒ was destroyed
   - Ⓓ destroyed

5. So long as she returns the book by Friday, I _____ it to you with pleasure.
   - Ⓐ lend
   - Ⓑ will lend
   - Ⓒ shall lend
   - Ⓓ would lend

6. Several famous actresses involved in the scandal _____ before the ceremony begins.
   - Ⓐ will to appear
   - Ⓑ are suppose to appear
   - Ⓒ supposed to make an appearance
   - Ⓓ are to appear

7. The moment they met, they knew that _____.
   - Ⓐ friendship would be happen
   - Ⓑ friendship they would have
   - Ⓒ they would be friends
   - Ⓓ they would have friendliness

8. Food prices have <u>raised</u> <u>so rapidly</u> in the past few weeks <u>that</u> many people
           A   B   C
   have been <u>forced to alter their eating habits</u>.
                                   D

9. After Jim <u>had searched</u> <u>for</u> twenty minutes, he found that his jacket had
                    A   B
   been <u>laying</u> on the table <u>the entire time</u>.
              C   D

10. Let <u>Nancy and Eddy</u> <u>to make</u> all the plans for the party, and you and
             A   B
    I <u>will prepare</u> <u>the refreshments</u> and entertainment.
            C   D

11. Jane's professor had her <u>to rewrite</u> her thesis <u>many times</u> before
                                  A   B
    <u>allowing her</u> to present <u>it to the committee</u>.
           C   D

12. Frederic Jameson <u>did</u> a fortune <u>in</u> the grocery, furniture, and iron
                       A   B
    businesses before <u>he went</u> into <u>politics</u>.
                          C   D

13. <u>More than</u> five million copies of <u>George Orwell's</u> novel *Nineteen Eighty*
          A   B
    Four <u>have been sold</u> in English alone since it <u>has been</u> first published in 1945.
                  C   D

14. In 1939 Amelia Earhart, the well-known aviatrix, <u>disappears</u> <u>during</u>
                                                          A   B
    her <u>attempt</u> <u>to fly</u> around the world.
              C   D

15. After 1970 <u>many</u> technological advances <u>have been made</u> in the
                   A   B
    field of computer science, <u>which</u> resulted in <u>more efficient</u> computer.
                                    C   D

16. <u>Even though</u> Minsu <u>has been studying</u> English for five years before
          A   B
    he came <u>to the United States</u>, it is still difficult <u>for him</u> to express himself.
                      C   D

17. A desert area that <u>has been</u> without <u>water</u> for five years will <u>still</u> bloom when
                            A   B   C
    rain <u>will come</u>.
              D

Unit 16

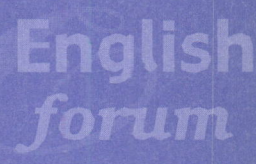

조동사

◀ 조동사의 기능

조동사의 1차 기능

각 조동사의 사전적 의미 그대로의 기능

[능력 : can/could]　　　　　　I can lift. I can type.
[허락 : may/might]　　　　　　You may leave early.
[예측 : will/would/shall]　　　　I will rain soon.
[책임/의무 : should/ought to]　You should do/ought to do as you're told.
[당위성 : must]　　　　　　　You must be quiet.
[방임 : don't/doesn't need]　　You don't need wait.

조동사의 2차 기능

어떤 가능성에 대하여 말하는 이가 느끼는 확실성의 정도를 표현하는 기능이다.

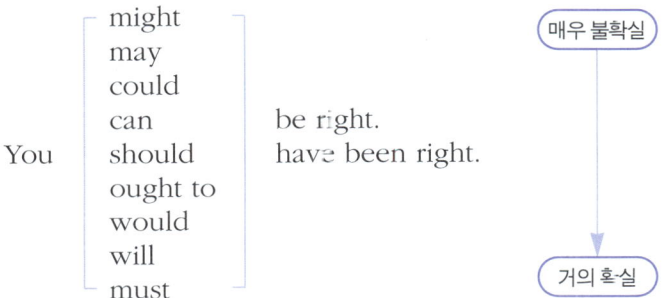

must의 경우 : 당위성을 표현할 때는 본동사 have to를 사용한다.

	1차 기능(당위성)	2차 기능(확실성)
부정사	They have to leave.	-
-ing	They are having to leave.	-
현재	They must leave.	They must be right.
미래	They must leave tomorrow.	-
현재완료	They have had to leave.	-
과거	They had to leave.	They must have been right.
과거완료	They had had to leave.	-
미래완료	They will have had to leave.	-
조건	They would have had to leave.	-

be, have, do 등과 다른 특징

1. 불완전동사로서의 특징

    (1) 조동사는 to부정사를 만들 수 없다. (cf. to be/to have/to do)

    You have to be able to type at least 60 words a minute.
    You have to can type at least 69 words a minute. (x)

    (2) 조동사 뒤에는 to부정사를 쓸 수 없다. (cf. be to do/ have to do)

    You must/mustn't phone him this evening.
    You must to phone him this evening. (x)

    (3) 조동사는 -ing 형으로 만들 수 없다. (cf. being/having/doing)

    I couldn't go home by bus, so I took a taxi.
    I coulding not go home by bus, so I took a taxi. (x)

    (4) 조동사 뒤에서는 3인칭 단수현재형태를 갖출 필요 없다.

    The boss can see you now.
    The boss can sees you now. (x)

    (5) be, have, do 동사에 비해 조동사는 스스로 기본의미를 가지고 있다.
    조동사 뒤에는 언제나 동사원형이 온다.

2. 한 시제에 조동사가 복수로 같이 쓸 수 없다.

    It may be necessary to call a doctor.
    It has been necessary to call a doctor.
    We may call the doctor.

We must call the doctor.
We may must call the doctor. (x)

◀ 조동사의 시제 표현

미래시제

[단순미래]   I will see you.
[미래진행]   I will be seeing you.
[미래완료]   I will have seen you.
[미래완료진행] I will have been seeing you.

<능동>   <수동>
I may see you.   I may be seen.
I may be seeing you.   -
I may have seen you.   I may have been seen.
I may have been seeing you.   -

현재시제

I can/may phone now.
I can/may phone tomorrow.

진행형

Jane is phoning her mother.
Jane may be phoning her mother.
Jane may have been phoning her mother.

과거시제

would, could, might, should 등의 형태가 있지만, 뜻으로나 실제사용에는 현재형과 거의 차이가 없다.

⎡ He says you can/will/may leave early.
⎣ He said you could/would/might leave early.

⎡ I hope you will succeed.
⎣ I had hoped you would succeed.

⎡ I may see you tomorrow.
⎣ I might see you tomorrow.

⎡ Can you tell me your name please?
⎣ Could you tell me your name please?

◀ 능력(ability)의 조동사 : can/could

능력(ability)을 표현하는 조동사의 종류와 형태

[현재]   I can/can't hear music. 음악을 들을 수 있다/없다.
[과거]   He could/couldn't play baduk. 바둑을 둘 수 있었다/없었다.
[과거완료] You could/couldn't have danced all night. 밤새 춤출 수 있었다/없었다.
[미래]- 없다. 대신, You **will be able to** play baduk. 바둑을 둘 수 있을 것이다.

수동태의 표현

This car can only be driven by my wife. 이차는 아내만 몰 수 있어요.
The lecture couldn't be understood by anyone present. 강의는 참석한 누구들 이해할 수 없었어요.

'가능성'(capability, probability) 표현 : (~일 수도 있다. ~일지도 모른다.)

It can be quite cold in Chicago in January. 1월에 시카고는 아주 추울지도 모릅니다.
He can be very naughty. 그는 매우 장난꾸러기일지도 모릅니다.
He could be very naughty when he was a little boy. 어렸을 때 그는 아주 장난꾸러기였을지도 모릅니다.

◀ 허락(permission)/금지(prohibition)의 표현

can/could/may/might (~해도 되나요? → ~할 수 없다. 안 된다.)
Can/Could/May/Might I borrow your umbrella (please)?

	Can I stay out late?	Of course, you can.
	Could I stay out late?	No, you can't/mustn't.
(가장 공손)	May I stay out late?	Of course, you may.
	Might I stay out late?	No, you may not/mustn't.

늦게까지 밖에서 놀아도 돼요? 물론, 돼지. /안 돼.

1. 매우 공손한 요구 표현

   Can/Could I use your phone ?
   Do you think I could/might use your phone?
   I wonder if I could/might use your phone?

2. 수용과 거절 표현

   You can/may watch TV for as long as you like.
   You can't/may not watch TV for as long as you like.
   Johnny can/may stay up late.
   Johnny can't/may not/mustn't stay up late.

   텔레비전을 마음껏 오래 봐도 돼. / 텔레비전을 마음대로 오래보면 안돼요. / 조니는 밤늦도록 안 자도 돼요. / 조니는 밤늦도록 안 자면 안돼요.

허락/금지의 다른 표현

(not) be allowed to	- You're (not) allowed to stay out late. 늦도록 밖에 있으면 (안)돼
(not) be permitted to	- You're (not) permitted to stay out late.
be forbidden to	- You're forbidden to stay out late. 늦도록 밖에 있는 것은 금지야.
be prohibited	- Smoking is (strictly) prohibited. 흡연은 금지됩니다.
be not to	- You're not to smoke. 담배 피면 안 돼.
부정명령형	- Don't smoke! 담배 피지마!

Basic Grammar for English Tests

◀ 확실성(certainty)/가능성(possibility)의 표현 : may/might/could

확실성과 가능성 표현 비교

Jane was at home yesterday.
Jane is at home. ⎫ 확실성
Jane will be at home tomorrow. ⎭
Jane may/might/could have been at home yesterday.
Jane may/might/could be at home. ⎫ 가능성
Jane may/might/could be at home tomorrow. ⎭

제인은 어제 집에 있었어요. / 제인은 (지금) 집에 있어요. / 제인은 내일 집에 있을 거예요. / 제인은 어제 집에 있었을 지도 몰라요. / 제인은 (지금) 집에 있을 지도 몰라요. / 제인은 내일 집에 있을 지도 몰라요.

가능성 표현 문장

1. should be/ought to be

   John should/ought to be at home. 존이 집에 있어야 했는데.
   John should/ought to be working. 존이 공부하고 있어야 했는데.
   John should/ought to have left by tomorrow. 존이 내일까지는 떠났어야 하는데.

2. 의문문

   Might/Could/Can this be true? 이것이 사실일까요?
   Might/Could/Can he still be working? 그가 아직 공부하고 있을까요?
   Might/Could/Can he have been waiting long? 그가 오래 기다리고 있었을까요?

3. 부정문

   He may not be here. 그는 여기 없을 거예요.
   He may not have been here. 그는 여기 없었을 거예요.
   He may not be working late. 그는 늦게까지 공부하지 않을 거예요.
   He may not have been working late. 그는 늦게까지 공부하지 않았을 거예요.

확실성의 정도

He is at home.   He isn't at home.
He could be at home.   확실한 사실   He can't be at home.
He should be at home.   He couldn't be at home.
He ought to be at home.
He may be at home.   He may not be at home.
He might be at home.   확실성 희박   He might not be at home.

◀ 추론/추측(deduction)의 표현

must/can't - 현재시제
must have p.p./can't have p.p.' - 현재완료, 과거시제

* 확실한 추측일 경우   (긍정) '~임에 틀림없다.'
                    (부정) '~일리가 없다.'

현재시제에서

1. 확실

He is here.   He lives here.   He is leaving.
He isn't here.   He doesn't live here.   He isn't leaving.

2. 추론(추측)

He must be here.   He must live here.   He must be leaving.
He can't be here.   He can't live here.   He can't be leaving.

그는 분명 여기 있어요. / 그는 분명 여기 살아요. / 그는 분명 떠나요. / 그가 여기 있을 리 없어요. / 그가 여기 살 리 없어요. / 그가 떠날 리 없어요.

현재완료/과거시제에서

1. 확실

He has left.   He has been working late.
He left early.   He was working late.

2. 추측(추론)

He must have left early.   He must have been working late.
He can't have left early.   He can't have been working late.
He couldn't have left early.   He couldn't have been working late.

그는 분명 일찍 떠났어요. 그가 늦게까지 공부했음이 분명해요. / 그가 일찍 떠났을 리가 없어요. 그가 늦게까지 공부했을 리가 없어요. / 그가 일찍 떠났을 리가 없었을 거예요. 그가 늦게까지 공부했을 리가 없었을 거예요.

◀ 제공(offers)/요구(requests)/제안(suggestions)의 표현

사물을 제공하는 표현 (offer something)

Can/Could I offer you some coffee?
Will/Won't you have some coffee?
(공손) Would/Wouldn't you like some coffee?

Yes, I'd like/love some please.
No, I won't.

사물을 요구하는 표현 (request something)

----------▶ (공손)

Can/Could/May/Might I have some coffee please?
  Of course, you can/may.
  No, you can't.
  You may not, I'm afraid.

제안(suggestion)이나 초대(invitation)

(공손)
Will you
Won't you
Would you
Wouldn't you like to
come for a walk with me?

  Yes, I'd like/love to.
  No, I'd prefer not to, thank you.

일을 시킬 때 (서비스를 요구할 때)

(공손)
Will you please
Can/Could you please
Would you please
Would you like to
open the window for me?

Would you mind opening the window for me?
  Yes, of course (I will).
  No, I'm afraid I can't (at the moment).

다른 사람에게 서비스를 제공할 때

Can/Could/Shall I open the window (for you)?
Would you like me to open the window (for you)?
 ─Yes please. /No thank you.

* What shall/can I do for you?

권유

Shall we go for a swim?

We can/could/might go for a swim.
- Yes, let's, (shall we)?
- No, I'd rather we didn't.
- No, I'd rather not.

What shall/can/could we do this afternoon?

◀ 소망(wishes) 표현 : I wish / if only

현재시제 표현

I wish / If only Jane was/were here now.
I wish / If only I knew the answer to your question.
cf. I hope he is on time.
　　 I hope he won't be late.

제인이 지금 여기 있다면 좋겠는데. / 내가 자네 질문의 답을 알고 있다면 좋겠네. / 그가 정각에 오기를 바랍니다. / 그가 늦지 않기를 바랍니다.

과거시제 표현

I wish/If only I had been here yesterday.
I wish/If only you had let me know earlier.
cf. If only I had been here yesterday, the accident would never have happened.

내가 어제 여기 있었다면 좋을 것을. / 자네가 내게 좀더 일찍 알려줬더라면 좋을 것을. / 내가 어제 여기 있었다면, 사고가 나지 않았을 지도 몰라.

would/could 사용

1. 정중한 명령

   I wish you would be quiet. 좀 조용해 주시기 바랍니다.
   I wish you wouldn't make so much noise. 좀 조용해 주시기 바랍니다.

2. 희망

   I wish I could be you. 내가 자네였으면 좋겠어.
   If only we could be together. 우리가 함께 할 수 있다면.
   I wish I could swim. 내가 수영을 할 수 있다면.
   I wish he would come tomorrow. 내일 그가 온다면 좋겠는데.

Basic Grammar for English Tests

3. 유감

   I wish I could have been with you. (함께 할 수 없었다)
   I wish Teresa could have come to my party. (올 수 없었다)

   내가 너와 함께 할 수 있었다면 좋았을 것을. / 테레사가 내 파티에 올 수 있었으면 좋았을 것을.

4. It's (high) time / It's about time

   It's **(high) time** he **was/were** taught a lesson.
   It's **about time** he **learned** to look after himself.

   그가 수업을 받을 시간입니다. / 그가 자신을 돌볼 줄 알 때가 되었어요.

   cf. We've enjoyed the evening, but **it's time (for us) to go**. (가야할 시간이 왔다.)
       We've enjoyed the evening, but **it's time we went**. (벌써 갔어야 했는데 늦은 것 같다.)

◀ **would rather / would sooner :** 어느 한쪽을 더 선호하는 표현

단문에서

1. 현재표현 : would rather+원형동사

   Jim would rather **go** to class tomorrow than today.
   I'd rather/sooner **be** a miner than a bank clerk.
   John would rather **not go** to class tomorrow.

   짐은 오늘보다는 차라리 내일 수업에 가려고 합니다. / 저는 은행직원보다는 차라리 광부가 되겠어요. / 존은 차라리 내일 수업에 가지 않으려 해요.

2. 과거표현 : would rather+have p.p.

   John would rather **have gone** to class yesterday than today.
   John would rather **not have gone** to class yesterday.

   존은 오늘보다는 차라리 어제 수업에 갔으면 좋았다고 해요. / 존은 어제 수업에 가지 말았어요 했다고 해요.

복문에서

1. 현재표현 : would rather that S+동사원형

   I would rather that you **call** me tomorrow.
   We would rather that he **take** this train.
   John would rather that you **not call** me tomorrow.

   나는 네가 내일 내게 전화해주면 좋겠어. / 우리는 그가 이 열차를 탔으면 좋겠어. / 존은 네가 내일 내게 전화하지 말기를 바래.

2. 현재사실의 반대표현 would rather that S+동사과거형

   Jane would rather that it **were** winter now. (=It is not winter now.)
   I'd rather you **were/weren't** happy.
   I'd rather she **sat/didn't sit** next to me.

   제인은 지금 겨울이라면 하고 바랍니다. / 저는 당신이 행복했으면/행복하지 않았으면 합니다. / 저는 그녀가 내 옆에 앉았으면/앉지 말았으면 좋겠어요.

3. 과거표현 : would rather that S+had p.p.(과거사실의 반대)

   Jim would rather that Jane **had gone** to class yesterday.
   (= Jill did **not** go to class yesterday.)
   Robert would rather that we **hadn't left** yesterday.

   짐은 제인이 어제 수업에 갔더라면 하고 있어요. / 로버트는 우리가 어제 떠나지 말았으면 했어요.

◀ 충고성 ← '의무/임무' → 필연성

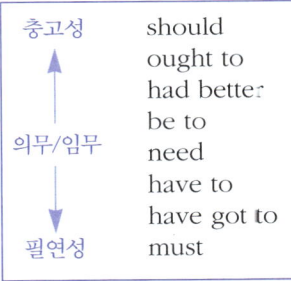

현재표현	과거표현
You should stop smoking.	You should have stopped smoking.(후회)
You ought to stop smoking.	You ought to have stopping.('굿했다'- 후회)
You'd better stop smoking.	-
You're to report for duty at 7.	-
Need I type this letter again?	Need you have told him about my plans?
- No, you needn't. (부정문과 의문문에서만)	- You needn't have told him about my plans. (필요 없는데 했다.)
I have (got) to check the oil level in the car.	I had to check the oil level in the car. (그래서 점검했다.)
You must phone home at once.	You had to phone home at once. (그래서 전화했다.)

Basic Grammar for English Tests

필연성 표현 : must/have to/have got to

We have (got) to send these boxes. 우리는 이 상자들을 보내야해요.
I really must do something about the weeds in the garden.
정원의 잡초를 정말이지 어떻게든 해야 되요.
You must phone home at once. It's urgent. 너 집에 당장 전화해야해. 급해

본동사로 취급하여 쓰는 경우 *

1. 생물 주어

   I need/needed to go to the dentist this morning. 나 오늘 아침에 치과에 가야겠어.
   I don't/didn't need to go to the dentist. 치과에 갈 필요 없어.
   Why did you need to go to the dentist? 너 치과에는 왜 가야되는 거니?

2. 무생물 주어인 경우

   The grass needs cutting/to be cut. 잔디를 깎아야겠어요.
   The television needs repairing/to be repaired. 텔레비전은 수리해야겠어요.
   The composition needs rewriting/to be rewritten. 작문을 다시 해야겠어요.

◀ '금지'와 '불필요' 표현

금지의 표현

현재표현	과거표현
You shouldn't start smoking. You ought not to start smoking.	You shouldn't have started smoking. You ought not to have started smoking. (충고를 무시한 것을 후회)
You can't park here. You must not park here.	You shouldn't have parked there. You ought not to have parked there.

(금지의 강도)

약　shouldn't-　　　　You shouldn't be late tomorrow.
　　ought not to-　　You ought not to be late tomorrow.
　　had better not -　You had better not be late tomorrow.
　　can't-　　　　　You can't be late tomorrow.
강　must not-　　　　You must not be late tomorrow.

불필요 표현

현재표현	과거표현
You needn't go there. (= You don't need to go there.) You don't have to go there. You haven't got to go there.	You needn't have gone there. (쓸데없이 갔다.) You didn't have to go there. (or You didn't need to go there. 그곳에 갔든지 안 갔든지 그것이 중요하지 않고, 갈 필요가 없었다는 것이다.)

◀ '습관'을 표현하는 조동사

- will - 현재습관
- would/used to - 과거습관

특징적 습관이나 행동 표현 : will/would

In fine weather, he will often sit in the sun for hours. (~하곤 한다.)
As he grew older, he would often talk about his war experience. (~하곤 했다.)

날씨가 좋으면, 그는 몇 시간 동안 자주 햇볕에 나와 앉아있곤 해요. / 늙어가면서 그는 자신의 전쟁경험을 자주 이야기하곤 했어요.

Boys will be boys. 애들은 그냥 애들일 뿐이죠.
Accidents will happen. 사고는 생길 수 있게 마련이다.
He would say a thing like that. 그 사람이 그런 것을 말하곤 했지요.

과거의 습관 표현 : used to/would

I **used to** smoke, but I don't any more.
I **never used to** eat a large breakfast, but I do now.
When I worked on a farm, I **always used to** get up at 5 a.m. (규칙적)
When I worked on a farm, I **would always** get up at 5 a.m (불규칙적)
When we were students, we **would often** stay up all night.

전 담배를 피웠는데, 더 이상 안 피워요. / 저는 아침을 많이 먹지 않았는데, 지금은 많이 먹어요. / 농장에서 일할 때, 저는 항상 5시에 일어났어요. / 학생일 때, 우리는 자주 밤을 새우곤 했지요.

과거상태 표현 : used to

I used to be a waiter, but now I'm a taxi-driver.

I used to have a beard, but I've shaved it off.

저는 전에는 웨이터였는데, 지금은 택시를 운전합니다. / 저는 전에는 턱수염이 있었는데 면도를 했습니다.

used to/juːst/ 의 유의할 점

1. 단순과거형에만 쓴다.

   Sally used to make all her own dresses.
   Did he use to live in London?
   You didn't use to smoke.
   Peter never used to be so difficult.

   샐리는 자신의 모든 옷을 만들곤 했습니다. / 그 사람이 런던에서 살았나요? / 너는 담배를 피지 않았잖아. / 피터는 그렇게 어려웠던 적이 없었습니다.

2. Did you use to smoke? - Yes, I did. (지금도 그렇다.)
   　　　　　　　　　　　　No, I didn't. (지금도 그러지 않는다.)
   　　　　　　　　　　　　Yes, I used to. (지금은 그렇지 않다.)
   　　　　　　　　　　　　No, I didn't use to. (지금은 그렇다.)

   cf. ┌ S+**be used**/juːzd/ **to do** : 일반동사 use의 수동태
   　　　└ S+**be/get used**/juːst/ **to -ing** : ~에 익숙해져 있다./익숙해지다.
   　　　　　= be/get accustomed to -ing

   ┌ These brushes are used to paint big picture.
   └ This broom is used to clean the floor.

   이 붓들은 큰 그림을 그리는데 사용됩니다. / 이 빗자루는 바닥을 쓰는데 사용됩니다.

   ┌ George **is used to** eating at 7:00 p.m. (= is accustomed to)
   │ We **got used to** cooking our own food when we had to live alone.
   │ (= become accustomed to)
   └ Mary **was used to** driving to school. (= was accustomed to)

   조지는 오후 7시에 밥을 먹는 데 익숙합니다. / 우리는 혼자 살아야 해서 직접 요리를 하는 데 익숙해졌습니다. / 메리는 학교에 차를 몰고 가는데 익숙했습니다.

◀ 조동사의 기타 용법

may/might

1. 기원 : May God be with you! 신의 가호가 있기를!
   May you succeed! 성공하시길!
   May you live long! 만수무강하시길!
   May you be happy! 행복하시길!
   May you live to be a hundred! 만수무강하시길!
   May he rest in peace! 평화로이 잠드소서!

2. 선택 : may as well / might as well (= had better)

   It's not very far, so we may/might as well go on foot. (둘은 차이가 없다.)
   Shall we walk or take a bus?
   — We may/might as well walk. (둘은 차이가 없다.)
   What a slow bus this is!
   — Yes, we might just as well walk. (걷는 것이 더 빠를 것 같다. may 사용불가)

   그리 멀지 않으므로 우리는 걸어가는 것이 낫겠어요. / 걸을까요, 버스를 탈까요? - 우리는 걷는 것이 좋겠어요. / 이 버스는 왜 이리 느려! - 맞아 우리는 걷는 게 낫겠어.

3. 당연 : may well/might well/could well (당연히 ~ 하다)

   He **may/might/could well** find that the course is too difficult.

   그는 그 과정이 너무 어렵다는 것을 당연히 알게 될 것입니다.

shall

[위협] You shall pay for this. 너는 여기에 대가를 지불해야 해.
[약속] You shall have a car for your birthday. 네 생일날 자동차를 마련해주마.
[결정] They shall not pass! 그들이 통과하지 못하게 하겠어.
[명령] When he comes in nobody shall say a word. 그가 들어올 때 아무도 말하지마!

won't/wouldn't(거절)

Drink your milk, John! - I won't.
I offered John some milk, but he wouldn't drink it.
The car won't start
The car wouldn't start this morning.

존, 우유 마셔라. - 싫어요. / 난 존에게 우유를 줬는데도 걔는 마시지 않으려 했어요. / 자동차가 출발을 안 해요. / 오늘 아침에는 자동차가 출발을 하지 않았어요.

should : 명사절에서 가정법현재로 취급 - 주로 생략한다.

1. 제안, 명령, 결정, 요구, 충고, 주장, 동의 등의 동사 뒤에서

   advise, ask, command, decide, decree, demand, insist, instruct, move, offer, prefer, persuade, propose, recommend, request, require, stipulate, suggest, urge

   * **S+V(위의 동사들)+that+S+(should)+ 동사원형**

   I **suggest** that he **should / shouldn't apply** for the job.
   = I **suggest** that he **apply / not apply** for the job.
   The judge **insisted** that the jury **(should) return** a verdict immediately.
   The university **requires** that all its students **(should) take** this course.
   The doctor **suggested** that his patient **(should) stop** smoking.
   We **proposed** that he **(should) take** a vacation.
   I **move** that we **(should) adjourn** until this afternoon.

   저는 그가 그 일에 지원할/하지 말 것을 제안합니다. / 판사는 배심원이 즉시 평결을 내려줄 것을 주장했습니다. / 대학은 모든 학생들이 이 과목을 선택할 것을 요구합니다. / 의사는 환자가 금연할 것을 제안했습니다. / 우리는 그가 휴가를 가질 것을 제안했습니다. / 저는 우리가 오후까지 휴회할 것을 동의합니다.

2. 형용사 뒤에서

   형용사 종류 : essential, imperative, important, mandatory, necessary, obligatory, urgent, vital

   * **It is 형용사 that S+(should)+ 동사원형**

   It was important that he (should) apply for the job.
   It is necessary that he (should) find the books.
   It was urgent that she (should) leave at once.
   It has been proposed that we (should) change the topic.
   It has been suggested that he (should) forget the election.
   It was recommended that we (should) wait for the authorities.

   그가 그 일에 지원하는 것이 중요했습니다. / 그가 책을 찾는 것이 필요합니다. / 그녀가 즉시 떠나는 것이 시급했습니다. / 우리가 화제를 바꾸자는 안이 제안되었습니다. / 그가 선거를 잊어야 한다는 의견이 제시되었습니다. / 우리가 당국자들을 기다리자는 권유가 있었습니다.

There+조동사

There can't be anyone waiting outside. 밖에 기다리는 사람이 있을 리가 없어.
There could be no doubt about it. 의심할 여지가 없을 거야.
There won't be an election in June. 6월에 선거는 없을 거야.
There must be a mistake. 분명히 실수일거야.
There can't have been any doubt about it. 의심할 여지가 없었던 거야.
There might have been a strike. 파업이 생겼을 거야.
There could have been someone crossing the road. 누군가 길을 건넌 자가 있었을 거야.

Actual Test 20

다음 각 문장을 읽고 빈칸에는 알맞은 단어를 넣고, 밑줄 친 부분에서는 잘못된 부분을 찾아내시오.

1. Most species of octopus _____ the color quickly.
   - Ⓐ can change
   - Ⓑ can be changed
   - Ⓒ changing
   - Ⓓ that change

2. My holiday was ruined by the bad weather; _____ have stayed at home!
   - Ⓐ it may be as well to
   - Ⓑ it was just as well I
   - Ⓒ I might just as well
   - Ⓓ I might do as well as I

3. I didn't want to go alone, and no one _____ with me.
   - Ⓐ went
   - Ⓑ has gone
   - Ⓒ had gone
   - Ⓓ would go

4. George has been sick for a long time, so he _____ pain.
   - Ⓐ used to
   - Ⓑ is used to
   - Ⓒ use to
   - Ⓓ is use to

5. You _____ your passport extended before it expires.
   - Ⓐ had better to get
   - Ⓑ had to get better
   - Ⓒ had better get
   - Ⓓ had better got

6. In fact, Jane would rather have left for Chicago _____ in New York.
   - Ⓐ by staying
   - Ⓑ than stay
   - Ⓒ than have stayed
   - Ⓓ to stay

7. The judge agreed to the suggestion that _____.
   - Ⓐ both of the criminals will soon be set freedom
   - Ⓑ some of the criminals there are of guilt only
   - Ⓒ the prisoner be sentenced to death
   - Ⓓ the prisoner to be given life-long sentence

8. It is so natural that an employee _____ his work on time.
   Ⓐ finishes
   Ⓑ finished
   Ⓒ can finish
   Ⓓ should finish

9. It was most urgent that the patient of the car accident _____ sent to hospital.
   Ⓐ must be
   Ⓑ should be
   Ⓒ would be
   Ⓓ was

10. If there is social or political change in <u>a region</u> where <u>a standard language</u>
                                                                  A   B
    is used, <u>local varieties</u> of the language may <u>developing</u>.
              C   D

11. They would come out to attack and then <u>went</u> <u>back</u> into the <u>deep</u> forests,
                                                        A   B   C
    where their opponents <u>were</u> at a disadvantage.
                                D

12. Since his blood pressure is <u>much</u> higher <u>than</u> it <u>should be</u>, his doctor
                                  A   B   C
    maintains that he <u>will not</u> smoke.
                       D

13. He said <u>softly</u> that he would rather <u>starve</u> than <u>stealing</u> to have <u>what</u>
             A   B   C   D
    he needed.

14. You had better <u>to review</u> this chapter <u>carefully</u> because You will have
                     A   B
    <u>some</u> questions <u>on it on your</u> test tomorrow.
      C   D

15. Our English professor would like <u>us</u> <u>spending</u> more time <u>in the</u>
                                              A   B   B
    laboratory <u>practicing</u> our pronunciation.
                D

16. John used to <u>living</u> in Georgia, <u>but</u> his company <u>had him transferred</u>
                A   B   C
    to <u>a better position</u> in Michigun.
          D

17. Jack would rather <u>to be fishing</u> <u>from his boat</u> in the sea <u>than</u> sitting
                        A   B   C
    <u>at his desk</u> in the office.
        D

18. I would rather <u>that</u> he <u>does not travel</u> during <u>the bad</u> weather, but
    　　　　　　　　　A　　　　　B　　　　　　　　　C

    he insists that <u>he must return</u> home tonight.
    　　　　　　　　　　D

19. It is <u>most</u> important that <u>he</u> <u>speaks</u> to the dean before <u>leaving</u> for his
    　　　　A　　　　　　　　　B　　C　　　　　　　　　　　D

    summer vacation.

20. The piano teacher requires <u>that</u> her student <u>practices</u> at least <u>fifty</u> minutes
    　　　　　　　　　　　　　　　A　　　　　　　　　B　　　　　　　　C

    every day <u>in preparation</u> for next week's recital.
    　　　　　　　　D

Unit 17

부정사와 동명사

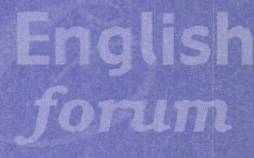

◀ 원형부정사 용법

조동사+원형부정사 : 조동사 뒤에는 항상 동사원형(원형부정사)이 온다.

I [can/could / may/might / will/would / shall/should / must] leave soon.

사역동사(let/make)뒤에는 항상 원형부정사

1. let가 조동사로 쓰이는 경우 : Let's ...

    Let's take a taxi, shall we? 택시를 탈까요?
    Let's not argue about it. (= Don't let's argue about it.) 그 문제로 다투지 맙시다.
    Let them eat cake. 그분들 케이크 드시게 해요.

2. let가 본동사로 쓰이는 경우 : let+O+원형부정사

    Please **let** us **have** more time, will you? 우리에게 시간을 좀 더 주시겠어요?
    Don't **let** the children **annoy** you. 애들이 그분을 귀찮게 하지 않게 해요.
    I won't **let** you **ride** my bicycle. 내 자전거 타게 못하게 할 거야.

3. make+O+원형부정사

    Miss Kim **made** the boys **stay** in after school.

Basic Grammar for English Tests

The beard **makes** you **look** much older than you are.
He was **made to work** sixteen hours a day. (사역동사의 수동태)
* Rules were made to be broken. (이때는 make가 사역동사가 아니다. = created)

<small>김선생은 방과후에 아이들을 남게 했습니다. / 턱수염은 당신을 실제보다 나이 들어 보이게 합니다. / 그는 하루에 16시간 일하게 되었습니다. / 규칙은 어기게 마련이야.</small>

4. 관용표현

The dog's got a stick between his teeth and he won't **let go**.
You'll have to **make** your pocket money **do**. I can't give you more.

<small>개가 막대기를 입에 물면 놓아주지 않습니다. / 네가 가진 돈으로 해결해. 더 이상 줄 수 없어.</small>

let go 놓아주다, 석방하다	let fall 떨어뜨리다
let me see 글쎄, 뭐랄까, 그런데	let slip 기회를 놓치다, 개를 풀어놓다
make believe ~인 체하다, ~라고 정하다	make do 해결하다, 때우다
live and let live 나도 살고 남도 살게 하자	

would rather
would sooner   + 원형부정사
had better
had best

I'd rather work on the land than work in a factory.
I'd rather be told the truth than be lied to.
You'd better not go near the edge.

<small>공장에서 일하느니 차라리 밭에서 일하고 싶습니다. / 거짓말을 듣느니 진실을 듣고 싶습니다. / 가장자리 가까이 가지 않는 게 좋겠어요.</small>

◀ 원형부정사 또는 to부정사를 받는 경우 : help/know

help

Mother **helped** me **(to) do** my homework.
How can I **help** my children **not to worry** about their exams?
(부정형에는 to를 생략할 수 없다.)
Everyone in the village **helped (to) build** the civil auditorium.

<small>어머니는 내가 숙제하는 것을 도와주셨어요. / 우리 애들이 시험걱정을 하지 않도록 내가 어떻게 도와야 할지? / 마을의 모든 사람들이 마을회관을 짓는 것을 도왔습니다.</small>

know

I've never **known** her **(to) be** late before.
I've never **known** her **not (to) be** late!

저는 그녀가 전에 늦었음을 전혀 몰랐습니다. / 저는 그녀가 늦지 않았음을 전혀 몰랐습니다.

and, but except, or, than : 병렬구문(Parallel Structure)에서

Which would you prefer: **to win** a million dollars **or (to) have** a brain like Einstein's?
I'd like **to be flying** over the Alps **and (to be) looking** / **be looking** down the mountains.
I'd like **to lie down and go** to sleep. (to go를 쓰지 않는다)

백만 달러를 얻는 것과 아인슈타인 같은 머리를 갖는 것 중에 어느 것이 더 좋으니? / 알프스로 날아올라 산맥 아래를 내려다보고 싶습니다. / 누워 잠들고 싶습니다.

◀ 원형부정사 또는 -ing를 받는 경우

지각동사 뒤에

see, hear, feel, smell, look at, listen to, notice, observe, watch

1. S+V+O

   We could **hear shouting** in the distance.
   People can stand on this platform and **watch building** in progress.

   우리는 멀리서 고함소리를 들을 수 있었습니다. / 사람들은 플랫폼에 서서 짓고있는 건물을 바라보았습니다.

2. S+V+O+C

   ⎡ I **watched** an artist **draw** a portrait in crayons. (처음부터 끝까지 지켜봄)
   ⎣ I **watched** an artist **drawing** a portrait in crayons. (진행중인 행위를 강조)

   ⎡ I **heard** someone **unlock** the door.
   ⎣ I **heard** someone **unlocking** the door. (진행중인 행위 강조)

   ⎡ I **heard** him **cough**. (한번 들음)
   ⎣ I **heard** him **coughing**. (반복적으로 기침하는 것을 들음)

   저는 화가가 크레용으로 초상화를 그리는 것을 지켜보았습니다. / 저는 누가 문을 따는 소리를 들었습니다. / 저는 그가 기침하는 소리를 들었습니다.

Basic Grammar for English Tests

3. 수동태

They **were seen waiting** on the corner. (진행중인 행위)
They **were seen to climb** through the window. (완성된 행위)

그들이 모퉁이에서 기다리는 것이 보였습니다. / 그들이 창을 통해 기어오른 것이 보였습니다.

have+원형부정사/-ing

1. have+O+원형부정사

Mary had John wash the car.
"Have the next patient come in now please, nurse."
I'll have you know that I'm a qualified engineer.

메리는 존에게 세차를 시켰습니다. / "간호사, 이제 다음 환자 들어오시게 해요." / 귀하에게 제가 능력 있는 엔지니어라는 것을 알려드리겠습니다.

2. have+O+-ing

I'll have you speaking English in six months.
Within five minutes, Jane had us all playing hide and seek.
I won't/can't have you speaking like that about your father.

저는 6개월 내에 당신이 영어를 말하도록 하겠습니다. / 5분 안에, 제인은 우리 모두 숨바꼭질을 하게 만들었습니다. / 나는 네 아버지에 대해 네가 그렇게 말하게 할 수 없어.

cf. have+O+p.p

I had my watch repaired.
Jane had her house painted.
Alice stopped at the service station to have the tank filled.

저는 시계를 수리 맡겼습니다. / 제인은 집을 도색하게 하였습니다. / 엘리스는 주유소에 정차하여 연료를 넣게 하였습니다.

Exercise 1 다음 각 문장의 빈칸에 주어진 동사의 적당한 꼴을 넣으시오.

1. Have him *bring* his car to the airport. (bring)
2. "I will not have students _____ on the walls of this school," the principal said. (draw)
3. I'll have you _____ I'm a qualified accountant. (know)
4. He had her _____ he was a millionaire. (believe)
5. We have people _____ us up all hours of the day and night.(ring)
6. The film had them _____ right from the first few minutes.(laugh)

7. He's an excellent piano teacher. He'll have you _____ in about a year. (play)
8. I'll have the plumber _____ the central heating boiler. (look at)
9. The sergeant had all the recruits _____ like real soldiers inside a month. (march)
10. The president had his advisors _____ a press conference. (arrange)

◀ to부정사

to부정사의 일반용법

1. 목적 표현 (to/in order to/so as to : ~하기 위하여)

   I went to live in France (in order/so as) **to learn** French.
   I went to France **not to study** French, **but to study** architecture.
   I shut the door quietly, **so as not to wake** the baby.
   I bought a second car (**in order**) **for my son to learn** to drive.
   I bought a new car **in order that** my wife might learn to drive.

   저는 불어를 배우려고 프랑스에 살러 갔습니다. / 저는 불어를 배우려는 게 아니고 건축을 공부하러 프랑스에 갔습니다. / 저는 아기를 깨우지 않으려고 조용히 문을 닫았습니다. / 저는 아들이 운전을 배우도록 두 번째 차를 샀습니다. / 저는 아내가 운전을 배우도록 새 차를 샀습니다.

2. 결과 표현 (~해서 그래서 ~하다)

   One morning he *awoke* **to find** himself famous. (= and found)
   He *grew up* **to be** a great scholar. (= and became)
   He *went* to Africa **never to return**. (= and never returned)
   I *came* home **to find** my garden neat and tidy. (= and found)

   어느 날 아침 그가 깨어보니 유명해졌습니다. / 그는 커서 위대한 학자가 되었습니다. / 그는 아프리카에 가서 돌아오지 않았습니다. / 제가 집에 와보니 정원이 깔끔하게 단장되어 있었습니다.

to부정사 부정하기 : to부정사 바로 앞에 not/never를 붙인다.

I soon learned *not/never* **to** swim near coral reefs.
(*cf.* I didn't learn/never learned to swim when I was a child.)
He told me *not* **to** feed the animals. (*cf.* He didn't tell me to feed the animals.)

⎡ I wasn't sorry to go. (= I went.)
⎣ I was sorry *not* to go. (= I didn't go.)

Basic Grammar for English Tests

It wasn't a surprise to hear from him. (= I heard from him.)
It was a surprise *not* to hear from him. (= I didn't hear from him.)

저는 산호초 근처에서 수영하지 않아야 하는 것을 곧 알게 되었습니다. (cf. 저는 어렸을 때 수영하는 법을 배우지 못했습니다.)
그는 제게 동물들에게 먹이를 주지 말라고 했습니다. (cf. 그는 제게 동물들에게 먹이를 주라고 말하지 않았습니다.)
제가 간 것이 유감이었습니다. / 제가 못 간 것이 유감이었습니다. / 그에게서 소식을 들은 것이 놀라운 일은 아니었습니다. / 그에게서 소식을 듣지 못한 것이 놀라웠습니다.

부정사 수식하기(to do의 분리)

I want you **to read** the last sentence **clearly**.
I want you **to clearly understand** what I'm telling you.
It's difficult **to really understand** the theory of relativity.

나는 네가 마지막 문장을 정확하게 읽기를 원해. / 내가 네게 말하는 것을 정확하게 이해해주기를 나는 원해. / 상대성원리를 실제로 이해하기란 어렵습니다.

be to do의 용법

1. 명사 역할

   Your mistake was to write that letter.
   What you do is to mix the eggs with flour.
   All I did was to press this button.

   자네의 실수는 그 편지를 쓴 것이었어. / 자네가 할 일은 밀가루에 계란을 반죽하는 것이야. / 내가 한 일이라곤 이 단추를 누르는 것이었어.

2. 형용사 역할

   This house is to let/to be let.
   Who is to blame/to be blamed?
   He's only to be admired/envied/pitied.
   All this is to be sold.

   이 집은 세를 놓습니다. / 비난받을 자가 누구인가요? / 그는 다만 존경/부러움/동정을 받아야 할 따름입니다. / 이것 몽땅 팔 것입니다.

관용구(독립부정사)

to be honest 정직하게 말하면, to begin with 우선, to cut a long story short 간추리면, to get (back) to the point 요점을 말하자면, to tell you the truth 사실을 말하면

동사의 목적어로서 to부정사

I want to leave.
I want to be left alone.

나는 떠나고/남고 싶어요. / 나는 혼자 남고 싶어요.

* to부정사를 목적어로 받는 동사

<1> V+to do

- afford : I can't afford to buy it. 난 그걸 살 여유가 못됩니다.
- agree : They agreed to help us. 그들은 우리를 돕기로 합의했어요.
- appear : He appeared to be tired. 그는 지쳐 보였습니다.
- ask : She asked to come with us. 그녀는 우리와 함께 가기를 요구했습니다.
- beg : He begged to come with us. 그는 우리와 함께 가기를 간청했습니다.
- care : I don't care to see that show. 전 그 쇼를 보는 것이 상관없어요.
- decide : I have decided to leave on Monday. 저는 월요일에 떠나기로 결정했어요.
- demand : I demand to know who is responsible. 저는 누구에게 책임이 있는지를 알고자 합니다.
- deserve : He deserves to win the prize. 그는 우승할 만 해요.
- expect : I expect to enter graduate school in the fall. 저는 가을에 대학원에 진학하려고 합니다.
- fail : I failed to return the book to the library on time.
  저는 도서관에 책을 정시에 반납하지 못했습니다.
- forget : I forgot to mail the letter. 저는 편지 부치는 것을 까먹었습니다.
- hope : Jane hopes to arrive next week. 제인은 다음주에 도착하기를 원합니다.
- manage : He managed to finish his work early. 그는 그럭저럭 자기 일을 일찍 마쳤습니다.
- mean : I didn't mean to hurt your feelings. 네 감정을 상하게 하려던 건 아니었어.
- need : I need to have your opinion. 나는 네 의견을 받아들일 필요가 있어.
- plan : I am planning to have a party. 난 파티를 열 계획이야.
- prepare : We prepared to welcome them. 우리는 그들을 환영할 준비를 했어.
- promise : I promise not to be late. 나 늦지 않을 것을 약속해.
- refuse : I refuse to believe his story. 저는 그의 이야기는 믿지 않겠어요.
- regret : I regret to tell you that you failed. 난 네가 실패했다고 말한 것을 후회해.
- remember : I remembered to lock the door. 저는 문을 잠그는 것을 기억했어요.
- seem : He seems to be friendly. 그는 우호적으로 보입니다.
- wait : I will wait to hear from you. 난 네 소식을 기다릴게.
- want : I want to tell you something. 네게 뭘 좀 이야기하고 싶어.
- wish : She wishes to come with us. 그녀는 우리와 같이 가기를 원해요.

<2> V+O+to do

- advise : I advised him to wait until tomorrow. 저는 그에게 내일까지 기다리라고 충고했습니다.
- allow : She allowed me to use her car. 그녀는 제가 자기 차를 쓰는 것을 허락했습니다.
- ask : I asked John to help us. 저는 존에게 우리를 도와줄 것을 요청했습니다.
- beg : They begged us to come. 그들은 우리에게 오라고 간청했습니다.
- cause : His laziness caused him to fail. 그의 게으름이 그를 실패하게 만들었습니다.
- convince : I couldn't convince her to accept our help.
  저는 그녀가 우리의 도움을 받아들이도록 확신시킬 수 없었습니다.

Basic Grammar for English Tests

encourage :	She encouraged me to try again. 그녀는 제게 다시 시도하도록 격려하였습니다.
expect :	I expect you to be on time. 나는 네가 시간을 지키리라 기대하네.
force :	They forced him to tell the truth. 그들은 그에게 진실을 말하라고 압박하였습니다.
invite :	Tom invited the Johnsons to come to his party. 톰은 존슨씨 가족을 자기 파티에 오라고 초대하였습니다.
permit :	She permitted the children to stay up late. 그녀는 아이들이 밤늦게 놀도록 허락하였습니다.
persuade :	I persuaded her to come for a visit. 저는 그녀에게 잠시 방문할 것을 설득하였습니다.
remind :	He reminded me to lock the door. 그는 방문을 잠글 것을 제게 상기시켰습니다.
require :	Our teacher requires us to be on time. 우리 선생님은 우리에게 시간을 지킬 것을 요구합니다.
urge :	I urged him to apply for the job. 저는 그에게 그 일자리에 지원할 것을 촉구하였습니다.
want :	I want you to be happy. 나는 네가 행복하기를 원해.
warn :	I warned you not to drive too fast. 난 네가 너무 과속운전하지 않기를 경고한다.

<3> **V+O(선택적)+to do**

ask, beg, chose, expect, hate, help, intend, like, love, need, prefer, prepare, promise, want, wish

- I want to speak to the manager. (= I will speak.) 저는 부장에게 말하려고 합니다.
- I want you to speak to the manager. (= You will speak.)
  저는 당신이 부장에게 말하기를 원해요.

- I like to keep everything tidy. (my action) 저는 모든 것을 깔끔하게 하는 걸 좋아해요.
- I like you to keep everything tidy. (your action) 저는 당신이 모든 것을 깔끔하게 했으면 좋 겠어요.

- I'd like to find you a job. (= I will do it for you.) 나는 네게 직장을 찾아주고 싶어.
- I'd like you to find him a job. (= You will do it.) 나는 네가 직장을 찾았으면 좋겠어.
 - It takes (me) ten minutes **to walk** to the station. 역까지 걸어가면 10분 걸립니다.

◀ V+ [to do / that S+V] 문형

V+ [to do / that S+V] 형태를 취하는 동사

agree, arrange, beg, care, choose, claim, contrive, decide, demand, determine, expect, hope, intend, learn, plan, prefer, pretend, promise, resolve, swear, threaten, wish

I decided to ask for my money back. 나는 내 돈을 돌려주기를 요구하기로 했어요.
= I decided that I would ask for my money back.

V+ ⎡ **wh-의문사+to do**
　　⎣ **wh-의문사+S+V**

consider, decide, discover, explain, find out, forget, hear, (not) know, learn, observe, perceive, remember, see, understand, wonder

I don't **know what to choose**. 저는 뭘 골라야 할지 모르겠어요.
I **wondered how to get** in touch with them. 저는 그들과 어떻게 접촉해야 할지 모르겠어요.

(비교) ⎡ I don't **know why** the accident happened. 왜 사고가 났는지 저는 모르겠어요.
　　　⎣ I didn't **know that** there had been an accident. 사고가 있었는지 저는 몰랐어요.

　- I haven't **decided** ⎡ **whether I should go** to England.
　　　　　　　　　　　　⎣ **whether to go** to England.
　영국에 가야할지 결정을 못했어요.

I **remembered to switch** off the lights. 저는 전등을 끄는 것을 기억하고 있었어요.
I **forgot to switch** off the lights. 저는 전등을 끄는 것을 까먹었어요.
I **learned to ride** a bicycle when I was four. 저는 4살 때 자전거 타는 것을 배웠어요.
I **learned how to ride** a bicycle when I was four.

V+O+ ⎡ **wh-의문사 to do**
　　　⎣ **wh-의문사 S+V**

advise, ask, instruct, remind, teach, tell, show

The receptionist **told me where to** wait.
The union leader **told the men when they** should go back to work.
Please **show me how to** start the engine.
You haven't **told me whether** to sign this form.

안내원은 내게 기다릴 곳을 말해주었습니다. / 노조 지도자는 남자들에게 직장에 돌아가야 한다고 말했습니다. / 엔진을 어떻게 거는 지 보여주세요. / 당신은 이 서류에 서명할 것인지 내게 말하지 않았어요.

Basic Grammar for English Tests

◀ 형용사+to do 형태

I'm pleased to meet you. 당신을 만나 기뻐요.
I'm glad to help you. 당신을 돕게 되어 기뻐요.
I'm sorry to have missed you. 당신을 놓친 것이 안타까워요.
I'm nice to be sitting by the fire. 저는 불가에 앉게 되어 좋아요.
I was surprised to see Tom at the meeting. 회의에서 톰을 만나 놀랐어요.

사람의 성격이나 특징을 나타내는 형용사

> brave, careless(not careful), clever, foolish, generous, good, (un)kind, polite, right/wrong, rude, (un)selfish, silly, wicked

1. S+be+형용사+to do : 문장의 주어가 to do의 주어를 겸한다.

    He was very **kind to help** us. (= He was kindly helped us.)
    John was **foolish not to accept** their offer.
    Would you be **so good as to let** me know as soon as possible?
    = Would you be **good enough to let** me know as soon as possible?
    그는 친절하게도 우리를 도와주었어요. / 존은 바보같이 그들의 제안을 받아들이지 않았습니다. / 가능한 빨리 알려주시면 참 고맙겠어요.

2. It+be+형용사+of+목적어 to 형태 : 목적어가 to do의 주어 역할
    (annoying, boring, trying 등의 형용사가 첨가된다.)

    It was **kind of her to help** us.
    It was **silly (of us) to believe** him.
    It was almost **selfish of him not to contribute** anything.
    It was **annoying of John to lose** my keys.
    그녀는 친절하게도 우리를 도와주었습니다. / 우리는 바보같이 그를 믿었습니다. / 그는 참 이기적이게도 아무 것도 기부하지 않았습니다. / 성가시게도 존이 내 열쇠를 잃어버렸습니다.

It+is+형용사+to do (It (가주어) = to do (진주어))

대부분의 형용사는 이 문형이 가능하다.

It is good to be here. (= To be here is good.)
It won't be easy for Tom to find a new job.
It would be foolish to accept their offer. (To accept their offer would be foolish.)
It would look rude to refuse their invitation. (가주어-진주어)

It is important to reply to their letter.
It is important that we (should) reply to her letter.

여기 있는 것이 좋겠어요. / 톰이 새 직장을 찾는 것은 쉽지 않을 것입니다. / 그들의 제안을 받아들이는 것은 바보짓일 거예요. / 그들의 초대를 거절하는 것은 무례하게 보일 것입니다. / 그들에 편지에 답하는 것은 중요합니다. / 우리가 그녀의 편지에 답하는 것은 중요합니다.

too+형용사+to do 문형

He is too weak to lift it.
I'm too tired to stay up longer.
The ring is too expensive for me to buy.
The race was almost too exciting to watch.

그는 너무 약해서 그걸 들어올릴 수 없어요. / 저는 너무 지쳐서 더 이상 지 않을 수 없어요. / 반지는 내가 사기에는 너무 비쌉니다. / 경주는 너무 흥분해서 볼 수 없을 지경이었어요.

형용사+enough+to do 문형

He's strong enough to lift it.
= He has enough strength to lift it.
= He has strength enough to lift it.
It is ripe enough (for me) to eat.
She was very kind enough to help the old.
* There's not **enough** work for me to do. (enough는 형용사)

그는 그것을 들어 올릴 만큼 힘이 셉니다. / 그건 (내가) 먹을 수 있을 만큼 익었습니다. / 그녀는 노인들을 도울 만큼 매우 친절했습니다. / 내가 할 만한 일이 없습니다.

◀ 명사+to do형태

to do가 뒤에서 명사를 수식하는 형용사 역할

I've got **an essay to write**.
I want **a machine to answer** the phone.
There was **a lot to do/to be done**.
There was **nothing to do** so we played computer games.

저는 써야될 작문이 있습니다. / 전화응답기를 원합니다. / 할 일이 많았습니다. / 할 일이 없어서 우리는 컴퓨터게임을 했습니다.

Basic Grammar for English Tests

◀ 동명사 ('-ing'; gerund)

* -ing ┌ 동명사 - 명사 역할: I like coffee/swimming/flying.
       └ 현재분사 - 형용사 역할: This is a wide/running stream.

동명사 '-ing'의 역할

1. 문장에서 be동사의 보어 역할

   My favorite pastime is bird-watching.
   My hobby is drawing pictures.
   The only thing that he likes is watching TV.

   제가 가장 좋아하는 여가활동은 조류관찰입니다. / 제 취미는 그림 그리기입니다. / 그가 좋아하는 유일한 것은 TV시청입니다.

2. 문장에서 주어 역할

   Walking is good exercise.
   Playing tennis is fun.
   Jogging isn't much fun.
   Being lost can be a terrifying experience.

   걷기는 좋은 운동입니다. / 테니스 치는 것은 재미있습니다. / 조깅은 그리 재미있지 않습니다. / 길을 잃는 것은 끔찍한 경험입니다

3. 목적어 역할

   We enjoy playing tennis.
   I hear shouting.
   He doesn't like not being taken seriously.

   우리는 테니스 치기를 좋아합니다. / 고함소리가 들립니다. / 그는 진지하게 되는 것을 좋아하지 않습니다.

4. do+-ing

   do the cooking 요리하다
   do the shopping 쇼핑하다

5. 전치사의 목적어 역할

   The skill of speaking a foreign language takes time to acquire.
   Why don't you find something to do, like cleaning the car for me?
   It's a tool for making holes in metal.

   외국어 회화술은 습득하기에 시간이 걸립니다. / 나대신 세차를 한다든지, 뭔가 할 일을 찾아보지 않을래? / 그건 금속에 구멍을 내는 연장입니다.

6. 기타 표현

A ringing of bells marked the end of the old year.
No smoking. No parking.
Slow cooking makes tough meat tender.
What about / How about sending them a postcard?

종을 울려서 지난해의 끝을 고했습니다. / 금연. 주차금지. / 천천히 요리를 하면 질긴 고기를 부드럽게 해줍니다. / 그들에게 엽서를 보내는 게 어떨까요?

현재분사 '-ing'와의 구별

Walking in the park the other day, I saw a bird building a nest. (현재분사)
(= When I was walking, the bird was building a nest.)
Here are your running shoes. (동명사)
I love the sight of running water. (현재분사)

하루는 공원을 걷다가 둥지를 짓고 있는 새 한 마리를 보았습니다. / 네 운동화 여기 있어. / 저는 물 흐르는 모습이 좋아요.

[동명사]		[현재분사]
a sleeping car	-	a sleeping baby
a dinning room	-	an exciting game
a sleeping bag	-	a rolling stone

◀ V+동명사

동명사를 목적어로 받는 동사

admit : She admitted stealing the money. 그녀는 돈을 훔친 것을 인정했습니다.
advise : He advised waiting until tomorrow. 그는 내일까지 기다릴 것을 충고했습니다.
anticipate : I anticipate having a good time on vacation.
저는 방학 때 좋은 시간을 갖기를 기대합니다.
appreciate : I appreciated hearing from them. 그들의 소식을 들은 것을 감사합니다.
avoid : She avoided answering my question. 그녀는 제 질문에 답을 회피했습니다.
complete : She finally completed writing her term paper.
그녀는 드디어 학기말 논문 작성을 끝냈습니다.
consider : I will consider going with you. 저는 당신과 함께 갈 것을 고려하겠습니다.
delay : She delayed leaving for school. 그녀는 학교로 떠나는 것을 연기했습니다.
deny : He denied committing the crime. 그녀는 범행을 부인했습니다.
discuss : They discussed opening a new business. 그들은 새로운 사업 착수를 논의했습니다.
dislike : I dislike driving long distance. 저는 장거리 운전을 싫어합니다.

Basic Grammar for English Tests

enjoy :	We enjoyed visiting them. 우리는 그들을 방문하는 것이 즐거웠습니다.
finish :	He finished studying about ten. 그는 10시경에 공부를 마쳤습니다.
forget :	I'll never forget visiting Napoleon's tomb. 저는 나폴레옹의 묘를 방문했던 일을 결코 잊지 않을 것입니다.
can't help :	I can't help worrying about it. 저는 그것을 걱정하지 않을 수 없습니다.
keep :	I keep hoping she will come. 저는 그녀가 오리라는 희망을 간직하고 있어요.
mind :	Would you mind helping me with this? 저를 도와 이것 좀 해주시겠어요?
miss :	I miss being with my family. 가족과 함께 했던 때가 그립습니다.
postpone :	Let's postpone leaving until tomorrow. 떠나는 것을 내일까지 연기합시다.
practice :	The player practiced throwing the ball. 선수는 공 던지는 연습을 했습니다.
quit :	She quit trying to solve the problem. 그녀는 그 문제 푸는 노력을 그쳤습니다.
recollect :	I don't recollect meeting her before. 저는 전에 그녀를 만난 것을 기억하지 못합니다.
regret :	I regret telling her my secret. 저는 그녀에게 제 비밀을 말한 것을 후회합니다.
remember :	I can remember meeting her when I was a child. 저는 어렸을 때 그녀를 만난 것을 기억할 수 있어요.
resent :	I resent her interfering in my business. 저는 제 일에 그녀가 끼어 드는 것을 못 참겠어요.
resist :	I couldn't resist eating the dessert. 저는 디저트 먹기를 거부하지 못했습니다.
stop :	He stopped going to classes when he got sick. 그녀는 아파서 수업에 가는 것을 그만두었습니다.
suggest :	He suggested going to a movie. 그녀는 영화 보러가자고 제안했습니다.
tolerate :	He won't tolerate cheating during an examination. 그는 시험 중에 부정행위 하는 것을 참지 못합니다.
understand :	I don't understand her leaving school. 저는 그녀가 학교를 떠나는 것을 이해하지 못합니다.

go/come + -ing

[제안] Why don't we go swimming? 수영하러가지 않겠니?
[초대] Come dancing this evening. 오늘 저녁에 춤추러 가자.
[서술] Yesterday we went sightseeing. 어제 우리는 관광을 갔어요.

> go boating, go bowling, go camping, go dancing, go fishing, go hiking,
> go hunting, go jogging, go mountain climbing, go running, go shopping,
> go sightseeing, go skating, go skiing, go swimming, go window shopping

◀ 형용사/명사+동명사

형용사+동명사

It's nice seeing him again.

It's difficult finding your way around in a strange city.
Sarah is happy getting everything ready for the wedding.
It's strange his behaving like that.

그를 다시 보게되어 기쁩니다. / 낯선 도시에서 길을 찾기란 어렵습니다. / 사라는 결혼을 위한 모든 준비가 완료되어 행복합니다. / 그가 그렇게 행동하는 것은 이상합니다.

명사+동명사

> a catastrophe(파국), a disaster(재난), fun, hell(지옥), luck, a mistake,
> a pain(고통), a pleasure, a relief(안심), a tragedy

It's a nightmare worrying where the children might be.
It's a tedious business attending so many meetings.
It's a catastrophe their shutting all those factories.

아이들이 어디에 있을지 걱정하는 게 악몽입니다. / 너무 많은 회의에 참석하는 것은 지겨운 일입니다. / 그들이 저 모든 공장의 문을 닫는다는 것은 파국입니다.

We had a good time / fun ┐ playing baseball.

I had trouble / difficulty / a difficult time / a hard time ┐ finding his house.

우리는 야구를 하며 즐거운 시간을 가졌습니다. / 저는 그의 집을 찾는데 어려움을 겪었습니다.

관용적인 표현

It is no good -ing : ~하는 것이 좋지 않다
It is no use -ing : ~해봐야 소용없다
It is not worth -ing : ~할 가치가 없다
It is worth while -ing : ~할 가치가 있다
It is hardly/scarcely worth -ing : ~할 가치가 거의 없다
There is no -ing : (도저히) ~할 수 없다, ~는 불가능하다
There is no point -ing : ~해봐야 아무런 의미가 없다
There is nothing worse than -ing : ~보다 더 나쁠 게 없다
spend / waste ┐ time -ing / money -ing : ~하는데 시간/돈을 소비/낭비하다

It is no good complaining.
It is no use crying over spilt milk.

Basic Grammar for English Tests

It's just not worth worrying about it.
It's worth while reading a lot of books.
This clock is hardly worth repairing.
There is no telling what will happen.
There's no point trying to persuade him.
Don't waste time talking.
She spend most of her money gambling.

불평해봐야 좋은 게 없습니다. / 우유를 엎질러 놓고 울어봐야 소용없습니다. / 그런 걱정은 쓸데없습니다. / 책은 많이 읽을 가치가 있습니다. / 이 시계는 수리할 가치가 거의 없습니다. / 무슨 일이 일어날지 알 수 없습니다. / 그를 설득해봐야 아무런 의미 없습니다. / 말하는 데 시간을 낭비하지 마라. / 그녀는 자신의 많은 돈을 도박으로 낭비합니다.

◀ 전치사+동명사

전치사+동명사

> about, after, by, for, instead of, to, without ...

I have learned a lot **about gardening** from my father.
After changing some money, I went sightseeing.
I opened this door **by turning** the key twice in the lock.
The teacher punished Jimmy **for talking** in class.
You shouldn't try to leave the restaurant **without paying**.
* It goes without saying that knowledge is power.

아버지에게서 정원조경에 대해 많이 배웠습니다. / 돈을 좀 환전한 뒤에 저는 관광에 나섰습니다. / 저는 자물통에 열쇠를 두 번 돌려서 문을 열었습니다. / 선생님은 수업 중에 떠들었다고 지미를 벌주었습니다. / 식대도 지불하지 않고 식당을 떠나려고 해서는 안됩니다. / 지식이 힘이라는 것은 말할 필요도 없습니다.

형용사/명사+전치사+동명사

afraid of -ing (~을 염려하는),	bored with -ing (~에 싫증난),
concern about -ing (~을 염려하는),	fear of -ing (~을 두려워하는),
fond of -ing (~을 좋아하는),	good at -ing (~을 잘하는),
interested in -ing (~에 흥미가 있는),	sorry for -ing (~이 유감인),
be used to -ing (~에 익숙한),	worried about -ing (~을 걱정하는),
surprised at -ing (~에 놀란)	

I'm interested in dancing.
I'm bored with playing cards.

He's good at skiing.
She's fond of collecting stamps.
I was afraid of disturbing you.

저는 춤이 재미있어요. / 저는 카드놀이가 싫증났어요. / 그는 스키를 잘 탑니다. / 그녀는 우표수집을 좋아합니다. / 당신을 방해했을까봐 겁이 났어요.

to+-ing : (이때 to는 전치사)

be accustomed to -ing (~에 익숙해지다)   be used to -ing (~에 익숙해지다)
look forward to -ing (~을 기대하다)   object to -ing (~에 반대하다)
be resigned to -ing (~에 따르다, ~에 몸을 맡기다)

I'm accustomed to living on my own. 저는 자립에 익숙해있습니다.
I'm used to doing the shopping. 저는 쇼핑에 익숙합니다.
I'm looking forward to seeing you. 저는 당신을 만나기를 고대하고 있습니다.
I object to being kept waiting. 저는 계속 기다리는 것을 반대합니다.
I'm resigned to being criticized. 저는 비판에 따르겠습니다.

◀ V+to부정사/동명사

의미변화가 없는 동사

attempt to do/-ing, begin to do/-ing, can't bear to do/-ing (참지 못하다)
cease to do/-ing, commence to do/-ing (시작하다), continue to do/-ing
intend to do/-ing, omit to do/-ing, start to do/-ing

It begins to rain/raining.
I can't bear to see/seeing people suffering.
I can't bear you to shout in that way.
= I can't bear your shouting in that way.

비가 오기 시작합니다. / 사람들이 고통받는 것을 차마 못 보겠어요. / 저는 당신이 그런 식으로 고함지르는 것을 못 참겠어요.

| allow | -ing / someone to do | advise | -ing / someone to do |
| permit | -ing / someone to do | forbid | -ing / someone to do |

Would you **advise phoning**, or shall I wait a bit longer?

Basic Grammar for English Tests

Would you **advice me to phone**, or shall I wait a bit longer?
전화를 하게 해주시겠어요, 아니면 제가 좀 더 기다릴까요? / 제가 전화를 하게 해주시겠어요, 아니면 제가 조금 더 기다릴까요?

뜻이 변하는 동사

> dread to do/-ing, hate to do/-ing, like to do/-ing,
> love to do/doing, prefer to do/-ing

1. I love/like to watch TV.
   I love/like watching TV.
2. I hate to disturb you. (싫지만, 폐를 끼치려 한다.)
   I hate disturbing you. (지금 폐를 끼치고 있음에 미안한 마음이 든다.)
3. I dread to think what has happened to him. (생각하기 두렵다.)
   I dread going to the dentist. (치과 가는 일이 두렵다.)
4. I prefer to wait here. (여기서 기다리려 한다.)
   I prefer waiting here. (지금 기다리고 있다.)
   I prefer swimming to cycling.

1. 저는 TV시청을 좋아합니다. / 2. 저는 당신을 방해하는 것이 싫습니다 / 3. 그에게 무슨 일이 무슨 일이 일어날지 생각하면 두렵습니다. / 치과에 가는 것이 두렵습니다. / 4. 여기서 기다리겠습니다. / 여기서 기다리는 것이 좋아요. / 자전거 타기보다는 수영을 더 좋아합니다.

뜻이 전혀 다른 경우

> remember to do/-ing, forget to do/-ing, regret to do/-ing,
> try to do/-ing, stop to do/-ing, go on to do/-ing

Remember *to post* the letter. (Don't forget to : 미래)
I **remember** *to post* the letters. (I didn't forget to)
I **remember** *posting/having posted* the letters.
(I remember the fact that I posted them.)

편지 부치는 것을 잊지 마라. / 저는 편지 부칠 일을 기억하고 있습니다. / 저는 편지 부친 일을 기억하고 있습니다.

Don't **forget** *to ask* Tom. (Remember to ask : 미래)
I **forget** *to ask* Tom. (I didn't ask.)
Have you **forgotten** *meeting/having met* her? (You met her.)

톰에게 물어볼 것을 잊지 마라. / 저는 톰에게 물어볼 일을 잊어버렸습니다. / 그녀를 만난 것을 잊어버렸나요?

We **regret** *to inform* you that your account is overdrawn.
(유감스럽게도 ~을 알려드립니다.)
I **regret** *leaving* the company after twenty years. (떠난걸 후회한다.)

유감스럽지만 손님의 계좌가 초과출금 되었음을 알려드립니다. / 저는 20년 후에 회사를 떠난 것을 후회합니다.

You really must **try** *to overcome* your shyness. (= make an effort)
Try *holding* your breath to stop sneezing. (= experience)

당신은 정말이지 수줍음을 극복하려고 노력해야 합니다. / 재채기를 그치게 하려면 숨 멈추기를 해보세요.

On the way to the station I **stopped** *to buy* a paper. (~하기 위하여)
When he told us the story, we just couldn't **stop** *laughing*. (목적어)

역으로 가는 길에 저는 신문을 사려고 멈췄어요. / 그가 우리에게 이야기를 말할 때 우리는 웃음을 그칠 수가 없었어요.

After approving the agenda, we **went on** *to discuss* finance. (다른 일을 하다.)
We **went on** *talking* till after midnight. (하던 일을 중단 없이 계속하다.)

의제를 통과시킨 후에 우리는 계속해서 재정문제를 논의하였습니다. / 우리는 자정이 지나서까지 계속 이야기했습니다.

Exercise **2** 다음 각 문장에 들어갈 적당한 표현을 고르시오.

1. The teacher decided (accepting/*to accept*) the paper.
2. His father doesn't approve of his (going/to go) to Europe.
3. We found it very difficult (reaching/to reach) a decision.
4. Donna is interested in (to open/opening) a bar.
5. George has no intention of (to leave/leaving) the city now.
6. We are eager (to return/returning) to school in the fall.
7. You would be better off (to buy/buying) this car.
8. She refused (to accept/accepting) the gift.
9. Mary regrets (to be/being) the one to have to tell him.
10. George pretended (to be/being) sick yesterday.
11. Carlos hopes (to finish/finishing) his thesis this year.
12. They agreed (to leave/leaving) early.
13. We are not ready (to stop/stopping) this research at this time.
14. You shouldn't risk (to drive/driving) so fast.
15. He demands (to know/knowing) what is going on.

Actual Test 21

다음 각 문장을 읽고 빈칸에는 알맞은 단어를 넣고, 밑줄 친 부분에서는 잘못된 부분을 찾으시오.

1. Since the air pollution was greatly reduced, Chicago is still _____.
   - Ⓐ a good place in which to live
   - Ⓑ lived as a good place
   - Ⓒ a good place to live in
   - Ⓓ living in as a good place

2. Having received over eighty percent of the vote, Jane Lyon became the first woman _____ elected mayor of San Francisco.
   - A who she
   - B she was
   - C was to
   - D to be

3. The stupid mother _____ that they are never safe.
   - Ⓐ causes her children feel
   - Ⓑ causes he children feeling
   - Ⓒ causes her children to feel
   - Ⓓ feels her children cause

4. On hearing the bell ring, _____.
   - Ⓐ the students' departure was hasty
   - Ⓑ our departure was hasty
   - Ⓒ they departed hastily
   - Ⓓ the classroom was filled immediately

5. It seems very difficult _____.
   - Ⓐ to stop the baby to cry
   - Ⓑ restraining the baby to cry
   - Ⓒ to keep the baby from crying
   - Ⓓ holding the baby's crying

6. I had a lot of trouble _____ through the heavy snow this morning.
   - Ⓐ drove
   - Ⓑ drive
   - Ⓒ driving
   - Ⓓ to drive

7. When the teacher fell off the slide, other children _____.
   - Ⓐ couldn't help laughing
   - Ⓑ weren't able to stop laughter
   - Ⓒ could not avoid to laugh
   - Ⓓ could not stop but laughing

8. London <u>is</u> one of the many cities in the world that <u>are currently</u> developing
          A   B
   programs <u>of restoring</u> <u>their</u> historical buildings.
                C   D

9. The <u>goal</u> of the skylab mission was <u>to studying</u> <u>a person's ability</u> to live
        A   B   C
   and <u>work for</u> extended periods in the weightless conditions of space.
          D

10. <u>To formation</u> a layer of coal one foot <u>thick</u>, <u>about</u> fifty feet of <u>original</u> plant
        A   B   C   D
    material must be compacted.

11. <u>Hopping</u> to distract me <u>from my grief</u>, my daughter and her friend
        A   B
    <u>invited me</u> <u>go</u> to the movies with them.
         C   D

12. Because I was <u>unaware of</u> his <u>interest in</u> the building, I did not understand
                    A   B
    why he <u>felt so bad</u> about <u>it's being</u> condemned.
            C   D

13. Amy <u>did not have</u> time <u>to go</u> to the concert last night because she was
          A   B
    busy <u>to prepare</u> <u>for her trip</u> to Europe and Chile
         C   D

14. Many people complain that the costs of establishing a <u>business</u> <u>are</u>
                                                  A   B
    <u>so much</u> that only the rich can afford <u>running</u> a company.
      C   D

15. <u>As time</u> <u>went on</u>, Michael suffered <u>such heavy</u> losses that he was forced
     A   B   C
    <u>giving up</u> his business.
       D

16. Some artists tended <u>considering</u> <u>artistic</u> invention and imagination more
                              A   B
    important than the <u>faithful</u> <u>reproduction</u> of nature.
                        C   D

17. After I <u>had</u> finished <u>to read</u> the newspaper, I began <u>to think</u> about <u>the</u>
           A   B   C   D
    terrible accident reported in the paper.

18. Mr. Smith often <u>wore</u> a <u>heavy coat</u> because he was not used <u>to live</u> in
                    A   B   C
    <u>such a</u> cold climate.
       D

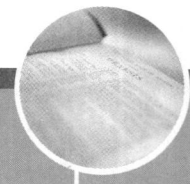

ENGLISH FORUM

Basic Grammar for English Tests

Translations and Explanatory Answers

정답과 해설

Translations and Explanatory Answers

Part I 구문편

Unit 1 문장구조

[EXERCISE 1]

(At) certain times men were fascinated (by) more particular problems (within) the general philosophic framework (of) these larger questions. For example, towards the end (of) the Middle Ages, that is (in) the fourteenth and fifteenth centuries, some critics (of) the then accepted Aristotelian system became specially interested (in) the problems (of) movement—why did a projectile continue to move after it had left the bow or sling and why did it gradually fall (to) the ground? Aristotle's explanations were no longer accepted (as) satisfactory, and the way was opened (for) a whole new philosophy to creep (into) men's minds through the small hole made (in) the accepted theory (of) motion.

[EXERCISE 2]

1. to laugh (부정사)
2. to town (전치사구)
3. to trip (부정사)
4. to notify (부정사)
5. to the park (전치사구)
6. to be angry (부정사)
7. to park (부정사)
8. to shout (부정사)
9. to the shore (전치사구)
10. to the supermarket (전치사구)
11. to save (부정사)
12. to drive (부정사)
13. to run (부정사)
14. to the drive (전치사구)
15. to peace (전치사구)
16. to the walk (전치사구)
17. to her laugh (전치사구)
18. to pieces (전치사구)
19. to his shout (전치사구)
20. to tear (부정사)

[EXERCISE 3]

1. Many students *have to work* during school vacations.
   (명사구)   (동사구)   (전치사구)
   많은 학생들이 방학 동안 일을 해야 합니다.

2. All of us *hoped to remain* calm during the test.
   (전치사구)   (동사구)   (전치사구)
   우리 모두는 시험치는 동안 조용히 있기를 바랬습니다.

3. Having finished the work, the agent *sent* for a heavy meal.
   (분사구)   (명사구)
                                        (전치사구)
   작업을 끝마친 후, 그 요원은 푸짐한 식사를 가지러 보냈습니다.

4. At last a heavy rain *fell* on the parched ground.
   (전치사구) (명사구)   (전치사구)
   드디어 메마른 대지 위에 소나기가 쏟아졌습니다.

5. An attitude of anxiety *does not appeal* to anyone.
   (명사구)   (전치사구)   (동사구)   (전치사구)
   화난 태도는 어떤 사람에게도 받아들여지지 않습니다.

6. Teaching a small puppy *is* a good way to develop patience.
   (동명사구)   (명사구)
                                 (부정사구)
   조그만 강아지를 훈련시키는 것은 인내심을 기르는 좋은 방법입니다.

7. To get an A *is* the goal of many students.
   (부정사구)   (명사구)   (전치사구)
   A학점을 받는 것은 많은 학생들의 목표입니다.

8. Putting all her strength into the effort, Ann *did* her best.
   (분사구)   (전치사구)
                                              (명사구)
   자기의 모든 힘을 다해 노력을 하여, 앤은 최선을 다 하였습니다.

9. He *has* a large family to support.
        (명사구)   (전치사구)
   그에게는 부양할 대가족이 있습니다.

10. The student *remained* in the library for two hours.
    (명사구)   (전치사구)   (전치사구)
    학생들은 2시간 동안 도서관에 남아 있었습니다.

[EXERCISE 4]

1. cars *cost* a lot of money (절)
   자동차는 돈이 많이 든다
2. in terms of population (구)
   인구에 관하여
3. walking home *takes* time (절)
   집으로 걸어가는 것은 시간이 걸린다
4. spelling irregular verbs (구)
   불규칙동사 철자쓰기
5. to dream of better days (구)
   좋은 날을 꿈꾸기
6. the man *ate* quickly (절)
   그 남자는 빨리 식사를 하였다
7. cars needing many repairs (구)
   수리를 많이 해야 하는 자동차
8. winter nights *chill* the bones (절)
   겨울밤은 뼈를 시리게 한다
9. to enter *costs* ten dollars (절)
   입장료는 10달러가 든다
10. after the last dance (구)
    마지막 춤을 춘 후
11. radial tires *are* expensive (절)
    방사형(레디얼) 타이어는 비싸다
12. from ten to twenty years (구)
    10년에서 20년까지

irregular [irégjulər] *adj.* 불규칙한 repair [ripέər] *n.* 보수, 수리 chill [tʃil] *v.* 춥게 하다, 시리다 radial [réidiəl] *adj.* 광선의, 방사(복사)상의

[EXERCISE 5]

1. before finishing dinner (구)
   만찬을 마치기 전에
2. if the doctors *operate* soon (종속절)
   의사들이 곧 수술한다면
3. whom the committee *chose* (종속절)
   위원회가 선출한
4. after the last class (구)
   마지막 수업 후에
5. as the sun *set* behind the hill (종속절)
   해가 서산에 질 때
6. because he *was born* in Texas (종속절)
   그가 텍사스에서 태어났기 때문에
7. standing in a long line (구)
   긴 행렬 속에 서 있기
8. which the driver *hit* (종속절)
   그 운전사가 충돌한
9. an inexpensive Japanese model (구)
   비싸지 않은 일본인 모델
10. before the rain *had stopped* (종속절)
    비가 그치기 전에
11. driving fifty-five miles an hour (구)
    시속 55마일로 운전하기
12. which he *passed* easily (종속절)
    그가 일찍 통과한

[EXERCISE 6]

1. the water *is used* for irrigation (주절)
   그 물은 관개용으로 이용된다
2. which *is used* to make chewing gum (종속절)
   껌을 만드는 데 사용되는
3. a famous talk show host (구)
   유명한 토크쇼 진행자
4. her hopes for the future (구)
   미래에 대한 그녀의 희망
5. the population *increased* greatly (주절)
   인구가 크게 증가하였다
6. a brain infection causing jerking (구)
   경련을 일으키는 뇌염
7. the fourth largest city of the state (구)
   그 주에서 네번째 큰 도시
8. although the law *was repealed* (종속절)
   비록 그 법률이 철회될지라도
9. who *lived* in Oregon (종속절)
   오리건에 살았던 (사람)
10. several different writing systems (구)
    몇 개의 서로 다른 작문체계
11. when the radio *was invented* (종속절)
    라디오가 발명되었을 때
12. the first ships *were* only logs (주절)
    최초의 배는 단순한 통나무였다

irrigatioin [irigéiʃən] *n.* 관개, 물대기 brain infection : 뇌염 jerking [dʒə́:rkiŋ] *n.* 경련

[EXERCISE 7]

1. Courtesy demands a prompt apology.
   즉시 사과하는 것이 예의입니다.
2. He is the new director of the institute.
   그는 그 연구원의 새 원장입니다.
3. To drive more than fifty five miles per hour is illegal.
   시속 55마일 이상의 속도로 운전하는 것은 위법이다.
4. Walking to the university takes twenty minutes.
   대학까지 걸어가면 20분 걸립니다.
5. Whoever wins the race will receive a trophy.
   경주에 이기는 사람이 트로피를 받을 것입니다.

Translations and Explanatory Answers

6. Cemeteries are frightening places at night.
   공동묘지는 밤에 무서운 곳입니다.
7. Rollerskating has recently become very popular.
   롤러스케이팅은 근래에 매우 인기가 있습니다.
8. That all the passengers survived the crash is miraculous.
   충돌사고에서 모든 승객들이 살아남은 것은 기적이었습니다.
9. To get angry is not the solution.
   화내는 것은 해결책이 아닙니다.
10. These appear to be photographs of a North African village.
    이것들은 북아프리카의 어느 마을의 사진 같습니다.

cóurtesy [kə́:rtəsi] n. 예의 prompt = quick ínstitute [ínstətju:t] n. 기관, 연구원 illégal [ilí:gəl] adj. 불법의 cémetery [sémətəri] n. 공동묘지 pássanger : 승객 survíve [sərváiv] v. ~에서 살아남다 crash [kræʃ] n. 충돌사고 miráculous [mirǽkjələs] adj. 기적적인

[EXERCISE 8]

1. The municipal auditorium *is located* on the shores of Town Lake.
   시민회관은 타운레이크 호반에 자리잡고 있습니다.
2. That new book *will interest* football fans.
   그 새책은 축구팬들의 관심을 끌 것입니다.
3. There *are* several new apartment complexes west of the university.
   대학의 서쪽에는 몇 개의 아파트단지가 있습니다.
4. Near the auditorium *stand* the city coliseum and the fair grounds.
   회관 근처에 시립경기장과 멋진 운동장이 서 있습니다.
5. Buses *depart* from the station every half hour.
   버스는 30분마다 역을 출발합니다.
6. Many career opportunities *are* available to a lawyer. 경험을 많이 쌓을 기회는 변호사에게 좋습니다.
7. The cable television company *has* recently *installed* lines to the suburbs.
   유선TV방송사는 근래에 교외에다 선을 설치하였다.
8. That new book *has been checked out* and *read* by a dozen people this week.
   그 새책은 이번 주에 10여 명에 의해 검토되고 읽혀졌습니다.
9. Through the branches of the tree *shone* the light of the full moon.
   나뭇가지 사이로 보름달빛이 비쳤습니다.
10. The new highway *will have been completed* by January of next year.
    새 고속도로가 내년 1월까지는 완성되어 있을 것이다.

munícipal auditórium : 시민회관 compléx [kəmpléks] n. 복합체, 복합단지 caréer opportúnity : 활동기회 aváilable [əvéiləbəl] adj. 쓸모있는, 유용한 instáll [instɔ́:l] v. 설치하다 súburb [sʌ́bə:rb] n. 교외 branch [bræntʃ] n. 나뭇가지 full moon : 보름달

[EXERCISE 9]

1. Mittens *warm* the hands.
   장갑은 손을 따뜻하게 합니다.
2. The smoke *rose* to the ceiling.
   연기가 천장으로 올라갔습니다.
3. Those dormitories *house* the men.
   저 기숙사들은 남자들을 수용합니다.
4. Her laugh *hurt* my ears.
   그녀의 웃음이 내 귀에 거슬렸습니다.
5. The will *interests* the lawyer.
   그 유언장은 변호사의 관심을 끈다.
6. His cries *fell* on deaf ears.
   그의 울음소리는 벙어리의 귀에까지 들렸습니다.
7. One can *fell* on the floor.
   깡통이 하나 마루바닥에 떨어졌습니다.
8. The experiments *require* live organs.
   그 실험은 살아있는 장기기관을 필요로 합니다.
9. Secretaries *book* appointments.
   비서들은 약속을 정합니다.
10. Her dreams *came* true.
    그녀의 꿈은 실현되었습니다.

mítten [mítn] n. 장갑 warm [wɔ:rm] v. 따뜻하게 하다 céiling [sí:liŋ] n. 천장 dórmitory [dɔ́:rmətɔ:ri] n. 기숙사 house [hauz] v. 수용하다 deaf [def] adj. 귀먹은 live órgan : 살아있는 장기기관 book v. 예약하다, 기록하다 come trúe : 실현되다

[EXERCISE 10]

1. In the desert the *need* for water *is* of primary importance. (명사)
   사막에서는 물의 필요성이 첫째로 중요합니다.
2. Out of the darkness *came* a woman's *cry* for help. (명사)
   어둠 속에서 도와달라는 여자의 울음소리가 들렸다.
3. On a dark night *dreams* *can seem* larger than life. (명사)
   어두운 밤에는 꿈이 삶보다 더 커 보입니다.
4. A safe place for a *will* *is* in a bank deposit box. (명사)
   유언장을 위해 안전한 곳은 은행 개인금고 속입니다.

Basic Grammar for English Tests

5. Coaches *time* exercises with a watch. (동사)
 코치들은 시계로 운동시간을 잽니다.

6. For a novice backpacker, an all-day climb on this mountain *is* strenuous. (명사)
 초보 등반인들에게는 산에서 종일 등반하는 것이 힘듭니다.

7. After a day on the slopes, skiers *warm* their feet by the fire. (명사)
 스키장에서 하루를 보낸 후에 스키어들은 난로가에서 발을 따뜻하게 합니다.

8. A rat *mothers* her young carefully during their first weeks. (동사)
 어미쥐는 첫 주 동안 태어난 새끼들을 정성껏 돌본다.

9. At the last minute, a swift kick by one player *tied* the game. (명사)
 마지막 순간에 한 선수의 재빠른 킥이 경기를 동점으로 만들었습니다.

10. For the engineering student recent studies *are* the most relevant. (명사)
 공학도에게는 최근의 연구가 가장 관련이 깊습니다.

will *n.* 유언 bank deposit box : 은행(개인)금고 time *v.* 시간을 재다 exercise [éksərsaiz] *n.* 운동 nóvice [návis] *v.* 초보자(= begínner) báckpacker [bǽkpækər] *n.* 등산인(= climber) strénuous [strénjuəs] *adj.* 노력을 요하는, 격렬한, 힘든 slope [sloup] *n.* 스키장 mother *v.* 어머니처럼 돌보다 young *n.* 새끼 swift [swift] *adj.* 재빠른(= rápid) rélevant [réləvənt] *adj.* 관련이 있는

[Actual Test **1**]

1. (C, cells die) 주어-동사를 갖춘 절이 와야 문장이 완성된다.
 다른 모든 생명체와 같이 세포도 죽습니다.

2. (B, was the) 빈칸에 주절의 동사가 들어가야 한다. discovered와 was established는 주절의 동사가 아니다.
 molecular [moulékjulər] *adj.* 분자의, 분자로 된
 1920년에 발견된 비타민A는 분자구조가 수립된 최초의 비타민이었습니다.

3. (B, encouraged) 문장의 동사가 들어가야 하되 능동임을 유의할 것.
 repertory theater 레퍼토리 극장 (전속극단을 보유하고 여러 가지 연극을 공연하는 극장)
 연극제작자 제임스 모리스는 미국에서 직업적인 레퍼토리극장 설립을 도모하였습니다.

4. (A, served) 능동인 동사가 있어야 문장이 완성된다.
 delegate *n.* 대표
 1960년에 메리 잭슨은 유엔대표로 나라에 봉사하였습니다.

5. (B, it 제거) 주어가 Boston, ~, it is ~로 중복되어 있다.

hub [hʌb] *n.* 중심(= center, core)
 뉴잉글랜드의 중심지인 보스톤은 매사추세츠주의 수도이자 그 지방에서 가장 큰 도시입니다.

6. (C, is → are) 주어 seeds가 복수이므로 동사도 복수형 are
 seed [siːd] *n.* 씨앗 crack [kræk] *v.* 부수다, 빻다 feed [fiːd] *n.* 먹이 *v.* 먹이다
 으깬 옥수수, 땅콩, 해바라기씨 등을 혼합한 씨앗들은 겨울 철새들에게 인기있는 먹이입니다.

7. (B, it was → was) 주어가 Washington it was로 중복되어 있다.
 house *v.* 수용하다
 대부분의 수도와는 달리 워싱턴은 정부 청사들을 수용하기 위해 특별히 건설되었습니다.

8. (B, being → is) 이 문장에 동사가 없다. being은 동사가 될 수 없다.
 bórax [bóuræks] *n.* (화학) 붕사 sóftener [sɔ́fənər] *n.* 묽게 하는 재료, 연화제 láundry *n.* 빨래
 일반적으로 사막에서 발견되는 붕사는 세탁업에서 수질 연화제로 사용됩니다.

9. (A, they → 제거) 주어가 중복되어 있다.
 초기 단추와 달리 오늘날의 단추는 흔히 대량 생산되고, 보통 플라스틱으로 만들어집니다.

10. (B, it 제거) 주어가 중복되어 있다.
 oríginate [ərídʒəneit] *v.* 발생되다, 기원하다
 철자 A는 아마 집의 상형기호에서 기원한 것 같습니다.

11. (A, deterministic → determine) 동사역할을 해야 한다.
 by means of ~ : (수단) ~에 의하여, ~로써 echolocátion [ekouloukéiʃən] *n.* 박쥐의 음향탐지장치 relý on ~ : ~에 의존하다 (= depénd on) sight [sait] *n.* 시각 (*v.* see)
 박쥐들은 시각에 의존하지 않는 체계인 방향탐지기능으로 자신들의 위치를 결정합니다.

12. (A, Thai farmers → Thai are farmers) 주절이 성립되려면 동사가 필요하다.
 cultivátion [kʌltəvéiʃən] *n.* 경작
 국토의 10%만이 경작되고 있음에도 불구하고 태국 국민의 65%가 농부들입니다.

13. (A, who 제거) 문장(주절)의 주어 John Bunyan에 대한 동사가 없다.
 másterpiece [mǽstərpiːs] *n.* 걸작, 명작 extrémely [ikstríːmli] *adv.* 몹시, 대단히
 1678년에 존 번연은 300년 이상이나 대단히 인기가 있었던 그의 역작 『천로역정』을 출간하였습니다.

14. (C, to having been → it's been)
 그 약이 시중에 나온지 겨우 2년밖에 되지 않기 때문에, 과학자들은 그 약의 장기적인 효능에 대해 거의 알지 못합니다.

Unit 2 문장의 종류

[EXERCISE 1]

1. (o) 나는 돈이 없습니다.
2. (x) → I don't need any help.
   나는 어떤 도움도 필요없습니다.
3. (x) → I didn't see anybody.
   나는 아무도 보지 못했습니다.
4. (x) → I can never understand him.
   나는 도무지 그를 이해할 수가 없습니다.
5. (o) 나는 누구도 믿지 않습니다.
6. (x) → He doesn't like either coffee or tea.
   그는 커피도 차도 다 좋아하지 않습니다.
7. (x) → I can hardly hear the radio.
   나는 라디오 소리를 거의 들을 수가 없었습니다.
8. (o) 그의 방에는 아무도 없었습니다.
9. (x) → We couldn't see anything but sand in the desert.
   사막에서 우리는 모래밖에 아무것도 볼 수가 없었습니다.
10. (o) 지난 8세기 동안 말을 훈련시키는 방법은 전혀 변하지 않았습니다.

désert [dézərt] n. 사막, 황무지 desért [dizə́:rt] v. 버리다, 유기하다
dessért [dizə́:rt] n. 후식

[EXERCISE 2]

everyone, no one, hardly ever, no, anywhere, anything, nothing

예티는 히말라야에서 사는 이상한 생물일 것으로 생각된다. 거의 모든 사람들이 예티에 대해 들었다. 그러나 아무도 실제로 보지는 못했다. 최근에 한 무리의 등산객들이 예티를 찾아 존리산을 등정하였다. 많은 유명한 산들과는 달리, 존리는 사람들이 거의 등반하지 않았다. 등반대는 어디에서도 예티를 볼 수가 없었다. 어느 날 밤 흥분의 한순간이 있었으니, 한 대원이 2음조의 이상한 소리를 들었다. 그는 천막 밖으로 뛰쳐나가서 티벳인 안내원에게 무슨 소리를 들었느냐고 물었다. "아뇨, 아무 소리도 못 들었습니다" 하고 안내원이 대답하였다. "그런데, 저는 방금 어떤 이상한 소리를 들었습니다." 그 대원이 말했다. "그건 예티가 아닙니다." 안내원이 웃었다. "그건 저였어요. 제가 코를 풀었거든요."

be supposed to do : ~라고 생각되다, ~로 소문나 있다 créature [krí:tʃər] n. 피조물 excítement [iksáitmənt] n. 흥분 two-note sound : 두 음조의 소리 rush out of ~ : ~를 뛰쳐나가다 blow one's nose : 코를 풀다

[EXERCISE 3]

1. 그들은 휴일이죠, 안 그래요? : aren't they?
2. 클라라는 집에 있죠, 안 그래요? : wasn't she?
3. 당신은 끝내쳤요, 안 그래요? : haven't you?
4. 제인은 외출했어요, 그렇지 않아요? : hasn't she?
5. 제가 하는 일은 늘 잘 못돼요, 안 그래요? : don't I?
6. 당신은 파리에 가본 적이 없죠, 그렇습니까? : have you?
7. 오늘 제인에게 무슨 일이 있나봐요, 안 그래요? : isn't it?
8. 아무도 시험에서 부정행위를 하지는 않아요, 그렇죠? : did they?
9. 제가 가버린 동안 잘못된 일은 아무것도 없어요, 안 그래요? : did it?
10. 모두가 수영하는 법을 배울 수 있어요, 안 그래요? : can't they?

[EXERCISE 4]

1. (is interested in) 캐롤은 고대역사에 흥미가 있습니다.
2. (is composed of) 물은 수소와 산소로 구성되어 있습니다.
3. (am accustomed to) 저는 여기서 사는 데 익숙합니다.
4. (is terrified at(with)) 우리 아들은 개를 무서워합니다.
5. (is finished with) 패트는 작문을 마쳤습니다.
6. (is covered with) 겨울입니다. 땅이 눈으로 덮였습니다.
7. (am satisfied with) 저는 제가 해낸 발전에 만족합니다.
8. (am tired of) 저는 여기 앉아있는 것에 싫증이 났습니다.
9. (Are related to) 당신 이름이 메리 스미스이지요, 존 스미스와 친척입니까?
10. (is dedicated to) 로빈슨 부인은 고아원에서 일합니다. 그녀는 자기 일에 헌신합니다.

be ínterested in ~ : ~에 흥미가 있는 hýdrogen n. 수소 óxygen n. 산소 be compósed of ~ : ~로 구성되다 be accústomed to ~ : ~에 익숙해지다 composítion n. 작문 be fínished with ~ : ~을 끝마치다 be cóvered with ~ : ~로 덮이다 prógress [prágres] n. 진보, [prəgrés] v. 진보하다 be sátisfied with ~ : ~에 만족하다 be tired of ~ : ~에 싫증나다 be reláted to ~ : ~와 친척이다 órphanage [ɔ́:rfənidʒ] n. 고아원

[Actual Test 2]

1. (C, did not begin) 일반동사를 부정할 때는 do+not를 사용한다.
   astronómical adj. 천문학의 astrophýsical adj. 천체물리학의
   캐더린 존스여사는 65세가 될 때까지 천문학과 천체물리학 연구의 지원을 시작하지 않았습니다.
2. (C, no) 명사를 부정할 때는 no를 쓴다.
   fíngerprint n. 지문 idéntical adj. 똑같은
   어떤 지문도 똑같은 것은 없다는 것이 확실했습니다.
3. (D, do cellular phone calls cost) 의문사 의문문의 주어-동사 어순문제. 주어 calls가 복수임을 주의할 것.
   휴대전화료는 얼마죠?
4. (B, is there) 의문사 의문문의 주어-동사 어순문제.
   여러분이 기말시험을 준비할 시간이 얼마나 있나요?
5. (A, didn't we) have to는 do로 받는다.
   우리가 12장을 읽어야 하죠, 그렇지 않으요?

6. (D, isn't) 주절의 동사가 긍정이면 부가의문문은 부정으로.
아뇨, 그는 당신을 보려고 해요, 안 그래요?

7. (A, Work hard) '명령문..., and ...(~하라, 그러면 ~하리라)'구문이다.
"기말고사에 실패했어요." "다음에 열심히 하게. 그러면 성공할 거야."

8. (B, was organized) 'by (someone)'로 보아 수동태 동사임.
미국적십자사는 낸시 존슨에 의해 조직되었습니다.

9. (B, can easily be) 주어가 사물이고 동사 measured의 목적어가 없는 것으로 보아 수동태임.
오늘날 지구에서 화성까지의 거리를 레이다로 쉽게저빔으로 쉽게 잴 수 있습니다.

10. (D, derived from legend) be derived from ~에서 유래하다
나무와 관련된 많은 상징이 전설과 민속에서 유래합니다.

11. (C, they were → were they) 의문절의 어순은 '의문사+be/have+주어 …?'
monolíthic [mɔnəlíθik] *adj.* 돌 하나로 된 비석 stóne statúe : 석상
이스터 섬의 석상에 관한 의문점 가운데 하나는 "어째서 그들 모두가 똑같이 생겼을까"이다.

12. (D, none → no) none은 대명사이다. 명사인 living traces를 부정(수식)하는 것은 no이다.
inhábit [inhǽbit] *v.* ~에 살다, 서식하다 trace [treis] *n.* 자취
화성은 한때 오늘날 전혀 생명의 흔적이 없는 동식물들이 서식하였다.

13. (B, too → either) 'not~either' : ~도 또한 아니다.
ríde a bus : 버스를 타다
제가 너무 멀리 떨어져 살지만 않았다면, 저는 회사까지 버스를 타려고 하지 않았을 거예요.

14. (D, never takes → ever takes) 'hardly never'는 이중 부정이므로 틀리는 표현이다.
mánager [mǽnidʒər] *n.* 부장, 관리자 staff *n.* 스태프, 중역, 보좌
지점장님은 자기 직원들이 휴가시간을 몽땅 이용할 것이라고 주장하시지만, 그는 휴가를 혼자 가져본 적이 거의 없습니다.

15. (D, been disappeared → disappeared) disappeared는 자동사이므로 수동태로 하지 않는다.
invént *v.* 발명하다 líver [lívər] *n.* 간
새로 발명된 백신 덕택에 간질환은 이제 사라지게 되었습니다.

16. (C, reflection → reflected) '반영되다': be reflected in
líberal [líbərəl] *adj.* 자유주의적인, 자유분방한 polítical opínion : 정치적인 견해
제인 오스틴은 자유주의적인 정치견해를 가지고 있는데, 그녀의 소설과 시에 반영되어 있습니다.

17. (B, described → been described) '주어+동사 관계인 This phenomenon과 described는 수동관계라야 한다.
phenómenon [finámənən] *n.* 현상 describe [diskráiv] *v.* 묘사하다, 기술하다 cliché [kliʃéi] *n.* 상투적인 문구
이 현상은 너무도 자주 묘사되어서 여기서 그 작품에 대한 더 이상의 상투어구를 필요로 하지 않을 정도입니다.

18. (D, borned → was born) '태어나다' : be born
sócial wórker 사회사업가 oríginator [ərídʒəneitər] *n.* 창시자
사회사업가이자 '키친가든' 운동의 창시자인 에밀리 존스는 코네티컷주 레바논에서 태어났습니다.

19. (C, extending → extended) 수동진행형: 'be+being +p.p.'
advántage [ædvǽntidʒ] *n.* 이점 édit [édit] *v.* 편집하다 exténd [iksténd] *v.* 확장시키다 wrítten lánguage : 문어, 글어
컴퓨터화에 의한 타자와 편집의 이점은 현재 세계의 모든 문자로 확산되고 있습니다.

20. (B, to an → as an/to be) '~로 임명되다': be appointed as/to be
appóint *v.* 지명하다 assóciate [əsóuʃieit] *v.* 제휴하다, 협력하다 Suprème Cóurt : (미국의) 연방대법원
우디 마셜은 1967년 미국 대법원의 판사에 임명되었습니다.

Unit 3 단문

[EXERCISE 1]

1. (terrible) 내 감기는 무서운 것 같구나.
2. (well) 그 피아니스트는 연주를 아주 잘 합니다.
3. (good) 그 식당의 음식은 언제나 맛이 좋습니다.
4. (calm) 야영객들은 뇌우에도 조용히 있었다.
5. (sick) 그들은 상한 음식을 먹은 후 병이 났습니다.
6. (quickly) 앤더슨 교수는 학생들의 스케치를 재빨리 보았습니다.
7. (diligently) 존은 그 프로젝트에 열심히 일하고 있었습니다.
8. (vehemently) 폴은 새로운 제안에 대해 격렬히 항의하였습니다.
9. (relaxed) 우리 이웃들은 휴가를 다녀온 후 편안해 보였습니다.
10. (noisy) 그 음악은 너무 시끄러워서 고전음악이 될 수가 없습니다.
11. (sweet) 계절의 절정 때에는 장미 향기가 좋습니다.
12. (silent) 어린이는 자기 아버지가 방에 들어오자 조용해졌습니다.
13. (rapidly) 물은 폭포 위를 급속하게 흘러갔습니다.
14. (angrily) 그의 팀이 공을 헛잡자 코치는 그들을 향해 화가 나서 고함을 질렀습니다.
15. (easily) 혹독한 훈련과정을 마친 뒤에 소년은 역기를 쉽게 들어 올릴 수 있었습니다.
16. (pale) 시험 이야기가 나오자 어린이는 안색이 창백해졌습니다.

17. (false) 경찰이 그 남자의 이야기를 조사하자 거짓으로 드러났습니다.
18. (easily) 알루미늄은 쉽게 구부려집니다.
19. (crazy) 그들의 작은 아파트에서는 미칠 지경이라서, 부부는 이사가기로 결심하였습니다.
20. (good) 저 끓는 수프는 아주 맛있는 냄새가 나는군요.

cámper v. 야영하는 사람 despíte [dispáit] prep. ~에도 불구하고 contáminate [kəntǽməneit] v. 오염시키다 contaminated food : 상한 음식 díligent [díləʤənt] adj. 부지런한 véhement [víəmənt] adj. 격렬한 propósal [prəpóuzəl] n. 제안 at the height of ~ : ~의 절정에, 한창 때에 falls n. 폭포 fúmble [fʌ́mbəl] v. (야구)공을 헛잡다 rígorous [rígərəs] adj. 엄격한, 혹독한 lift the weights : 역기를 들어올리다 cf. wéightlifting : 역도 at the méntion of ~ : ~의 이야기가 나오면 turn pále : 창백해지다 bend v. 구부리다 (bend-bent-bent) búbble [bʌ́bəl] v. 거품이 일다, 끓다

[EXERCISE 2]

1. (to accept) 선생님은 그 숙제를 받아들이기로 결정하셨습니다.
2. (having) 그들은 이 정보를 얻게되어 고마워합니다.
3. (going) 그의 아버지는 그의 유럽행을 허락하지 않습니다.
4. (to reach) 우리는 결정을 내리기가 매우 어렵다는 사실을 알았습니다.
5. (opening) 도너는 술집을 개업하는 일에 관심이 있습니다.
6. (leaving) 조지는 현재 도시를 떠날 생각이 없습니다.
7. (to turn) 우리는 가을에 학교로 돌아가기를 열망합니다.
8. (buying) 당신은 이 자동차를 살 만큼 형편이 좋아질 겁니다.
9. (to accept) 그녀는 선물 받기를 거절하였습니다.
10. (being) 메리는 자신이 그에게 말을 해줘야 하는 사람이 된 것을 후회합니다.

apprécíate = thank appróve [əprúːv] v. 승인하다 reach a decísion : 결론짓다 inténtion n. 의도 be éager to do : ~하기를 열망하다 be better óff : 부유해지다

[EXERCISE 3]

1. (leave) 선생님은 제인에게 방을 떠나도록 하였습니다.
2. (repaired) 톰은 자동차를 기계공에게 수리를 시켰습니다.
3. (to type) 제인은 존에게 자기 논문을 타자치도록 하였습니다.
4. (call) 저는 제인이 자기 친구들에게 전화걸도록 했습니다.
5. (painted) 우리는 지난주에 우리 집을 페인트 칠하였습니다.
6. (write) 앤더슨 박사님은 학생들에게 작문을 시키고 있습니다.
7. (sent) 마크는 자신의 성적증명서를 대학에 제출하였습니다.
8. (cut) 마라이는 내일 자신의 머리를 자르려고 합니다.
9. (to sign) 우리는 학장님이 이 서류에 서명하시도록 해야 합니다.
10. (find) 우리는 자넷이 열쇠를 찾는 것을 도와야 합니다.

mechánic [məkǽnik] n. 기계공 write a composítion : 작문을 하다 transcript [trǽnskript] n. 성적증명서 cut-cut-cut dean [diːn] n. 학장

[Actual Test 3]

1. (D, stay late) stay는 완전자동사이므로 부사로 수식. (lately: 최근에, late: 늦게, 늦도록)
   조지는 늦도록 남아 있을 지도 모르지만, 우리는 곧 가야해요.
2. (A, slightly) increased는 완전자동사이므로 부사로 수식이 가능함.
   지난주에 식품요가 아주 조금 인상되었습니다.
3. (A, sweet and soothing) 감각동사 sound는 형용사를 보어로 받는다.
   soothing adj. 위로하는, 진정하는
   저는 아름답고 부드러워서 브람스의 음악을 아주 좋아합니다.
4. (C, resemble) resemble은 타동사로 be like 또는 be similar to의 뜻.
   resemble v. 닮다
   마을의 모든 사람들이 붉은 머리입니다. 그들은 모두 서로 닮았습니다.
5. (C, I found my watch missing) 5형식의 문장으로 missing이 목적보어이다.
   집에 돌아와서야 저는 시계가 없어진 것을 알았습니다.
6. (C, visible) 'S+make+O+C'구문에서 목적어 (details that ...)가 길어서 뒤로 가고 보어와 도치된 경우이다.
   pass through 통과하다
   X레이는 사물을 통과하여 보기가 불가능한 것들을 볼 수 있게 합니다.
7. (D, to subscribe) urge (some) to do (누구에게) ~하기를 촉구하다
   subscribe v. 기부하다
   오늘 아침 라디오 연설에서 대통령은 사람들에게 적십자사에 기부하기를 촉구하였습니다.
8. (C, two men robbing a bank) see가 지각동사이지만 보어가 동작의 진행을 나타내므로 현재분사형이 보어로 왔다.
   "라이언양, 어젯밤에 정확히 무엇을 보았습니까?" "예, 두 남자가 은행을 터는 것을 보았습니다."
9. (A, fame → famous) 'become+형용사'가 옳은 표현이다.
   áccurate [ǽkjərit] adj. 정확한 shot n. 사수 pístol n. 권총 rífle [ráifəl] n. 장총 shótgun [ʃɑ́tgʌn] n. 엽총
   제임스 오클리는 권총과 장총, 엽총으로 세계최고 명사수의 한 사람으로 유명해졌습니다.
10. (D, to be instinctive → instinctive) call이 타동사로 쓰일 때는 명사, 형용사가 직접 보어로 쓰인다.
    reáction [riǽkʃən] n. 반응 instínctive [instíŋktiv] adj. 본능적인, 직감적인
    제 반응은 본능적이라고 부를 수 있었을 것이라고 생각합니다.
11. (B, possibly → possible) a remarkable leap은 동사 make의 목적어이고, 보어는 형용사 possible이다.

leap n. 뜀, 도약 proficiency[prəfíʃənsi] n. 숙달
컴퓨터는 인간의 진보에 엄청난 도약을 가능케하였습니다.

12. (B, strongly enough → strong enough)
'make+목적어+목적보어(형용사)'
cart n. 수레, 마차
그는 이 마차를 어른 다섯 사람을 충분히 태울 수 있도록 튼튼하게 만들었습니다.

13. (B, to be → as) define은 전치사 as로 연결되는 동사이다.
épigram [épigræm] n. 경구 defíne [difáin] v. 규정하다, 정의하다 bright adj. 똑똑한
경구란 흔히 간단하게 표현된 명석하고 위트있는 사상으로 정의됩니다.

14. (C, paying → to pay)
depósiter [dipázitər] n. 예금주, 기탁자 in full : 전액 at one time : 한 번에
어떤 은행도 모든 예금주들에게 한꺼번에 전액 지불할 수 있는 현금을 충분히 보유하고 있지는 않습니다.

15. (A, spontaneously → spontaneous) 어미가 -ly 라고 해서 모두가 부사인 것은 아니다. lively처럼 형용사인 것도 있다.
quilt [kwilt] n. 퀼트, 서양자수 lively [láivli] adj. 활기찬, 생동감있는 spontáneous [spantéiniəs] adj. 동시발생적인, 자발적인
재즈처럼 미국혹인 퀼트는 생동감이 있고 자연발생적이다. 그러나 재즈와 달리 퀼트는 이제 막 알려지기 시작했습니다.

16. (B, obstinately → obstinate) 동사 prove는 형용사를 보어로 취한다.
pórtion [pɔ́:rʃən] n. 일부분 óbstinate [ábstənit] adj. 완고한, 단단한 máson [méisən] n. 석공 árchway [á:rtʃwei] n. 아치길 wéaken v. 약화시키다 suppórt [səpɔ́:rt] n. 지주, 버팀
벽의 일부분이 단단한 것으로 드러났습니다. 석공은 그 지탱을 약하게 하는 쪽에서 아치길을 공격해갔습니다.

17. (B, interest → interested) be interested in
génesis [dʒénəsis] n. 기원 (= órigin) sólar sýstem : 태양계
달의 기원은 그 자체로 흥미가 있을 뿐 아니라 지구와 태양계의 더 큰 기원의 일부로서도 흥미로운 것입니다.

18. (C, covers it → covers) cover는 타동사로 바로 목적어를 받는다. it는 필요없다.
square feet : 평방피트
성인의 피부는 무게가 약 8파운드 나가고, 면적은 39평방피트나 됩니다.

19. (D, bitterly → bitter) '감각동사(taste)+형용사'
버터를 사는 데 남은 돈을 써버린 후, 그에게는 맛이 고약했지만, 그는 그걸 몽땅 먹기로 결심하였습니다.

20. (D, credibly → credible) '연결동사(seem)+형용사'
fume [fju:m] n. 향기, 가스 detéct [ditékt] v. 발견하다, 찾아내다 crédible [krédəbl] adv. 확실한, 신뢰할 만한
암모니아가스가 전혀 발견되지 않았기 때문에 이 이론은 신뢰성이 없어 보입니다.

Unit 4 중문

[EXERCISE 1]

(1) and (2) and (3) and (4) as well
(5) and (6) but (7) yet (8) either
(9) or (10) for (11) and (12) and
(13) but (14) and

놀이공원의 고객들이 떠나고 불빛이 꺼졌습니다. 소형자동차를 타고 놀던 마지막 두 사람은 돈을 내고 떠났습니다. 대관람 풍차가 멈췄고, 회전목마도 섰습니다. 회전목마 가게는 문을 닫고 주인도 귀가하였습니다. 새벽 2시이 야간경비원 네 사람이 공원을 순찰하고 있었습니다. 그런데 아무도 보이지 않았습니다. "나는 순찰도는 게 지겨워." 한 사람이 말했습니다. "그럼 우리가 할 수 있는 일이 뭐가 있겠어?" "카드놀이를 하든지 앉아서 이야기를 할 수도 있잖아." 그들은 따분하였습니다. 왜냐하면 이렇게 고요하고 더운 밤에 할 일은 아무것도 없었기 때문이죠. "우리가 회전목마는 탈 수 있겠어!" 한 사람이 소리쳤습니다. "재미있을 거야!" 세 사람이 회전목마에 올라탔고, 한 사람이 시동을 걸었습니다. 그 다음 그도 올라타고서 돌았습니다. 그들은 매우 즐거운 한때를 보내고 있었습니다. 그런데 갑자기 기계를 멈출 사람이 아무도 없다는 것을 알았습니다. 그들은 아침까지 구조되지 못했고 그때까지 심하게 멀미를 하였습니다!

custómer n. 고객 amúsement park : 놀이공원, 유원지 dódgem car : 도젬카, 유원지에서 다른 차와 부딪히면서 노는 소형 전기자동차 big wheel : 풍차놀이 mérry-go-round : 회전목마 stall[stɔ:l] n. 회전목마를 설치한 가게 tired of ~ : ~ 에 싫증난, 지겨운(= bored) time of their lives : 인생에서 즐거운 때 réscue [réskju:] v. 구조하다

[EXERCISE 2]

1 (not only) 줄리아는 스페인어를 말할 뿐 아니라 프랑스어도 말합니다.
2 (as well as) 그녀는 베이지색 치마뿐 아니라 노란색 스웨터도 샀습니다
3 (both) 그들은 시골과 도시에 집을 가지고 있습니다.
4 (but also) 그는 부지런할 뿐 아니라 재능도 있습니다.
5 (as well as) 그녀의 아이들은 미국 사촌과 스페인 사촌들이 있습니다.
6 (not only) 그들의 유럽여행은 독일과 오스트리아뿐 아니라 스위스도 포함되어 있습니다.
7 (and) 그는 단단히 그리고 신속하게 팔에 붕대감았습니다.
8 (but also) 클라크는 변호사 일을 할 뿐 아니라 법률을 가르치기도 합니다.
9 (as well as) 톰은 배우이자 극작가입니다.
10 (as well as) 신부의 부케에는 장미와 난초가 들어있습니다.

beige [beiʒ] n. 베이지색 indústrious [indʌ́striəs] adj. 부지런한 ingénious [indʒí:njəs] adj. 재능 있는, 영리한 bándage [bǽndidʒ] v. 붕대를 감다 pláywright [pléirait] n. 극작가 bouquét [bu:kéi] n. 부케 órchid [ɔ́:rkid] n. 난초

[EXERCISE 3]

1. (politics → a politician) 벤저민 프랭클린은 작가이자, 과학자, 정치가였습니다.
2. (accuracy → accurate) 펠레는 빠르고 노련하고 정확한 축구선수였습니다.
3. (alcoholic → alcohol) 그의 악행 가운데는 담배와 알코올, 마약이 있습니다.
4. (hunger → hungry) 호수에서 하루를 보낸 뒤, 아이들은 지치고, 볕에 타고, 허기져서 돌아왔습니다.
5. (wine → a glass of wine) 저녁식사 후 마리아는 늘 커피 한 잔과 차 한 잔, 와인 한 잔을 합니다.
6. (poetic → poetry) 이 미국문학선집은 시와 단편소설, 장편소설을 담고 있습니다.
7. (third → three) 문장 하나가 두세 가지 또는 네 가지의 소재를 담을 수 있습니다.
8. (equal → equality) 프랑스혁명의 모토는 자유, 평등, 박애였습니다.
9. (careful → carefully) 좋은 작가는 자기 작품을 천천히, 주의깊게 그리고 일정하게 편집합니다.
10. (agree → agreement) 영어시험에서 여러분은 모든 동사를 일치, 시제, 격의 측면에서 점검해야 합니다.

pólitics [pάlitiks] n. 정치학 politician [pɑlətíʃən] n. 정치가 áccuracy [ǽkjərəsi] n. 정확성 áccurate [ǽkjərit] adj. 정확한 vice n. 해악 alcohólic [ӕlkəhɔ́lik] adj. 알코올 중독의 álcohol n. drug n. 마약류 cf. médicine [médəsən] n. 약, 의약품 súnburned [sʌ́nbəːrnd] adj. 햇볕에 탄 anthólogy [ӕnθɔ́lədʒi] n. 시선, 선집 French revolútion : 프랑스 혁명 fratérnity [frətə́ːrnəti] n. 우애 édit [édit] v. 편집하다

[EXERCISE 4]

1. b) 냇물은 흘러가면서 침식하기도 하고 물질을 퇴적하기도 합니다.
2. b) 이끼류는 광합성과 호흡 둘 다 수행합니다.
3. a) 기후는 습기와 온도뿐만 아니라 그것이 허용하는 식물을 통해서도 토양형성에 영향을 미칩니다.
4. b) 컴퓨터 언어는 고급 또는 초급으로 분류됩니다.
5. b) 침식은 물이나 바람의 작용을 통해 일어날 수 있습니다.
6. a) 에드먼드 핼리는 최초의 바람지도를 처음 출간하였을뿐더러 바람을 열에 관련지음으로써 날씨를 아는 데 공헌하기도 하였습니다.
7. a) 컴퓨터 언어는 문제중심이나 절차중심으로 더 깊이있게 분류될 수 있습니다.
8. b) 달의 분화구는 화산의 붕괴나 큰 운석의 충격으로 비롯되었을 것입니다.

stream n. 냇물 eróde [iróud] v. 침식하다 depósit [dipάzit] v. 적립하다, 퇴적하다 líchen [láikən] n. 이끼류 식물 carry on : 수행하다 photosýnthesis [fòutousínθəsis] n. 광합성 respirátion [rèspəréiʃən] n. 호흡 soil formátion : 토양생성 móisture [mɔ́istʃər] n. 습기 vegetátion [vèdʒətéiʃən] n. 식물 permít [pəːrmít] v. 허용하다 clássify [klǽsəfai] v. 분류하다 erósion n. 침식 públish [pʌ́bliʃ] v. 출판하다 contríbute [kəntríbjut] v. 공헌하다 reláte A to B : A를 B에 연결하다 próblem-óriented : 문제지향적 procédure-óriented : 절차지향적

[Actual Test 4]

1. (B, listening to music also gave him great pleasure) 등위접속사 but가 있으므로 뒤의 절도 앞의 절과 같이 동명사가 주어이어야 함.
   pastime n. 여가활동, 취미
   우표수집이 그녀의 최고 여가활동이지만, 음악감상도 그녀에게 큰 즐거움을 주었습니다.
2. (C, for she was tired and afraid to drive at night) ', for'는 등위접속사로 쓰였으므로, 양쪽이 같은 구문이어야 할 것.
   낸시는 아침까지 출발을 늦추었는데, 너무 지쳐서 밤에 운전하기 두려웠기 때문입니다.
3. (B, but) not ... but
   antelope n. 영양
   미국 로키산맥의 염소는 진짜 염소가 아니고 영양입니다.
4. (D, both) both ... and ...
   피아니스트 조지 윈스턴은 자신의 재즈와 클래식음악 음반으로 그레미상을 받았습니다.
5. (C, American eagles not only protect) not only ... but also ...
   미국 독수리는 둥지를 잘 지킬 뿐 아니라, 잘 만들기도 합니다.
6. (C, visited his daughter) 'A, B, and C' 병렬구문 ─ 동사가 3개 연결되었다.
   프로스트씨는 시카고에 가서 책을 몇 권 사고는 딸에게 갔습니다.
7. (A, the job in New York) neither the assignment ... nor the job ...
   메리는 런던에서의 임무도, 뉴욕에서의 일도 원치 않았습니다.
8. (B, than being antisocial) 'more -ing than -ing' 구문
   친구를 사귀는 것은 반사회적인 것보다는 더 좋습니다.
9. (B, turning → turn) 조동사 would에 이어지는 동사원형의 병렬구조
   매일 밤 경비원은 문을 잠그고, 점조등을 켜고, 건물 주위를 걸어갑니다.
10. (A, making → to make) 'to do'의 병렬구조
    contról quálity : 품질을 관리하다 make a decísion : 결심하다
    품질관리와 생산에 관한 의사결정은 산업기술자들의 수많은 책임에 속하는 것입니다.
11. (A, being introduced → to be introduced) 'to do'의 병렬구조
    líterature [lítərətʃər] n. 문학
    외국 문학을 읽고 다른 문화를 소개받는 것은 외국어를 공부

Basic Grammar for English Tests

러시아도 미국도 점진적 군비축소에 대해 상호 만족스런 계획을 발견할 수가 없었습니다.

12. (C, and not → nor) 'neither~nor~'의 병렬구조
    propósed *adj.* 제안된, 예상된 utílity rate : 이용률 fair requést : 타당한 요구
    제안된 이용률 증가는 타당한 요구도 아니고 실용적인 것도 아니었습니다.

13. (D, the operation was begun → began the operation) 접속어 'and then'으로 연결된 등위절
    súrgeon [sə́:rdʒən] *n.* 외과의사 exámine [igzǽmin] *v.* 검사하다, 진찰하다 operátion *n.* 수술, 작전
    의사는 환자를 신속하게 검사하고서 수술을 시작하였습니다.

14. (C, warning → to warn) 'whether to do~or to do …'
    cheat [tʃi:t] *v.* 속이다 cheating *n.* (시험의) 부정행위 warn *v.* 경고하다
    조교는 그 학생을 부정행위로 보고할 것인지, 먼저 그에게 경고를 할 것인지 몰랐습니다.

15. (D, less → least) 최상급의 형용사가 병렬구조로 연결되어 있다.
    aváilable *adj.* 유용한
    자네에게 있는 가장 작고, 가장 최근에 출간된, 가장 값싼 사전을 내게 좀 빌려주게.

16. (D, the House of Representative → by the House of Representative) 'not only~ but also~'의 상관관계를 잘 살필 것
    Sénate [sénit] *n.* (미 국회) 상원 Hóuse of Represéntative (미 국회) 하원
    미국에서 법률이 되기 위해서 법안은 상원뿐 아니라 하원에서도 통과되어야 합니다.

17. (C, permanent → permanence) 'because of 명사+명사'의 구조
    inténse [inténs] *adj.* 강렬한, 열띤 útilize [jú:təlaiz] *v.* 활용하다 exténsively [iksténsivli] *adv.* 광범위하게
    진한 흑색과 영구성 때문에, 인디언 잉크는 건축가들과 기술자들에 의해 광범위하게 활용됩니다.

18. (B, point → pointed) 'be동사'의 보어인 형용사들의 병렬구조
    yúcca : (식물이름) 유카 stiff [stif] *adj.* 뻣뻣한 sáwlike *adj.* 톱니모양의 fíbrous [fáibrəs] *adj.* 섬유질의
    유카나무잎은 톱니모양이거나 섬유모양의 끝을 가지고 있어, 뽀족하고 뻣뻣하며 가느다랗습니다.

19. (C, when → but) 앞뒤 문장이 대조되는 문제이므로 when자리는 역접의 등위접속사 자리이다.
    investigátion [investəɡéiʃən] *n.* 조사, 수사
    소방수들은 화재원인을 정확히 결정할 수가 없었습니다. 그러나 그들은 수사를 포함시킬 것이라고 말했습니다.

20. (B, have been able → has been able) 주어가 'neither A nor B' 구문인 문장에서 동사는 뒤쪽 'nor B'만을 받는다. 그런데 the United States는 단수이다.
    mútually [mjú:tʃuəli] *adv.* 서로 satisfáctory [sætisfǽktəri] *adj.* 만족스런 grádual disármament : 점진적인 군비축소

Unit 5 복문

[EXERCISE **1**]

1. it *started* to rain (주절)
   비가 내리기 시작하였습니다

2. after the runner *fell* down (종속절)
   달리기 선수가 쓰러진 후에

3. before the telephone *was invented* (종속절)
   전화가 발명되기 전에

4. which no one clearly *understood* (종속절)
   아무도 분명하게 이해하지 못한

5. she *left* because of you (주절)
   그녀는 당신 때문에 떠났어요

6. what you *said* to me (종속절)
   당신이 제게 말씀하신 것

7. a singer *performed* after dinner (주절)
   한 가수가 저녁식사 후에 공연을 하였습니다

8. because the chicken *was burned* (종속절)
   닭고기가 탔기 때문에

9. she *has been crying* a lot (주절)
   그녀는 많이 울었습니다

10. when you *left* town (종속절)
    당신이 마을을 떠났을 때

11. the cost of chicken *has gone* up (주절)
    닭고기 값이 올랐습니다

12. whom he *saw* at the theater (종속절)
    그가 극장에서 본 (사람)

13. exercise *promotes* health (주절)
    운동이 건강을 증진시킵니다

14. walking *develops* leg muscles (주절)
    걷기가 다리 근육을 발달시킵니다

15. winning *is* not everything (주절)
    승리가 전부는 아닙니다

16. that apples *are* very nutritious (종속절)
    사과는 영양이 풍부합니다

17. while the choir *was singing* (종속절)
    합창단이 노래를 부르고 있을 동안

18. if prices *continue* to climb (종속절)
    가격이 계속 오른다면

19. they *arrived* after the deadline (주절)
    그들은 마감시한 후에 도착하였습니다

20. although there *was* ice on the road (종속절)
    비록 길 위에 얼음이 있었지만

fall down : 쓰러지다 perfórm [pərfɔ́ːrm] v. 공연하다 promóte [prəmóut] v. 증진시키다 múscle [mʌ́səl] n. 근육 nutrítious [njuːtríʃəs] adj. 영양이 있는 chóir [kwáiər] n. 합창단(= chórus) deadline n. 마감시한

[**EXERCISE 2**]

1. When the seasons *change*, many small animals *change* their colors. (o)
   계절이 바뀔 때 많은 작은 동물들은 색깔을 바꿉니다.

2. When winter *approaches* and the landscape *turns* white with snow. (x)
   겨울이 다가오고 풍경이 눈으로 하얗게 변할 때

3. Nature *has given* different types of creatures different types of camouflage. (o)
   자연은 여러 가지 동물들에게 여러 가지 보호색을 부여하였습니다.

4. Camouflage which *refers* to an animal's ability to hide itself. (x)
   스스로를 숨기는 동물의 능력을 말하는 보호색

5. Because many insects and small lizards *have* no way to protect themselves. (x)
   많은 곤충과 작은 도마뱀은 스스로를 보호하는 방법이 없기 때문에

6. Unless a camouflaged insect *is seen* against a contrasting background, it *may be* completely invisible. (o)
   위장한 곤충은 대조되는 배경에 비추어 보지 않으면, 그것은 완전히 보이지 않습니다.

7. A small insect *needs* camouflage so that its enemies *cannot find* it. (o)
   작은 곤충은 적이 발견할 수 없도록 보호색을 필요로 합니다.

8. Although some fish *can become* almost transparent. (x)
   비록 어떤 물고기가 거의 투명해질 수 있다고 해도

9. Many species of fish which *protect* themselves through camouflage. (x)
   보호색을 통해 자신을 보호하는 많은 물고기류

10. Reef fish *can escape* an enemy by changing their appearance to match almost any background. (o)
    수초어는 자신의 외모를 배경과 거의 맞추어 바꿈으로써 적으로부터 탈출할 수 있습니다.

appróach [əpróutʃ] v. 다가오다 lándscape [lǽndskeip] n. 풍경 turn white : 하얗게 변하다 cámouflage [kǽmuflɑːʒ] n. 위장, 변장 v. 위장하다 hide [haid] v. 숨기다 lízard [lízərd] n. 도마뱀 protéct [prətékt] v. 보호하다

[**EXERCISE 3**]

1. Where the dog *went is* a mystery. (주어)
   개가 어디 갔느냐가 의문입니다.

2. My father *doesn't know* how much money I spent. (목적어)
   아버지께서는 제가 돈을 얼마나 많이 쓰는지를 모르십니다.

3. What you *said hurt* my feeling. (주어)
   당신이 말한 것은 내 감정을 상하게 하였습니다.

4. Harry *knows* how he *did* on the test. (목적어)
   해리는 그가 시험에서 어떻게 했는지 알고 있습니다.

5. What the reporter *asked was* not polite. (주어)
   기자가 물은 것은 공손하지 못했습니다.

6. The babysitter *knows* what the children *like to eat*. (목적어)
   보모는 어린이들이 무엇을 잘 먹는지를 알고 있습니다.

7. Where we *spend* our vacation *is* not far from here. (주어)
   우리가 휴가를 보낼 장소는 여기서 멀지 않습니다.

8. The advertisement *doesn't say* how much the car *costs*. (목적어) 그 광고는 그 자동차의 가격이 얼마인지 말하지 않고 있습니다.

9. Even his parents *don't know* why he *ran* away from home. (목적어) 심지어 그의 부모님들도 그가 왜 집을 뛰쳐나갔는지를 모릅니다.

10. The class *will explore* how children *learn*. (목적어)
    수업은 어린이들이 어떻게 학습을 하는지 탐구할 것입니다.

11. The tropics *are* where the study of biology really *begins*. (보어)
    열대지방은 생물학연구가 실제로 시작하는 곳입니다.

12. How I *spent* my summer vacation *is* a boring topic. (주어)
    제가 어떻게 여름방학을 보냈는지는 지겨운 화제입니다.

13. The pamphlet *explains* where students *can get* a library card. (목적어)
    그 소책자는 학생들이 도서관카드를 어디서 발급받을 수 있는지를 설명하고 있습니다.

14. The subject of the film *is* how dolphins *communicate*. (보어)
    영화의 주제는 돌고래가 의사소통하는 방법입니다.

15. The officer *asked* where I *lived*. (목적어)
    그 관리는 제가 어디 사는지 물었습니다.

políte [pəláit] adj. 공손한, 예의바른 bábysitter [béibisitər] n. 집 지키며 아이를 돌보는 사람 advertísement [ædvərtáizmənt] n. 광고, 줄여서 ad라고 쓰기도 함 explóre [ikspló:r] v. 조사하다, 탐구하다 trópics [trɑ́piks] n. (남북)회귀선, 열대지방 biólogy n. 생물학 bóring [bɔ́ːriŋ] adj. 따분한 pámphlet [pǽmfliːt] n. 소책자

Basic Grammar for English Tests

[EXERCISE 4]

1. Ambitious students *feel* hard work *is* ultimately *rewarded*. 야망이 있는 학생들은 열심히 공부하면 결국 보답이 있다고 느낍니다.

2. The pilot *said* his plane *was* in good condition. 비행사는 자기 비행기는 상태가 양호하다고 말했습니다.

3. The fire inspector *stated* the building *lacked* sufficient safety equipment. 화재조사관은 건물이 충분한 안전장비를 갖지 못하였다고 말했습니다.

4. Result of the garbage study *reveal* fifteen percent of the city's edible food *is wasted*. 쓰레기문제 연구결과는 시의 먹을 수 있는 음식물 15%가 버려진다고 밝히고 있습니다.

5. Search parties *reported* they *had found* the lost hikers. 탐사대는 조난 등산객을 찾았다고 보고하였습니다.

6. The chief of the police *said* his men *have arrested* a suspect. 경찰대장은 자기 부하들이 혐의자를 체포하였다고 말했습니다.

7. The instruction booklet *says* the appliance should *not be dropped* in water. 설명서는 그 기구가 물 속에 빠지면 안된다고 합니다.

8. Few *believe* the report *is* accurate. 그 보고가 정확하다고 믿는 사람은 거의 없습니다.

9. The city council *believes* the planning committee *has been* heavily *influenced* by developers. 시의회는 기획위원회가 개발업자들의 영향을 심하게 받았다고 믿고 있습니다.

10. The upholsterer *felt* the old couch *was* not worth repairing. 실내장식업자는 그 낡은 침상을 수리할 가치가 없는 것이라고 느꼈습니다.

últimately [ʌ́ltəmitli] adv. 궁극적으로, 결국 be rewárded : 보답받다 fire inspéctor : 화재검사관 lack v. ~을 결여하다, ~을 가지고 있지 않다 suffícient [səfíʃənt] adj. 충분한 sáfety equípment : 안전장비 gárbage study : 쓰레기연구 revéal [riví:l] v. 드러내다, 노출하다 édible [édəbəl] adj. 먹을 수 있는 séarch party : 탐사대 lost híkers : 조난 등반객들 chief of the políce : 경찰대장(반장) arrést [ərést] v. 체포하다 suspéct [səspékt] n. 혐의자, 피의자 instrúction bóoklet : 설명서, 안내서 appliánce [əpláiəns] n. 기구, 기계장치 áccurate [ǽkjərit] adj. 정확한 city cóuncil : 시의회 plánning commíttee : 기획위원회 devéloper [divéləpər] n. 개발업자 uphólster [ʌphóulstər] n. 실내장식업자 couch [kautʃ] n. 카우치, 침대 겸용 소파 be worth -ing : ~할 가치가 있는

[EXERCISE 5]

1. (left → leave) 선생님은 그 학생이 교실을 떠날 것을 요구하셨습니다.

2. (called → call) 그가 그녀에게 즉시 전화하는 것은 긴급하였다.

3. (틀린 부분 없음) 우리가 논의를 지연시키는 것은 아주 중요합니다.

4. (suspends → suspend) 그녀는 위원회가 이 문제에 대한 논의를 중지하는 것에 동의하려고 합니다.

5. (took → take) 임금님은 새로운 법률을 다음 달에 발효한다고 공표하였습니다.

6. (should stop → stop) 저는 당신이 이 집회를 중단시켜 주기를 제안합니다.

7. (틀린 부분 없음) 저는 당신이 이 과정에 등록하기 전에 필수조건들을 갖출 것을 충고합니다.

8. (attends → attend) 그의 아버지는 그가 다른 대학에 다니기를 좋아합니다.

9. (틀린 부분 없음) 교수단은 그 규정이 폐지되어야 한다고 요구했습니다.

10. (found → find) 그녀는 우리에게 다른 대안을 찾을 것을 촉구하였습니다.

deláy [diléi] v. 연기하다, 미루다 suspénd [səspénd] v. 중지하다 take effect : 발효하다 rálly [rǽli] n. 집회 prerequisite [pri:rékwəzit] n. 필수조건 régister [rédʒəstər] v. 등록하다 fáculty [fǽkəlti] n. 교수회, 교사회 stípulate [stípjəleit] v. 규정하다, 요구하다 altérnative [ɔːltə́rnətiv] n. 대안, 차선책

[EXERCISE 6]

1. One archeologist *thinks* that human beings *did not develope* the idea of numbers until after 3100 B.C. 어느 고고학자는 인간이 기원전 3100년 후까지는 숫자의 개념을 발전시키지 못했다고 생각합니다.

2. That Samuel Colt *developed* a practical handgun in 1836 *has had* a great influence on modern society. 새뮤얼 콜트가 1836년에 실용적인 권총을 개발한 것은 현대사회에 커다란 영향을 끼쳤습니다.

3. Christians' belief that Jesus Christ *rose* from the dead *is* one of the bases of their religion. 예수가 죽은 자 가운데서 살아났다는 기독교의 믿음은 그들 종교의 근본 중에 하나입니다.

4. The fact that he *proved* unreliable *made* them reluctant to employ him again. 그가 믿을 수 없는 사람으로 드러난 사실은 사람들에게 그를 다시는 고용하기를 꺼리게 만들었습니다.

5. Recent news articles *have reported* that fifty to eighty percent of all handguns *are used* for criminal purposes. 권총의 50-80%가 범죄목적으로 사용된다고 최근의 신문기사는 보고하였습니다.

6. Why man *sleeps has been* the subject of much research. 인간이 잠을 자는 이유는 많은 연구의 주제였습니다.

7. There *is* a biologist at Boston University who *believes* that insects *developed* wings in order to collect solar heat.
   보스턴 대학에는 태양열을 집적하기 위해 곤충들이 날개를 발달시켰다고 믿는 생물학자가 한 사람 있습니다.
8. What *caused* dinosaurs to disappear from the earth *is* still *unknown*.
   무엇이 공룡들을 지구상에서 사라지게 했느냐가 아직도 알려지지 않고 있습니다.
9. Few people *realize* that there *are* only six landing strips in the world long enough for the space shuttle to land safely.
   우주선이 안전하게 착륙할 만큼 충분히 긴 활주로는 세계에 6개밖에 없다는 사실을 사람들은 거의 깨닫지 못합니다.
10. A computer program called 'Eliza' *acts* as a personal counselor and *asks* 'her clients' how they *are feeling*.
    '엘리사'라고 하는 컴퓨터 프로그램은 개인상담역으로 활동하고 '고객들'에게 어떻게 느끼는지를 묻기도 합니다.

archeólogist [ɑ:rkiáləd3ist] n. 고고학자 hándgun [hǽndgʌn] n. 권총 ínfluence [ínfluəns] n. 영향 v. 영향을 미치다 rise from the dead : 죽음에서 살아나다, 부활하다 (rise—rose—risen) religion [rilídʒən] n. 종교 relúctant [relʌ́ktənt] adj. 꺼리는 news árticle : 뉴스기사 críminal púrpose : 범죄목적 reséarch [risə́:rtʃ] n. 연구 dínosaur [dáinəsɔ:r] n. 공룡 land v. 착륙하다 landing strips : 활주로 space shuttle : 우주선 cóunselor [káunsələr] n. 상담원 clíent [kláiənt] n. 고객

[EXERCISE **7**]

1. whom the doctors treated (형용사절)
   그 의사가 치료한
2. whom did they visit (주절)
   그들이 누구를 방문했는가?
3. who failed the last exam (둘 다)
   마지막 시험에서 실패한 사람
4. that one is an old photograph (주절)
   하나가 옛날 사진이다
5. which dog bit the child (주절)
   어느 개가 아이를 물었는가?
6. that scientists recently discovered (형용사절)
   과학자들이 최근에 발견한
7. which movie did he see (주절)
   그가 무슨 영화를 보았는가?
8. whose test had the teacher misplaced (주절)
   선생님이 누구의 시험을 잘못 놓았는가?
9. whom they saw at the hotel (형용사절)
   그들이 호텔에서 본
10. that the sailors threw overboard (형용사절)
    선원들이 배 밖으로 던진

11. those people have recently moved in (주절)
    저 사람들이 최근에 이사를 왔다
12. who babysits for the next-door neighbors (둘 다) 이웃사람들을 위해 아기를 봐주는 사람
13. whose name he had forgotten (형용사절)
    이름이 생각나지 않는
14. at what time did he leave (주절)
    그가 몇 시에 떠났는가?
15. for which he carefully looked (형용사절)
    그가 주의 깊게 찾은

treat [tri:t] v. 치료하다 bite [bait] v. 물다 (bite—bit—bit/bitten) thraw óverboard : 배 밖으로 던지다, 버리다

[EXERCISE **8**]

1. a) (that) 세인트 헬렌산이 분화했다는 소식
   b) (which) 잡지가 펴낸 소식
2. a) (that) 권총이 위험하다는 사실
   b) (which) 학생이 잊어버리고 말을 못한 사실
3. a) (which) 그 상원의원이 제기한 주장
   b) (that) 인삼이 암을 치료한다는 주장
4. a) (that) 하나님이 존재한다는 믿음
   b) (which) 그 여자가 표현한 믿음
5. a) (that) 화성에 생명이 있다는 증거
   b) (which) 과학자들이 찾고 있던 증거
6. a) (which) 그 남자가 한 진술
   b) (that) 돌고래가 의사전달을 할 수 있다는 진술
7. a) (that) 그 남자가 살아날 것이라는 희망
   b) (which) 선생님이 나타낸 희망
8. a) (which) 프로이트가 분석한 꿈
   b) (that) 세계가 평화롭게 지내는 꿈
9. a) (that) 우주에 블랙홀이 있다는 이론
   b) (which) 심리학자가 설명한 이론
10. a) (that) 그 남자가 결백하다는 주장
    b) (which) 그 변호사가 법정에서 활용한 주장

erúpt [irʌ́pt] v. (화산이) 분출하다 ánalyze [ǽnəlaiz] v. 분석하다 psychólogist [saikáləd3ist] n. 심리학자

[EXERCISE **9**]

1. Newspapers *reported* the fact that a major earthquake *had occurred* in Algeria.
   주 지진이 알제리아에서 발생하였다는 사실을 신문이 보도하였습니다.
2. The beliefs (that Moslems *hold*) *are based* on the teachings of Mohammed.
   회교도들이 지닌 믿음은 모하메드의 가르침에 기반을 두고 있습니다.

Basic Grammar for English Tests

3. The lawyer *expressed* his belief that his client *was* innocent.
   변호사는 자신의 고객이 결백하다는 믿음을 나타냈습니다.

4. The facts (that the witness *concealed*) *would have saved* the defendant from being convicted.
   증인이 숨긴 사실들은 피고가 유죄선고를 받는 것을 구해주었습니다.

5. Searchers *have given up* hope that the hikers *will be found* before nightfall.
   수색대원들은 등반인들이 해지기 전에 발견되리라는 희망을 포기하였습니다.

6. The newspaper frequently *misquoted* the statements (that the governor *made*).
   정부가 발표한 진술을 신문이 흔히 잘못 인용하기도 하였습니다.

7. The jurors *seemed* unconvinced by the witness's statements that he *had seen* an armed man running from the house.
   배심원들은 그 집에서 달아나는 무장한 남자를 보았다는 증인의 진술에 확신을 가지지 못하는 것 같았습니다.

8. Several people *overheard* the argument (that the couple *had*).
   여러 사람이 부부가 한 언쟁을 우연히 엿들었습니다.

9. News that a ship *had sunk* off the Georgia coast *reached* the Coast Guard very quickly.
   배 한 척이 조지아 해안가에 가라앉았다는 소식이 매우 빨리 해안경비대에 도착했습니다.

10. The hope (that all students *have*) *is* to pass their exams
    모든 학생들이 가진 희망은 시험에 통과하는 것입니다.

éarthquake [ə́ːrθkweik] n. 지진 móslem [mázləm] n. 회교도 (= múslim, muslem) clíent [kláiənt] n. 고객 wítness [wítnis] n. 증인 concéal [kənsíːl] v. 숨기다, 비밀로 하다 deféndant [diféndənt] n. 피고 convíct [kənvíkt] v. 유죄선고하다 séarcher [sə́ːrtʃər] n. 수색자 níghtfall [náitfɔːl] n. 해질녘, 황혼(= dusk) misquóte [miskwóut] v. 잘못 인용하다 júror [dʒúərər] n. 배심원 unconvínced [ʌnkənvínst] adj. 납득되지 않은 ármed man : 무장한 남자 overhéar [ouvərhíər] v. 어쩌다 듣다, 엿듣다 sink [siŋk] v. (물 속에) 가라앉다, 잠기다 the Coast Guard : (미) 해안경비대

[EXERCISE 10]

1. (so) 태양이 너무 밝게 빛나서 마리아는 선글라스를 써야 했습니다.
2. (such) 팀은 너무도 강력한 수영선수라서 언제나 레이스에서 우승을 합니다.
3. (so) 등록된 학생들이 너무도 없어서 그 수업은 취소되었습니다.
4. (such) 우리는 그곳에 대해 너무도 멋진 기억을 가져서 우리는 돌아가기로 결정하였습니다.
5. (so) 우리는 파티에서 너무도 좋은 시간을 보내서 떠나기가 싫었습니다.
6. (so) 이익이 너무도 대단한 성공이어서 프로모터들은 그것을 반복하기로 결정하였습니다.
7. (such) 너무 좋은 날이어서 우리는 해변에 가기로 결정하였습니다.
8. (so) 제인은 너무 아픈 것 같아서 간호사가 그녀에게 집에 가라고 말했습니다.
9. (such) 너무 어려운 숙제들이 있어서 우리는 그것들을 마치는 데 2주일을 보냈습니다.
10. (so) 버스에 사람들이 너무 많아서 우리는 걸어가기로 결정하였습니다.

shine—shone—shone put on : 입다, 쓰다 régister [rédʒəstər] v. 등록하다 bénefit [bénəfit] v. 이익 promóter [prəmóutər] n. 지지자, 후원자 assígnment [əsáinmənt] n. 숙제, 할당

[EXERCISE 11]

1. (Until cable television was invented) (시간절)
   케이블 텔레비전이 발명되기까지 많은 시청자들이 깨끗한 화면을 받지 못했습니다.

2. (provided that their files are complete before the deadline) (조건절)
   그들의 파일이 마감시한 전에 완성된다면 원서들이 검토될 것입니다.

3. (whether or not he voluntarily turns in his resignation) (조건절)
   윌리암슨씨는 자발적으로 사직서를 내든 말든 곧 회사를 떠날 것입니다.

4. (As water vapor cools) (시간절)
   수증기가 차가워질 때는, 기체에서 액체로 변하고 나중에는 고체인 얼음으로 변합니다.

5. (Because Neptune orbits the sun only once every 165 years) (원인절)
   (since it was discovered in 1946) (시간절)
   해왕성이 태양궤도를 겨우 165년마다 한 번 돌기 때문에 1946년에 그것이 발견된 후 해왕성은 아직 완전한 일주를 끝내지 못했습니다.

6. (While vision is the dominant sense in sighted people) (대조절)
   시각이 정상인에게 주요한 감각인 반면, 맹인들에게는 촉각이 가장 중요합니다.

7. (although the percentage of murders committed with handguns increased) (양보절)
   비록 총기로 자행된 살인율은 증가했지만, 1800년대 후반 미국의 살인사건 수는 떨어졌습니다.

8. (Unless the sewing machine is repaired by Monday) (조건절)

정답과 해설 363

재봉틀이 월요일까지 수리되지 않으면, 의상이 첫 공연에 맞춰 준비되지 못할 것입니다.

9. (as if it has been vacant for quite some time) (태도절)
저 마당의 잡초와 키 큰 풀들이 그 집을 마치 한동안 비어있었던 것처럼 보이게 합니다.

10. (so that it can be repainted) (목절)
(before the summer season begins) (시간절)
여름철이 시작하기 전에 페인트칠을 할 수 있도록 스테이시 수영장은 일주일간 문을 닫을 것입니다.

invént [invént] v. 창안하다 víewer [vjú:ər] n. 시청자 get clear recéption : 깨끗한 화면을 수신하다 applicátion [æplikéiʃən] n. 지원서 firm [fə:rm] n. 회사 vóluntarily [válənterili] adv. 자발적으로 turn in : 제출하다 resignátion [rezignéiʃən] n. 사직(서) water vápor : 수증기 líquid [líkwid] n. 액체 sólid [sálid] n. 단단한, 고체 Néptune [néptju:n] n. 해왕성 órbit [ɔ́:rbit] v. 궤도를 돌다 n. 궤도 a full revolútion : 한 번 일주 dóminant [dámənənt] adj. 유력한 dóminant sénse : 주도 감각 síghted people : 볼 수 있는 사람 the blind : 맹인들 sénse of tóuch : 촉감 séwing machíne : 재봉틀 cóstume [kástju:m] n. 옷, 의복 in time : 시간에 맞춰 perfórmance [pərfɔ́:rməns] n. 공연 weed [wi:d] n. 잡초 vácant [véikənt] adj. 비어 있는

[EXERCISE 12]

1. (형용사절) 그들이 지난주에 방문한
2. (부사절) 시냇물이 넘쳐서
3. (명사절) 사람들이 했던 것
4. (형용사절) 연구원들이 연구한 ~의 언어
5. (명사절) 그 후보들이 쓴 돈이 얼마인지
6. (부사절) 그가 그것들을 배우는 데 전념하는 한
7. (부사절) 유럽인들이 북미대륙에 왔을 때
8. (형용사절) 초기 정착민들이 아무것도 몰랐던
9. (형용사절) 구조하러 온
10. (명사절) 그가 마지막 시험에서 얼마나 잘했는지
11. (명사절) 그가 그 질문의 답을 알았다는 사실
12. (형용사절) 그가 어제 이야기한
13. (부사절) 학생들이 숙제를 하지 못하면
14. (부사절) 마감시한이 지날 때까지
15. (형용사절) 각 지원자들에게 주어진

creek [kri:k] n. 시냇물 reséarcher [risə́:rtʃər] n. 연구원 take to ~ : ~에 전념하다 séttler [sétlər] n. 정착민 réscue [réskju:] n. 구조 v. 구조하다 ápplicant [ǽplikənt] n. 응모자, 지원자

[Actual Test 5]

1. (C, That the) 두 번째 is가 주절의 동사이므로, 앞의 절은 주어가 될 명사절이어야 한다.
제인 라이언에 의한 찰스 국왕의 구출 이야기는 일부 역사가들의 의혹을 받고 있습니다.

2. (B, your grandfather retired) years ago를 보아서 완료형일 필요는 없다.
자네 할아버지가 몇 년 전에 퇴직하셨는지 궁금해.

3. (D, How) 동사 is not known에 대한 주어 역할을 할 명사절을 만들 수 있는 접속사가 필요.
일부 포유류가 어떻게 바다에 살게 되었는지는 알려지지 않습니다.

4. (D, What) What A is to B, C is to D: A와 B의 관계는 C와 D의 관계와 같다.
시간과 공간이 물리학과 가지는 관계는, 자유와 평등이 민주주의와 가지는 과거와 현재까지의 관계와 같습니다.

5. (B, Whatever) 주절의 동사는 has, brings about은 종속절의 동사. 선행사까지 포함하는 관계대명사를 찾을 것.
공리주의 이론에 따르면, 행복을 가져오는 것은 무엇이나 공익을 가지고 있습니다.

6. (D, lived) 선행사 Jane Lyon이 주어이므로 동사가 필요함.
1876년에서 1945까지 살았던 제인 라이언씨가 매사추세츠주에 세인트폴 대학을 설립했습니다.

7. (B, whose) 주어 Tom Jones와 wrist and arm의 관계를 보면 소유관계이다.
톰 존스씨는 2차 세계대전에서 손목과 팔을 심하게 다쳤지만 훌륭한 예술가가 되었습니다.

8. (D, in which) players hit wooden balls ... in the sport
크로킷은 선수들이 위킷이라고 하는 아치를 통해 나무 공을 치는 인기 있는 잔디구장 스포츠입니다.

9. (D, that gave her a great deal of pleasure) a hobby를 수식하는 형용사절
동전수집은 그녀에게 많은 즐거움을 주는 취미였습니다.

10. (D, where the air is warm) 선행사 low altitude를 수식하는 관계부사절.
차나무는 공기가 따뜻한 저고도에서 빨리 자랍니다.

11. (D, There have been moments) when 이하는 종속절이므로 주어—동사가 있는 주절이 필요하다.
역사에는 비교적 짧은 기간에 위대한 진보가 이루어진 순간들이 있었습니다.

12. (D, Although) 뒤의 절이 주절이므로 앞의 절은 부사절(양보절)이다.
dance company 무용단 sculpture n. 조각
미술가 앤 랜더스는 마사 그래험 무용단의 놀라운 무대디자인을 만들었지만, 그녀는 조각으로 더 유명합니다.

13. (A, dry a desert may be) 양보절의 바른 어순
사막이 아무리 건조해도 완전히 무가치한 것은 아닙니다.

14. (A, which → who) 선행사가 사람이므로 who를 쓰는 것이 옳다.
metropólitan area : 대도시 지역, 수도권 political únity : 정치적 일체감

대도시 지역에 살고 있는 대부분의 사람들은 흔히 그들에게 정치적 일체감이 거의 없습니다.

15. (B, those whom → those who) '주격관계대명사 +동사'
prime mínister : 국무총리 cábinet [kǽbənit] n. 내각
대통령은 내각에 지명된 사람들의 이름을 발표하였습니다.

16. (A, whom → who) The woman who they think did it has been taken
take to : ~을 찾아가다, ~에 의지하다
그것을 했다고 생각되는 남자는 상담을 위해 변호사를 찾아갔다.

17. (B, that → whether/if) 'whether/if~or'
have trouble -ing : ~하는데 고생을 하다 lie—lay—lain
cóastal área : 해안지대
그는 그 주의 수도가 해안지역에 있는지 산지에 있는지를 알아내는 데 고생을 했습니다.

18. (B, which → whose) '선행사+whose+명사+V'
organizátion [ɔːrgənəzéiʃən] n. 조직 sole = only méntally retárded children : 저능아들, 정신적 저진아동
유일한 목적이 지진아들을 돕는 것인 단체들이 많이 있습니다.

19. (A, who → whom)
best math student : 수학도사 dórmitory [dɔ́ːrmətɔːri] n. 기숙사
네가 지금 당장 만나야 할 녀석은 칼 해리스로, 우리 기숙사에서 수학 도사야.

20. (D, which → that) 선행사가 'the only~'일 경우, 관계대명사 that를 쓴다.
coming year : 내년
그린 여사는 내년도 사회위원회의 위원으로 승용차를 가진 유일한 여성입니다.

21. (C, until → before) 문맥상 'not~before ~'
not more than : 고작, 기껏 (= at most)
그 나라에서 겨우 사흘이 지나서 우리는 안내원이 필요하다는 것을 알게되었습니다.

22. (D, that looks → that it may look)
méasuring worm : 자벌레 hold (itself) straight : (자신)을 꼿꼿이 세우다 branch [bræntʃ] n. 나뭇가지, (기업의) 지사 twig [twig] n. 잔가지
자벌레는 잔가지처럼 보이도록 나뭇가지에서 몸을 똑바로 세울 수 있습니다.

23. (A, as rapidly → so rapidly) 'so~that'
beyónd the réach of ~ : ~의 능력을 넘어선
대학교육비가 지난 10년 동안 너무 급히 올라서 이제는 많은 사람들의 능력을 넘어섰습니다.

24. (C, where → when) 부사절의 성격과 그 접속사를 잘못 쓰고 있다.
repúblican párty : 공화당
박대통령이 1962년에 정치권력의 중심에 있을 때, 그때 그는 공화당의 지도자가 되었습니다.

25. (A, which → 제거) which가 있는 부분이 주절이어야 한다.
perféct [pərfékt] v. 완성하다 suspénsion brídge : 현수교
브룩클린 다리는 현수교를 완성한 존 로블링에 의해 건설되었습니다.

Unit 6 특수문형

[EXERCISE 1]

1. That (hanging) basket contains a rare species of fruit.
저기 걸려있는 바구니는 희귀종의 과일을 담고 있습니다.

2. People (suffering) from a severe depression should seek help from a licensed psychologist.
심한 우울증에 시달리는 사람들은 허가 받은 심리치료사에게서 도움을 구해야 합니다.

3. A (crying) child is easily comforted by a few (soothing) words.
우는 아이는 달래는 말 몇 마디에 쉽게 위안을 받습니다.

4. The homes (destroyed) by the hurricane will be restored by one of the city's (wrecking) crews during the (coming) weeks.
허리케인으로 파괴된 집들은 다음주에 시의 조난구조대에 의해 복구될 것입니다.

5. The number of vacation days (provided) by the school is adequate for most people.
학교에서 주어진 방학일수는 대부분의 학생들에게 적당합니다.

6. (Baked) potatoes are frequently served with sour cream, (grated) cheese, and bits of (fried) bacon.
구운 감자는 흔히 신 크림과 으깬 치즈, 튀긴 베이컨 조각들과 함께 나옵니다.

7. The old movies (shown) late at night are frequently better than movies (produced) in the last five years.
심야에 방영되는 옛날 영화들이 최근 5년간 제작된 영화들보다 더 훌륭합니다.

8. Badly (torn) clothes should be mended by an (experienced) tailor.
심하게 찢어진 옷은 경험 있는 양복점에서 수선되어야 합니다.

9. Volunteers (recruited) by the sheriff searched for the (lost) hikers for several (exhausting) days.
보안관에 의해 모집된 자원봉사자들이 힘든 며칠 동안 조난 등반객들을 수색하였습니다.

10. People (walking) in poorly (lighted) areas atnight should be extremely careful.
밤에 조명이 부실한 지역을 걸어다니는 사람들은 매우 조심해야 합니다.

a ráre spécies : 희귀종 sevére depréssion : 심한 우울증 seek v. 찾다, 구하다 licénsed psychólogist : 허가 받은 심리치료사 cómfort [kʌ́mfərt] v. 위안을 주다 soothe [suːð] v. 달래다 restóre [ristɔ́ːr] v. 복구하다, 회복하다 wreck [rek] v. 난파하다, 조난을 구조하다 wrécking créw : 조난구조대 ádequate [ǽdikwit] adj. 적당한 sóur [sáuər] cream : 신 크림 grated cheese : 뭉개진 치즈 bit n. 조각 recrúit [rikrúːt] v. 모집하다 shériff [ʃérif] n. 보안관 search for ~ : ~을 찾다 lost hiker : 조난 등반객 exháusting days : 힘겨운 날들 póorly líghted área : 조명이 부실한 지역

[EXERCISE 2]

1. (filling → filled) 신선하게 구워진 쿠키가 가득한 큰 병은 배고픈 아이들에 의해 금방 비워졌습니다.
2. (o) 인공감미된 청량음료수들은 살을 빼려고 애쓰는 사람들에 의해 구매됩니다.
3. (boring → bored) 시즌이 끝날 때 보여주는 재상영물에 지겨운 텔레비전 시청자들은 더 재미있는 프로그램을 위해 공영방송으로 돌립니다.
4. (o) 배심원들에 의해 언도된 평결은 사건에 관계된 변호사들 중 아무도 놀라게 하지 못했습니다.
5. (o) 벼룩이 옮은 가정의 애완동물들은 특별히 준비된 벼룩비누로 매주 목욕시켜야 합니다.
6. (aspired → aspiring) 출판사들은 유명한 젊은 작가들로부터 꾸준히 원고를 받습니다.
7. (assigning → assigned) 당월 1일이 지나서 접수된 추천장은 여러분의 파일에 배정된 모집관에 의해 검토되지 않습니다.
8. (o) 검댕으로 가득 찬 굴뚝은 숙달된 굴뚝청소부의 작업을 필요로 합니다.
9. (o) 꾸준한 관심을 필요로 하는 실내식물들은 여유시간이 거의 없는 맞벌이 부부들에게는 적당하지 않습니다.
10. (boiling → boiled) 데친 채소가 삶은 것보다는 영양분을 더 많이 함유하고 있습니다.

émpty [émpti] v. 비우다 artificially-swéetened béverages : 인공감미 음료수 púrchase [pə́ːrtʃəs] v. 구매하다 lose weight : 몸무게를 줄이다 rerún n. (영화의) 재방영 vérdict [vɔ́ːrdikt] n. (배심원의) 평결 hand down : 언도하다, 전달하다 invólve [inválv] v. 연루시키다, 포함시키다 case n. 소송사건 hóusehold pet : 집 보는 애완동물 inféct [infékt] v. 감염시키다, 옮기다 flea [fliː] n. 벼룩 bathe [beið] v. 목욕시키다 spécially-prepáred flea soap : 특별히 준비된 벼룩비누 públishing house : 출판사 cónstantly [kánstəntli] adv. 꾸준히

mánuscript [mǽnjəskript] n. 원고 aspíre [əspáiər] v. 열망하다 aspíring young writer : 유명한 젊은 작가 letter of recommendátion : 추천장 revíew [rivjúː] v. 검토하다 recrúiting ófficer : 모집관 soot [suːt] n. 검댕 quálified [kwáləfaid] adj. 자격 있는 chímneysweep [tʃímnisswiːp] n. 굴뚝청소부 hóuseplant [háusplænt] n. 실내에 놓는 화분식물 súitable [súːtəbəl] adj. 적절한 working couple : 맞벌이 부부 spare time : 여유시간 steam [stiːm] v. 찌다 boil [bɔil] v. 끓이다 retáin [ritéin] v. 보유하다, 함유하다 nútrient [njúːtriənt] n. 영양분

[EXERCISE 3]

1. b) 주차권을 신청할 때, 학생들은 학교경찰에게 적절한 신분증을 보여주어야 합니다.
2. b) 1950년에 25억에서 증가하여, 세계인구가 1970년대 말에는 42억 5천만에 달했습니다.
3. a) 납세자들의 돈을 절약해주기 위해 생물학자들은 운하를 맑게 하는 초식성고기를 실험하고 있습니다.
4. b) 자연의 모양을 따서, 엔지니어들이 안전하고 연료 효율적인 기름탱크를 디자인하고 있습니다.
5. b) 아파트를 임대할 때, 세입자는 임대계약에 서명하기를 요구받습니다.

párking sticker : 주차권 próper identificátion : 적절한 신분증 roast [roust] n. 로스비프 v. (고기를) 굽다 chef [ʃef] n. 주방장, 요리사 táxpayer [tǽkspeiər] n. 납세자 biólogist [baiálədʒist] n. 생물학자 expériment [ikspérəmənt] v. 실험하다 weed-eating fish : 초식어 canál [kənǽl] n. 운하 bio-médical adj. 생체의학의 stable [stéibl] adj. 안정감 있는 fuel-efficient adj. 연료 효율적인 lease [liːs] n. 리스, 임대계약 ténant [ténənt] n. 임차인, 세입자

[EXERCISE 4]

1. (o) 1965년 독립전쟁에서 승리하기 전에, 알제리는 많은 청년들을 잃었습니다.
2. (x) 1901년에 수상한, 설리 프루덤은 첫 노벨문학상을 받았습니다.
3. (x) 복잡한 기하학문양으로 장식하여, 회교도 금속노동자들은 구리와 양철, 동으로 된 아름다운 쟁반들을 생산합니다.
4. (x) 메카에서 도망친 뒤에, 모하메드와 추종자들은 기원 후 622년에 메디나 시를 건설하였습니다.
5. (o) 노틀담 사원은 세느강 안의 섬에 자리잡고 있어서, 파리에서 가장 유명한 기념물들의 하나입니다.
6. (x) 여러 해 동안 사망원인으로 기각되었는데도, 광부들의 미망인들은 흑폐증에 대한 보상을 받고 있습니다.
7. (x) 원하는 만큼의 물을 마신 후에, 낙타는 거의 두 주일 동안 물 없이 견디는 것이 가능합니다.
8. (o) 구리로 형성될 때, 알루미늄 합금은 아주 강합니다.
9. (o) 햇빛에 직접 노출되었을 때, 식물들은 시드는 경향이 있습니다.
10. (x) 눈 속을 통과하여 집으로 달려와서 그녀는 코감기가 심하게 걸렸습니다.

the war for indepéndence : 독립전쟁 awárd [əwɔ́ːrd] v. 수상하다

décorate [dékəreit] v. 장식하다 íntricate [íntrəkət] cdj. 복잡한
geométric desígn : 기하학적 도안 métal wórker : 금속노동자 tray [trei] n. 쟁반 cópper n. 구리 tin n. 양철 bronze n. 동 lándmark [lǽndmɑːrk] n. 표지물, 기념물 rejéct [ridʒékt] v. 거부하다 míners' wídows : 광부들의 미망인들 compensátion [kɑmpənséiʃən] n. 보상 black-lung diséase : 흑폐진증

[Actual Test 6]

1. (C, being) Football and baseball (which are) being played ... today
   오늘날 미국에서 하고 있는 야구나 미식축구는 기본적으로 영국에서 생긴 경기들의 변형입니다.

2. (B, joined together) lenses (which are) joined together
   잠자리는 수백 개의 렌즈가 결합되어 이루어진 복잡적인 눈을 가지고 있습니다.

3. (C, although) 양보의 의미가 강하여 분사구문의 접속사를 생략하지 않았다.
   프란시스 존슨은 오하이오주에서 태어났지만, 미시간주에서 살며 변호사를 개업하였습니다.

4. (A, Jane Lyon turned to writing for her livelihood) 앞의 표현이 분사구문이므로 주절이 필요하다.
   turn to ~에 의존하다
   1937년에 심한 재정적인 위기를 맞아서 제인 라이언은 생활을 위해 글쓰기에 의존했습니다.

5. (A, Found) 뒤의 절이 주절이므로 앞부분은 부사절이거나 분사구문.
   위스콘신주 어디에서 발견되는 소나무는 그 주에서 가장 흔한 나무입니다.

6. (A, Jane Smith was stimulated by the social reform movement)
   제인 스미스는 유럽을 여행하면서 사회개혁운동에 고무되었습니다.

7. (C, live → living) 하나의 문장에 동사가 둘일 수는 없다. 하나는 분사이다.
   institútion [ìnstətjúːʃən] n. 기관 províde [prəváid] v. 제공하다(= give) educátional assístance : 교육적인 도움 depréssed commúnities : 침체된 지역사회
   제시잭슨에 의해 1961년에 세워진 그 기관은 경제적으로 침체된 지역사회에 살고 있는 어린이들에게 교육적인 도움을 제공합니다.

8. (C, grow → growing) 이 문장의 동사는 is 이다.
   Mediterránean [mèdətəréiniən] n. 지중해
   오늘날 자라고 있는 지중해 올리브 나무의 평균수명은 3백년입니다.

9. (B, publish by → published by) publish는 앞의 명사 story를 수식하는 과거분사이다.
   워싱턴 어빙이 출간한 첫 단편소설은 1829년에 나온 'Rip van Winkle'이었습니다.

Basic Grammar for English Tests

10. (C, is required → required) 두 개의 동사구 중에 하나는 분사임이 분명하다.
    fúrnace [fɚːrnɪs] n. 용광로 exténsively [iksténsivli] adv. 광범위하게, 널리 steel álloys : 철합금
    전기용광로는 철합금 제조에 필요한 고급 철을 생산하는 데 널리 쓰입니다.

11. (B, covering → covered) '진행의미'인 covering 보다는 '상태의미'인 covered가 바르다.
    abándon [əbǽndən] v. 버리다 pórtion [pɔ́ːrʃən] n. 부분, 비율 vines and bushes : 덩굴과 풀숲 tráceable [tréisəbəl] adj. 찾을 수 있는, 더듬을 수 있는 córnfield n. 옥수수밭 órchard [ɔ́ːrtʃəd] n. 과수원 thícket [θíkit] n. 덤불숲, 관목림
    그 언덕의 많은 버려진 부분은 덩굴과 풀숲으로 덮여있어서 옥수수밭을 건너서 또는 과수원과 잡목림을 지나면 여전히 쉽게 찾을 수 있습니다.

12. (A, Standing in the driveway, → When we were standing in the driveway,) 주절과 주어가 다르다.
    dríveway n. 진입로
    진입로에 서 있을 때, 그 교회가 수년 전 어린 시절에 우리가 봤던 것보다 훨씬 더 작아 보였습니다.

13. (A, was known → known) A는 이 문장의 동사가 아니다.
    méntal institútion : 정신요양원 superinténdent [sùːpərinténdənt] n. 감독
    정신요양원을 개선하기 위한 힘든 노력으로 유명한 엘리자베스 테일러는 미국 남북전쟁 때 간호사들의 감독으로 근무하였습니다.

14. (C, broken → breaking) 문장의 주어는 분사와 능동적인 관계이므로 현재분사가 옳다.
    contínually [kəntínjuəli] adv. 점점 párticle [pɑ́ːrtikl] n. 작은 조각
    비바람은 큰 나무들을 더 작은 조각들로 부수면서 끊임없이 지구표면을 때립니다.

15. (B, and employed → and employing) 주어인 the organization은 employ에 능동적인 관계이다.
    éstimated [éstəmeitid] adj. 어림잡은, 대충의 gain a reputation : 명성을 얻다 brutality [bruːtǽləti] n. 잔인성, 포악성
    1971년에 창설되었고, 대략 40,000명을 고용하고 있는 그 조직은 잔인성으로 명성을 얻었습니다.

16. (A, saw → seen) 주어인 the moon은 분사의 동사 see에 대해 수동적인 관계이다.
    strikingly [stráikiŋli] adv. 두드러지게, 상당히
    달이 수평선 근처에서 보일 때는, 머리 위에서 보일 때보다 상당히 커 보입니다.

[EXERCISE 5]

1. (understood) 헨리는 자기 개에게 마치 자기 말을 알아듣는 것처럼 말을 합니다.

2. (had) 만약 그가 돈을 가지고 있다면, 그는 내게 줄 것이다.

3. (would stop) 제가 집중을 할 수 있도록 그들이 너무 시끄럽게 떠들지 말았으면 좋겠어요.
4. (needed) 만약 도움이 필요하다면, 그녀는 당신에게 즉시 전화를 할 것입니다.
5. (would have found) 세일에 일찍 도착했더라면, 그들은 더 좋은 물건을 골랐을 것입니다.
6. (enjoyed) 우리는 당신이 어젯밤 파티를 즐겁게 보냈기를 바랍니다.
7. (paint) 충분한 시간이 있으시면, 당신이 떠나기 전에 의자에 페인트칠을 해주세요.
8. (were) 오늘이 토요일이라면 우리는 드라이브를 갈 수 있을 거예요.
9. (writes) 그녀가 상을 받는다면, 그것은 그녀가 글을 잘 쓰기 때문일 것입니다.
10. (would permit/had permitted) 마이크는 편집자들이 그에게 그들의 자료 일부를 복사하도록 허락해주기를 원했습니다.

make a noise : 떠들다 cóncentrate [kánsəntreit] v. 집중하다 find a (better) seléction : (더 좋은) 물건을 고르다 go for a drive : 드라이브 가다 win the prize : 상을 받다 éditor [édətər] n. 편집자

[Actual Test **7**]

1. (B, if only) 내용이 강한 소망이나 후회를 나타내고 있으므로 if only가 적절하다.
   누가 책을 마지막으로 빌렸는지 내가 기억하기만 한다면 네게 줄텐데.
2. (D, you would have met Tom) if절의 시제가 had p.p.이므로 가정법과거완료
   어젯밤 파티에 조지와 함께 가지 않았더라면 너는 톰을 만났을 텐데.
3. (D, I'd have been glad) you'd let = you had let (let-let-let). 가정법과거완료
   그녀가 내게 시간을 알려줬더라면 내가 그녀를 반갑게 만났을 텐데.
4. (C, had accepted) 조건절에는 then, 주절에는 now로 보아 가정법과거완료와 과거가 혼재하고 있다.
   내가 그때 그녀의 충고를 받아들였더라면 지금쯤 더 행복할 텐데.
5. (B, wish) I wish 가정법 - I am sorry (that) Professor Miller didn't teach me ...
   equation n. 방정식
   밀러교수가 이 방정식을 가르쳐 주셨다면 좋았을 텐데.
6. (D, didn't make) I wish가정법이지만 every day가 있음을 유의할 것.
   내가 또 실수를 저질렀어. 매일 실수 좀 하지 않았으면 좋겠어.
7. (B, didn't do) would rather (that) 구문은 과거시제이다.
   나는 잠시 동안 그것에 대해 아무 것도 하지 않고 싶어.

8. (B, has) save는 except/but/if ... not의 역할을 한다.
   the white dress save it has a stain = the white dress if it had not a stain
   앞에 때가 묻지 않았다면 난 그 하얀 드레스를 입을 텐데.
9. (D, would have had → would have) 조건절과 주절의 시제를 비교해 보면 알 수 있다.
   resign [rizáin] v. 사임하다 take one's place : ~의 자리를 차지하다 vígorous [vígərəs] adj. 왕성한, 활기찬
   만일 존이 사임을 하고, 해리가 피선되어 그 자리를 차지한다면, 우리는 좀더 강력한 지도력을 가지게 될 것입니다.
10. (A, would have tried → had tried) 조건절과 주절의 동사시제가 바른 짝인지 확인한다.
    ópposite [ápəzit] adj. 반대편의
    존이 좀더 노력하여 반대편 해변에 도착했더라면, 우리가 그를 배에 태울 필요는 없었을 것입니다.
11. (A, did not filter out → had not filtered out) 주절의 시제가 would not have evolved 임을 유의한다.
    átmosphere [ǽtməsfiər] n. 대기 filter out : 여과시키다 ultravíolet [Ʌltrəváiəlit] n. 자외선(의) evólve [iválv] v. 발전시키다, 진화하다
    대기의 오존가스가 태양의 자외선을 여과하지 않았다면, 우리가 알다시피, 생물은 지구상에서 발달하지 못했다는 것입니다.
12. (B, would have study → would have studied) ... have study라는 표현은 없다.
    제인이 시험에 합격을 했다면, 그는 시험공부를 아주 많이 했을 것입니다.
13. (A, would have → had) 주절의 시제가 would have p.p.이면, 조건절의 시제는 had p.p.이다.
    경찰이 좀더 일찍 도착하였더라면, 그는 교통사고를 보았을 것입니다.
14. (A, you have learned → you had learned) 주절에 있는 today를 주의할 것. 혼합시제의 문장이다.
    속독을 배웠더라면, 너는 지금 훌륭한 독자가 되어있을 것입니다.
15. (A, saw → had seen) 혼합시제의 문장이다. this morning을 참고한다.
    오늘 아침에 그녀가 아침식사로 먹은 식사량을 보셨다면, 당신은 그녀가 왜 그렇게 살이 쪘는지 이해하실 것입니다.
16. (A, I knew → I had known) 주절의 시제 would have met을 유의한다.
    저는 당신이 오늘 올 줄을 알았더라면 좋았을 것입니다. 제가 공항에 마중나갔을 거예요.
17. (A, looked like → looked as if) look는 자동사이고, 또 조건절에 if가 필요하다.
    advance [ædvǽns] v. 나아가다 at a double pace : 두 배의 속도로
    그는 마치 나이가 두 배의 속도로 진행된 이상한 곳에 있었던 것처럼 보였습니다.
18. (C, was → were smiling) 가정법 조건절의 be동사는 항상 were이다.

Basic Grammar for English Tests

제인은 자기를 즐겁게 하는 어떤 것에 관해 마치 미소를 짓는 것처럼 얼굴에 묘한 표정을 짓고 있습니다.

19. (C, couldn't → can't) 주절이 'while I am now in Boston'로 보아 현재시제임을 유의한다.
get in touch with ~ : ~와 연락하다
제가 그 아름다운 산에 갈 것입니다만, 지금은 제가 시카고에 있어서 당신과 연락을 할 수가 없군요.

[EXERCISE 6]

1. (best) 드레스 네 벌 중에서, 저는 빨간 것을 가장 좋아합니다.
2. (happiest) 그는 내가 아는 사람 중에 가장 행복한 사람입니다.
3. (faster) 제인의 자동차는 댄의 자동차보다 더 빠릅니다.
4. (creamist) 이것은 오랫동안 제가 먹어보았던 것 중 가장 부드러운 아이스크림입니다.
5. (more colorful) 이 포스터는 홀에 있는 것보다 더 화려합니다.
6. (better) 프레드는 어제보다 오늘 더 나아졌습니까?
7. (good) 이 채소수프는 아주 맛이 좋습니다.
8. (more awkwardly) 머리 위 바구니의 균형을 맞추려고 하다 보니, 그 여자는 뜻보다 더 어색하게 걸었습니다.
9. (least) 제인은 여자들 중에서 가장 약합니다.
10. (prettier) 둘 중에 우리 고양이가 더 예쁩니다.
11. (the better) 둘 중에 이 요약이 더 훌륭합니다.
12. (from) 당신의 유산은 제것과 다릅니다.
13. (less impressive) 이 그림은 다른 화랑에 있는 것보다 덜 인상적입니다.
14. (the sicker) 날씨가 추워질수록 더 아프게 느낍니다.
15. (than) 편지를 받자마자 그는 마리아에게 전화를 하였습니다.
16. (twice as much as) 밍크코트는 담비코트보다 두 배나 비쌉니다.
17. (few) 짐은 저보다 테니스 칠 기회가 거의 없습니다.
18. (much) 그 조리법은 제 요리법보다 훨씬 많은 설탕을 요구합니다.
19. (farthest) 박물관은 세 건물 중에서 가장 멀리 떨어져 있습니다.
20. (more famous) 조지 워싱턴은 존 제이보다 더 유명합니다.

créamy [krí:mi] adj. 매끈매끈한 athlétic [æθlétik] adj 강건한, 운동선수 같은 héritage [héritidʒ] n. 유산 sable coat : 담비코트 récipe [résəpi:] n. 조리법

[EXERCISE 7]

1. b) 알래스카는 다른 어느 주보다 더 큽니다.
2. b) 존은 자기 학급의 어느 아이보다 큽니다.
3. b) 알래스카 지역은 텍사스 지역보다 더 큽니다.
4. a) 간이 아파트의 임대료는 원룸아파트 임대료보다 훨씬 쌉니다.
5. b) 우리 학원에서는 아침수업이 오후수업보다 훨씬 더 인기가 있습니다.

6. b) 최근의 도본조사에 따르면, CBS뉴스가 NBC뉴스보다 더 많은 시청자를 가지고 있습니다.
7. b) 대학의 본부건물은 캠퍼스 내에 있는 다른 어느 건물보다 더 큽니다.
8. b) 원숭이들은 사람을 제외한 다른 어떤 동물보다 더 지적입니다.

efficiency apártment : 간이 아파트(부엌이 있는 방 하나와 욕실이 있는 아파트) institútion n. 학원 survéy [sə:rvéi] n. (표본)조사, 검사

[EXERCISE 8]

1. a) 라텍스화는 더 훌륭하지는 않더라도, 유화만큼 훌륭합니다.
2. b) 낡은 카뷰레터의 수리는 더 비싸지는 않더라도, 새것을 사는 것만큼이나 비쌀 것입니다.
3. b) 타자수로서 그녀의 기술은 그녀의 전임자의 기술과 같거나 능가합니다.
4. a) 존 필립은 자기 학급의 다른 이들의 성적보다 더 높지는 않지만, 같은 높은 성적을 받았습니다.
5. b) 트랙조명은 오늘날 시장에서 가장 인기있는 조명형태는 아니라도, 그중 하나입니다.
6. a) 비록 세일 중이지만, 이 냉장고들은 다른 가게에 있는 것들과 가격에서 더 비싸지는 않지만, 같습니다.
7. a) 저타르 담배는 일반 담배보다 더 유해하지는 않더라도, 그만큼 유해합니다.
8. b) 방사형 타이어의 보증은 네 겹 타이어의 보증보다 더 좋지는 않더라도 그만큼 좋습니다.

látex paint : 라텍스화 oil-based paint : 유화 worn-out : 낡은 cárburetor [kɑ́:rbəretər] n. 카뷰레터, 기화기 excéed [iksí:d] v. 능가하다 predecéssor [predisésər] n. 조상, 선배, 전임자 track lighting : 트랙조명 wárranty [wɔ́:rənti] n. 보증 rádial tire : 방사형 타이어 four-ply tire : 네 겹 타이어 ply [plai] n. 겹, 층, 가닥

[Actual Test 8]

1. (B, less than piston turbines) steam engines와 piston turbines를 비교한다.
증기기관은 같은 양의 힘을 생산하는 피스톤터빈보다 무게가 적게 나갑니다.
2. (C, more immediate social change than) than 이하 절이 도치된 문장.
자유당이 보수당에 비해 신속한 사회변화에 좀 더 호의적인 경향이 있습니다.
3. (A, faster through water than through) through water와 through air가 비교되고 있다.
소리는 물 속에서 보다 공기 중에서 더 빨리 이동합니다.
4. (A, than that at last year's baseball game) 비교되는 것은 올해와 작년의 crowd
관중이 작년 야구경기 때보다 훨씬 더 많았습니다.

5. (C, the more isolated one) Of the two가 단서이다.
두 집 가운데 아내는 좀 더 떨어진 집을 선호합니다.

6. (D, greater the amount of gold used) the 비교급+명사, the 비교급+명사
생활수준이 높고 국부가 클수록 황금의 소비량도 많아집니다.

7. (A, as rapidly that → as rapidly as) 'as 부사 as'
inhábitant [inhǽbətənt] n. (거)주민 cúrrently [kə́rəntli] adv. 현재
미국의 도시들 중 1850년에 주민이 1,610명이었다가 현재 약 400만의 인구를 가진 로스엔젤레스만큼 빨리 성장한 도시는 거의 없습니다.

8. (B, as good as → as good) as가 중복되어 잘못 들어간 것이 있다.
éxercise n. 운동(하다) unwánted weight : 원치 않은 몸무게
운동이 원치않은 몸무게를 줄이는 데는 어떤 것만큼이나 좋은 방법입니다.

9. (D, as any → as that in any) 비교하는 대상이 같아야 한다.
discríminating [diskrímǝneitiŋ] adj. 구별되는, 혜안의, 심미안 있는 góurmet [gúərmei] n. 미식가, 식도락가
심지어 최고의 미식가도 동부의 음식이 이 나라 다른 어느 지역의 음식만큼이나 훌륭하다는 데 동의합니다.

10. (B, as → than) fewer~than
ímport [ímpɔːrt] n. 수입품 énergy crísis : 에너지 위기
작년에 국가는 경제위기 때문에 그전해보다 수입품을 더 적게 들여왔습니다.

11. (A, largest → larger) 둘 중의 비교는 비교급으로 한다.
take down : (높은 곳에서) 끄집어내리다
그녀는 사전 두 권 중에 더 큰 것을 내려서 자기가 철자를 잘못 쓴 단어를 찾기 시작하였습니다.

12. (D, as that → than that) 앞에 비교급 more가 있음을 유의한다.
학생이 완수해야 하는 것으로 작문을 잘하는 기술보다 더 중요한 것은 아무것도 없습니다.

13. (D, any another → any other) 'any another'라는 표현은 없다.
handle v. 취급하다 freight [freit] n. 화물
시카고 오해어공항은 미국의 다른 어느 공항보다 더 많은 화물과 우편물을 취급합니다.

14. (B, more wilder than → wilder than) 'more wilder'처럼 비교급을 중복하지 않는다.
the Smokies : 스모키산(Great Smokie Mountain)
스모키산 외부의 다른 어느 동부지역보다 더 황량한 지역이 펜실바니아 북부에 많이 있습니다.

15. (B, best of all → best) like-best
fishing rod : 낚싯대
자신의 모든 외부활동 중에서, 존은 낚시를 가장 좋아합니다. 그러나 그는 나중에 낚싯대를 정리하는 것은 좋아하지 않습니다.

16. (B, him → he) 비교대상은 Nobody와 같은 주어이다.
fréquently : 흔히 make out : 이해하다(= comprehend)
그 사람보다 더 명료하게 말하는 사람은 아무도 없지만, 그의 글은 흔히 알아보기 힘듭니다.

17. (D, his life → during his life) 비교대상이 시간이다. 'after his death'와 'during his life'
인간의 마음에 미치는 그 철학자의 영향은 그가 살아있는 동안보다 죽은 후에 훨씬 더 위대해졌습니다.

18. (C, as more superior → as superior) 'regard~as'
마이클 잭슨의 노래는 그를 다른 가수들보다 낫다고 여기는 젊은이들 사이에서 매우 인기가 있습니다.

19. (D, highest → higher) 'rising higher'라고 비교급을 쓴다.
세계시장의 금값은 매일 올랐습니다.

20. (B, better necessary → more necessary) 적절한 의미의 비교급을 사용했는지 유의한다.
주제가 복잡할수록, 그 주제를 독자가 이해할 수 있는 많은 부분으로 쪼개주는 것이 더욱 필요합니다.

21. (C, worst → worse) 'the 비교급~, the 비교급~.'
제가 저의 잘못을 설명하려고 할수록, 저의 이야기는 더 나쁘게 들렸습니다.

22. (C, hard → hardness) 'the same 명사 and 명사'
artifícial [ɑːrtəfíʃəl] adj. 인조의 hárdness [hάːrdnis] n. 경도, 단단함 composítion n. 구성
인조 루비는 실제 보석과 같은 경도와 구성을 가지고 있습니다.

[**EXERCISE 9**]

1. (o) 그런 행동은 이 교실에서는 용납되지 않습니다.
2. (the boy was → was the boy)
소년은 너무 피곤하여 곧바로 잠이 들었습니다.
3. (o) 십대들은 그들이 얼마나 많이 배워야 하는지 거의 깨닫지 못합니다.
4. (the gas station are → are the gas station)
길게 뻗은 도로상에 주유소들이 멀리 떨어져 있고, 거의 있지도 않았습니다.
5. (So old the book was → So old was the book)
그 책은 너무 오래되어서 페이지가 노랗게 변색되었습니다.
6. (Little the boy realizes → Little does the boy realize)
그 남자는 자기가 어떻게 아픈지 거의 깨닫지 못했습니다.
7. (o) 그 외국인의 억양은 아주 완벽해서 모두가 그 사람을 원어민으로 생각하였습니다.
8. (o) 그가 한밤이 되기 전에 잠자리에 든 밤은 거의 없었습니다.
9. (o) 그런 범죄는 그 나라에서는 사형의 처벌을 받습니다.
10. (So great her love was → So great was her love)
그녀의 사랑은 너무도 대단해서 자기 자식들을 위해서 모든 것을 희생하였습니다.

Basic Grammar for English Tests

behávior [bihéivjər] *n.* 행동 gas station : 주유소 stretch [stretʃ] *n.* (뻗은) 길, 연속 crime [kraim] *n.* 범죄 púnish [pʌ́niʃ] *v.* 처벌하다 sácrifice [sǽkrəfais] *v.* 희생하다

[Actual Test 9]

1. (D, evolved the abstract algebra) 부사구가 문두에 놓임으로서 주어-동사가 도치된 문장이다
   algebra [ǽldʒəbrə] *n.* 대수학
   오늘날 사용되는 추상대수학과 대수학적 구조의 개념은 기초 대수학의 기본요소들에서 발전하였습니다.

2. (A, does the marine gyrocompass) 뒤의 절에 nor가 있어서 동사-주어로 도치된다.
   poles 나침반 또는 지구의 남북 양극 magnetic poles 나침반의 양극 geographic poles 지구의 남북 양극 gyrocompass [dʒáiərouk˄mpəs] *n.* 회전나침반
   자기나침반은 자극 근처에서 잘 작동되지 않듯이 해도 회전나침반 역시 극지방에 가까이서는 잘 작동되지 않습니다.

3. (D, had a state governor refused to step down) never가 강조되어 문두에 주어-동사가 나가면서 도치된 문장이다. 시제는 과거완료시제.
   step down 사임하다
   과거 비슷한 상황에서 어떤 주지사도 사임하기를 거절한 사람은 없었습니다.

4. (C, do meteors blaze) 부정어 Rarely가 문두에 와서 주어-동사가 도치되는 문장.
   meteor [míːtiər] *n.* 유성, 별똥별
   별똥별이 지구 대기권에 일단 들어오면 불과 몇 초간 불타다가 사라집니다.

5. (B, So successful was Grace Miller) so ... that 구문에서 'so+형용사'가 강조되어 앞으로 나간 문장이다.
   그레이스 밀러씨는 탄탄한 플롯과 현대적인 등장인물을 통해 자신의 메시지를 전달하는 데 아주 성공적이었기에 1950년까지 그녀의 책은 100만 부나 팔렸습니다.

6. (B, children are → are children) 도치구문의 어순은 동사가 주어 앞에 놓인다.
   ínstitute [ínsətitjuːt] *n.* 학원
   13세 이하의 어린이들은 이 학원의 수업에 좀처럼 등록되지 않습니다.

7. (C, it begins → does it begin) 도치구문이 복문인 경우 주절의 '주어-동사' 어순이 바뀐다.
   pouch [pautʃ] *n.* 주머니, 어미 캥거루의 배에 있는 주거니
   아기 캥거루는 생후 6개월이 되어서야, 어미의 몸 밖에서 살기 시작합니다.

8. (C, it will learn → will it learn) 주절의 '주어-동사' 어순에 주의한다.
   seal [siːl] *n.* 물개
   아기 물개는 어미 물개에 의해 바닷속으로 일단 밀어 넣어진 후에야 수영을 배우게 됩니다.

9. (A, were → was) 도치된 문장이지만, 주어(the predominant land life)는 단수이다.
   predóminant [pridάmənənt] *adj.* 우월한, 현저한 Mesozóic [mesəzóuik] *adj.* 중생대의
   주라기의 대표적 육지생물은 그러했습니다.

10. (A, was → were) 주어(one hundred and eighty men)가 복수이다.
    mígrate [máigreit] *v.* 이주하다
    알라모 요새 안에는 인근 주에서 최근에 이주해온 사람들의 2/3가 넘는 250명이 있었습니다.

11. (A, his luggage had → had his luggage) 동사가 부사를 따라 주어 앞으로 나간다.
    그의 짐이 실리자마자 트럭은 출발을 했습니다.

12. (A, Rarely meteors → Rarely do meteors) 부사를 따라 동사가 주어 앞으로 나간다.
    méteor [míːtiər] *n.* 유성, 운석 blaze bleiz] *n.* 불꽃, 폭발 átmosphere [ǽtməsfiər] *n.* 대기
    유성은 일단 대기권에 진입한 다음에, 드물게 잠시 불꽃을 발합니다.

13. (C, nor → does nor) does not … does nor …
    magnétic cómpass : 자기컴퍼스 magnetic pole : 자기극 óperate *v.* 작동하다 geográphic pole : 지리학적 극
    자기극 근처에서는 자기 나침반이 잘 작동하지 않고, 지도상의 양극 근처에서 해도 나침반 역시 잘 작동하지 않습니다.

14. (B, the force is → is the force) 부사가 도치된 문장에서 동사는 주어 앞에 놓인다.
    exért [igzə́ːrt] *v.* 발휘하다 locomótive [loukəmóutiv] *n.* 전동차
    토네이도에 의해 발휘되는 힘은 워낙 대단해서, 토네이도는 열차를 철로에서 들어올리는 것으로 알려져 있습니다.

15. (B, dreams were → were dreams) 주어, 동사의 도치에 주의
    scrútinize [skrúːtənaiz] *v.* 검토하다, 자세히 살피다
    20세기 초반에 와서야 겨우 꿈이 처음으로 분석되었습니다.

[EXERCISE 10]

1. (does) 로즈는 비행을 좋아하고, 그녀의 오빠 역시 좋아합니다.
2. (will) 그들은 정오에 떠날 것이고, 저도 그럴 것입니다.
3. (do) 그는 일찍 약속이 있는데, 저도 그렇습니다.
4. (have) 그녀는 자신의 작문을 이미 썼고, 그녀의 친구들도 그렇습니다.
5. (is) 그들의 비행기는 9시에 도착을 하고, 제것도 그렇습니다.

[Actual Test 10]

1. (A, So) 긍정문에서는 확인과 동의 뜻인 so를 사용한다.
   "존스씨 가족은 하루 종일 텔레비전을 봅니다." "밀러씨 가족도 그렇습니다."

2. (D, and so did his brother) 긍정문의 확인, 동의 표현은 'So+동사+주어'
   조지가 콘서트에 갔고, 그의 동생도 갔습니다.

3. (C, Neither can I) 부정문의 확인, 동의 표현은 'Neither+동사+주어'
   "톰은 내일까지 떠날 수 없습니다." "압니다. 저도 그렇습니다."

4. (A, I wasn't, either) not ... either
   "제인은 대학원생이 아닙니다." "예. 저도 아닙니다."

5. (D, the Bushes do → do the Bushes) 부가의문의 바른 어순에 유의
   존스 가족은 늘 텔레비전을 시청합니다. 부시씨 가족도 마찬가지입니다.

6. (C, did so → so did) 어순 주의
   조지는 영화 보러 갔고, 그의 동생도 그랬습니다.

7. (D, so does John → so is John) 부가동의문의 동사는 주절의 동사와 일치한다.
   샐리는 대학에서 법률을 공부하고 있고, 존도 그렇습니다.

8. (D, neither they are → neither are they) 어순 주의
   그녀는 6월에 그 회의에 가지 않을 것이고, 그들도 그럴 것입니다.

9. (D, would I → had I) 'd met = had met
   cf. would +원형동사, had+p.p.
   저는 전에 여러 차례 제인을 만났습니다. 저도 그랬습니다.

10. (D, neither → either) not~either = neither
    조지는 대학생이 아니었습니다. 예, 저도 아니었습니다.

Unit 7 일치

[EXERCISE 1]

1. (were → was) 과일과 채소는 각각 독자적으로 자랐습니다.
2. (have → has) 아침에는 모두 8시30분에 도착해야 합니다.
3. (were → was) 유리창을 깬 것은 그 어린이들이었습니다.
4. (are → is) 집 안의 모든 것을 팔 것입니다.
5. (want → wants) 모든 학생은 입학시험에 합격하고 싶어합니다.
6. (has → have) 육상경주에 선수들이 이렇게 많은 적이 결코 없었습니다.
7. (are → is) 큰 여행가방뿐 아니라 책 상자가 침대 밑에 있습니다.
8. (have → has) 보좌관들과 함께 대통령은 뉴욕으로 떠났습니다.
9. (are → is) 그 노래에는 가사뿐 아니라 곡도 있습니다.
10. (speak → speaks) 두 학급의 모두가 영어를 아주 잘 말합니다.

[EXERCISE 2]

1. (aren't) 오늘은 당신 우편물에 편지가 하나도 없습니다.
2. (isn't) 오늘은 당신 우편물이 아무것도 없습니다.
3. (are) 세상에는 60만 종이 넘는 곤충이 있습니다.
4. (are) 얼마나 많은 종류의 새가 세상에 있습니까?
5. (isn't) 왜 저 마을에 가까운 병원이 없습니까?

[EXERCISE 3]

1. (are) 경주를 끝낼 만큼 충분히 강한 사람은 거의 없습니다.
2. (is) 바닥에 선글라스가 놓여 있습니다.
3. (are) 내 멋진 바지와 낡은 청바지는 둘 다 세탁 중입니다.
4. (are) 여러분 중 많은 사람이 입학시험에 합격할 것입니다.
5. (are) 서가 꼭대기에 책이 몇 권 있습니다.
6. (are) 의사도 간호사들도 여기 없습니다.
7. (is) 도시의 간호사 수가 매우 많습니다.
8. (are) 간호사들 모두가 매우 훌륭합니다.
9. (is) 의약품이 모두 없어졌습니다.
10. (is) 약간의 물이 관개에 쓰입니다.
11. (is) 대부분의 돈이 모조품입니다.
12. (are) 돈뿐 아니라 보석도 금고 안에 잠겨 있습니다.
13. (is) 보석뿐 아니라 돈도 제것입니다.
14. (are) 쿠키가 몽땅 없어졌습니다.
15. (is) 가구의 절반이 트럭에 있습니다.

be at the laundry : 빨래 중인 irrigation [irəgéiʃən] n. 관개 counterfeit [káuntərfit] n. 모조품, 복제품 lock up : 잠그다 safe n. 금고

[EXERCISE 4]

1. (causes) 독일 홍역이 가슴과 팔에 붉은 반점을 만들었습니다.
2. (has) 평화회담 소식이 아직 섬에 도착하지 않았습니다.
3. (attracts) 정치는 언제나 야망있는 사람들을 매료시킵니다.
4. (were) 모든 사무실에 뉴욕타임스 신문 여분이 있었습니다.
5. (is) 2주일은 주립공원으로 캠프여행을 가기에 충분한 시간입니다.
6. (is) 챔피언에 따르면, 1백 파운드는 들기 쉽다고 합니다.
7. (is) 2천 달러는 그가 수업료로 내기에는 많은 돈입니다.
8. (are) 수학과 물리학은 둘 다 재미있습니다.
9. (was) 상어에 관한 영화인 「죠스」는 기록적으로 많은 사람들이 보았습니다.
10. (is) 백신의 발달에도 불구하고, 홍역은 여전히 성인들에게 대단히 위험합니다.

spot n. 반점 ámple [ǽmpl] adj. 충분한, 풍부한 (= much) túition [tjúːiʃən] n. 수업료

[EXERCISE 5]

1. (astounds) 다양하고 복잡한 주제에 대해 제인이 가진 지식의 범위는 저를 놀라게 합니다.
2. (are) 이 과목에서 당신이 공부할 주제들은 강의배정표에 적혀 있습니다.
3. (are) 메사추세츠주와 코네티컷주는 뉴잉글랜드에 자리잡고 있습니다.
4. (has) 미국의 모든 거미들 중에 검은 과부거미들 만이 인간을 죽게 할 수가 있습니다.
5. (are) 오렌지, 토마토, 신선한 딸기, 양배추, 푸른 상추 등은 비타민C가 풍부합니다.
6. (agree) 선생님과 학생이 그 점에서 동의를 합니다.
7. (approves) 그 대학의 거의 모든 교수와 학생이 새 총장으로 브라운 박사의 선택을 찬성합니다.
8. (has) 6학년 학급의 모든 남녀학생들은 과학프로젝트를 작업해야 합니다.
9. (is) 파이와 케이크를 만드는 일은 리드 부인의 특별요리입니다.
10. (is) 전세계에서 온 학생들을 알게 되는 것은 저의 일 중에서 가장 좋은 부분의 하나입니다.

exténd [ikstént] n. 범위, 정도 astóund [əstáund] v. 놀라게 하다
sýllabus [síləbəs] n. 강의요목, 시간배정(표) wídow [wídou] n. 과부
opp. wídower : 홀아비 spécialty [spéʃəlti] n. 특별요리

[EXERCISE 6]

1. (whom → who) 어젯밤에 당신에게 전화를 한 것은 저였습니다.
2. (him → he) 제가 그이보다 더 크다는 것은 사실입니다.
3. (him → he) 경찰이 체포한 사람은 분명 그 사람이었을 것입니다.
4. (me → I) 당신이 저라면, 그에게 돈을 빌려주시겠습니까?
5. (him → he) 우리 선생님은 내가 그 친구보다 더 똑똑하다고 생각하신다.
6. (whom → who) 길 건너에 살고 있는 남자들이 많이 떠듭니다.
7. (I → me) 너, 해리 그리고 나를 제외하고는 무슨 일이 있었는지 아무도 몰라.
8. (him → he) 우리가 영화에서 본 것은 분명 그 사람이었습니다.
9. (he → him) 이것은 그 사람을 찍은 훌륭한 사진입니다.
10. (whom → who) 저는 이 사진들을 찍은 사람을 선생님이 알고 계신다고 생각합니다.

arrést [ərést] v. 체포하다 intélligent [intélədʒənt] adj. 똑똑한, 지적인 make a noise : 떠들다

[EXERCISE 7]

1. (me → my) 내가 점심을 다 먹을 때까지 기다리지 못하면 너는 혼자 가야 할 거야.
2. (whom → who) 자기 책을 잊고 온 학생은 오늘밤 기분이 나쁠 것입니다.
3. (us → our) 우리 선생님은 우리가 학급에서 스페인어를 말하는 것을 좋아하지 않으십니다.
4. (me → mine) 네 고양이는 내것보다 훨씬 더 크다.
5. (him → his) 조지는 어제 자기 친구 한 사람을 학급으로 데려왔습니다.
6. (me → mine) 빌은 연필 가져오는 것을 잊어버리고, 내게 빌렸습니다.
7. (your → yours) 내가 내 숙제를 할 수 있으면, 너도 분명히 네 숙제를 할 수 있을 거야.
8. (hisself → himself) 그의 아들은 자주 말썽을 부립니다.
9. (ourself → ourselves) 형과 나는 늘 직접 운전하여 극장에 갑니다.
10. (yourself → yourselves) 너희 둘은 시간을 낭비하기보다는 공부를 하여 더욱 스스로를 도울 수 있어.

[EXERCISE 8]

1. (who) 감독은 최고 자격을 갖춘 사람을 고용할 것입니다.
2. (her) 그녀 외에는 누구도 걱정을 가져오지 않았습니다.
3. (he) 맨 앞줄에 있는 사람들은 낸시, 짐 그리고 그 사람이었습니다.
4. (Whom) 당신은 오스틴으로 누구를 찾아갔습니까?
5. (whom) 브라이언은 누구와 이야기하고 있습니까?
6. (hers) 그의 신발은 그녀의 신발보다는 훨씬 새 겁니다.
7. (me) 그들은 당신과 내게 자기들의 자리를 제공하였습니다.
8. (she) 질문을 한 것은 그녀였습니다.
9. (his) 아무도 그녀가 콘테스트에서 우승한 것에 놀라지 않았습니다.
10. (him) 당신과 그 사이에는 아무런 비밀이 없어야 합니다.
11. (Who) 그 질문을 한 것은 누구였지요?
12. (he) 오직 그 사람만이 시험에 대해 잊어버렸습니다.
13. (mine) 비쉬는 저의 좋은 친구입니다.
14. (who) 그녀는 누가 파티를 여는지 알고 싶어합니다.
15. (them) 당신과 그들이 없으면 소풍은 아무런 재미가 없을 것입니다.
16. (who) 누가 통화 중인지 저는 알 수가 없습니다.
17. (himself) 존은 모든 숙제를 혼자서 했습니다.
18. (me) 이것은 스코트와 그의 구이, 그리고 나를 찍은 사진입니다.
19. (him) 그를 제외한 모든 사람들이 시험을 잘 보았습니다.
20. (I) 당신이 저라면, 휴가를 어디로 가시겠습니까?

credéntial [kridénʃəl] n. 자격(= qualification) give a party : 파티를 열다 figure out : 파악하다

Translations and Explanatory Answers

[**EXERCISE 9**]

1. (their → his) 미국문학반의 모든 이는 내일 자기들의 교재를 받을 것입니다.
2. (their → his) 누군가 자기 담배를 싱크대 안에다 꺼버렸습니다.
3. (her → their) 여왕과 딸은 승마를 하며 많은 자유시간을 보냅니다.
4. (my → our) 형과 저는 호수가에서 주말을 보낼 것입니다.
5. (their → his) 아무도 자기 논문을 제때에 제출하지 않은 것이 놀랍습니다.
6. (their → his) 남자들 중에 아무도 최근에 머리를 깎은 사람이 없습니다.
7. (their → its) 그 가족은 자기네 여름 집을 팔았습니다.
8. (his → their) 빌과 톰이 최근에 자기 식구들을 방문했던 것을 아무도 몰랐습니다.
9. (their → his) 마틴이나 존스는 자기 기사를 다음에 낼 것입니다.
10. (their → its) 교수단은 월례회의를 취소하였습니다.

put out : (불을) 끄다   on horseback : 승마로

[**EXERCISE 10**]

1. (o) 텍사스와 멕시코를 나누는 강은 리오그란데입니다.
2. (which → who) 한 친구가 제 아들을 치료하고 있는 의사를 추천하였습니다.
3. (o) 그녀의 머리를 만지는 미용사는 매우 좋은 분입니다.
4. (which → who) 그 법안을 소개한 상원의원이 지난 선거에서 패배하였습니다.
5. (who → which) 아프리카에 살고 있는 호랑이들은 위험에 처해 있습니다.
6. (o) 작품이 전시 중인 화가는 텍사스 토박이입니다.
7. (o) 문을 열어둔 골동품가게를 누군가 털었습니다.
8. (o) 필리스가 빌린 녹음기는 제것입니다.
9. (whom → which) 농작물이 필요로 하는 비는 결코 오지 않았습니다.
10. (o) 그가 말한 이점들은 수없이 많습니다.

treat [tri:t] v. 치료하다 beautícian [bju:tíʃən] n. 미용사 senator n. (미) 상원의원 bill n. 법안 deféat [difí:t] v. 물리치다 endánger [endéindʒər] v. 위태롭게 하다 be on the display : 전시중인 Texan n. 텍사스주 사람 antique shop : 골동품가게 leave unlócked : 열어두다 crop [krɔp] n. 농작물, 수확 advántage [ædvǽntidʒ] n. 이점 númerous [njú:mərəs] adj. 수많은

[**Actual Test 11**]

1. (D, has been announced) 주어 schedule이 비인칭, 단수이므로 동사 역시 단수이며 수동일 것.

이번 강의 스케줄이 강의위원회에서 발표되었습니다.

2. (C, go) 'Here/There+V+S' 구문에서 뒤의 주어가 복수이다.

자, 마지막 남은 케이크와 아이스크림이 나갑니다.

3. (A, is not known) where to do and how to do는 단수로 취급한다.

그녀를 어디서 어떻게 찾을 것인지 우리에게 알려지지 않았습니다.

4. (B, enable → enables) 주어(The ability)・동사(enables)가 일치하는지 확인할 것

concéal [kənsí:l] v. 숨기다 cámouflage [kǽmɑflɑ:ʒ] n. 위장 defénceless [difénslis] adj. 무방비의

위장으로 자신들을 숨기는 능력은 어떤 다른 방어능력이 없는 동물들이 살아남는 것을 가능하게 합니다.

5. (A, were → was) 주어・동사의 일치 확인

그 학교의 가장 유명한 동창생은 5월말에 잡혀있는 졸업식과 관련행사에 초대되었습니다.

6. (D, industry → industries) 'one of 복수' (여럿 중에 하나)

ádvertising [ǽdvərtaiziŋ] n. 광고(= ad.) strictly adv. 엄격히 régulate [régjuleit] v. 규제하다

현재, 광고는 미국에서 가장 엄격히 규제되는 산업 중의 하나입니다.

7. (D, move → moved) 시제일치 문제. last September로 과거시제임을 알 수 있다.

스미스 가족은 지난 1월에 이사를 온 이래 작은 아파트에서 살아왔습니다.

8. (B, have searching → have searched) 시제일치 문제. Over the past few years로 완료형시제 문장임을 확인한다.

means n. 수단 hérpes vírus : 포진 바이러스

지난 몇 년 동안, 의학연구원들은 독감바이러스를 통제할 수 있는 수단을 연구해왔습니다.

9. (C, is → will be) 시제일치 문제. For some time now로 미래시제 문장임을 확인

tightly adv. 단단히 National Advertising Committee : 국립광고위원회

현재 당분간, 텔레비전 광고는 광고위원회로부터 단단히 통제를 받게 됩니다.

10. (B, you → one/he) 대명사 one은 3인칭으로 받는다.

만약 누군가 자신을 존중하지 않으면, 그는 다른 사람들이 자신을 존중하기를 기대할 수 없습니다.

11. (C, were → was) 주어・동사의 일치 확인

1980년에 뉴욕주에서 일어난 일은 대통령의 캄보디아 침공명령의 결과였습니다.

12. (C, their → our) 인칭대명사의 일치 확인

renéw v. 갱신하다

유학생문제 전국연합에 소속되어 있는 우리들은 회원증을 3월에 갱신해야 합니다.

13. (B, are → is) 주절의 주어는 the money이다.

Basic Grammar for English Tests

traveler's check : 여행자 수표 cable [kéibl] v. 송신하다, 송금하다 sufficient [səfíʃənt] adj. 충분한

내 여행자 수표도, 아버지가 송금해주신 돈도 표를 구입하기엔 충분하지 않습니다.

14. (A, have been → has been) 주어가 little rain이다.
high préssure área : 고압지대
그 주의 대부분을 차지하는 고압지대 때문에 최근 2주일 동안 비가 거의 내리지 않았습니다.

15. (C, their → his) 주어는 Everyone이고, 단수로 취급받는다.
시험을 치는 모든 이는 3주일 후에 성적표를 받을 것입니다.

16. (D, their → its) 'the eagle's = its'
objéct [əbdʒékt] v. 반대하다(—to) prédatory [prédətɔri] adj. 약탈적인
그는 독수리의 약탈적인 본성 때문에 독수리가 국가 상징새로 선정되는 것에 강하게 반대하였습니다.

17. (A, is → are) few airports가 주어로 복수이다.
미국에서 뉴욕의 비행장만큼 현대적인 것은 거의 없습니다.

18. (B, develop → develops) 주어인 Not one은 단수이다.
seed n. 종자, 씨 devélop v. 성장하다(= grow)
1천 개의 씨앗에서 건강한 식물로 성장하는 것은 하나도 없습니다. 실험실의 조건에서도 그렇습니다.

19. (C, were → was) 'neither of~'는 단수로 받는다.
altérnative [ɔːltə́ːrnətiv] n. 선택안, 택일안 óutline v. 구체화하다, 윤곽을 잡다 accéptable [əkséptəbl] adj. 수용 가능한 exécutive commíttee : 집행위원회
지난번 회의에서 계획된 두 개의 안 중에 어느 것도 집행위원회에 받아들여지지 않았습니다.

20. (B, were → was) 종속절의 주어는 a serious objection이다.
objéction n. 반대 regulátion [regjuléiʃən] n. 규정(= rule) consúlt [kənsʌ́lt] v. 자문을 구하다
관리들에게 자문을 구하지도 않고 그들이 장기대여의 규정을 바꾼 데에 심각한 반대가 없는 것이 놀랍습니다.

Part II 품사편

Unit 8 명사

[EXERCISE 1]

(1) — (2) a(—) (3) a (4) a (5) a (6) a (7) a
(8) — (9) a (10) a (11) some (12) a
merchant [mə́ːrtʃənt] n. 상인, 업자 a wine testing : 포도주 감정

포도주가 값싸지는 않습니다. 좋은 포도주는 요즈음 돈이 많이 듭니다. 뉴욕의 한 포도주 업자인 브라운씨는 최근에 7만 달러짜리 포도주 한 병을 잃었습니다. 그것은 한 때 미국의 3대 대통령인 토마스 제퍼슨씨의 소유였던 1784년 산 샤토 마르조였습니다. 브라운씨는 그것을 포도주 감정소에 가져가서 탁자 위에 올려놓았습니다. 그 포도주 병은 검은 유리로 만들어져 있어서 웨이터가 그것을 열어치리지 못했습니다. 그가 쟁반으로 병을 쳐서 커다란 구멍을 냈습니다. 포도주의 대부분이 없어졌습니다만 브라운씨는 그 일부를 맛볼 수 있었습니다. 그는 "그리 훌륭하지 않군" 하고 말했습니다만, 그 포도주 병을 잃은 것은 '엄청난 비극'으로 묘사되었습니다.

[EXERCISE 2]

1. (are) 모든 정부들은 범죄를 억제하는 노력을 하고 있습니다.
2. (are) 이 식당에 해충이 있습니다.
3. (have) 군대가 그 집을 점령하였습니다.
4. (are) 경찰이 이 사건에 관심을 가지고 있습니다.
5. (have) 많은 사람들이 그 청원서에 서명을 하였습니다.
6. (are) 이 방의 음향은 매우 좋습니다.
7. (Are) 이 계역에 개 사육장이 있나요?
8. (are) 이 보고서의 통계는 정확하지 않습니다.
9. (Are) 도로사고에 대한 어떤 통계가 있습니까?
10. (have) 많은 종의 나방이 사라졌습니다.
11. (has) 이 종은 초록과 흰색의 반점을 가지고 있습니다.
12. (has) 우리 공장에는 훌륭한 기숙사가 있습니다.
13. (has) 제 수학은 점점 나빠졌습니다.
14. (are) 1마일마다 교차로가 있습니다.
15. (are) 가위가 어디 있어요?

contról crime : 범죄를 억제하다 vérmin [və́ːrmin] n. 해충, 별레 óccupy [ɔ́kjəpài] v. 점령하다, 차지하다 case n. 사건, 사례 petition n. 청원서 acóustics [əkúːstiks] n. 음향효과, 음향학 kénnels n. 개사육장 statístics [stətístiks] n. 통계 spécies [spíːʃi(ː)z] n. 종(류) moth n. 나방 dórmitory [dɔ́ːrmitɔ̀ːri] n. 기숙사 láundry basket : 빨래바구니 belóngings [bilɔ́(ː)ŋiŋz] n. 소유물, 재산 earning n. 소득

[EXERCISE 3]

1. (she) 제인은 훌륭한 음악가입니다. 그녀는 교향악단에서 연주합니다.
2. (he) 제 변호사는 제가 원하는 정보를 자기가 얻었을 때는 제게 전화를 할 것이라고 말했습니다.
3. (his) 당신의 손님이 어제 여기 왔을 때 안경을 두고 갔습니다.
4. (She) 존슨 교수는 훌륭한 과학자입니다. 그녀는 자신의 학문에 대해 노벨상을 받아야 합니다.
5. (her) 영어선생님인 라이언 부인은 실제로 자신의 문법을 알고 있습니다!
6. (his) 화가인 렘브란트는 자기 아내 그림을 여러 장 그렸습니다.
7. (she) 그녀를 어떻게 설명하시겠습니까? 음, 그녀는 열여덟 살쯤의 학생입니다.
8. (her) 이 여권이 어떤 여자 것인지 어떻게 아십니까? - 주인이 그 속에 사진을 가지고 있지요.

9. (she) 제 딸은 언론인으로 일하면서 매우 성공했습니다.
10. (her) 너는 그녀를 모르니까 편지를 쓸 때 'Dear Madam'이라고 시작해야 한다.

[Actual Test **12**]

1. (B, is) acoustics와 같이 -ics로 끝나는 학문명칭들은 단수로 취급한다.
   acoustics [əkúːstiks] *n.* 음향학
   음향학은 자연과학 가운데서도 가장 오래된 것 가운데 하나입니다.

2. (C, are) deer는 단수/복수 동일형인데, 보어인 animals가 복수임이 단서이다.
   antler [ǽntlər] *n.* (사슴의) 가지모양의 뿔
   사슴은 세상에서 가지 모양의 뿔을 가진 유일한 동물입니다.

3. (D, a boyfriend of my sister's) 이중소유격 of one's
   쇼핑센터에서 누이의 남자친구를 보았습니다.

4. (A, a stone's throw) within a stone's throw
   within a stone's throw 돌을 던지면 닿을 만한 거리에 있는
   그녀의 아파트는 우리 집에서 돌 던지면 닿을 거리에 있습니다.

5. (C, book store) 복합명사 : 명사+명사

6. (D, newspaper reporters) 'one of+복수명사'
   로저 브라운은 미국에서 가장 성공한 신문기자들 가운데 한 사람입니다.

7. (A, Ann Landers was mayor of Austin, Texas) A Republican과 동격인 주어와 동사, 보어가 모두 필요하다.
   공화당원인 앤 랜더스는 1946년부터 1958년까지 텍사스주 오스틴의 시장이었습니다.

8. (C, the ideas of → the idea of) 여기서 idea는 단수개념이 옳다.
   patent [pǽtənt] *n.* 특허 relay [ríːlei] *v.* 전달하다, 중계하다 via [vai] *prep.* -을 거쳐, 경유하여
   벨 박사는 전화를 통해서 소리를 전달하기 위해 빛을 사용하는 아이디어로 1888년에 특허를 받았습니다.

9. (A, man → men) they라는 복수대명사로 받았으므로 주어는 복수이다.
   pioneer [pàiəníər] *n.* 개척자, 선구자
   서부의 개척자적인 남성들은 동부에서보다 일할 기회를 더 많이 가졌습니다.

10. (C, century ago → centuries ago) '수세기 전'이라는 복수의미로 표현해야 한다.
    fireworks [fáiərwə̀ːrk] *n.* 폭죽, 불꽃놀이
    불꽃놀이는 수세기 전에 중국에서 비롯되었는데, 마르코 폴로에 의해 유럽으로 전해졌습니다.

11. (A, characteristics → characteristic) 부정관사 a가 붙어있으므로 단수이다.

predator [prédətər] *n.* 육식동물 parasite [pǽrəsàit] *n.* 기생충 characteristic [kæ̀riktərístik] *n.* 특징 at the expense of ~을 희생하여, ~을 비용으로
육식동물과 기생충은 공통된 기본 특징을 함께 가지고 있습니다. 둘 다 다른 생물들을 희생하여 생존한다는 것입니다.

12. (C, they include → it includes) mathematics는 복수형이 아니다.
    classify [klǽsəfài] *v.* 분류하다 include [inklúːd] *v.* 포함하다 element [éləmənt] *n.* 요소
    수학은 예술이나 과학이라고 단순히 분류하기 어렵습니다. 왜냐하면 둘의 요소를 다 가지고 있기 때문입니다.

13. (C, their → its) 종속절의 주어가 the friendship이므로 단수 its로 받아야 한다.
    reach a highest point : 최고점에 달하다
    헤밍웨이와 피처럴드의 우정이 최고조에 달한 것은 1930년대였습니다.

14. (B, equipments → equipment) equipment는 집합명사로 복수형이 없다.
    manufacture [mæ̀njəfǽktʃər] *v.* 제조 transportation [træ̀nspərtéiʃən] *n.* 교통 equipment [ikwípmənt] *n.* 장비 *cf.* 복수형이 없다.
    교통장비 제조는 캘리포니아 주의 주요한 산업으로 자리합니다.

15. (D, they are → he is) a famous movie star는 단수로 받아야 한다.
    just as ~ : ~와 꼭 같이
    사람들은 흔히 유명 영화배우를 마치 실제생활의 인물인 것처럼 그들을 보는 것에 흥미를 가집니다.

16. (A, its → his) a scientist → his
    hypotheses [haipéθəsis] *n.* 가설 experimentation *n.* 실험
    과학자는 자신의 학문을 주의 깊은 실험을 거친 가설을 바탕으로 수립합니다.

17. (A, Jane's and John's → Jane and John's) car는 한 대로 표현되어 있다.(it)
    break down : 고장나다 fix *v.* 수리하다
    제인과 존의 자동차가 다시 고장났지만, 다행히도 그들은 어떻게 정비를 해야할지 알고 있었습니다.

18. (C, Clinton winning → Clinton's winning) 동명사의 의미상 주어인 소유격
    파티의 회원들은 클린턴이 선거를 아주 쉽게 이긴 것에 놀랐습니다.

Unit *9*   관사

[EXERCISE **1**]

1. (An/The, The, the) 개인은 개인적인 자유를 기대할 모든 권리를 가지고 있습니다. 개인의 자유는 쟁취할 가치가 있습니다.

Basic Grammar for English Tests

2. (the, the) 문간에 있는 사람은 누구지요? 우체부입니다.
3. (the) 외출할 때 슈퍼에 가서 버터 좀 사오시겠어요?
4. (an, the) 저는 오후에 진찰예약이 있습니다. 병원에 가야 해요.
5. (the, a) 우리는 간밤에 극장에 가서 《햄릿》을 보았습니다. 멋진 연극이었습니다.
6. (the, the, the) 우리는 공휴일을 시골이나 산, 또는 바닷가에서 보내고 싶습니다.
7. (The, the, the, a) 이게 앞방입니다. 천장과 벽은 장식이 필요한데 마루는 정돈이 잘되어 있습니다. 우리는 카펫을 깔게 될 겁니다.
8. (The, the, he, —) 세계의 역사는 전쟁의 역사입니다.
9. (a, the) 우리 시내 한복판에 새로운 슈퍼를 짓고 있습니다.
10. (the, the) 지금 네 어머니 어디 계시니? 부엌에 계신 것 같아요.

[EXERCISE 2]

1. (—) 우리는 자정이 되기 전에 집에 가야 합니다.
2. (—) 우리는 석양이 되기 전에 마을에 도착했습니다.
3. (The) 내가 주문한 점심이 타버렸습니다.
4. (—) 테라스에서 점심을 먹습니다.
5. (—) 늘 4시에 차를 마시나요?
6. (the) 우리는 석양을 보러 여기 왔습니다.
7. (a) 저는 리츠호텔에서 멋진 점심을 먹었습니다.
8. (—) 저는 정말 피곤해서 자야겠어요.
9. (the) 네 신발은 침대 밑에 있어.
10. (a) 우리는 예쁜 새 침대를 샀어요.
11. (the) 우리는 교회 밖에서 사진을 찍었습니다.
12. (—) 우리는 일요일에 항상 교회에 갑니다.
13. (a) 공장에서 일해 본적이 있습니까?
14. (—) 수잔은 지금 수업을 듣고 있습니다.
15. (—) 우리 아버지는 14살 때 어부로 바다에 나가셨어요.
16. (—) 언제 대학에 가기를 원하나요?
17. (—) 그녀가 얼마동안 입원해 있을 건가요?
18. (the) 병원에서 파업이 있어요.
19. (the) 직장에서 언제 퇴근하나요?
20. (the, —) 저는 나폴레옹의 생애에 대해 잘 모릅니다.

[Actual Test 13]

1. (B, a dress) 여기서 a는 any의 뜻.
  제인은 붉은 색의 드레스를 입었을 때 언제나 가장 잘 보입니다.
2. (B, a) William Phillip과 a United States senator가 동격이다.
  미국 미네소타주 상원의원인 윌리엄 필립이 1860년대 공화당의 설립을 도왔습니다.
3. (B, by the hour) 계량의 단위 by the
  일반적으로 이 회사의 노동자들은 급여를 시간당으로 받습니다.
4. (C, The rarely) clover 전체를 대표할 때는 the
  보기 힘든 네 잎 클로버는 흔히 행운의 증표로 생각됩니다.
5. (D, the) 'the+비교급+the+명사, the+비교급+the+명사' 구문
  자기장이 셀수록, 발전기가 생산하는 전압이 높습니다.
6. (C, the day → a day/each day) a를 붙여 측정단위의 빈도 수를 나타낸다.
  in length 길이 gain weight 살이 찌다 at the rate of ~비율로 nursing n.(adj). 수유(하는), 양육(하는), 간호(하는)
  푸른 고래는 태어날 때 길이가 20~30피트 정도이고, 수유기에는 하루에 200파운드씩이나 몸무게가 늘어납니다.
7. (A, an unit → a unit) a/an은 모음의 철자가 아니고 발음에 따라 변한다.
  joule [dʒuːl] n. 줄 (에너지의 절대 단위)
  와트는 초당 1줄에 해당하는 힘의 단위이다.
8. (A, a honest → an honest) h는 묵음이다.
  hold an opin on 어떤 생각을 가지다, 의견을 가지다 bring up 기르다, 양육하다
  저는 결혼하여 가족을 부양하는 정직한 남자가 인구를 걱정하면서 독신을 고집하는 남자보다 더 많은 봉사를 한다는 의견을 가졌습니다.
9. (D, clue → a/the clue) clue에 관사를 붙인다.
  dacktyloscopy n. 지문학, 지문학 (= the study of fingerprints)
  지문학은 의학자들에게 알츠하이머병을 탐구하는 단서를 제공합니다.
10. (A, is remarkably → is a remarkably) a remarkably capable organism
  infant [ínfənt] n. 유아 organism [ɔ́ːrgənìzəm] n. 유기체, 생물, 기관
  어떤 과학자들은 갓난아기가 숨쉬기 시작하는 순간부터 놀라운 능력을 가진 생명체라고 주장합니다.
11. (D, a → the)
  physicist [fízisist] n. 물리학자 celebrate [séləbrèit] v. 기리다, 축하하다 centennial [senténiəl] adj. 100주년의
  전 세계의 저명한 물리학자들이 아인슈타인 탄생 100주년을 기념하여 미국에 왔습니다.
12. (B, an → the) old house는 의미상 재 언급되고 있다
  바닥에 먼지가 두껍게 앉아 있었지만 그것은 그 낡은 집이 한때 대단한 저택이었으리라는 증거였습니다.
13. (A, Since beginning → Since the beginning) 동명사가 전치사구의 수식을 받고 있다.
  reproduce [rìːprədúːs] v. 재생하다
  사진이 시작된 이래 발명가들은 자연의 색을 재생하는 사진을 만들려고 노력하였습니다.
14. (A, At end → At the end) 시간의 추이에는 the를 붙인다.
  roar [rɔːr] v. 으르렁거리다, 고함치다 surge [səːrdʒ] n. 큰 파도, 격랑

남북전쟁이 끝날 때, 미국은 4년간 중단되었던 서부확장을 노도와 같이 다시 시작할 준비가 되어있었습니다.

15. (C, of universe → of the universe) 유일한 곳에 the를 붙인다.
    우주의 구조를 이해하려는 사람들의 초기 노력은 신화의 형식을 띄었습니다.

16. (A, the Louisiana → Louisiana) 지명을 나타내는 고유명사는 무관사
    루이지애나주에 있는 뉴올리언스는 미시피강의 입구에 있는 큰 항구입니다.

17. (D, the law and order → law and order) 불가산명사는 무관사
    supposedly adv. 아마, 필경, 소문으로는
    세 사람 이상이 모이는 것은 필경 법과 질서의 이름으로 금지되었을 것입니다.

18. (A, the church → church) 명사의 본래목적
    church 교회·예배
    예배를 마치고 여자들은 그가 미쳤을 거라고 말하며 교회당에 모여 있었습니다.

Unit 10 대명사

[EXERCISE 1]

1. (him) 매일 그와 함께 학교 갑니다.
2. (our) 우리는 새 차를 아주 좋아합니다.
3. (her) 개가 그녀의 다리를 물었습니다.
4. (himself) 존은 회의에 갔습니다.
5. (yourself) 조심하지 않으면 핀에 찔릴 거야.
6. (I) 메리와 저는 영화 보러 갈 것입니다.
7. (his) 각자 자신의 연구를 해야 합니다.
8. (me) 우리끼리 말인데, 난 이 음식이 싫어.
9. (us) 월요일은 우리 교사들을 위한 휴일입니다.
10. (Her, ours) 그녀의 자동차는 우리 차만큼 빠르지 않습니다.

[EXERCISE 2]

1. (nothing) 옷 바구니에 아무것도 없습니다. 비어있어요.
2. (anything) 옷 바구니에 뭔가 있나요? – 아뇨, 비어있어요.
3. (no one/nobody) 통화를 하려해도 전화할 때마다 아무도 없었습니다.
4. (something) 당신이 아주 좋아할 저녁을 준비했어요.
5. (anyone/anybody) 난 너처럼 고집 센 사람은 못 봤어.
6. (something/anything) 본 요리를 주문하시기 전에 뭘 좀 하시겠습니까?
7. (someone/somebody/no one/nobody) 자네를 도울 수 있는 사람을 알고 있어/몰라.
8. (anything) 그는 식탁에 앉았으나 먹을 것이 없었습니다.
9. (anyone/anybody/no one/nobody) 여기 한국말 할 수 있는 사람 있어요/없어요?
10. (anyone/anybody/no one/nobody) 잠시 도와주실 분 누구 있나요/없나요?

[Actual Test 14]

1. (A, she) as ... as she (is kindhearted)
   저는 클럽에서 그녀만큼 마음씨 따뜻한 여자를 알지 못합니다.

2. (A, all of them have their tickets) the party of students는 복수이다.
   브라운 선생님은 학생들의 데리고 역에 가서 모두 표를 가지고 있는지 확인할 것입니다.

3. (C, it) 주어 heat를 받는 대명사는 it이다.
   conduction [kəndʌ́kʃən] n. (열의) 전도
   열이 전도에 의해 이동을 할 때는, 어떤 물질도 동반하지 않고 물질을 통과해서 이동합니다.

4. (D, It is believed) 'It(가주어) ... that 이하 (진주어) ...' 구문
   condensation [kàndənséiʃən] n. 응축, 응고
   태양, 행성, 그리고 다른 별들의 생성은 우주 가스구름의 응축과 함께 시작되었다고 믿어집니다.

5. (B, it easier) 동사 made의 목적어는 it(가목적어)와 to store(진목적어)이다.
   테이프레코드, CD, 컴퓨터 등은 데이터를 편리하고 정확하게 저장하게 하였습니다.

6. (C, of mine) 소유대명사의 형식문제
   He's a favorite of mine. = He is one of my favorites. = He's my favorite.
   어젯밤 오페라의 테너는 내가 가장 좋아하는 사람입니다.

7. (B, that of the United States) budget 대신 that를 씀. 앞의 절에는 여러 나라의 budget라서 복수(budgets)로 썼지만, 미국은 한 국가이므로 단수(that)로 받았다.
   일부 국가들의 예산과는 달리 미국의 그것은 주로 지출에 초점을 맞추고 있습니다.

8. (C, me → I) he와 같은 격. 목적격이 아니라 주격이 들어가는 강조구문
   분명, 행사 취소를 권한 사람은 내가 아니고 그였습니다.

9. (D, they are → he is) no one은 단수로 받는다.
   administrator [ædmínəstrèitər] n. 행정가, 관리
   어떤 관리나 방문객도 교사의 초청을 받지 않고 교실에 들어갈 수는 없습니다.

10. (C, you are → he is) the best of drivers는 he로 받는다.
    아무리 모범운전자라도 피곤하거나 운전상태가 나쁘면 사고

를 낼 수 있습니다.

11. (C, for him → for his) for his work
    physician n. 의사, 특히 내과의사 dermatology [də̀ːrmətɑ́lədʒi] n. 피부학
    의사인 조지 밀러씨는 피부의학 분야에서 자신의 업적으로 유명해졌다.

12. (D, them → it) The field of를 받으므로 단수 it
    infancy n. 초기, 유년기
    사라 해처씨가 지도와 상담 분야에 입문했던 1928년에는 그곳이 아직 초기 단계에 있었습니다.

13. (D, oneself → itself) 무생물(the vine)의 재귀대명사는 itself로 받는다.
    vanilla vine 바닐라 덩굴 rootlets 잔뿌리
    바닐라 덩굴은 잔뿌리를 뻗어내어서 나무에 달라붙습니다.

14. (C, his → their) the other people → their
    deserve [dizə́ːrv] v. …할 가치가 있다, …할 만하다
    다른 사람들의 능력개발을 도우려 하지 않는 사람은 누구도 친구를 가질 가치가 없습니다.

15. (C, them → those (whom)) from conquer의 목적어이어야 함.
    정복자 찰스는 자신을 정복한 사람들로부터 자신을 보호하기 위해 런던탑을 세웠습니다.

16. (A, them → those) interested in의 주어 역할 – those (who are) interested in …
    자연에 관심을 가진 사람들을 위해 그 클럽은 여름에 매주 하이킹과 캠핑을 제공합니다.

17. (B, them → those) those who …
    premise [prémis] n. (논리) 전제 (pl.) 토지나 집의 경내, 구내
    valid [vǽlid] adj. 확실한, 타당한 identification card 신분증 (ID card)
    고용인들과 확실한 신분증이 있는 사람들을 제외하고 누구도 건물 내에 들어올 수 없습니다.

11. (a few) 이 방을 밝게 하려면 그림이 몇 점 필요합니다.
12. (Several) 올해 여러 기업이 파산했습니다.
13. (any) 초콜릿이 남아 있지 않잖아!
14. (any) 낭비할 시간이 없어요.
15. (enough) 우린 벌써 이 기계 때문에 많은 속을 썩었습니다.
16. (Hardly any) 올해는 이 모퉁이에서 사고가 거의 없었습니다.
17. (Neither) 우리는 그 평가를 수용할 수 없습니다. 어느 평가도 충분히 낮지 않습니다.
18. (Both) 두 가지 예 모두 제가 옳다는 것을 증명합니다.
19. (no) 신판에서는 아무런 수정이 없었습니다.
20. (no) 신판에서는 아무런 수정이 없었습니다.

[EXERCISE 2]
1. (some) 바구니에 계란이 약간 있습니다.
2. (some) 그분은 89세신데, 아직도 그에게는 활력이 있습니다.
3. (some) 주말을 대비해 고기와 샐러드를 구입해오세요.
4. (any) 어떤 사람들은 고기를 전혀 먹지 않습니다.
5. (any) 그 깡통에는 비스킷이 전혀 없을 것입니다.
6. (some) 외출하거든 빵을 좀 사오너라.
7. (some) 자녀는 돈을 좀 벌 필요가 있어.
8. (any) 그 사람에 대한 소식이 없어요.
9. (some) 감자 더 있나요? — 예, 접시에 감자가 좀 있어요.
10. (some) 차 좀 더 주시겠어요? — 예.

[EXERCISE 3]
1. (few) 이 대학은 학생들을 위한 장학금이 아주 적습니다.
2. (a little) 미안합니다만, 잠시 이 계산서를 지불하실 것을 요청합니다.
3. (little) 서두르지 않는다면 우리는 열차를 놓칠 것입니다. 남은 시간이 없습니다.
4. (a few) 어려운 텍스트입니다. 사전에서 적지 않은 단어들을 찾아봐야 했습니다.
5. (a few) 이 카탈로그들은 남겨둘 수가 없어요. 남은 게 몇 권밖에 없습니다.
6. (a little) 네가 이 향수를 많이 쓰지 못하게 하겠어. 병에 겨우 조금밖에 없어.
7. (little) 당신이 하는 말이 진실이라도 우리가 할 수 있는 일은 거의 없어요.

[EXERCISE 4]
1. (every) 시글의 거의 모든 가정에 텔레비전을 가지고 있습니다.
2. (each) 여러분 각자를 위한 것이 여기 있습니다.
3. (every) 모든 학생이 영어학습 능력이 있는 것은 아닙니다.

Unit 11 한정사와 수량표시

[EXERCISE 1]
1. (fewer) 우리는 비디오를 작년보다 올해 더 적게 수입했습니다.
2. (less) 올해는 작년보다 비디오의 수요가 더 적었습니다.
3. (A lot of) 많은 자동차가 디자인 결함으로 리콜됩니다.
4. (A lot of) 이 프로젝트에 많은 노력이 들었습니다.
5. (much) 난파선을 찾을 희망이 그리 많지 않습니다.
6. (many) 이것과 비교할 수 있는 사전이 많지 않습니다.
7. (Most of) 그 책의 대부분은 다른 누군가에 의해 쓰여졌습니다.
8. (Most) 대부분의 잡지는 광고를 싣고 있습니다.
9. (Most) 대부분의 금속은 녹슬기 쉽습니다.
10. (a little) 이 커피에 우유를 조금 넣어주세요.

4. (every) 우리 자동차여행 단체는 여러분이 힘들 때 모든 지원을 해드릴 것입니다.
5. (each) 입장권은 각 7달러씩입니다.
6. (every) 시골의 모든 도로를 보수하는 것 같습니다.
7. (each) 그들이 각자 인생에서 그렇게 새로운 출발을 하는 것은 행운입니다.
8. (each) 그 둘은 잘 했고, 각자 상을 받을 것입니다.
9. (every) 당신은 이 회사에서 잘 할 수 있는 모든 기회를 얻을 것입니다.
10. (each) 그에게 두 번씩이나 전화를 했는데 매번 외출 중이었습니다.

[EXERCISE 5]

1. (the other) 존이 하루는 저를 보러왔습니다. 금요일로 생각됩니다.
2. (the other) 회사로 가는 길에 낯선 두 사람을 보았어요. 한사람은 제게 인사를 했고 다른 사람은 하지 않았습니다.
3. (others) 어떤 사람들은 항상 창문을 열어두는 것을 좋아하는데 다른 사람들은 그렇지 않습니다.
4. (another) 오늘은 그를 볼 수 없습니다. 다른 날 만나야겠어요.
5. (the next) 우리는 작은 마을에서 그날밤을 보내고 다음 날 여행을 계속 했습니다.
6. (another/the other, the other) 빌과 (또)다른 소년은 마당에서 놀고 있고, 다른 소녀들은 앞방에 있습니다.
7. (another) 시내 중심가로 향하는 또 다른 도로가 있을 것입니다.
8. (other) 시내 중심가로 향하는 다른 도로들이 있을 것입니다.

[EXERCISE 6]

1. (Either) 언제 만날까요? 7시 아니면 7시 반? — 상관없어요. 저는 둘 다 괜찮아요.
2. (Neither) 저 스크루드라이버들을 쓸 수 없어요. 둘 다 그 일에는 맞지 않아요.
3. (either) 통화자가 누군지 모르겠어. 자네 어머니 아니면 숙모일거야.
4. (neither) 1년 전에 존을 만났는데, 이후로는 보지도 듣지도 못했습니다.
5. (either) 저 두 지원자들에 대해 자네가 좋은 사람을 말해보게. 나는 두 사람 다 싫어!
6. (neither) 당신이 우리에게 편지를 두통 보낸 것으로 아는데, 우리는 둘 다 못 받았습니다.

[EXERCISE 7]

1. much   2. a little   3. those   4. fewer
5. too much   6. this   7. too much   8. few
9. less   10. too much

[EXERCISE 8]

1. is   2. are   3. are   4. belongs   5. are   6. is
7. is   8. Do   9. Does   10. Do

[Actual Test 15]

1. (B, anyone else) anyone else는 강조의 표시
   제인은 어느 누가 말하든지 관심이 전혀 없었습니다.
2. (A, each state) 주절의 동사가 has이므로 주어는 단수이어야 한다.
   미국 상원에서 각 주는 인구에 상관없이 균등하게 한 명씩의 상원의원을 가집니다.
3. (B, each other) 둘이 서로의 뜻은 each other
   에이미와 로라는 아주 친한 친구들이어서 서로 자주 선물을 주고받았습니다.
4. (D, Unlike most) '거의 다, 대부분'의 여러 가지 표현: most 명사, most of the 명사, most of them, almost all (of) -
   cat family 고양이과
   고양이과의 다른 대부분의 동물들과 달리 표범은 나무를 잘 오릅니다.
5. (A, Almost all of) '대부분, 거의 다'의 표현
   opponent [əpóunənt] n. 상대, 적
   부시는 선거를 이기지 못할 것으로 생각돼요, 확실해요. 그 나라 사람들 대부분이 그의 상대에게 투표했어요.
6. (A, five times as hard as ordinary glass) 배수비교 five times as ... as / than
   temper [témpər] v. 불리다, 담금질하다
   담금질한 유리는 일반유리 강도의 5배나 올라갈 수 있습니다.
7. (C, chapter fifteen) chapter fifteen = the fifteenth chapter
   기말고사가 교재의 전편 절반에서 나올 거야. 이건 우리가 15장을 끝내야 한다는 뜻이지.
8. (A, Few artists) few는 부정어이고, more ... than 구문임
   뉴욕의 현대미술관에서 데이비드 로렌스보다 더 행운의 기회를 잡았던 화가는 거의 없었습니다.
9. (B, a lot of) furniture는 불가산명사
   큰 아파트를 샀기 때문에 그는 가구도 많이 사야할 것입니다.
10. (C, tens of thousands of) 부정확한 수는 수에 복수형 -s를 붙인다.
    jubilant [dʒúːbələnt] adj. 기쁨에 넘치는, 환성을 지르는

몇 분만에 수만 명의 환호하는 한국인들이 거리에 쏟아져 들어왔습니다.

11. (C, Only a loaf of French bread) 물질명사의 수량표시
저는 오늘 할인점에서 프랑스빵 한 덩이만 샀습니다.

12. (C, has been → have been) 'half of 복수명사'는 복수로 받는다.
meteor [míːtiər] n. 운석, 별똥 crater [kréitər] n. 분화구, 운석구멍
고대 운석구멍의 거의 절반이 캘리포니아 주 중부-동부에서 발견되었습니다.

13. (A, All the day long → All day long) 무관사 All day long
unsuspecting adj. 의심하지 않는, 수상히 여기지 않는
총으로 어느 무심한 동물을 쏜 때를 제외하면, 하루종일 그는 한번도 아내를 걱정시키거나 두렵게도 하지 않았습니다.

14. (A, Some the → Some (of the)) Some of the ...가 맞는 표현
일부 대형 제지기계는 하루에 3백만 파운드 이상의 종이를 생산할 수 있습니다.

15. (A, hardly no sign of → hardly any sign of) hardly가 이미 부정어이다. (부정어 ... any)
the management 경영진 the union 노동조합 dispute n. 싸움, 논쟁
임금과 노동조건에 대한 싸움에서 경영진과 노조 사이에 아직까지 어떤 합의의 징후도 없었습니다.

16. (D, the Chapter 6 → Chapter 6/the 6th Chapter) 서수를 표기할 때는 정관사 동반
evaluate [ivǽljuèit] v. 평가하다, 가치를 검토하다
어떤 시험을 평가하는데 포함되는 다른 많은 그런 점들은 제6장에서 논의되고 있습니다.

17. (B, seven-days → seven-day) 수를 포함하여 한정사 역할을 할 때는 단수로 표기한다. a ten year old boy, a two-week vacation ...
그는 다른 노동자들이 더 많이 쉰다는 사실에도 불구하고 올해 7일간의 휴가만 가졌습니다.

18. (B, much → many) 복수인 the billions of stars를 받는 말
galaxy n. 우리은하계 stable adj. 안정된
우리은하계의 수십억 개의 별 가운데 그 행성들에서 생명체를 생성시키기에 충분히 안정적인 것들이 얼마나 될까요?

19. (A, exit → exists) 양을 표현하는 much는 단수를 받는다.
인간과 동물에게 있어서 여러 가지 체소들과 그 가치에 관해 알아야 할 것이 많이 있습니다.

20. (C, much → many) required courses는 복수보통명사이므로 수를 받는 many
required courses 필수과목

심리학과는 이번 학기에 개설된 필수과목이 많지 않아서 비난받았습니다.

21. (C, in few cases → in a few cases) 부정인 few cases가 아니고 긍정인 a few cases가 바르다.
tax return 세금신고(서) file v. 정리하다, 기록하다, 제출하다 annually [ǽnjuəli] adv. 매년, 해마다 submit [səbmít] v. 제출하다
일반적으로, 세금신고서는 매년 부과되지만 어떤 경우에는 6개월마다 부과됩니다.

22. (B, the number → the amount) sugar는 대표적인 불가산명사이므로 number(수)가 아니고 amount(양)가 바르다.
최근의 보고에 따르면, 미국인들이 소비하는 설탕의 양은 해마다 크게 변하지 않습니다.

23. (B, thousands interview → thousand interview) 형용사로 쓰일 때 수의 표현은 단수로
Federal Writers Project 미국작가연맹
1950년대에는 옛 노예들에 대한 인터뷰의 3천 건 이상이 작가연맹 회원들에 의해 실시되었습니다.

24. (B, kinds of person → kinds of persons) 동사가 복수인 are이므로 수를 일치할 것.
앞서가는 학자들은 흔히 평생 지적인 도전을 즐긴 사람들입니다.

25. (D, herb → herbs)
valerian n. 쥐오줌풀 perennial adj/n. 다년생의/다년생 식물 shrub n. 덤불, 잡목
쥐오줌풀군은 200여 종의 다년생 또는 1년생 허브와 몇 종의 덤불을 포함하고 있습니다.

Unit 12 형용사

[EXERCISE 1]

1. (broken) 깨진 접시들이 바닥에 놓여있었습니다.
2. (trembling) 떨고있는 어린이들에게 보온을 위해 담요가 지급되었습니다.
3. (crying) 온정적인 친구들은 사고로 울부짖는 희생자들을 위로하려고 하였습니다.
4. (interesting) 재미있는 테니스경기는 많은 흥분을 자아냅니다.
5. (burning) 제인은 불타는 건물을 보자 즉시 소방서에 알렸습니다.
6. (excited) 배가 가라앉는다는 것을 알아차렸을 때 흥분한 승객들이 구명정에 뛰어들었습니다.
7. (smiling) 웃고 있는 모나리자가 파리의 루브르박물관에 전시되어 있습니다.
8. (frightening) 바람이 아주 무서운 소리를 내서 어린이들은 부모님 방으로 뛰어들어갔습니다.
9. (frightened) 겁에 질린 인질들은 오로지 혼자 있고 싶었습니다.

10. (advancing) 우리는 시내 건너편에서 전진하는 군대를 보았습니다.
11. (approving) 우리는 해리스 부인의 만족스런 미소로 우리의 연설이 좋았다는 것을 알았습니다.
12. (approved) 우리의 대표는 대중들에게 인가된 계획을 발표하였습니다.
13. (blowing) 허리케인 몰아치는 바람이 해안구조물을 파괴하였습니다.
14. (boring) 우리는 중앙극장에서 영화를 보려고 했는데 친구들이 재미없는 영화라고 말했습니다.
15. (cleaning) 메리의 청소서비스는 매주 수요일에 옵니다.
16. (cleaned) 세탁한 신발은 말리려고 햇볕에 놓여있었습니다
17. (closed) 열쇠 없이 닫힌 방을 들어가는 것이 어렵다는 것을 우리는 알았습니다.
18. (crowded) 우리가 그 붐비는 방에 들어갔을 때 저는 사촌들을 발견했습니다.
19. (aching) 제임슨 의사는 동생에게 아픈 발을 올려보라고 말했습니다.
20. (parked) 경찰은 입구를 막고 있는 주차된 자동차들을 견인하였습니다.

tremble [trémbəl] v. 떨다 warmth [wɔːrmθ] n. 온기, 따뜻함 compassionate [kəmpǽʃənit] adj. 자비로운, 온정적인 console [kənsóul] v. 달래다, 위로하다 excitement [iksáitmənt] n. 흥분, 흥미 notice v. 알아차리다, 통지하다 on display 전시중인, 진열하는 hostage [hástidʒ] n. 볼모, 인질 advancing 전진하는 advanced 앞서간, 진보의 approving 만족하는, 찬성하는 approved 승인된, 인가된 representative [rèprizentéitiv] n. 대표 present v. 발표하다 blowing (바람이) 불어오는 blown 부푼, 숨이 찬, 결판난 waterfront n. 해안, 물가; 부두, 선창

[EXERCISE 2]

1. nicely 2. nice 3. badly 4. bad 5. good
6. well 7. smoothly 8. smooth

[EXERCISE 3]

1. (least → less) 그 우주선은 재활용이기에 다른 우주선보다 덜 비쌉니다.
2. (quick → quickly) 공연이 끝나자 군중들은 서둘러 떠났습니다.
3. (real → really) 신부는 새로운 시댁 식구들에게 아주 공손하였습니다.
4. (sweetly → sweet) 모두가 좋은 향기가 났기에 좋은 향수를 고르기가 어려웠습니다.
5. (considerable → considerably) 상당히 오래 기다린 끝에 선생님들은 급여를 인상 받았습니다.
6. (probable → probably) 코끼리들은 정부가 현 법규를 고치지 않으면 아마 멸종할 것입니다.

in-laws (구어) 결혼, 재혼 등으로 맺어지는 새 식구들. son-in-law, mother-in-law 등의 총칭 grant v. 수여하다, 부여하다 become extinct 멸종하다

[EXERCISE 4]

1. farther/further 2. oldest 3. worse 4. lesser
5. latest 6. further 7. well 8. last 9. oldest
10. smaller 11. less 12. older 13. more/most
14. better 15. best 16. farthest/furthest
17. oldest/eldest 18. elder/older 19. least 20. most

[EXERCISE 5]

1. (with) 같은 나이 또래의 어린이들과 비교해서 제인은 아주 큽니다.
2. (best) 아픈 이후에 그는 시험에서 최선을 다하는 것 같지 않습니다.
3. (the most) 유치원의 모든 어린이들 가운데, 찰스가 가장 활동적입니다.
4. (more) 열심히 공부할수록 더 많은 것을 학습하게 됩니다.
5. (less) 이 시험은 첫 번째 것보다 훨씬 덜 어렵습니다.
6. (better) 두 번의 시축 가운데 두 번째가 분명히 더 나왔습니다.
7. (faster) 빨리 달릴수록 그는 숨쉬기가 더 어려워졌습니다.
8. (less) 등반을 높이 할수록 호흡할 수 있는 산소가 더 적어집니다.
9. (easier) 그는 역사가 화학보다 더 쉽습니다.
10. (to) 그녀의 시험점수는 그보다 나았습니다.
11. (wilder) 아이를 많이 꾸짖을수록 아이는 더 거칠어집니다.
12. (worst) 미적분학을 들은 것은 그의 인생에서 최악의 경험이었습니다.

compare to ~에 비유하다 compare with ~와 비교하다 definitely adv. 명백히, 확실히, 분명 calculus [kǽlkjələs] n. 미적분학

[EXERCISE 6]

1. (with → to) 직사각형은 정사각형과 비슷합니다.
2. (same → the same) 진호와 미나는 같은 나라 출신입니다.
3. (to → from) 소녀와 소년은 다릅니다. 소녀들은 소년과 다릅니다.
4. (with → as) 제 막내 동생은 사촌과 동갑입니다.
5. (with → to) 늑대는 개와 비슷합니다.
6. (same → the same) 제인과 빌은 동시에 말을 시작했습니다.
7. (like → alike) 너와 나는 비슷한 책을 가지고 있어. 우리 책은 같아.
8. (alike → like) 어떤 의미에서 타운은 시티와 같습니다.
9. (alike → like) 어떤 의미에서 오토바이는 자전거와 같습니다.
10. (like → alike) 기숙사와 아파트는 많은 부분 같습니다.

Basic Grammar for English Tests

[Actual Test **16**]

1. (B, enough) enough가 형용사로 명사 앞에서 수식하는 경우이다.
   모퉁이 서점은 우리 학급의 모든 학생들을 위한 충분한 교과서를 준비하지 못했습니다.

2. (C, enough to make) enough가 부사로 쓰인 경우.
   make the point that ~을 주장하다 case of sour grapes (이솝우화의) 신 포도 이야기
   네 것은 신 포도의 사례가 아니라고 주장하기에는 충분하지 않아.

3. (C, asleep) asleep은 서술용법으로만 쓰인다.
   아메리칸 드림은 잠자는 사람에게는 오지 않습니다.

4. (B, worth the price) be worth 명사 또는 be worthy of -ing
   자네 컴퓨터는 값어치를 못하는 것 같아.

5. (B, a typical public) 형용사의 어순: 일반 성질 → 특수 성질
   public company 주식회사, 법인, 상장 회사 (cf. private company 비상장 회사 또는 개인기업)
   전형적인 주식회사에서 사장이 주식을 그렇게 조금 보유하고 있다는 것을 국민의 몇 퍼센트나 알고 있을까요?

6. (D, the southernmost city) 방위나 위치의 최상급은 east/west/south/north에다 -most/-ernmost를 붙여 만든다.
   플로리다주 마이애미는 미국에서 가장 남쪽 도시입니다.

7. (C, more strawberries than) more ... than 구문으로 최상급의 뜻을 표현한다.
   캘리포니아주는 미국에서 다른 어떤 주보다 딸기를 많이 생산합니다.

8. (C, lively → a live) tree alive 또는 living tree가 맞는 표현이다.
   과학자들은 살아 있는 가장 오래된 나무를 연구하는데, 이유는 그것이 여러 문제에 관해 많은 것을 알려줄 수 있기 때문입니다.

9. (D, awake wide → wide awake) wide는 부사로서 형용사 awake 앞에 위치
   꿈을 꾸는 동안 인체는 잠을 자지만, 두뇌의 생각하는 부분은 활짝 깨어있습니다.

10. (C, like → alike) alike가 맞다.
    antibiotic [æntibaiótik] n. 항생물질 treatment [trí:tmənt] n. 치료 fingi [fíŋgi] n. fungus(버섯)의 복수
    인간의 질병 치료에 쓰이는 일부 항생물질들은 버섯과 박테리아에서 얻어진다는 점에서는 같습니다.

11. (D, similar with → similar to) similar to가 맞는 표현
    Afrikaans (남아프리카) 표준 네덜란드 말 (Dutch) Flemish 플란더즈 말
    아프리칸어는 유럽에서 사용되지 않는 유럽 어원의 유일한 언어로서, 플란더즈 말과 비슷한 네덜란드 어원을 가지고 있습니다.

12. (A, to move → of moving) be capable of -ing (= be able to do = have the capability of -ing)
    인간의 갈비뼈는 움직일 수 있어서 숨쉴 때 폐가 확대될 수 있도록 합니다.

13. (C, of → with) concerned with (명사)
    be concerned with (명사) ~에 관심을 가지다, 관련이 있다 be concerned about ~을 걱정하다/염려하다 birth control pills 피임약
    많은 의사들이 피임약의 장기적인 잠재 효과에 관심을 가지게 되었습니다.

14. (D, convincing → convinced) be convinced of가 맞다
    broad-minded adj. 마음이 넓은, 도량이 큰 be convinced of ~을 확신하는
    워싱턴은 그들의 태도를 알았지만, 그는 그들의 능력을 확신했기 때문에 그런 사람들을 중요한 직책에 임명할 만큼 마음이 넓었습니다.

15. (C, world new → new world) 명사를 수식하는 형용사의 순서. 일반적인 표현이 특정한 표현보다 앞선다.
    set a record 기록을 수립하다
    1936년 올림픽 경기에서 제시 오웬스는 트랙경기에서 세계 신기록을 수립하고 금메달 4개를 땄습니다.

16. (C, great first → first great) 같은 형용사 가운데서도 서수가 앞에 온다.
    relief [rilí:f] n. 구조, 구원 sanitary [sǽnətèri] n/adj. 위생의, 보건/의
    우리나라 최초의 훌륭한 개인구조단체인 미국위생위원회에 여성들이 큰 역할을 하였습니다.

17. (A, As → Like) like (명사) ~처럼
    currency [kə́:rənsi] n. 통화, 화폐 the gold standard 금본위제
    다른 모든 국가들처럼 미국도 금본위제에 따라 달러를 통화 단위로 규정하곤 했습니다.

18. (B, like → alike) A and B look alike ... A와 B가 같아 보이다
    rabbit 집토끼 hare 산토끼 mistake for 잘못보다, 착각하다
    집토끼와 산토끼는 아주 같아 보여서 서로 자주 착각합니다.

19. (C, mostly → most) most interested in으로 interest를 수식하는 최상급이 맞다.
    geologist [dʒiɑ́lədʒist] n. 지질학자
    달나라 여행에 가장 관심이 많은 과학자는 아마도 지질학자들일 것입니다.

20. (B, costlier → costly) more costly가 바른 표현
    microwave n. 극초단파, 마이크로웨이브 thermometer [θərmɑ́mitər] n. 온도계 costly adj. 비싼, 비용이 드는
    극초단파 오븐 온도계는 다른 종류의 온도계보다 훨씬 더 비쌉니다.

21. (D, more better → better) do well (well-better-best)
    숙제를 하기 전에 내 충고를 들었더라면, 자네는 더 잘 할 수 있었을 것이다.

정답과 해설 | 383

22. (B, worse → worst) 문장의 문맥상으로 최상급이 맞다.
    그녀는 최소한 재미는 있을 것이라는 바람에서 홧김에 최악의 영화를 골랐습니다.
23. (D, a most → the most) 최상급에는 the를 붙인다.
    tribe *n.* 부족, 종족 temporary [témpəreri] *adj.* 일시적인, 덧없는, 무상한, 짧은
    미국의 모든 토박이 부족들 가운데 쇼니인디언 부족이 가장 단명하였습니다.
24. (B, the bigger → the biggest) 최상급+of+명사
    목성은 태양에서 5번째이자, 지름이 지구의 약 7배나 되는, 태양계에서 가장 큰 행성입니다.
25. (A, most small → smallest)
    수성은 태양계에서 가장 작은 행성이고 태양에 가장 가깝습니다.

Unit 13 부사

[EXERCISE **1**]

1. (well) 제인은 바이올린을 잘 연주합니다.
2. (intense) 그건 열정적인 소설입니다.
3. (brightly) 태양이 밝게 빛납니다.
4. (fluent) 소녀들이 유창한 불어를 구사합니다.
5. (fluently) 소년들이 일본어를 유창하게 합니다.
6. (smooth) 탁자의 표면이 매끈합니다.
7. (accurately) 우리는 소득세 계산을 정확하게 산정해야 합니다.
8. (bitter) 우리는 강한 차를 마시는 것을 좋아하지 않습니다.
9. (soon) 비행기가 곧 도착합니다.
10. (fast) 그는 너무 과속 운전해서 사고를 냈습니다.

intense *adj.* 강렬한, 열정적인 fluent *adj.* 유창한, 유려한 figure *v.* 계산하다, 산정하다 income tax 소득세 tax return 세금신고서 accurate *adj.* 정확한 bitter *adj.* 심한, 강한, 독한

[EXERCISE **2**]

1. (hard) 농장일꾼들은 추수기에 아주 열심히 일해야 합니다.
2. (hardly) 농장일꾼들은 자신들의 생활비를 대기에 충분한 돈을 법니다.
3. (lately) 최근에 우리는 많은 쓸데없는 우편물을 받았습니다.
4. (late) 우편배달부가 제 우편을 너무 늦게 가져와서 제가 출근 전에는 좀처럼 볼 수 없습니다.
5. (highly) 나는 사장이 자네를 아주 좋게 생각하고 있는 것을 확신해.
6. (high) 자네가 성공하기를 원한다면, 목표를 높이 잡아야지.
7. (justly) 저는 당신이 아주 제대로 대접받았다고 생각지 않아.
8. (just) 저는 방금 멕시코에서 일자리를 제공받았습니다!

9. (near) 플랫폼 끝에 너무 가까이 가지 마라.
10. (nearly) 저는 플랫폼 끝에서 거의 떨어질 뻔했어요.

[EXERCISE **3**]

1. (till) 저는 이 편지에 답하기 전에 월요일까지 기다리겠습니다.
2. (till) 저는 내일 오전 10까지 잠잘 작정입니다.
3. (by) 손님 양복은 금요일까지 준비될 것입니다.
4. (by) 제가 월요일까지는 떠날 것을 확신합니다.
5. (during) 8월에는 아주 덥습니다.
6. (during) 군대시절에 저는 외국에 파병되었습니다.
7. (for) 한시간 동안 택시를 잡으려고 애썼습니다.
8. (during) 저는 연설하는 도중에 갑자기 아팠습니다.
9. (during) 레이스 도중에 사고가 났습니다.
10. (for) 2분 동안 숨을 멈출 수 있습니까?

[Actual Test **17**]

1. (A, looks rather like) 부사 rather의 위치 문제. (look like ~와 같다)
   kettledrum *n.* (악기) 팀파니(timpani)
   팀파니의 사발모양은 차라리 거대한 달걀껍질의 절반과 같습니다.
2. (A, greatly) 내용상 increased에 어울리는 것은 신분이나 가격, 칭찬 등에 쓰는 highly보다 greatly(= very much)가 적절하다.
   오늘날 미국의 자동차생산은 크게 증가했습니다.
3. (D, Tornadoes almost never occur) 부사 almost는 never occur 앞에서 수식한다.
   토네이도는 미국 서부해안에서는 거의 생기지 않습니다.
4. (B, People have long had) 시간의 부사 long의 위치는 have와 p.p. 사이에.
   superstitious [sù:pərstíʃəs] *adj.* 미신적인
   사람들은 산에 대해서 오랫동안 미신적인 믿음을 가져왔습니다.
5. (C, always caused problems in) 빈도부사는 조동사와 본동사 사이에 위치한다.
   drainage [dréinidʒ] *n.* 배수시설
   미시시피주는 훌륭한 농지를 가지고 있으나, 홍수와 부족한 배수시설은 이 지역에 문제들을 자주 야기합니다.
6. (C, seldom more than) 빈도부사 seldom은 수식하는 형용사 more 앞에 위치한다.
   life span 수명
   금붕어의 수명은 짧아서 좀처럼 5년이 넘지 못합니다.
7. (B, rapidly) a rapid change, a fast runner/train 등의 용례 참고할 것.
   미국의 서부가 급속히 변화하고 있습니다.
8. (D, late too much → much too late) too much

가 late를 수식하는 어순이 맞다.
그 날 아침 존스씨는 8시30분까지 일어나지 못했고, 회의에 너무 늦게 도착했습니다.

9. (D, many → much) 비교급을 수식하는 부사는 much
현악기인 만돌린은 아주 오래된 악기인 루트(14~17세기 때 현악기)를 모방한 것 같습니다.

10. (B, prompt and careful → promptly and carefully) 동사 handle은 부사를 수식어로 갖는다.
improve v. 향상시키다. 이 문장에서 식품을 향상시킨다는 것은 숙성시키는 것이다. processing n. 숙성, 과정
어떤 식품은 시간이 지나면 숙성되지만, 생선은 잡는 순간부터 마지막 공정까지 신속하고 조심해서 다루어야 합니다.

11. (A, many → much) way가 단수임을 주시할 것.
much the same way: 거의 비슷하게
안개는 수증기를 내는 주전자 주위에 구름이 생기는 것과 거의 같은 식으로 생깁니다.

12. (A, sometime → sometimes) sometime (후일의 언젠가), sometimes (가끔, 때때로)
disc 디스크 spinal [spáinl] adj. 나선형의 vertebra [və́ːrtəbrə] n. 척추
지나친 스트레스는 가끔 신경을 압박하는 나선형 척추 디스크를 유발하기도 합니다.

13. (D, already → yet) not ~ yet
저는 연기를 보자마자 소방서에 전화를 했지만, 아직 도착하지 않았습니다.

14. (A, only is → is only) 일반적으로 only는 수식할 단어 앞에 위치한다.
뉴욕의 Verranzano-Narrows 다리는 샌프란시스코의 금문교보다 겨우 50피트 더 깁니다.

15. (D, hardly → hard) 부정의 뜻이 있는 hardly는 as ~ as one can 문형으로 쓸 수 없음.
그녀가 아무리 열심히 일해도 그녀는 가능한 열심히 그 원칙을 주장할 것입니다.

16. (D, formerly → formally) formerly (이전에), formally (격식 있게, 정식으로)
dressed formally 정장을 입다
파티 초대장에는 모두 정장할 것을 명시하고 있었습니다.

17. (B, lately → late) lately (최근에= recently), late (늦게)
quite late 아주 늦게 lie unconscious 자고 있어서 의식이 없는
다음날 밤에 존은 아주 늦게 퇴근하여 돌아와 보니 어머니가 전화기 옆에서 모르고 누워있었습니다.

18. (A, Ordinary → Ordinarily) Ordinarily는 문장 전체를 수식하는 부사.
break up 발발하다, 발생하다 dissipate [dísəpèit] v. 흩어지다, 사라지다
일반적으로 토네이도는 갑자기 발생하여 형성된 지 5시간도 안되어서 사라집니다.

Basic Grammar for English Tests

Unit 14 전치사

[EXERCISE 1]
1. (me) 초대장은 남편과 저를 위한 것입니다.
2. (us) 그녀는 우리에게 이 선물들을 주었습니다.
3. (them) 이것을 그들과 공유하시오.
4. (us) 우리 구세대를 위해서 사회에 많은 변화가 있었습니다.
5. (me) 그 뉴스는 저 같은 사람에게는 아주 놀라운 것이었습니다.

[EXERCISE 2]
Animals live all over the world; on land, in water, and in the air. Some animals are common and well known, while others do not even look like animals. Many water animals look like plants growing on the rocks or in the sand beneath the water.
Plants and animals are different from each other in two important ways. First, plants can not move by their own power as animals can, and second, animals can not make their own food as plants do. There might be some doubt a sponge's being an animal, because a sponge can not move. The sponge, however, is an animal because it does not make its own food. It lives by feeding on small animals in the water. Because it can not move, the sponge does not fit the rule. Almost all other animals can move if they wish. Plants can make their food out of substances drawn in through their roots and leaves, but animals can not do this. Their food has to be ready-made in the form of plants or other animals.

[EXERCISE 3]
1. at 2. at 3. in 4. in 5. in 6. at 7. at
8. in 9. in 10. in 11. in 12. in 13. at 14. at
15. in 16. in 17. at 18. in

[EXERCISE 4]
1. (at, on) 나는 6월14일 월요일 10시30분에 너를 만날 것이다.
2. (in) 우리는 7월에 있을 공휴일을 이야기하고 있습니다.
3. (on) 저는 금요일에는 항상 일찍 일을 마칩니다.
4. (in) 2030년에 세계가 어떨지 누가 알아요?
5. (on) 당신도 결혼식 날에는 어느 것도 잘못되기를 원하지 않을 거요.
6. (In) 19세기에는 많은 어린이들이 생후 1년도 되기 전에 죽었습니다.

7. (at) 우리는 새벽에 일어나 정오에 정상에 도착하였습니다.
8. (At) 14살 때 저는 외과의사가 되지 못할 거라고 생각했습니다.
9. (in) 새들이 겨울에는 우리 정원에서 먹을 것을 많이 찾지 못합니다.
10. (in) 공휴일에 뭘 하실 건가요?
11. (on) 설날에 뭘 하실 건가요?
12. (At) 그 해는 1986년이었습니다. 당시에 저는 웨이터로 일하고 있었습니다.
13. (at) 우리는 성탄절에 여행을 떠날 생각입니다.
14. (in) 열흘이 지난 다음 당신을 만나겠어요.
15. (on) 그들은 제 생일날 사무실에서 저를 위해 깜짝 파티를 준비했어요.

[Actual Test 18]

1. (A, in) 장소/위치의 전치사 in
   temperate regions 온대지역
   에델바이스는 세계 대부분의 온대지역에서 야생으로 자랍니다.
2. (D, Throughout) 주어 the making of fine books, 동사 has required가 있으므로, 빈칸에는 history와 결합하여 부사구가 되는 전치사가 오면 된다.
   역사를 통해서 볼 때, 좋은 책을 만드는 일은 많은 예술적인 기술과 상상이 필요했습니다.
3. (D, during) 기간(period)을 나타낼 때는 전치사 during을 쓴다.
   coniferous trees 침엽수
   침엽수는 약 2억 년 전 쥬라기 초기 동안에 지구에 처음 등장하였습니다.
4. (D, With such a short time) 부대상황을 표현하는 with
   마감시한까지 시간이 아주 조금 남았는데도, 팀이 기사를 끝낼 것 같아 보이지 않습니다.
5. (C, from) 출처를 나타낼 때는 from이다.
   이 카펫을 저 쇼핑센터에서 샀지만 실제로는 이란산입니다.
6. (B, among the professors) 둘 이상은 among, 둘 사이는 between
   controversy [kάntrəvə̀ːrsi] n. 논쟁, 반론
   이 결론은 교수들 사이에 심한 논쟁을 불러일으켰습니다.
7. (C, Except for) 내용상 '～을 제외하고'의 뜻이다.
   단세포생물을 제외하고, 거의 모든 동물들이 어떤 종류의 신경계를 가지고 있습니다.
8. (A, to) 반주에 맞추는 경우, 전치사 to를 쓴다.
   dance to the music 음악에 맞춰 춤추다
   우리는 어젯밤 클럽에서 도로시 존슨 밴드의 음악에 맞춰 춤을 추었습니다.
9. (C, out from → out of/from) out of = from
   draw guns 총을 뽑다   holster n. 권총집
   영화에서는 카우보이들이 총집에서 권총을 잘못 뽑는 모습은 전혀 보이지 않습니다.
10. (B, over → above) above see level 해발
    카그뉴역은 해발 7,200피트의 높이, 적도에서 겨우 북위 30도에 위치해 있어서 그 나라에서는 독특한 위치를 점하고 있습니다.
11. (B, of → at) be situated at
    be situated at ~에 위치하다, ~에 자리잡다
    미시건주 북부의 매키낙섬은 휴런호의 매키낙 해협 입구에 자리잡고 있습니다.
12. (D, in → on) 특정한 날에는 on
    inspection n. 검사 table n. (고대 모세의 법전 등) 평판에 새긴 법전 predict v. 예상하다, 추측하다 eclipse [iklíps] n. 식 eclipse of the sun 일식 (= a solar eclipse), a lunar eclipse 월식, a total eclipse 개기식 be due on ~에 예정되다 (일정)
    바빌론의 법전을 철저히 검사해본 뒤에 그는 또 다른 일식이 기원전 650년 5월 25일에 있었음을 추측했습니다.
13. (D, at the → in the) in the near future 가까운 장래에
    incurable [inkjúərəbəl] adj. 고칠 수 없는, 불치의 detect v. 발견하다, 간파하다 tuberculosis [tjuːbə̀ːrkjəlóusis] n. 결핵(TB)
    의사들은 수많은 불치병을 알 수는 없지만, 가까운 장래에 결핵이나 암 종류는 알아낼 수 있을 것입니다.
14. (A, Since → Because of) 원인이나 이유를 뜻할 때는 접속사로 쓰인다.
    content n. 함량
    비타민이 풍부하고 칼로리 함량이 낮아서 토마토는 다이어트식품에 포함됩니다.
15. (A, with → by) 수단방법의 전치사 by
    20세기 초에 재봉틀을 발명되기까지는 모든 바느질을 손으로 하였습니다.
16. (D, by → with) 동반의 전치사 with
    lunar soil 달의 흙
    달의 흙의 샘플을 통해 달의 구조나 역사에 관해 우리들이 얼마나 많은 것을 알 수 있는지 놀랍습니다.
17. (D, with → of) in search of ~을 찾아서, ~을 추구하여
    be/become acquainted with ~를 알게되다, ~를 사귀다 roam v. 방랑하다, 여행하다 (= wander)
    몇 십년 전 제가 유럽을 여행할 때, 저는 모험을 찾아서 세계를 방랑한 한 남자를 알게 되었습니다.
18. (C, from → in) result in 결국 ~가 되다
    neglect n. 부주의, 소홀함, 방치
    캠프파이어를 끄지 않고 소홀한 것이 결국 200에이커가 넘는 숲을 파괴하였습니다.
19. (B, from the ten → out of the ten) two out of the ten 10 가운데 2
    그녀는 최소한 10편의 소설을 썼는데, 현재 알려진 그 10편 가운데 2편만이 살아생전에 출간되었습니다.
20. (A, Besides to be → Besides being)
    주 수도라는 것 외에도 몽고메리는 농업의 중심지이자 앨라

21. (A, with → of) 소유의 표현 of
대부분 사람들의 의견을 보면, 한 국가의 교사상은 혼히 높은 급여를 받을 때 향상됩니다.

22. (B, behalf to → behalf of) on behalf of ~을 위하여, ~을 대신하여
역사가인 자넷 존스는 여성들의 평화와 평등권을 위해 격렬히 운동을 벌였습니다.

23. (B, to → on) depend on
quarantine [kwɔ́:rənti:n] n. 격리, 검역
검역기간은 특정 질병의 확산을 방지하는데 필요한 시간에 달려있습니다.

24. (A, Opposite → Contrary) contrary to ~와는 반대로
일반적인 믿음과는 반대로 타조는 모래 속에 머리를 감추지 않고, 겁이 나면 달아납니다.

Unit 15 동사

[EXERCISE 1]

1. raised 2. rises 3. sat 4. set 5. lay
6. lying 7. laid 8. lie 9. lies 10. hung

[EXERCISE 2]

1. (terrible) 네 기침소리가 심각하구나.
2. (well) 그 피아니스트는 연주를 잘하는구나.
3. (good) 그 레스토랑의 음식은 항상 맛있어요.
4. (calm) 그 야영지는 뇌우가 쳐도 가만히 있었습니다.
5. (sick) 그들은 상한 음식을 먹고 아팠습니다.
6. (quickly) 베이커교수는 얼른 학생의 스케치를 보았습니다.
7. (diligently) 피터는 그 프로젝트를 열심히 하고 있었습니다.
8. (vehemently) 폴은 새로운 제안에 대해 격렬히 항의하였습니다.
9. (relaxed) 우리 이웃사람들은 휴가 뒤에 편안해 보입니다.
10. (noisy) 음악은 너무 시끄러워 클래식이 되지 못하겠습니다.

contaminate [kəntǽmənèit] v. 오염시키다, 더럽히다
vehement(ly) [ví:əmənt(li)] adj.(adv.) 격렬한(히), 맹렬한(히)

[EXERCISE 3]

1. (grow) 내가 늙어서 손자들이 많으면 좋겠어.
2. (get) 여행할 때는 아프지 않도록 아주 조심해야 해.
3. (has turned / is turning) 이 우유는 변한 것 같아요.
4. (goes) 더운 날씨에는 음식이 아주 빨리 상합니다.

5. (has run / is running) 여러 달 비가 오지 않아서 우리 지방의 강이 말랐습니다.
6. (becoming) 내가 네게 질문을 할 때마다 화를 내는 것은 좋지 않아.
7. (has come / came) 그녀는 늘 마흔이 되기 전에 은퇴하기를 원했는데 그 꿈이 이루어졌습니다.
8. (fell) 저는 아파서 여행을 단축해야 했습니다.
9. (get) 정치 방송을 듣는 게 넌 지겹지도 않니?
10. (make) 개인적으로 저는 아주 훌륭한 비행사가 될 거라 생각합니다.

[EXERCISE 4]

1. (leave) 선생님은 존에게 방을 나가게 했습니다.
2. (repaired) 제인은 정비공에게 자동차를 정비하게 했습니다.
3. (to type) 엘렌은 마빈을 시켜 자기 서류를 타자 치게 하였습니다.
4. (call) 저는 제인에게 자기 친구들에게 전화하도록 하였습니다.
5. (painted) 우리는 지난주에 우리 집을 페인트로 도색 했습니다.
6. (write) 브라운박사는 학생들에게 작문을 시키고 있습니다.
7. (lie) 경찰들은 피의자를 바닥에 엎드리게 하였습니다.
8. (sent) 마크는 자신의 원고를 대학에 보냈습니다.
9. (cut) 마리아는 내일 머리를 자를 것입니다.
10. (to sign) 우리는 학장님이 이 서류에 서명하시도록 할 것입니다.
11. (leave) 선생님은 앨에게 교실을 나가게 했습니다.
12. (fixed) 제인은 언제나 같은 정비공에게 차를 맡깁니다.
13. (find) 우리는 수가 열쇠 찾는 것을 도와야 합니다.

[EXERCISE 5]

1. (rang → rung) 종이 울리고, 학생들이 건물을 떠났습니다.
2. (o) 자정이 지나자마자 일본 선박이 해안 가까이에 가라앉았습니다.
3. (chose → chosen) 불행히도 풋볼 팀에 응시한 누구도 뽑히지 않았습니다.
4. (sworn → swore) 취임식에서 새 대통령은 헌법을 지킬 것을 맹세하였습니다.
5. (became → become) 죽은 여자의 가족들 누구도 그녀의 유언이 어떻게 되었는지 몰랐습니다.
6. (o) 대통령은 언제나 정부관리의 대표를 보내 귀한 손님들을 같이 합니다.
7. (bit → bitten) 부주의한 등산객이 독사에게 물렸습니다.
8. (shaken → shook) 가을이 되면, 늘 할아버지는 나무에 올라가 가능한 깊은 밤을 텁니다.
9. (o) 한번도 타보지 못한 사람들은 늙은 말을 고를 것을 충고합니다.
10. (feed → fed) 큰 개들과 달리, 강아지들은 하루에 두 차례 먹이를 줍니다.

try out for ~에 응시하다, ~에 시험보다 inauguration [inɔ́:gjəréiʃən] n. 취임식 uphold [ʌphóuld] v. 떠받치다, 지지하다 delegation [dèligéiʃən] n. 대표, 대표단

[Actual Test **19**]

1. (C, originates) 빈칸에는 동사 자리이고 originate는 자동사이다.
   igneous rock 화성암 solidification n. 응고 molten rock 용암 eruption n. 분출
   화성암은 화산분출에서 나온 용암이 식어 응고되는 과정에서 생깁니다.

2. (D, Since she went) 뒤에 주절의 시제가 현재완료이므로 Since로 유도되는 절이 적절함.
   그녀가 시카고를 간 뒤에 아버지는 그녀의 소식을 들어보지 못했습니다.

3. (A, has been used) since와 무생물주어임을 보면, 완료형에다 수동태이다.
   marble [má:rbəl] n. 대리석
   대리석은 고대 그리스 초기부터 조각의 재료로 사용되어 왔습니다.

4. (D, destroyed) 분명한 과거시간이 표현되어 있으므로 과거시제이다.
   1926년 11월의 시카고 화재는 도시의 많은 것을 파괴하고 5만 명의 이재민을 낳았습니다.

5. (B, will lend) so long as는 if와 같은 조건절으로서 시제는 가정법현재이다.
   with pleasure 기꺼이
   그녀가 금요일까지 그 책을 돌려준다면 나는 기꺼이 네게 빌려줄게요.

6. (D, are to appear) are to do '예정'(= will do)
   추문에 연루된 몇몇 여배우들이 행사가 시작되기 전에 나타나기로 되어 있습니다.

7. (C, they would be friends) 시제는 모두 과거로 맞으나, 표현이 바른 문장을 고를 것.
   그들은 만나자마자 친구라는 것을 알았습니다.

8. (A, raised → risen) 주어 Food prices에 자동사 rise가 맞음.
   alter [ɔ́:ltər] v. 바꾸다 (= change)
   지난 몇 주간 식품가격이 너무 빨리 올라서 많은 사람들은 식사습관을 바꾸어야 했습니다.

9. (C, laying → lying)
   짐은 20분간 찾은 뒤에야, 자기 재킷이 내내 탁자 위에 놓여 있었음을 알았습니다.

10. (B, to make → make) let ... make(동사원형)
    refreshment n. 다과, 작은 음식 (흔히 pl.) entertainment n. 여흥
    낸시와 에디에게 모든 파티계획을 맡기고 당신과 나는 다과와 여흥을 준비할 것입니다.

11. (A, to rewrite → rewrite) had(사역동사)+(someone)+원형동사
    thesis [θí:sis] n. 논제, 명제
    교수님은 제인이 위원회에 논제를 발표하는 것을 허락하기 전에 여러 차례 재 작성하도록 했습니다.

12. (A, did → made) make a fortune
    make a fortune 큰돈을 벌다, 횡재하다
    제임슨씨는 정계에 들기 전에 청과, 가구, 철강사업 등으로 큰돈을 벌었습니다.

13. (D, has been → was) 구체적인 일시가 명시되어 있어 현재완료보다는 단순과거형이 맞다.
    조지오웰의 소설 《1984년》은 1945년에 처음 출간된 이래 영국에서만 500만부가 넘게 팔리고 있습니다.

14. (A, disappears → disappeared) 1937년이라는 명백한 과거시제
    aviatrix [èiviétriks] n. 여류비행사
    1939년에 유명한 여류비행사인 아멜리아 에르하트는 세계일주비행을 시도하다가 사라졌습니다.

15. (B, have been made → had been made) 1970년 이전이라는 명시적 시간이 제시되어 있어서, 시간 종속절의 과거시제보다 더 먼 과거시제이어야 한다.
    1970년 이후에 컴퓨터공학 분야의 많은 기술적 진보가 이루어졌는데, 그 결과 더욱 효율적인 컴퓨터를 낳았습니다.

16. (B, has been studying → had been studying) 시간종속절 before 안의 시제가 과거이므로 더 먼 과거이어야 한다.
    민수는 미국에 오기 전에 5년이나 영어를 공부했었지만, 그는 자신을 표현하기가 여전히 어렵습니다.

17. (D, will come → comes) 시간의 종속절에는 현재 시제를 쓴다.
    5년간 물이 없이 지내온 사막지대도 비가 오면 꽃을 피울 것입니다.

Unit 16 조동사

[Actual Test **20**]

1. (A, can change) 주어와 동사는 능동의 관계이다.
   대부분의 문어류는 자기 색깔을 재빨리 바꿀 수 있습니다.

2. (C, I might just as well) might have stayed at home 집에 있었으면 좋았을 텐데 (과거의 가능성 추측) may/might just as well 차라리 ~하는 것이 더 낫다
   공휴일을 날씨가 나빠 망쳤는데, 나는 차라리 집에 있는 것이 더 나을 뻔했어요.

3. (D, would go) '거절이나 고집'의 would
   저는 혼자 가고 싶지 않아요. 아무도 저와 하지 않으려 하네요.

4. (B, is used to) be/get used to+(동)명사 ~에 익

숙하다, used to do ~하곤 했다 (습관)
조지는 오랫동안 아팠기 때문에 고통에 익숙해 있습니다.

5. (C, had better get) had better는 조동사로서 뒤에는 원형동사가 온다.
당신은 여권 기한이 만료되기 전에 연장신청을 하는 것이 좋을 겁니다.

6. (C, than have stayed) would rather have p.p.는 과거에 실현되지 않은 일. 'would rather ... than' 구문
사실, 제인은 뉴욕에 남아 있기보다는 오히려 시카고로 떠났어야 했습니다.

7. (C, the prisoner be sentenced to death) 종속절이므로 주어·동사가 있어야 하며, '제안(suggestion)'의 표현이 있어서 '(should)+동사원형'을 써야 한다.
판사는 죄수를 사형에 처하자는 제안에 동의하였습니다.

8. (D, should finish) 'It is imperative/important/natural/necessary/required/urgent ... that S+(should)+동사원형' 구문이다.
고용인이 자신의 일을 정해진 시간에 끝내는 것은 너무도 당연합니다.

9. (B, should be) urgent가 that절 동사 시제의 단서가 된다.
그 교통사고 환자를 병원으로 보내는 것이 가장 시급했습니다.

10. (D, developing → develop) 조동사 다음에는 반드시 동사원형이 온다.
표준어가 사용되는 지역에 사회적, 정치적 변화가 생기면, 그 언어의 지역적 다양성이 발전하기도 합니다.

11. (A, went → go) would come out ... and go back ... 2개의 동사가 and로 연결되어 있다.
opponent [əpóunənt] n. 적, 상대 be at a disadvantage (상황이나 위치가) 불리한
그들은 적들이 불리한 울창한 숲에서 나와 공격하는 숲으로 되돌아갔습니다.

12. (D, will not → (should) not) maintains that (should) not smoke ... 동사 insist에 주의할 것.
blood pressure 혈압
그는 혈압이 정상보다 너무 높아서 의사는 그가 금연할 것을 주장하고 있습니다.

13. (C, stealing → steal) would rather 역시 조동사이므로 다음에는 바로 앞의 starve와 같은 형태인 동사원형이 와야 한다.
그는 필요한 것을 가지려고 훔치느니 차라리 굶겠다고 부드럽게 말했습니다.

14. (A, to review → review) had better 역시 조동사이므로 다음에는 동사원형이 올 것.
내일 있을 여러분의 시험에서 그 장(章)에 대한 문제가 일부 나올 것이니 여러분은 주의해서 검토하는 것이 좋겠어요.

15. (B, spending → to spend) would like (someone) to do
laboratory [læbərətɔ̀ːri] n. 실험실, 어학실습실(lab)
우리 영어 교수는 우리가 어학실습실에서 발음연습을 하며 좀 더 많은 시간을 보냈으면 합니다.

16. (A, living → live) used to do
transfer [trænsfə́ːr] v. 옮기다, 전근시키다, 발령내다
존은 조지아주에서 살았는데, 그의 회사가 그를 미시건주에 더 나은 자리로 발령을 내렸습니다.

17. (A, to be fishing → be fishing) would rather - 동사원형
잭은 사무실 책상에 앉아있는 것보다는 오히려 바다에서 보트를 타고 낚시하고 싶어합니다.

18. (B, does not travel → did not travel) 뒤 문장이 today로 현재시제를 분명히 나타내고 있으므로, 문맥으로 보아 앞 문장의 시제는 과거시제임을 유추할 수 있다.
저는 그가 궂은 날씨에 여행하지 않기를 바랬지만, 오늘밤 그는 굳이 집으로 돌아오겠다고 합니다.

19. (C, speaks → speak) It be important that S+(동사원형) ...
dean n. (단과대학의) 학장
그가 여름방학을 떠나기 전에 학장님께 말씀드리는 것이 가장 중요합니다.

20. (B, practices → practice) S require that S+(동사원형) ...
in preparation for ~를 대비하여
피아노 교사는 다음 주의 연주회에 대비하여 학생이 적어도 매일 50분은 연습을 할 것을 요구합니다.

Unit 17 부정사와 동명사

[EXERCISE 1]

1. (bring) 그에게 공항으로 차를 가져오게 해.
2. (drawing) "나는 학생들이 이 학교 담장에 그림을 그리지 않게 하겠소."하고 교장선생님이 말씀하셨습니다.
3. (know) 제가 자격 있는 회계사라는 것을 알려드리겠습니다.
4. (believe) 그는 그녀가 자신을 백만장자라고 믿게 하였습니다.
5. (ringing) 우리는 사람들을 시켜 밤낮으로 우리에게 전화하도록 했습니다.
6. (laughing) 영화는 처음 5분에서 바로 사람들을 웃게 만들었습니다.
7. (playing) 그는 뛰어난 피아노 교사야. 그는 1년쯤 뒤에 네게 피아노를 치게 할거야.
8. (look at) 저는 배관공을 시켜 중앙난방 보일러를 보게 했습니다.
9. (marching) 상사는 모든 지원병들을 한달 안에 진짜 군인처럼 행군하게 만들었습니다.

10. (arrange) 사장은 자신의 고문들에게 기자회견을 조정하게 하였습니다.

plumber [plʌ́mər] n. 배관공 central heating boiler 중앙난방 보일러 sergeant [sáːrdʒənt] n. (군대) 하사관, 부사관 (경찰) 경사 recruit [rikrúːt] n. 보충병, 신병, 신입생 v. 모집하다 press conference 기자회견

[EXERCISE **2**]

1. (to accept) 선생님은 그 논문을 받아들이기로 결정하셨습니다.
2. (going) 그의 아버지는 그의 유럽행을 허락하지 않으십니다.
3. (to reach) 우리는 결정에 내리기가 어렵다는 것을 알았습니다.
4. (opening) 도나는 술집을 여는 일에 관심이 있습니다.
5. (leaving) 조지는 지금 도시를 떠날 생각이 없습니다.
6. (to return) 우리는 가을에 학교에 돌아가기를 간절히 바랍니다.
7. (buying) 자네는 형편이 좋아져 이차를 살 수 있을 거야.
8. (to accept) 그녀는 선물을 거절했습니다.
9. (being) 메리는 자기가 그에게 말해야 하는 사람이 된 것을 후회합니다.
10. (to be) 조지는 어제 꾀병을 앓았습니다.
11. (to finish) 카를로스는 올해 그의 논문을 마치려고 합니다.
12. (to leave) 그들은 일찍 떠나기로 합의했습니다.
13. (to stop) 우리는 이번에 이 연구를 중단할 준비가 되어있지 않습니다.
14. (driving) 자네는 과속 운전하는 위험은 감행하지 말게.
15. (to know) 그는 진행상황을 알기를 원합니다.

[Actual Test **21**]

1. (C, a good place to live in) to do는 뒤에서 앞의 place를 수식하는 형용사 용법이다.
대기오염이 크게 줄었기에 시카고는 여전히 살기 좋은 곳입니다.
2. (D, to be) the first woman *who was* elected = the first woman *to be* elected
유효투표의 80% 이상을 얻어서 제인 라이언은 샌프란시스코의 시장에 당선된 최초의 여성이 되었습니다.
3. (C, causes her children to feel) cause ... to do (cause, get, force, enable 등 to do를 받는 사역동사)
어리석은 어머니는 자신의 아이들이 불안하게 느끼도록 만듭니다.
4. (C, they departed hastily) 앞의 동명사 구문에서 생략된 주어와 뒤 주절의 주어가 같아야 한다.
종소리를 듣자마자, 그들은 서둘러 떠났습니다.
5. (C, to keep the baby from crying) keep ... from -ing keep/stop/restraining/hold the baby from crying 아기가 울지 못하게 하다
아기가 울지 않게 하는 것이 아주 어려운 것 같습니다.

6. (C, driving) have trouble (in) -ing
저는 오늘 아침에 심한 눈 속에서 운전하느라 애를 먹었습니다.
7. (A, couldn't help laughing) can not help -ing ~하지 않을 수 없다
선생님이 미끄러져 넘어지셨을 때, 아이들은 웃지 않을 수 없었습니다.
8. (C, of restoring → to restore) to restore가 뒤에서 programs를 수식하고 있다.
currently [kə́ːrəntli] adv. 현재 restore [ristɔ́ːr] v. 복구하다, 복원하다
런던은 역사적 건물들을 복구하기 위한 프로그램을 현재 개발하고 있는 세계 많은 도시들 가운데 하나입니다.
9. (B, to studying → to study) 주격보어로서 명사 역할 하는 to study가 옳다.
skylab mission 인공위성을 쏘아 올려 지구를 돌게 하는 계획, 스카이랩 계획. weightless condition 무중력상태
인공위성 계획의 목적은 우주의 무중력상태에서 장기간 지내면서 연구하는 개인의 능력을 연구하려는 것이었습니다.
10. (A, To formation → To form) formation(n.)과 form(v.)의 잘못 사용. one foot thick은 a layer of coal을 수식한다.
layer n. 단층, (한) 겹 compact v. 채워지다, (빽빽이) 들어차다
1피트 두께의 석탄층 한 장을 형성하기 위해서는 약 50피트의 식물 원재료가 퇴적되어야 합니다.
11. (D, go → to go) invite (someone) to go
distract [distrǽkt] v. (주의를) 딴 데로 돌리다, 흩트리다, 미혹케 하다
슬퍼하는 나의 관심을 돌려보려고 딸과 그 친구는 영화 보러 가자고 나를 초대하였습니다.
12. (D, it's being → its being) it's(= it is)와 its(소유격)를 착각하지 말 것.
be unaware of ~을 인식하지 못하다 condemn [kəndém] v. 비난하다
저는 그 건물에 대한 그의 관심을 알지 못했기에, 건물이 비난받는 것을 그가 왜 그리도 기분 나빠하는지 이해하지 못했습니다.
13. (C, to prepare → preparing) be busy -ing ~하느라 바쁘다
에이미는 유럽 여행 준비를 하느라 바빠서 어젯밤 콘서트에 갈 시간이 없었습니다.
14. (D, running → to run) can afford to do ~할 수 있는, ~할 능력이 있는
run v. (조직이나 단체를) 경영하다, 운영하다
많은 사람들은 기업을 설립할 비용이 너무 많아서 부자들만이 회사를 경영할 수 있다고 불평합니다.
15. (D, giving up → to give up) be forced to do ~하기를 압력 받다, 억지로 ~하다
시간이 흐르자 마이클은 너무나 큰 손실을 겪게 되어 자기 사업을 포기하게 되었습니다.
16. (A, considering → to consider) tend to do

invention *n.* 창안, 허구 reproduction *n.* 재생산

어떤 예술가들은 예술적인 허구와 상상을 자연의 충실한 재생보다 더 중요한 것으로 생각하곤 합니다.

17. (B, to read → reading) finish -ing

저는 신문 읽고 나서 신문에 난 끔찍한 사고에 대해 생각하기 시작했습니다.

18. (C, to live → to living) be used to -ing: ~에 익숙하다

스미스씨는 아주 추운 기후에 사는데 익숙하지 않아서 자주 두꺼운 코트를 입었습니다.